高等院校精品课程系列教材

国际商务英语

INTERNATIONAL BUSINESS ENGLISH

主 编 孙 莹
副主编 荣华英

图书在版编目（CIP）数据

国际商务英语 / 孙莹主编. —北京：机械工业出版社，2021.1（2024.11重印）
（高等院校精品课程系列教材）

ISBN 978-7-111-67213-5

I. 国… II. 孙… III. 国际商务 – 英语 – 高等学校 – 教材 IV. F740

中国版本图书馆 CIP 数据核字（2020）第 266360 号

本书介绍了常见的国际知名银行和国际经济组织、参与国际贸易必备的营销知识，并按国际贸易流程介绍了国际贸易的谈判过程、商务合同及其写作技巧。本书还介绍了国际商务礼仪及商务技巧，为读者参与商务活动提供了一定的指导。此外，本书对一些国家的文化和商务习俗进行了简单介绍，以让读者具有国际视角。每一部分都配有阅读材料，涵盖冶金、化工、纺织等行业，以便读者了解这些行业的基础知识，扩大知识面，提高阅读能力，满足未来的工作需要。书中有关外贸实务对话及口语的练习、商务英语考试（BEC）口语的练习，可以提高读者的口语及应用能力。

本书针对国际经济与贸易、国际商务等经管类专业的本科生、MBA 及国际贸易学的硕士生而编写，对参加自学考试的学生及其他从事或准备从事国际贸易的人员来说，也非常有参考价值。

出版发行：机械工业出版社（北京市西城区百万庄大街 22 号　邮政编码：100037）
责任编辑：施琳琳　　　　　　　　　　　　责任校对：李秋荣
印　　刷：北京建宏印刷有限公司
版　　次：2024 年 11 月第 1 版第 10 次印刷
开　　本：185mm×260mm　1/16
印　　张：22.5
书　　号：ISBN 978-7-111-67213-5
定　　价：55.00 元

客服电话：(010) 88361066　68326294

版权所有 · 侵权必究
封底无防伪标均为盗版

前 言
PREFACE

改革开放40多年来,中国对外贸易取得了举世瞩目的成就,中国目前已经成为全球第一大出口国和第二大经济体。在经济全球化和"一带一路"的背景下,亟须提高经济贸易人员的国际商务技能,培养通晓国际商务理论与实务、精通国际商务英语写作、熟悉跨文化交流的国际化综合型应用人才。

基于"一带一路"背景和国际贸易新形势,我们精心组织专业教师编写了这本《国际商务英语》。编写本书的目的是使广大读者了解国际商务的相关知识,掌握参与国际贸易必备的国际市场营销分析能力与国际贸易实务操作能力,具备一定的国际商务谈判技巧。

全书共五部分。第一部分是 WORLD RENOWNED BANKS AND INTERNATIONAL ORGANIZATIONS(世界知名银行和国际组织),主要介绍了国际贸易活动中常见的国际知名银行和国际经济组织。第二部分是 INTERNATIONAL MARKETING(国际市场营销),主要介绍了参与国际贸易必备的营销知识。第三部分是 PRACTICE OF INTERNATIONAL BUSINESS(国际贸易实务),按国际贸易流程重点介绍了整个国际贸易谈判磋商过程和外贸函电写作,包括建立业务关系、询盘与发盘、还盘与接受、装运、保险、索赔与理赔、国际贸易合同、修改信用证等内容。第四部分是 INTERNATIONAL TRADE THEORIES(国际贸易理论),主要包括古典、新古典和当代国际贸易理论及贸易政策工具。第五部分是 INTRODUCTION OF COUNTRIES ON THE BELT AND ROAD("一带一路"主要国家介绍),主要介绍这些国家的一般情况、经济概况、与中国的关系、商务礼仪和禁忌。每一部分都有相应的阅读材料,以提高读者的阅读能力并扩大知识面。第一部分和第二部分还附加了一些商务小贴士(Business Tips),为读者参与商务活动提供一定的技巧。第三部分附有大量的国际单证,绝大部分单证都是根据函电内容精心制作的,如商业发票、装箱单、海运提单、原产地证、品质检验证、健康证书、植物检疫证书、保险单、信用证、国际贸易合同等样本。第三部分还加入了新版国际贸易术语解释通则 Incoterms® 2020，体现了时效性，并配有 2009 版协会货物保险条款，真实地反映了国际商务和外贸行业的新动态；增加了对话及口语的练习，以提高读者的口语及应用能力。同时，第三部分有大量的案例和阅读材料，包括"一带一路"、世界主要港口、全球前十大集装箱运输公司、RAPEX（非食品类消费产品的快速警报系统）年报解析等。第四部分加入了小专栏，内容丰富、真实生动，介绍现实案例或趣味知识等，以拓宽学生的知识面，提高学生对理论部分的学习兴趣，促进学生延伸阅读和深入思考。第五部分入选国家包括 4 个丝绸之路经济带国家、7 个 21 世纪海上丝绸之路国家、2 个美洲国家，共 13 个国家。

本教材已列入北京科技大学"十三五"校级重点规划教材，在编写中得到了北京科技大学教材建设经费的资助。本书是在编者多年来从事教学与研究及参与国际贸易实践活动的基础上写成的。主要编写人员既有商务英语和国际贸易教学背景，又有丰富的国际贸易实务实践经验。本书语言地道规范，编者阅读了英美主流网站、报刊和书籍等大量外文相关资料；内容系统全面，注重理论联系实际，配套资源丰富，包含习题参考答案和 PPT 课件。

本书第一部分由孙莹编写，第二部分由孙莹、李晓东和盛晓娟编写，第三部分由孙莹和荣华英编写，第四部分由荣华英和孙莹编写，第五部分由孙莹、李侨敏、Aizhan Kaiypova、Komiljonova Asalkhon、Rodrigo Acevedo、Bleoca Darius-Daniel、Woo Pyung Ho、Ei Ei Khaing Ust、Teamrat Kahssay Gebremariam、Oumalkhair Ahmed Mohamed、Angela Wangechi Mwaniki、Lilian Wanjiru Kingori、Kyoyagala Linda、Oduka Safina、Nkolo Ezangono Marthe Christelle、Epede Mesumbe Bianca、Andrea Mishell Proaño Solís、David Rea Constante、Alison Azucena Izurieta Toala、Diana Erika Rodriguez Hernandez、Diana Denisse Lozano Rodriguez 编写。本书由孙莹主编，荣华英为副主编。李晓东参加了本书的修改工作。

在编写过程中，编者参考了国内外多种教材、著作和资料，引用了其中一些材料，并在书后的参考文献中列出。在此，我们向这些作者表示深深的感谢。

北京科技大学经济管理学院领导和同人及很多外贸公司的业务人员对本书的编写给予了大力支持和帮助，在此深表感谢。

感谢机械工业出版社编辑团队认真、细致、严谨地审稿。

为了紧贴国际贸易业务实际，本书中的单证、合同、图片等仿真文件的外观样式，采用虚拟的公司名称、地址、电话、人名、交易内容等。如不慎与真实生活中的人物、公司或事件有雷同之处，纯属巧合，特此声明。

由于时间仓促和编者水平与经验有限，书中难免有不足之处，欢迎广大读者在使用中提出宝贵建议和修改意见。

编者

2020 年 12 月

教学建议
SUGGESTIONS

教学目的

随着经济贸易的快速发展,我国与世界各国间的经济合作与贸易规模日益扩大,需要大量的国际贸易人才。本课程的教学目的在于让学生熟悉英文背景下的国际贸易业务、国际贸易理论与政策,了解国际通用的外贸术语,以及提高他们用英文进行商务谈判、书面交流的能力,以适应国际贸易的要求。

本书不仅介绍了全球化背景下世界知名银行和国际组织的简要情况,以及国际市场营销的基本知识,而且全面介绍了国际贸易实务中各环节的谈判、信函交流知识及国际贸易理论,还创新性地加入了"一带一路"及相关国家经贸背景与商务礼仪的介绍,使学生能够理论联系实际,很快融入实际工作中,为从事国际贸易工作打下坚实的基础。

前期需要掌握的知识

国际贸易实务、国际贸易理论等课程相关知识。

课时分布建议

本书适合国际经济与贸易、国际商务等经管类专业的本科生、MBA及国际贸易学的硕士生使用。在实际教学中,根据学生的层次和特点,分别做如下的课时分布和教学安排。

对于本科生和MBA学生的教学,课堂教学主要集中在PART 3和PART 5(见下表)。

教学内容	学习要点	课时安排 本科生	课时安排 MBA
Chapter 1~9 The Background of Globalization and International Marketing	1. Self-reading and learning to understand the world renowned banks and international organizations 2. Self-reading to understand the basic knowledge of international marketing	0	0
Chapter 10 Principles, Structure, and Layout of Business Letters	1. Brief introduction 2. Business tips in Chapter 1~9 3. General principles of business communication 4. Layout of business letters	4	4
Chapter 11 Establishing Business Relations	1. Introduction 2. Some business letters 3. Trade terms 4. Uses of some words and phrases	4	4
Chapter 12 Inquiries and Offers	1. Introduction 2. How to make inquiries and offers 3. Some business letters 4. Uses of some words and phrases	2	4
Chapter 13 Counter-offers	1. Introduction 2. Some business letters 3. Uses of some words and phrases	4	4
Chapter 14 Shipment	1. Introduction 2. Some business letters 3. Uses of some words and phrases in business	4	2
Chapter 15 Insurance	1. Introduction 2. Some business letters 3. Uses of some words and phrases in business	4	2
Chapter 16 Terms of Payment	1. Introduction 2. Some business letters 3. Uses of some words and phrases in business	4	4
Chapter 17 Complaints, Claims, and Settlement	1. Introduction 2. Some business letters 3. Uses of some words and phrases in business	2	0
Chapter 18 Conclusion of Business	1. How to make out a contract 2. Some exercises about contracts 3. How to make amendments to a L/C	4	2
Chapter 19, 20, 21 International Trade Theories	1. Classic trade theories 2. New classic trade theories 3. New trade theories	4	0
Chapter 22 Instruments of Trade Policy	1. Tariff barriers 2. Non-tariff barriers	4	2
Chapter 23 Countries on the Silk Road Economic Belt	1. To learn and understand the basics of the Belt and Road Initiative 2. To learn about the economic and business situations of the countries along the Belt and Road 3. To understand the business taboos in these countries	3	0.5

（续）

教学内容	学习要点	课时安排 本科生	MBA
Chapter 24 Countries on the 21st Century Maritime Silk Road	1. To learn and understand the basic policies of the 21st Century Maritime Silk Road 2. To learn about the economic and business situations of the 21st Century Maritime Silk Road 3. To understand the business taboos in these countries	3	3
Chapter 25 Other Countries in America	1. To learn and understand the basic policies of Mexico and Ecuador 2. To learn about the economic and business situations of Mexico and Ecuador 3. To understand the business taboos in these countries	2	0.5
课时总计		48	32

说明：

（1）在课时安排上，对于国际经济与贸易专业本科生，建议48学时；

（2）对于MBA，建议32学时；

（3）标注课时的内容建议要讲，其他内容不一定讲，或者选择性补充。

对于国际贸易学硕士生的教学，课堂教学主要集中在PART 3、PART 4，而且，根据硕士生的水平和特点，学生以小组讨论汇报的时间要占课时的1/3左右（见下表）。

教学内容	学习要点	课时安排 国际贸易学硕士生
Chapter 1~9 The Background of Globalization and International Marketing	1. Self-reading and learning to understand the world-renowned banks and international organizations 2. Self-reading to understand the basic knowledge of international marketing	0
Chapter 10 Principles, Structure, and Layout of Business Letters	1. Brief introduction 2. Business tips in Chapter 1~9 3. General principles of business communication 4. Layout of business letters	4
Chapter 11 Establishing Business Relations Chapter 12 Inquiries and Offers Chapter 13 Counter-offers	1. Introduction 2. Some business letters 3. Trade terms 4. How to make inquiries and offers	4
Chapter 14 Shipment Chapter 15 Insurance	1. Introduction 2. Some business letters 3. Ways of making shipment 4. Insurance coverage	4

（续）

教学内容	学习要点	课时安排 国际贸易学硕士生
Chapter 16 Terms of Payment Chapter 17 Complaints, Claims, and Settlement	1. Introduction 2. Payment ways in business 3. Uses of some words and phrases in business	4
Chapter 18 Conclusion of Business	1. How to make out a contract 2. Some exercises about contracts 3. How to make amendments to a L/C	4
Chapter 19 Classical Trade Theories	1. Mercantilism Theory 2. Absolute Advantage Theory 3. Comparative Advantage Theory	2（学生小组讲解讨论）
Chapter 20 New Classical Trade Theories	1. Heckscher-Ohlin Theory 2. The Leontief Paradox	2（学生小组讲解讨论）
Chapter 21 Modern Trade Theories	1. Product Life Cycle Theory 2. National Competitive Advantage Theory: Porter's Diamond Model 3. New Trade Theory 4. Economies of Scale Theory	2（学生小组讲解讨论）
Chapter 22 Instruments of Trade Policy	1. Tariff Barriers 2. Non-tariff Barriers	2（学生小组讲解讨论）
Chapter 23 Countries on the Silk Road Economic Belt Chapter 24 Countries on the 21st Century Maritime Silk Road Chapter 25 Other Countries in America	1. To learn and understand the basic policies of Mexico and Ecuador 2. To learn about the economic and business situations of Mexico and Ecuador 3. To understand the business taboos in these countries	4
课时总计		32

说明：

（1）在课时安排上，建议32学时；

（2）标注课时的内容建议要讲，其他内容不一定讲，或者选择性补充。

目 录
CONTENTS

前　言
教学建议

Introduction　Globalization ··· 1

PART 1
WORLD RENOWNED BANKS AND INTERNATIONAL ORGANIZATIONS

Chapter 1　The World-Renowned Banks ·· 6
  1.1　Citigroup ··· 6
  1.2　JPMorgan Chase ··· 7
  1.3　Bank of America ··· 7
  1.4　Barclays Bank ··· 8
  1.5　Hong Kong and Shanghai Banking Corp. Ltd. ··· 8
  1.6　Bank of China ··· 9
  1.7　Bank of Montréal ··· 9
  1.8　Swiss Bank Corp. ··· 10
  1.9　First Interstate Bank ·· 10
  1.10　Standard Chartered Bank ·· 11
  1.11　Deutsche Bank ··· 11
  1.12　Bank of England ·· 11
  1.13　Wells Fargo & Company ··· 12

    1.14 Industrial and Commercial Bank of China ················ 12
    1.15 China Construction Bank ································ 13
    1.16 Agricultural Bank of China ····························· 13

Chapter 2 International Economic Organizations ············ 17
    2.1 Comprehensive Economic Organizations ··············· 17
    2.2 Organizations in Trade ·································· 28
    2.3 Organizations in Finance ································ 31

PART 2
INTERNATIONAL MARKETING

Chapter 3 Introduction of Marketing ······················· 42

Chapter 4 Analysis of Market Environment ················ 47
    4.1 Background of Market Environment ···················· 47
    4.2 Relevant Knowledge ···································· 49

Chapter 5 Market Research ································· 52
    5.1 Pre-knowledge ·· 52
    5.2 Theory of Marketing ···································· 54

Chapter 6 Market Segmentation, Targeting and Positioning ········ 59
    6.1 Introduction ·· 59
    6.2 Relevant Knowledge ···································· 62

Chapter 7 The Marketing Mix ······························· 74
    7.1 4P's ··· 74
    7.2 Promotional Mix ·· 76

Chapter 8 Distribution ·· 92
    8.1 Channels of Distribution ································ 92
    8.2 Wholesaling ·· 95

Chapter 9 About E-commerce ······························· 99
    9.1 Marketing for E-commerce ······························ 99

9.2　Relevant Knowledge ········ 102

PART 3
PRACTICE OF INTERNATIONAL BUSINESS

Chapter 10　Principles, Structure, and Layout of Business Letters ········ 110

10.1　General Principles of Business Communication ········ 110
10.2　Structure of Business Letters ········ 111
10.3　Layout of Business Letters ········ 113

Chapter 11　Establishing Business Relations ········ 122

11.1　Pre-knowledge ········ 122
11.2　Correspondence Writing Guide and Specimen Letters ········ 123
11.3　Dialogues ········ 127

Chapter 12　Inquiries and Offers ········ 132

12.1　Pre-knowledge ········ 132
12.2　Correspondence Writing Guide and Specimen Letters ········ 133
12.3　Dialogues ········ 138

Chapter 13　Counter-offers ········ 143

13.1　Pre-knowledge ········ 143
13.2　Correspondence Writing Guide and Specimen Letters ········ 144
13.3　Dialogues ········ 147

Chapter 14　Shipment ········ 157

14.1　Pre-knowledge ········ 157
14.2　Correspondence Writing Guide and Specimen Letters ········ 159
14.3　Dialogues ········ 174

Chapter 15　Insurance ········ 184

15.1　Pre-knowledge ········ 184
15.2　Correspondence Writing Guide and Specimen Letters ········ 186

15.3 Dialogues ··· 191

Chapter 16 Terms of Payment ··· 196
  16.1 Pre-knowledge ··· 196
  16.2 Correspondence Writing Guide and Specimen Letters ··· 198
  16.3 Dialogues ··· 211

Chapter 17 Complaints, Claims, and Settlement ··· 223
  17.1 Pre-knowledge ··· 223
  17.2 Correspondence Writing Guide and Specimen Letters ··· 224
  17.3 Dialogues ··· 229

Chapter 18 Conclusion of Business ··· 235
  18.1 Pre-knowledge ··· 235
  18.2 Correspondence Writing Guide and Specimen Letters ··· 236
  18.3 Dialogues ··· 242

PART 4
INTERNATIONAL TRADE THEORIES

Chapter 19 Classical Trade Theories ··· 250
  19.1 Mercantilism Theory ··· 251
  19.2 Absolute Advantage Theory ··· 252
  19.3 Comparative Advantage Theory ··· 255

Chapter 20 New Classical Trade Theories ··· 263
  20.1 Heckscher-Ohlin Theory ··· 263
  20.2 The Leontief Paradox ··· 265

Chapter 21 Modern Trade Theories ··· 268
  21.1 Product Life Cycle Theory ··· 268
  21.2 National Competitive Advantage Theory: Porter's Diamond Model ··· 270
  21.3 New Trade Theory ··· 272
  21.4 Economies of Scale Theory ··· 274

Chapter 22   Instruments of Trade Policy 276

22.1 Tariff Barriers 277

22.2 Non-tariff Barriers 280

PART 5
INTRODUCTION OF COUNTRIES ON THE BELT AND ROAD

Chapter 23   Countries on the Silk Road Economic Belt 294

23.1 Kyrgyzstan 294

23.2 Uzbekistan 297

23.3 Czech 301

23.4 Germany 303

Chapter 24   Countries on the 21st Century Maritime Silk Road 311

24.1 Republic of Korea 311

24.2 Myanmar 313

24.3 Ethiopia 315

24.4 Djibouti 321

24.5 Kenya 323

24.6 Uganda 325

24.7 Cameroon 328

Chapter 25   Other Countries in America 333

25.1 Mexico 333

25.2 Ecuador 338

Reference Answers 344

Bibliography 345

Introduction

Globalization

A fundamental shift is occurring in the world economy. We are moving away from a world in which national economies were relatively self-contained entities, isolated from each other by barriers to cross-border trade and investment; by distance, time zone, and language; and by national differences in government regulation, culture, and business systems. We are moving toward a world in which barriers to cross-border trade and investment are tumbling; perceived distance is shrinking due to advances in transportation and telecommunications technology; material culture is starting to look similar the world over, and national economies are merging into an interdependent global economic system. We refer to this process as globalization.

Globalization refers to the shift toward a more integrated and interdependent world economy. Globalization has several different facets, including the globalization of the market and the globalization of production. The globalization of the market refers to the merging of historically distinct and separate national markets into one huge global marketplace. Falling barriers to cross-border trade have made it easier to sell internationally. The globalization of production refers to the sourcing of goods and services from locations around the world to take advantage of national differences in the cost and quality of factors of production (such as labor, energy, land, and capital). By doing this, companies hope to lower their overall cost structure and/or improve the quality or functionality of their product offering, thereby allowing them to compete more effectively.

It is a world where the volume of goods, services, and investment crossing national borders expand faster than world output every year during the last two decades of the 20th century. It is a world where more than $5 trillion in foreign exchange transactions are made every day (NASDAQ, 2019). It is a world in which international institutions such as the World Trade Organization and gatherings of leaders from the world's most powerful economies have called for even lower barriers to cross-border trade and investment. It is a world where the symbols of material and popular culture are increasingly global: from Coca-Cola and McDonald's to Sony PlayStations, Nokia cell phones, MTV shows, and Disney films. It is a world in which products are made from inputs that come from all over the world. It is a world in which an economic crisis in Asia can cause a recession in the United States, and a slowdown in the United States did help drive Japan's Nikkei index in 2001 to lows not seen since 1985. It is also a world in which a vigorous and vocal minority is protesting against globalization, which they blame for a list of ills, from unemployment in developed nations to environmental degradation and the Americanization of popular culture. Yes, these protests have turned violent.

For business, it is in many ways the best of times. Globalization has increased the opportunities for a firm to expand its revenues by selling around the world and reduce its cost by producing in nations where key inputs are cheap. Regulatory and administrative barriers to doing business in foreign lands have come down, while those nations have often transformed their economies, privatizing state-owned enterprises, deregulating markets, increasing competition, and welcoming investment by international businesses. Thus, globalization has allowed companies both large and small, from both advanced and developing nations, to expand internationally.

Is the shift toward a more integrated and interdependent global economy a good thing? Many influential economists, politicians, and business leaders seem to think so. They argue that falling barriers to international trade and investment are the twin engines driving the global economy toward greater prosperity. However, there are also some anti-globalization protests. One concern frequently voiced by opponents of globalization is that falling barriers to international trade destroy manufacturing jobs in wealthy advanced economies such as the United States and the United Kingdom. The critics argue that falling trade barriers allow firms to move their manufacturing activities to countries where wage rates are much lower. The second source of concern is that free trade encourages firms from advanced nations to move manufacturing facilities to less developed countries that lack adequate regulations to protect labor and the environment from abuse by the unscrupulous. Another concern voiced by critics of globalization is that today's increasingly interdependent global economy shifts economic power away from national governments and toward supranational organizations such as WTO, EU, and UN. As perceived by critics, unelected bureaucrats now impose policies on the democratically elected governments of nation-states, thereby undermining the sovereignty of those states and limiting the nation-states' ability to control their destinies.

After all, everything has two sides, so is globalization. Globalization brings us both opportunities and challenges. No matter how some protest it, globalization is in the trend. People and companies around the world should embrace those opportunities.

PART 1

WORLD RENOWNED BANKS AND INTERNATIONAL ORGANIZATIONS

Chapter 1

The World-Renowned Banks

1.1 Citigroup

Citigroup Inc. (branded Citi), is a major American financial services company based in New York, NY. Citigroup has two major segments—Citicorp and Citi Holdings. Citigroup's brands include Citi, Citibank, CitiFinancial, CitiMortgage, Citi Capital Advisors, Citi Cards, Citi Private Bank, Citi Institutional Clients Group, Citi Investment Research, Citi Microfinance, Ban AmEx, Women & Co. Citigroup was a result of one of the world's largest mergers in history by combining the banking giant Citicorp and financial conglomerate Travelers Group on April 7, 1998. Citigroup Inc. has the world's largest financial services network, spanning 140 countries with approximately 12,000 offices worldwide. The company employs about 200,000 staff around the world and holds over 200 million customer accounts in more than 160 countries. It is the world's largest bank by revenues as of 2008. It is a primary dealer in US Treasury securities.

Citigroup suffered huge losses during the global financial crisis of 2008 and was rescued in November 2008 by a massive bailout by the U.S. government. Its largest shareholders include funds from the Middle East and Singapore. On February 27, 2009, Citigroup announced that the United States government would be taking a 36% equity stake in the company by converting $25 billion in emergency aid into common shares.

1.2 JPMorgan Chase

JPMorgan Chase's corporate headquarters are in New York City. The retail financial services and commercial banking headquarters are in Chicago. The major legacy institutions—J.P. Morgan, Chase Manhattan, Chemical, Manufacturers Hanover, Bank One, First Chicago, and National Bank of Detroit—contributed significantly to the development of communities worldwide.

Principal transactions leading up to the formation of JPMorgan Chase include the followings:

- In 1991, Chemical Banking Corp. combined with Manufacturers Hanover Corp., keeping the name Chemical Banking Corp., then the second-largest banking institution in the United States.
- In 1995, First Chicago Corp. merged with National Bank of Detroit's parent NBD Bancorp., forming First Chicago NBD, the largest banking company based in the Midwest.
- In 1996, Chase Manhattan Corp. merged with Chemical Banking Corp., creating what was then the largest bank holding company in the United States.
- In 1998, Banc One Corp. merged with First Chicago NBD, taking the name Bank One Corp. Merging subsequently with Louisiana's First Commerce Corp., Bank One became the largest financial services firm in the Midwest, the fourth-largest bank in the U. S. and the world's largest Visa credit card issuer.
- In 2000, J. P. Morgan & Co. merged with Chase Manhattan Corp., in effect combining four of the largest and oldest money center banking institutions in New York City (J. P. Morgan, Chase, Chemical and Manufacturers Hanover) into one firm called J. P. Morgan Chase & Co.

These mergers culminated in July 2004 with the joining of J. P. Morgan Chase & Co. and Bank One Corp. to form today's JPMorgan Chase & Co.

JPMorgan Chase is ranked the first biggest bank in the United States and the sixth world's biggest bank by total assets with 2.687 trillion estimated total assets in 2019 (Wikipedia, 2020). According to Wikipedia (2020), JPMorgan Chase is also the world's largest bank by market capitalization. Besides, JPMorgan Chase's hedge fund is the world's third largest hedge fund (Wikipedia, 2020).

1.3 Bank of America

Bank of America is one of the world's largest financial institutions, serving individual consumers, small and middle-market businesses, and large corporations with a full range of banking, investing, asset management, and other financial and risk-management products and services. The company provides unmatched convenience in the United States, serving more than 55 million consumers and small business relationships with more than 5,700 retail banking offices, nearly 17,000 ATMs, and award-winning online banking with more than 20 million active users. Bank of America is the No. 1 overall Small Business Administration (SBA) lender in the United States and the No. 1 SBA lender to minority-owned small businesses. The company serves clients in 175 countries and has relationships with 98 percent of the U.S. Fortune 500 companies and 80 percent of the Global Fortune 500. Bank of America Corporation stock (NYSE: BAC) is listed on the New York Stock Exchange.

1.4 Barclays Bank

Barclays Bank is a financial services organization that moves, lends, invests, and protects money for more than 27 million customers and clients around the world—from large businesses to personal account holders. Approximately 50 percent of its profit now comes from outside UK.

Barclays Bank has two clusters, each of which has several business units.

1. Global Retail and Commercial Banking

- UK Banking: UK Retail Banking and Barclays Commercial Bank
- Barclaycard
- International Retail and Commercial Banking
- Absa

2. Investment Banking and Investment Management

- Barclays Capital
- Barclays Global Investors
- Barclays Wealth

1.5 Hong Kong and Shanghai Banking Corp. Ltd.

Hong Kong and Shanghai Banking Corp. Ltd., the HSBC Group, one of the world's largest banking and financial services organizations, had its beginnings in China Hong Kong more than 140 years ago. Today, the HSBC Group has over 10,000 offices in 82 countries and territories in Europe, the Asia-Pacific region, the Americas, the Middle East, and Africa.

At the Group's core around the world are domestic, commercial banking, and financial services, which fund themselves locally and do business locally. Highly efficient technology links these operations to deliver a wide range of international products and services adapted to local customers' needs.

1.6 Bank of China

Bank of China (BOC), or Bank of China Limited in full, is one of China's four state-owned commercial banks. Its businesses cover commercial banking, investment banking, and insurance. Members of the group include BOC Hong Kong, BOC International, BOCG Insurance, and other financial institutions. The bank provides a comprehensive range of high-quality financial services to individuals and corporate customers as well as financial institutions worldwide. In terms of tier one capital, it ranked 18th among the world's top 1,000 banks by *The Banker* magazine in 2005.

The bank is mainly engaged in commercial banking, including corporate and retail banking, treasury business, and financial institutions banking. Corporate banking is built upon credit products, to provide customers with personalized and innovative financial services as well as financing and financial solutions. Retail banking serves the financial needs of the bank's individual customers, focusing on providing them with such services as savings deposits, consumer credit bankcard, and wealth management businesses. Treasury business includes domestic and foreign-currency trading and investment, fund management, wealth management, value-secured debt business, local and overseas financing, and other fund operation and management services.

BOC reported $73.23 billion in revenues in 2018 and $3.091 trillion in total assets (Wikipedia, 2020). In 2009, it was ranked the second largest lender in China and world's fifth largest bank by market capitalization (Wikipedia, 2020). In 2017, BOC was in the top 4 biggest banks in the world along with 3 other Chinese banks (Wikipedia, 2020).

1.7 Bank of Montréal

The Bank of Montréal, with head offices in Montréal, is Canada's oldest chartered bank. Founded in 1817, the Bank of Montréal participated in many of the developments spurring the growth of Canada: the first CANALS, the TELEGRAPH, the CANADIAN PACIFIC RAILWAY, major hydroelectric projects, and the development of Canada's ENERGY and MINING industries. It was the banker in Canada for the Canadian government from 1863 until the founding of the Bank of Canada in 1935. It was also the first Canadian bank to establish representation outside the country, with correspondent agencies started in London and New York in 1818. In 1893, it was named the Canadian government fiscal agent in Britain, a function it still performs. Between 1903 and 1962, the Bank of Montréal purchased the assets and business of smaller banks, mainly in Atlantic Canada.

Today, the bank has over 1,300 branches in Canada and overseas, and it offers corporate, government, merchant, and personal banking services with a variety of commercial and international services. Canada's second-largest financial institution, the bank reported a net income of $1.3 billion in 1997, with $207.8 billion in total assets.

1.8 Swiss Bank Corp.

Swiss Bank Corporation (SBC) (German: Schweizerischer Bankverein (SBV), French: Société de Banque Suisse (SBS), Italian: Società di Banca Svizzera) is the name of a bank that existed between 1856 and 1998 when it merged with Union Bank of Switzerland (UBS/SBG) to form UBS AG.

The history of the Swiss Bank Corporation dates to 1856 and the constitution of an underwriting consortium, or "Bankverein", by six private banks in Basel—Bischoff zu St Alban, Ehinger & Cie., J. Merian-Forcart, Passavant & Cie., J. Riggenbach and von Speyr & Cie. These six members formed the Bankverein in Basel, Switzerland, and a consortium acted as underwriting for its member banks. The company formally organized as Basler Bankverein in 1871, later joined forces with Zürcher Bankverein in 1895 to become Basler & Zürcher Bankverein. The next year, Basler Depositenbank and Schweizerische Unionbank were acquired.

Following these acquisitions in 1896, the company changed its name to Schweizerischer Bankverein (Swiss Bank Corporation). The company grew through a series of mergers, including Basler Handelsbank in 1945, O'Connor & Associates in 1992, Brinson Partners Chicago in 1994, S.G. Warburg & Co in 1995, and Dillon, Read & Co. in 1997.

1.9 First Interstate Bank

First Interstate Bank is a multi-state, $5 billion banking organization headquartered in Billings, Montana. First Interstate Bank has evolved since 1968 from a single bank in Sheridan, Wyoming, to operating 50 branches and over 100 ATMs in Montana and Wyoming.

First Interstate Bank is the principal subsidiary of First Interstate Bank System, Inc., a financial holding company.

In 1984, the company purchased a franchise agreement with First Interstate Bancorp to use the First Interstate Bank name and logo. In 1996, when First Interstate Bancorp of California merged with another banking institution, our bank negotiated to retain the First Interstate name. It now serves 30 communities across Montana and Wyoming.

1.10 Standard Chartered Bank

Standard Chartered is a leading international bank, listed on the London, Hong Kong, and Mumbai stock exchanges. It has operated for over 150 years in some of the world's most dynamic markets and earns around 90 percent of its income and profits in Asia, Africa, and the Middle East. Its incomes and profits have more than doubled over the last few years primarily as a result of organic growth, supplemented by acquisitions.

Standard Chartered Bank PLC was formed in 1969 through the merger of two banks: the Standard Bank of British South Africa, founded in 1863, and the Chartered Bank of India, Australia, and China, founded in 1853. Both companies were keen to capitalize on the extensive expansion of trade and earn handsome profits to be made from financing the movement of goods between Europe, Asia, and Africa.

Its business includes Consumer Banking, Wholesale Banking, SME Banking (offers products and services to help small and medium enterprises manage the demands of a growing business, including the support of our international network and trade expertise), Islamic Banking, and the Standard Chartered Private Bank.

1.11 Deutsche Bank

Deutsche Bank is a leading global investment bank with a strong and profitable private clients franchise. Its businesses are mutually reinforcing. Founded in Berlin in 1870 to support the internationalization of business and to promote and facilitate trade relations between Germany, other European countries, and overseas markets, Deutsche Bank has developed into a leading global provider of financial services. As a leader in Germany and Europe, the bank is continuously growing in North America, Asia, and key emerging markets. Its products and services include Private & Business Clients, Private Wealth Management, Asset Management, Global Markets, and Global Banking.

1.12 Bank of England

Bank of England is the central bank of United Kingdom. Sometimes known as the "Old Lady" of Threadneedle Street, the bank was founded in 1694, nationalized on 1 March 1946, and gained independence in 1997. Standing at the center of the UK's financial system, the bank is committed to promoting and maintaining monetary and financial stability as its contribution to a healthy economy.

The bank's roles and functions have evolved and changed over its three-hundred-year history. Since its foundation, it has been the government's banker and, since the late 18th century, it has been banker to the banking system more generally—the bankers' bank. As well as providing banking services to its customers, Bank of England manages the UK's foreign exchange and gold reserves.

The bank has two core purposes—monetary stability and financial stability. The bank is perhaps most visible to the general public through its banknotes and, more recently, its interest rate decisions. The bank has had a monopoly on the issue of banknotes in England and Wales since the early 20th century. But it is only since 1997 that the bank has had statutory responsibility for setting the UK's official interest rate.

1.13 Wells Fargo & Company

Wells Fargo & Company (WFC) is a multinational financial services company founded in 1852. WFC has the headquarters complex in San-Francisco and several central offices throughout the United States.

In 2007, Wells Fargo was the only AAA-rated bank for a brief period (Wikipedia, 2020). In 2014, WFC was named the most valuable bank brand in the world for the second year in a row. In 2016, it was ranked 7th in the list of largest public companies by Forbes Global 2000 (Wikipedia, 2020).

However, in 2016, WFC admitted that it created more than 3.5 million fake accounts to meet sales quotas. As the result, there were resigned the CEO and fired 5300 employees, paid $1.5 billion penalties for federate and state authorities, and over $600 million to resolve lawsuits with the shareholders and customers (McFarlane, 2019). Thus, WFC and its CEO Tim Sloan took many different actions to restore trust in the brand (McFarlane, 2019).

Nowadays, Wells Fargo is one of the "Big Four Banks" of US along with JP Morgan Chase, Bank of America, and Citigroup; it had a market capitalization of almost $223 billion in 2019 (Wikipedia, 2020). By the year 2018, WFC had more than 8,000 branches and about 13,000 ATMs (Wikipedia, 2020). As was reported in 2019, Wells Fargo had about 260,000 employees and over 70 million customers in 35 countries (Wikipedia, 2020).

1.14 Industrial and Commercial Bank of China

Industrial and Commercial Bank of China (ICBC) is a state-owned commercial bank established in 1984 with headquarters in Beijing. ICBC mostly focuses on industry, offering loans in transportation, manufacturing, power, and retail (Berger, 2019).

In 2017 and 2018, ICBC was named the biggest bank in the world by total assets with $4,027.44 billion in total assets in 2017 (Wikipedia, 2020) and $4.3 trillion in 2018 (ADV Ratings, 2020). Additionally, it was the largest bank in the world by deposits, number of employees, and customers (ADV Ratings, 2020).

As of 2006, ICBC had 150 million individual and 2.5 million corporate customers (Wikipedia, 2020). In 2017, it had more than 450,000 employees (Berger, 2019). According to Wikipedia (2020), as for the year 2018, ICBC had revenues of $105.4 billion. Moreover, ICBC was positioned the 1st in the list of The Banker's Top 1,000 World Banks for seven consecutive years (2012-2019) and ranked as the first world's largest public company by the Forbes Global 2000 in 2019 (Wikipedia, 2020).

1.15 China Construction Bank

China Construction Bank (CCB) was founded in 1954 in Beijing. Nowadays, CCB is one of the "Big Four" banks in China with more than 13,000 branches throughout China (Wikipedia, 2020). Moreover, it also maintained many branches: in Barcelona, Frankfurt, Luxembourg, Hong Kong, Johannesburg, New York City, Seoul, Singapore, Tokyo, Melbourne, Kuala Lumpur, Sydney, and Auckland (Wikipedia, 2020).

CCB offers corporate banking (credit, e-banking, credit lines, and commercial loans) and personal banking (loans, credit cards, deposits, and wealth management) segments (Johnston, 2019). Besides, CCB also operates with Treasury stock, dealing with money markets, debt securities, and currencies (Johnston, 2019).

In 2015, CCB was ranked the second in the Forbes' Global 2,000 list of the largest and most valuable companies. In 2018, CCB's estimated revenue was $92.1 billion and total assets reached $3.375 trillion (Wikipedia, 2020).

1.16 Agricultural Bank of China

Agricultural Bank of China (ABC, also known as AG Bank) was established in 1951 with its headquarters in Beijing. ABC is one of China's "Big Four" banks with approximately 24,000 branches in China Mainland, China Hong Kong, Singapore, Tokyo, London, New York, Frankfurt, Sydney, and Seoul. According to Wikipedia (2020), Ag Bank has 2.7 million corporate and 320 million retail customers.

Agricultural Bank of China is state-owned. The bank's deals with small farmers, large agricultural companies, and non-agricultural companies; mid-sized companies—the bank's largest growth segment (Johnston, 2019).

In 2010, ABC became public and was named after the world's largest-ever initial public offering (IPO) by that time, after overtaking by Chinese company Alibaba

(Wikipedia, 2020). ABC was ranked third in the Forbes' Global 2000 in 2015 and fifth in 2017 (Wikipedia, 2020). Ag Bank employs more than 470,000 people (as for 2018); moreover, it had estimated revenues of $87.6 billion in 2018 (Wikipedia, 2020).

Reading Material

Part One: Nestlé Has a Winning Team
Carol Matlack

Shares of the Swiss food giant rebound after passed-over CFO Polman confirms he'll stay on with Nestlé veteran Bulcke as the chief.

Could Nestlé (NESN.F) have a winning recipe after all? Yes, shares in the world's biggest food company sank more than 3.5% on Sept. 20, on the news a longtime Nestlé executive, Paul Bulcke, 53, would replace Peter Brabeck as chief executive next April. The announcement surprised Nestlé-watchers who had expected the job to go to Chief Financial Officer Paul Polman, a relative newcomer who has won plaudits for his push to boost operating margins.

But analysts were relieved, and on Sept. 21, the stock regained about one-third of the ground it had lost, when Polman confirmed he'd stay on as CFO of the $83.6 billion Swiss-based company. The strengths of Polman, a veteran Procter & Gamble (PG) executive, are an excellent complement to those of Bulcke, a skilled manager, and strategic thinker, says James Amoroso, an analyst with the brokerage Helvea in Geneva. "It's the very best of both worlds." Amoroso says.

Polman, who arrived at Nestlé in 2005, had impressed investors with his honesty about the need to improve efficiency in the company's far-flung empire. On his watch, Nestlé has improved operating margins that historically lagged its rivals'. In the first-half results reported on Aug. 15, margins grew to 13.5%, not far behind those of competitors Danone (DANO.PA), Kraft (KFT), and Unilever (UN).

CEO Choice "Has Delivered Results"

Yet Bulcke shares in the credit for that improvement. Margins in the Americas region—which he has overseen for the past four years—grew faster than in any other area, to 14.5% during the first half.

Bulcke also spearheaded Nestlé's recent acquisition of baby-food maker Gerber, which is expected to accelerate the company's push into higher value-added specialty nutrition products (BusinessWeek.com, 6/22/06). In choosing Bulcke, Brabeck told analysts during a conference call on Sept. 21, "We have chosen the man who has delivered results."

One reason for the market's early skepticism about Bulcke maybe is his relatively low profile. In contrast to the dynamic and charismatic Polman, he has rarely met with analysts and investors. But Amoroso says he is impressed by Bulcke's keen understanding of the company and the food industry. "He is deliberate and thoughtful, but when he makes a decision, it is going to be quick," the analyst says.

Exercises

Translation: translate following English into Chinese.

1. The announcement surprised Nestlé-watchers who had expected the job to go to Chief Financial Officer Paul Polman, a relative newcomer who has won plaudits for his push to boost operating margins.

2. Margins in the Americas region—which he has overseen for the past four years—grew faster than in any other area, to 14.5% during the first half.

Part Two: Acquisition of 21st Century Fox by Disney

The Disney and 21st Century Fox acquisition was reported for the first time on November 6, 2017. After a nearly 2-year struggle toward the finish line, the $71 billion acquisition took place on March 20, 2019. The deal included the 104-year-old 20th Century Fox studio, cable and satellite channels such as the FX, Fox Networks Group, National Geographic cable networks, Indian TV broadcaster Star India, and an additional 30 percent of subscription streaming service Hulu (Disney already held a 30 percent stake before the acquisition). Many authors claim that this acquisition transforms things in more than one way and call this deal "the most massive transformation ever". According to MediaRadar data, the networks Disney bought from Fox should push Disney to the number 1 position in terms of market share for the national TV advertisement market (Media Radar, 2019).

This extraordinary and historic event created significant long-term value for the company and its shareholders. The deal also helped Disney to gain further control of television shows and movies from start to finish—from creating the programs to distributing them through TV channels, cinemas, streaming services, and other ways people use to watch entertainment. Therefore, Disney would get valuable data on customers and their entertainment habits, which further can be used to sell advertising. Moreover, the acquisition has ended Hollywood's era of "Big Six" cutting it to "Big Five": Warner Bros, Universal, Sony Pictures, and Paramount Pictures, and Disney (The Guardian, 2019).

Interestingly, in their research study, Sergi, Owers and Alexander (2019) claimed that the case of Disney and 21st Century Fox is not M&A, but divestiture (a transaction that results in a part of a company being sold). The authors explain that the main difference with acquisition here is the fact that in the whole process there has been experienced significant value changes for both parties. For the shareholders of 21st Century Fox, the transaction created an additional value of $36 billion. In M&A only selling firms gain benefit from a deal, but buying firm shareholders typically experience losses. Nonetheless, there was also major value creation for the shareholders of Disney at the end of the transaction: when the process started, the Market Cap of Disney was $149 billion, and by the time it was completed, the market cap increased to $164 billion. Thus, this divestiture transaction dramatically illustrates how both seller and buyer can gain from divestitures. Thus, many restructuring experts claim that divestitures having greater potential benefits for both transacting companies than M&A activity (Sergi, Owers, and Alexander, 2019).

Business Tip: Business Meeting

You've finally convinced your boss to think that you're perfect for that business meeting with that significant client. And during that meeting, you could have your one chance to get that long-pending promotion and prove yourself to your boss. Here are a few tips you should keep in mind when going for a business meeting.

- Reach the venue of the meeting well in advance. Whether it will be in your own office or your client's, make sure that you're present there at least a quarter of an hour before the stipulated time. You can run over your presentation, check if all the equipment is in place and fully functional, and be present in the boardroom when your business partner arrives.
- Make sure that you have everything you need for your presentation in place. Include your whole presentation with all the slides in the right order, all your paperwork, documents (if any) that the client would need to sign as well as all corporate financial figures that would be required.
- Lots of people who go to client meetings invariably forget to carry their business cards with them or make the mistake of taking just a few cards. Although this might not seem like a big deal, it is. Your business cards would be a physical reminder of you and your firm once the meeting is over.
- Dress appropriately, perhaps a little better than how you would when you go to work. Remember that when you go for a meeting, you're representing your entire organization, so you don't want to come off looking shabby and underdressed. No matter what anyone says, clothes and outward appearances do matter.
- Converse with your business partners either before or after the meeting. Many people prefer to do this a few minutes before the meeting as it helps them break the ice as well as makes them a little less nervous before the presentation. Breaking the ice is the best way to get your business partners to remember you the next time they're interacting with your firm.

Chapter 2

International Economic Organizations

2.1 Comprehensive Economic Organizations

2.1.1 WTO

World Trade Organization (WTO) is the only global international organization dealing with the rules of trade between members. At its core are the WTO agreements, negotiated and signed by the bulk of the world's trading members and ratified in their parliaments. The goal is to help producers of goods and services, exporters, and importers conduct their business.

WTO was formed on Jan. 1, 1995, as a successor to the General Agreement on Tariffs and Trade (GATT), which since 1947, had regulated tariffs worldwide. WTO's 23,000 pages of agreements control the following subjects:

- **Tariffs on trade in manufactured goods and agriculture:** Fundamental principles include national treatment, which requires members to monitor imported goods in the same way as domestic goods; a most favored nation which obligates countries to give equal treatment to all other members; and elimination of quotas.
- **Services:** Rules force members to open their banking, insurance, and telecommunications industries to foreign competition. U.S. firms have benefited greatly.
- **Intellectual property:** Copyrights, trademarks, and patents are crucial for the

U.S. computer, software, entertainment, and biotechnology industries, which lose billions of dollars each year from pirated goods.
- **Food:** The Sanitary and Phytosanitary Standards (SPS) Agreement covers food safety issues from pesticide regulations to product labeling and genetically engineered foods. Critics say SPS rulings undermine safety standards.
- **Government purchasing:** WTO bans members and their states or provinces from giving preference to local industries in government purchasing of goods and services.

WTO is the most powerful legislative and judicial body in the world. By promoting the "free trade" agenda of multinational corporations above the interests of local communities, working families, and the environment, WTO has systematically undermined democracy around the world.

Unlike the United Nations treaties, the International Labor Organization conventions, or multilateral environmental agreements, WTO can implement trade rules through sanctions. It gives WTO more power than any other international body. WTO's authority even eclipses national governments.

2.1.2 APEC

APEC (Asia-Pacific Economic Cooperation), the premier forum for facilitating economic growth, cooperation, trade, and investment in the Asia-Pacific region, was established in 1989 to further enhance economic growth and prosperity for the region and to strengthen the Asia-Pacific community,

APEC is the only intergovernmental grouping in the world operating based on non-binding commitments, open dialogue, and equal respect for the views of all participants. Unlike the WTO or other multilateral trade bodies, APEC has no treaty obligations required of its participants. Decisions made within APEC are reached by consensus and commitments are undertaken voluntarily.

APEC has 21 members, which account for approximately 41% of the world's population, approximately 56% of world GDP and about 49% of world trade. APEC's 21 Member Economies are Australia; Brunei Darussalam; Canada; Chile; China Mainland; China Hong Kong; Indonesia; Japan; Republic of Korea; Malaysia; Mexico; New Zealand; Papua New Guinea; Peru; The Republic of the Philippines; The Russian Federation; Singapore; China Taiwan; Thailand; United States of America; Viet Nam.

Since its inception, APEC has worked to reduce tariffs and other trade barriers across the Asia-Pacific region, creating efficient domestic economies and dramatically increasing exports. APEC also works to create an environment for the safe and efficient movement of goods, services, and people across borders in the region through policy alignment and economic and technical cooperation.

2.1.3 EU

European Union (EU) is a family of democratic European countries, committed to working together for peace and prosperity. It is not a State intended to replace existing States, nor is it just an organization for international cooperation. EU is, in fact, unique. Its member states have set up conventional institutions to which they delegate some of their sovereignty so that decisions on specific matters of joint interest can be made democratically at the European level.

The historical roots of the European Union lie in the Second World War. The idea was born because Europeans were determined to prevent such killing and destruction from ever happening again. In the early years, the cooperation was between six countries and mainly about trade and the economy. Now EU embraces 27 countries, and it deals with a wide range of issues of direct importance for our everyday life. The 27 members are:

- Austria (since 1995-01-01) (EUR)
- Belgium (EUR) (since 1958-01-01)
- Bulgaria (since 2007-01-01)
- Croatia (since 2013-01-01)
- Cyprus (Greek part) (since 2004-05-01) (EUR: 2008-01-01)
- Czech Republic (since 2004-05-01)
- Denmark (since 1973-01-01)
- Estonia (since 2004-05-01)
- Finland (since 1995-01-01) (EUR)
- France (EUR)
- Germany (EUR)
- Greece (EUR)
- Hungary (since 2004-05-01)
- Ireland (EUR)
- Italy (EUR)
- Latvia (since 2004-05-01)
- Lithuania (since 2004-05-01)
- Luxembourg (EUR)
- Malta (since 2004-05-01) (EUR: 2008-01-01)
- Netherlands (EUR)
- Poland (since 2004-05-01)

- Portugal (EUR)
- Romania (since 2007-01-01)
- Slovakia (since 2004-05-01) (EUR)
- Slovenia (since 2004-05-01) (EUR)
- Spain (EUR)
- Sweden (since 1995-01-01)

(P.S. : EUR means Euro)

Europe is a continent with many different traditions and languages, but also with shared values such as democracy, freedom, and social justice. EU defends these values. It fosters cooperation among the nations of Europe, promoting unity while preserving diversity and ensuring that decisions are taken as close as possible to the citizens.

In the increasingly interdependent world of the 21st century, it is more necessary than ever for every European citizen to work together with people from other countries in a spirit of curiosity, openness, and solidarity.

2.1.4 ASEAN

1. Establishment

Association of Southeast Asian Nations or ASEAN was established on 8 August 1967 in Bangkok by the five original member countries, namely, Indonesia, Malaysia, Philippines, Singapore, and Thailand. Brunei Darussalam joined on 8 January 1984, Vietnam on 28 July 1995, Lao PDR and Myanmar on 23 July 1997, and Cambodia on 30 April 1999.

2. Objectives

ASEAN Declaration states that the aims and purposes of the association are: (1) to accelerate economic growth, social progress, and cultural development in the region; (2) to promote regional peace and stability through abiding respect for justice and the rule of law in the relationship among countries in the area and adherence to the principles of the United Nations Charter.

ASEAN Vision 2020, adopted by ASEAN leaders on the 30th Anniversary of ASEAN, agreed on a shared vision of ASEAN as a concert of Southeast Asian nations, outward-looking, living in peace, stability and prosperity, bonded together in partnership for dynamic development, and a community of caring societies.

In 2003, ASEAN leaders resolved that an ASEAN Community shall be established comprising three pillars, namely, ASEAN Security Community, ASEAN Economic Community, and ASEAN Socio-Cultural Community.

3. Fundamental Principles

ASEAN member countries have adopted the following fundamental principles in their relations with one another, as contained in the Treaty of Amity and Cooperation in Southeast Asia (TAC):

- Mutual respect for the independence, sovereignty, equality, territorial integrity, and national identity of all nations;
- The right of every state to lead its national existence free from external interference, subversion, or coercion;
- Non-interference in the internal affairs of one another;
- Settlement of differences or disputes by peaceful manner;
- Renunciation of the threat or use of force, and effective cooperation among themselves.

4. ASEAN-China Free Trade Area

ASEAN-China Free Trade Area (ACFTA), also known as China-ASEAN Free Trade Area, is a free trade area among the ten member states of the Association of Southeast Asian Nations (ASEAN) and the People's Republic of China. The initial framework agreement was signed on 4 November 2002 in Phnom Penh, Cambodia, with the intent of establishing a free trade area among the eleven nations by 2010. The free trade area came into effect on 1 January 2010. ASEAN-China Free Trade Area is the largest free trade area in terms of population and the third largest in terms of nominal GDP.

The free trade agreement reduced tariffs on 7,881 product categories, or 90 percent of imported goods, to zero. This reduction took effect in China and the six original members of ASEAN: Brunei, Indonesia, Malaysia, the Philippines, Singapore, and Thailand. The remaining four countries followed suit in 2015. The average tariff rate on Chinese goods sold in ASEAN countries decreased from 12.8 to 0.6 percent on 1 January 2010, pending implementation of the free trade area by the remaining ASEAN members. Meanwhile, the average tariff rate on ASEAN goods sold in China decreased from 9.8 to 0.1 percent.

The six original ASEAN members also reduced tariffs on 99.11 percent of goods traded among them to zero.

2.1.5 USMCA (Former NAFTA)

North American Free Trade Agreement (NAFTA) was implemented on January 1, 1994. It was designed to remove tariff barriers between the U.S., Canada, and Mexico.

NAFTA included two significant side agreements on environmental and labor issues that extend into cooperative efforts to reconcile policies, and procedures for dispute resolution between the member states. NAFTA created the world's largest free trade area at that time, which linked 444 million people producing $17 trillion worth of goods and services.

NAFTA was a radical experiment—never before had a merger of three nations with such radically different levels of development been attempted. Plus, until NAFTA, "trade" agreements only dealt with cutting tariffs and lifting quotas to set the terms of trade in goods between countries. But NAFTA contained 900 pages of one-size-fits-all rules to which each nation was required to confirm all of its domestic laws—regardless of whether voters and their democratically-elected representatives had previously rejected the very same policies in Congress, state legislatures, or city councils.

However, NAFTA was widely criticized by the presidential candidates in 2016. Democratic candidate Bernie Sanders called it a "disastrous trade agreement", which depressed American wages and caused a huge job loss. US President Donald Trump called NAFTA a "worst trade deal ever appeared" in US and his campaign promised to renegotiate or break it. As the result, Trump proposed the new trade agreement and in November 2018, USMCA (United States-Mexico-Canada Agreement) has been signed by President Trump, Mexican President Enrique Peña Nieto, and Canadian Prime Minister Justin Trudeau. The USMCA is also called the "New NAFTA" or "NAFTA 2.0". The revised version of the agreement was signed in December 2019, and ratified by all three countries; the last ratification has taken place on March 13, 2020 (Wikipedia, 2020).

In comparison with NAFTA, USMCA has developed new environmental and working regulations, and shifted its focus more on domestic production of cars and trucks. There have been also updated intellectual property laws, increased access of US to the Canadian dairy market, and imposed a quota on automotive production of Canada and Mexico (Wikipedia, 2020). The full list of the updates can be found on the website of USTR (United States Trade Representative).

2.1.6 OECD

OECD, whose full name is Organization for Economic Co-operation and Development, was established in 1961 and is located in Paris, France. OECD now has 32 member countries, and its budget is EUR 328 million (2007). OECD brings together the governments of countries committed to democracy and the market economy from around the world to:

- Support sustainable economic growth
- Boost employment
- Raise living standards
- Maintain financial stability
- Assist other countries' economic development
- Contribute to growth in world trade

The OECD also shares expertise and exchanges views with more than 100 other countries and economies, from Brazil, China, and Russia to the least developed countries in Africa.

Chile became a member of the Organization on 7 May 2010, and Slovenia became a member on 21 July 2010. On 10 May 2010, the OECD invited Estonia and Israel to become members of the OECD. Each country's membership will become official once necessary formalities, including parliamentary approval, have been completed.

For more than 40 years, the OECD has been one of the world's largest and most reliable sources of comparable statistics, and economic and social data. As well as collecting data, the OECD monitors trends, analyses and forecasts economic developments and researches social changes or evolving patterns in trade, environment, agriculture, technology, taxation, and more.

The organization provides a setting where governments compare policy experiences, seek answers to common problems, identify good practices, and coordinate domestic and international policies.

The OECD is one of the world's largest publishers in the fields of economics and public policy. OECD publications are a prime vehicle for disseminating the organization's intellectual output, both on paper and online.

2.1.7 Main Organizations under UN

1. UNDP

United Nations Development Programme (UNDP) is the UN's global development network, an organization that advocates for change and connecting countries to knowledge, experience, and resources to help people build a better life.

World leaders have pledged to achieve the Millennium Development Goals, including the overarching goal of cutting poverty in half by 2015. UNDP's network links and coordinates global and national efforts to reach these goals. The focus is helping countries build and share solutions to the challenges of:

- Democratic governance
- Poverty reduction

- Crisis prevention and recovery
- Energy and environment
- HIV/AIDS

UNDP helps developing countries attract and use aid effectively. In all our activities, UNDP encourages the protection of human rights and the empowerment of women.

2. UNIDO

United Nations Industrial Development Organization (UNIDO) was set up in 1966 and became a specialized agency of the United Nations in 1985. As part of the United Nations conventional system, UNIDO has responsibility for promoting industrialization throughout the developing world, in cooperation with its 173 member states. Its headquarters are in Vienna, and it is represented in 35 developing countries. This representation and several specialized field offices, for investment and technology promotion and other specific aspects of its work, give UNIDO an active presence in the field.

UNIDO helps developing countries and countries with economies in transition in their fight against marginalization in today's globalized world. It mobilizes knowledge, skills, information, and technology to promote productive employment, a competitive economy, and a sound environment.

3. FAO

Food and Agriculture Organization (FAO) of the United Nations leads international efforts to defeat hunger. Serving both developed and developing countries, FAO acts as a neutral forum where all nations meet as equals to negotiate agreements and debate policy. FAO is also a source of knowledge and information. FAO helps developing countries and countries in transition modernize and improve agriculture, forestry, and fisheries practices and ensure proper nutrition for all. Since its founding in 1945, FAO has focused particular attention on developing rural areas, home to 70 percent of the world's poor and hungry people. FAO's activities comprise four main areas:

- Putting information within reach.
- Sharing policy expertise.
- Providing a meeting place for nations.
- Bringing knowledge to the field.

4. IFAD

International Fund for Agricultural Development (IFAD), a specialized agency of the United Nations, was established as an international financial institution in 1977 as one of the significant outcomes of the 1974 World Food Conference. The conference was organized in response to the food crises of the early 1970s that primarily affected the Sahelian countries of Africa. The conference resolved that "an International Fund for Agricultural Development should be established immediately to finance agricultural development projects primarily for food production in the developing countries". One of the most vital insights emerging from the conference was that the causes of food insecurity and famine were not so many failures in food production, but structural problems relating to poverty and to the fact that the majority of the developing world's poor populations were concentrated in rural areas.

IFAD is dedicated to eradicating rural poverty in developing countries. Seventy-five percent of the world's poorest people—800 million women, children, and men—live in rural areas and depend on agriculture and related activities for their livelihoods.

Working with rural poor people, governments, donors, non-governmental organizations, and many other partners, IFAD focuses on country-specific solutions, which can involve increasing rural poor people's access to financial services, markets, technology, land, and other natural resources.

5. ILO

International Labor Organization (ILO) was founded in 1919, in the wake of a destructive war, to pursue a vision based on the premise that universal, lasting peace can be established if it is only based upon the proper treatment of working people. ILO became the first specialized agency of the UN in 1946.

ILO is devoted to advancing opportunities for women and men to obtain decent and productive work in conditions of freedom, equity, security, and human dignity. Its main aims are to promote rights at work, encourage fair employment opportunities, enhance social protection, and strengthen dialogue in handling work-related issues.

In promoting social justice and internationally recognized human and labor rights, the organization continues to pursue its founding mission that labor peace is essential to prosperity. Today, ILO helps advance the creation of decent jobs and the kinds of economic and working conditions that give working people and business people a stake in lasting peace, prosperity, and progress.

6. WIPO

World Intellectual Property Organization (WIPO) is a specialized agency of the United Nations. It is dedicated to developing a balanced and accessible international intellectual property (IP) system, which rewards creativity, stimulates innovation, and contributes to economic development while safeguarding the public interest.

WIPO was established by the WIPO Convention in 1967 with a mandate from its member states to promote the protection of IP throughout the world through cooperation among states and in collaboration with other international organizations. Its headquarters are in Geneva, Switzerland. The five strategic goals are:

- To promote an IP culture;
- To integrate IP into national development policies and programs;
- To develop international IP laws and standards;
- To deliver quality services in global IP protection systems; and
- To increase the efficiency of WIPO's management and support processes.

WIPO's core tasks and program activities are all aimed at achieving these goals.

7. UNESCO

United Nations Educational, Scientific and Cultural Organization (UNESCO) is an agency of the United Nations based in Paris. UNESCO was founded in 1946 with the aim of developing international collaboration in the spheres of education, science, and culture (Wikipedia, 2020).

UNESCO has five major programs—education, natural science, social science, culture, and information. Among the projects financed by UNESCO, there are such projects as technical and international science programs, teacher-training programs, literacy, the promotion of freedom of the press, world's literature, fostering cultural diversity, international agreements to secure the world's natural and cultural heritage, history projects and promoting the development of the worldwide digital divide (Wikipedia, 2020).

8. WHO

World Health Organization (WHO) is a specialized agency of UN which is concerned with public health. WHO was founded in 1948 with the headquarters in Geneva, Switzerland. The constitution of WHO was signed by 61 countries.

According to Wikipedia (2020), the current priorities of WHO are the following:

- Communicable diseases—HIV/AIDS, malaria, Ebola, tuberculosis;
- Non-communicable diseases and their impact on reproductive health, development, and aging;
- Nutrition—food security and healthy eating;
- Dependence on an addictive substance, especially alcohol or drugs;
- Occupational health;
- Promoting the development of the publications, reporting, and networking.

Moreover, WHO is responsible for:

- World Health Report—annual reports, which include expert assessment of specific health issues related to all WHO's member countries. The reports are available in

multiple languages;
- World Health Survey—a survey developed by WHO to address the need of reliable information;
- World Health Day—celebrated on the 7th of April each year in order to draw worldwide attention to an important subject to global health. On this date the WHO normally organizes international, regional, and local events related to a particular theme (Wikipedia, 2020).

2.1.8 SCO

Shanghai Cooperation Organization (SCO) is a political, economic, and security alliance of the Eurasian countries. SCO was established in 2001 in Shanghai by the leaders of China, Kazakhstan, Kyrgyzstan, Russia, Tajikistan, and Uzbekistan. In 2017, the membership was expanded after joining India and Pakistan as full members. SCO is the world's largest regional organization in terms of population and geographical coverage since it covers 3/5 of the Eurasian continent and almost half of the human population (Wikipedia, 2020).

The top decision-making body in SCO is the Council of Heads of State, which currently are:

- Arif Alvi (Pakistan)
- Almazbek Atambayev (Kyrgyzstan)
- Emomali Rahmon (Tajikistan)
- Xi Jinping (China)
- Ram Nath Kovind (India)
- Shavkat Mirziyoyev (Uzbekistan)
- Vladimir Putin (Russia)
- Kassym-Jomart Tokayev (Kazakhstan)

The council meets at the annual SCO summits which are held in the capitals of the member countries (Wikipedia, 2020).

In accordance with Wikipedia (2020), besides the member states, which were listed above, there are also:

- Observer states—Afghanistan, Belarus, Iran, Mongolia;
- Dialogue partners—Armenia, Azerbaijan, Cambodia, Nepal, Sri Lanka, Turkey;
- Guest attendances—ASEAN, CIS, Turkmenistan, UN.

2.1.9 ISO

International Organization for Standardization (ISO) is an international, independent, and non-governmental standard-setting body, founded in 1947 in order to promote proprietary, industrial and commercial standards (Wikipedia, 2020). ISO is focusing on developing, coordinating, revising, and producing technical standards in order to address the needs of the affected adopters (Wikipedia, 2020). ISO is headquartered in Geneva and operates in 164 countries.

The use of the standards contributes to the creation of safe, reliable and good quality products and services. Moreover, it helps businesses to increase productivity and minimize errors and waste. The standards also serve as a safeguard for the consumers of products and services since the certified products meet the standards set internationally (Wikipedia, 2020).

ISO has three official languages: English, French and Russian (Wikipedia, 2020).

2.2 Organizations in Trade

2.2.1 ICC

International Chamber of Commerce (ICC), also known as the world business organization, was founded in 1919 to promote peace among countries through trade and prosperity. ICC grew throughout the century to become the leading body of representation for enterprises around the globe. Its rules and guidelines, while being voluntary, govern international business actions and have become a standard used by ICC members, which include businesses and associations in over 130 countries involved in international trade. ICC was given the highest level of consultative status with the United Nations shortly after its formation.

ICC is involved in business-related issues such as trade and investment policies, financial services, information technologies, telecommunications, marketing ethics, the environment, transportation, competition law, and intellectual property. As an increasing number of business transactions began taking place on the World Wide Web throughout the 1990s, ICC started to focus on Internet-related issues and formed the Commission on Telecommunications and Information Technologies. The commission was founded to "formulate policy on issues such as electronic business, information security, telecommunications, and competition," according to ICC. Upon its formation, its agenda included advising governments on competition in the telecommunications industry and pushing for the implementation and increased development of the World Trade Organization telecommunications agreement, along with aiding developing countries in meeting telecommunications objectives.

Now ICC has proposed UCP 600 to guide the behaviors in trade.

2.2.2 UNCTAD

Established in 1964, United Nations Conference on Trade and Development (UNCTAD), promotes the development-friendly integration of developing countries into the world economy. UNCTAD has progressively evolved into an authoritative knowledge-based institution whose work aims to help shape current policy debates and thinking on development, with a particular focus on ensuring that domestic policies and international actions are mutually supportive in bringing about sustainable development.

The organization works to fulfill this mandate by carrying out three essential functions:

- It functions as a forum for intergovernmental deliberations, supported by discussions with experts and exchanges of experience, aimed at consensus building.
- It undertakes research, policy analysis, and data collection for the debates of government representatives and experts.
- It provides technical assistance tailored to the specific requirements of developing countries, with particular attention to the needs of the least developed countries and of economies in transition. When appropriate, UNCTAD cooperates with other organizations and donor countries in the delivery of technical assistance.

2.2.3 OPEC

Organization of the Petroleum Exporting Countries (OPEC) is a permanent, intergovernmental organization, created at the Baghdad Conference on September 10-14, 1960, by Iran, Iraq, Kuwait, Saudi Arabia, and Venezuela. Nine other members later joined the five founding members: Qatar (1961), Indonesia (1962-2008), Socialist People's Libyan Arab Jamahiriya (1962), United Arab Emirates (1967), Algeria (1969), Nigeria (1971), Ecuador (1973-1992, 2007), Gabon (1975-1994), and Angola (2007). From December 1992 until October 2007, Ecuador suspended its membership. Gabon terminated its membership in 1995. Indonesia suspended its membership effective in January 2009. Currently, the organization has a total of 12 member countries. OPEC had its headquarters in Geneva, Switzerland, in the first five years of its existence, then moved to Vienna, Austria, on September 1, 1965.

OPEC's objective is to co-ordinate and unify petroleum policies among member countries, to secure fair and stable prices for petroleum producers; an efficient, economical, and regular supply of petroleum to consuming nations; and a decent return on capital to those investing in the industry.

The ministers of energy and hydrocarbon affairs meet twice a year to review the status of the international oil market and the forecasts for the future to agree upon appropriate actions that will promote stability in the oil market.

The member countries also hold other meetings at various levels of interest, including meetings of petroleum and economic experts, country representatives, and special-purpose bodies such as committees to address environmental affairs.

Decisions about matching oil production to expected demand are taken at the Meeting of the OPEC Conference. Details of such arrangements are communicated in the form of OPEC Press Releases.

The OPEC Secretariat is a permanent intergovernmental body. The Secretariat, which has been based in Vienna since 1965, provides research and administrative support to the MCs. The Secretariat also disseminates news and information to the world at large. The official language of the Secretariat is English.

2.2.4 African Continental Free Trade Agreement

African Continental Free Trade Agreement (AfCFTA) is a free trade agreement which was created in 2018 by 28 African countries. As of July 2019, 54 of the 55 African Union states had signed the agreement; Eritrea is the only country which has not signed the agreement. This free-trade area is the largest in the world in terms of the number of participating countries since the establishment of the World Trade Organization (Wikipedia, 2020).

The main objectives of the AfCFTA are the following:

- To create a single liberalized market, which will deepen the economic integration of the African countries;
- To stimulate the movement of capital and people;
- To facilitate investment;
- To develop future continental customs union;
- To achieve sustainable and inclusive socio-economic development, gender equality, and structural transformations within member states;
- To enhance the competitiveness of member states within Africa and in the global market;
- To encourage industrial development;
- To diversify and develop regional value chain;
- To develop agricultural and food security;
- To resolve challenges of multiple and overlapping memberships.

2.2.5 Mercosur (Southern Common Market)

Mercosur (in Spanish)—officially Southern Common Market—is a South American trade bloc established by the Treaty of Asunción in 1991 and Protocol of Ouro Preto in 1994. Full members are Argentina, Brazil, Paraguay, and Uruguay. Venezuela is a full member but has been suspended since 2016. Bolivia, Chile, Colombia, Ecuador, Guyana, Peru, and Suriname are associate countries. New Zealand and Mexico are observer countries.

The official languages of Mercosur are Spanish, Portuguese, and Guarani.

The main purpose of Mercosur is to promote free trade and the fluid movement of goods, people, and currency in its member countries. Since its establishment, functions of the Mercosur have been updated and amended several times. Currently, Mercosur confines itself to a customs union, in which there are free intra-zone trade and a common trade policy between member countries. In 2019, the Mercosur had generated a nominal gross domestic product (GDP) of around 4.6 trillion US dollars, placing the bloc as the 5th economy of the world. Furthermore, the bloc places high on the human development index. In addition, it has signed free trade agreements with several countries or organization: Israel, Egypt, Japan, and European Union, among others.

2.3 Organizations in Finance

2.3.1 World Bank Group

1. IBRD

Founded in 1944 to help Europe recover from World War II, International Bank for Reconstruction and Development (IBRD) is one of five institutions that make up the World Bank Group. IBRD is the part of the World Bank (IBRD/IDA) that works with middle-income and creditworthy poorer countries to promote sustainable, equitable, and job-creating growth, reduce poverty, and address issues of regional and global importance.

Structured something like a cooperative, IBRD is owned and operated for the benefit of its 187 members. Delivering flexible, timely, and tailored financial products, knowledge, and technical services and strategic advice helps its members achieve results. Through the World Bank Treasury, IBRD clients also have access to capital on favorable terms in larger volumes, with longer maturities, and more sustainably than world financial markets typically provide.

Specifically, IBRD:

- supports long-term human and social development needs that private creditors do not finance;

- preserves borrowers' financial strength by providing support in crisis periods, which is when poor people are most adversely affected;
- uses the leverage of financing to promote key policy and institutional reforms (such as safety net or anti-corruption reforms);
- creates a favorable investment climate to catalyze the provision of private capital;
- provides financial support (in the form of grants made available from IBRD's net income) in areas that are critical to the well-being of poor people in all countries.

IBRD aims to reduce poverty in middle-income and creditworthy poorer countries by promoting sustainable development through loans, guarantees, risk management products, and analytical and advisory services. Established in 1944 as the first institution of the World Bank Group, IBRD is structured like a cooperative that is owned and operated for the benefit of its 187 member countries.

IBRD raises most of its funds on the world's financial markets and has become one of the most established borrowers since issuing its first bond in 1947. The income that IBRD has generated over the years has allowed it to fund development activities and to ensure its financial strength, which enables it to borrow at low cost and offer clients good borrowing terms.

2. IDA

International Development Association (IDA) is the part of the World Bank that helps the world's poorest countries. Established in 1960, IDA aims to reduce poverty by providing interest-free credits and grants for programs that boost economic growth, reduce inequalities, and improve people's living conditions.

IDA complements the World Bank's other lending arm—International Bank for Reconstruction and Development (IBRD)—which serves middle-income countries with capital investment and advisory services. IBRD and IDA share the same staff and headquarters and evaluate projects with the same rigorous standards.

IDA is one of the largest sources of assistance for the world's 80 poorest countries, 39 of which are in Africa. It is the single largest source of donor funds for essential social services in the poorest countries.

IDA lends money (known as credits) on concessional terms, which means that IDA credits have no interest charge, and repayments are stretched over 35 to 40 years, including a 10-year grace period. IDA also provides grants to countries at risk of debt distress.

Since its inception, IDA credits and grants have totaled US$182 billion, averaging US$10 billion a year in recent years and directing the largest share, about 50 percent, to Africa.

3. IFC

The full name of IFC is International Finance Corporation, whose vision is that poor people have the opportunity to escape poverty and to improve their lives and whose values are excellence, commitment, integrity, and teamwork. The purpose of IFC is to:

- Promote open and competitive markets in developing countries;
- Support companies and other private sector partners;
- Generate productive jobs and deliver essential services;
- Create an opportunity for people to escape poverty and improve their lives.

IFC promotes sustainable private sector development in developing countries. The particular focus is to promote economic development by encouraging the growth of productive enterprise and efficient capital markets in its member countries.

IFC's investments in emerging-market companies and financial institutions create jobs, build economies, and generate tax revenues. It also recognizes that economic growth is sustainable only if it is environmentally and socially sound and helps improve the quality of life for those living in the developing world.

IFC invests in enterprises majority-owned by the private sector throughout most developing countries in the world. Developing regions include:

- Sub-Saharan Africa
- East Asia & the Pacific
- South Asia
- Europe & Central Asia
- Latin America & the Caribbean
- The Middle East & North Africa

4. MIGA

As a member of the World Bank Group, the mission of Multilateral Investment Guarantee Agency (MIGA) is to promote foreign direct investment (FDI) into developing countries to help support economic growth, reduce poverty, and improve people's lives.

Concerns about investment environments and perceptions of political risk often inhibit foreign direct investment. MIGA addresses these concerns by providing three essential services: political risk insurance for foreign investments in developing countries, technical assistance to improve investment climates and promote investment opportunities in developing countries, and dispute mediation services, to remove possible obstacles to future investment.

MIGA's operational strategy plays to our foremost strength in the marketplace—attracting investors and private insurers into challenging operating environments. The agency's approach focuses on specific areas:

- *Infrastructure development* is an essential priority for MIGA, given the estimated need

for $230 billion a year solely for new investment to deal with the rapidly growing urban centers and underserved rural populations in developing countries.
- *Frontier markets*—high-risk and/or low-income countries and markets—represent both a challenge and an opportunity for the agency. These markets typically have the most need and stand to benefit the most from foreign investment, but are not well served by the private market.
- Investment in *conflict-affected countries* is another operational priority for the agency. While these countries tend to attract considerable donor goodwill once the conflict ends, aid flows eventually start to decline, making private investment critical for reconstruction and growth. With many investors wary of potential risks, political risk insurance becomes essential to move investments forward.
- *South-South investments* (investments between developing countries or regions) are contributing to a higher proportion of FDI flows. But the private insurance market in these countries is not always sufficiently developed, and national export credit agencies often lack the ability and capacity to offer political risk insurance.

5. ICSID

The World Bank, as an institution and the President of the Bank, assisted in mediation or conciliation of investment disputes between governments and private foreign investors. The creation of International Centre for Settlement of Investment Disputes (ICSID) in 1966 was, in part, intended to relieve the President and the staff of the burden of becoming involved in such disputes. But the Bank's overriding consideration in creating ICSID was the belief that an institution specially designed to facilitate the settlement of investment disputes between governments and foreign investors could help to promote increased flows of international investment.

2.3.2 IMF

International Monetary Fund (IMF) was conceived in July 1944, when representatives of 45 governments meeting in the town of Bretton Woods, New Hampshire, in the northeastern United States, agreed on a framework for international economic cooperation. It was established to promote international monetary cooperation, exchange stability, and orderly exchange arrangements; to foster economic growth and high levels of employment, and to provide temporary financial assistance to countries to help ease balance of payments adjustment. IMF now has 187 members.

IMF is the world's central organization for international monetary cooperation. It is an organization in which almost all countries and regions in the world work together to promote the common good.

IMF's primary purpose is to ensure the stability of the international monetary system—the system of exchange rates and international payments that enables members (and their citizens) to buy goods and services from each other. It is essential for sustainable economic growth and rising living standards.

To maintain stability and prevent crises in the international monetary system, IMF reviews national, regional, and global economic and financial developments. It provides advice to its 184 members, encouraging them to adopt policies that foster economic stability, reduce their vulnerability to economic and financial crises, and raise living standards, and serves as a forum where they can discuss the national, regional, and global consequences of their policies.

IMF also makes financing temporarily available to members to help them address the balance of payments problems—that is when they find themselves short of foreign exchange because their payments to other countries exceed their foreign exchange earnings.

And it provides technical assistance and training to help members build the expertise and institutions they need for economic stability and growth.

IMF performs three main activities:

- monitoring national, global, and regional economic and financial developments and advising members on their economic policies ("surveillance");
- lending members hard currencies to support policy programs designed to correct balance of payments problems;
- offering technical assistance in its areas of expertise, as well as training for government and central bank officials.

2.3.3 ADB

Asian Development Bank (ADB), a multilateral development finance institution, was founded in 1966 by 31 member governments to promote the social and economic progress of the Asian and Pacific region. Over the past 31 years, the Bank's membership has grown to 67. 48 of 67 members are from within the region and 19 from outside the region. ADB is a non-governmental organization providing funding and technical assistance throughout the Asian region.

The Bank gives special attention to the needs of the smaller or less-developed members and priority to regional, sub-regional, and national projects and programs.

The Bank's principal functions are: (i) to extend loans and equity investments for the economic and social development of its developing members; (ii) to provide technical assistance for the preparation and execution of development projects and programs, and for advisory services; (iii) to promote and facilitate the investment of public and private capital for development purposes; and (iv) to respond to requests for assistance in coordinating development policies and plans of its developing members.

The work of ADB is to improve the welfare of the people in Asia and the Pacific, particularly the 1.9 billion who live on less than $2 a day. Despite many success stories, Asia and the Pacific remains home to two-thirds of the world's poor.

ADB's vision is a region free of poverty. Its mission is to help its developing members reduce poverty and improve the quality of life of their citizens.

ADB's main instruments for providing help to its developing members are:

- policy dialogue;
- loans;
- technical assistance;
- grants;
- guarantees;
- equity investments.

2.3.4 BIS

Bank for International Settlements (BIS) was established on 17 May 1930. It is the world's oldest international financial institution and remains the principal center for international central bank cooperation.

BIS is an international organization which fosters international monetary and financial cooperation and serves as a bank for central banks.

BIS fulfills this mandate by acting as:

- a forum to promote discussion and policy analysis among central banks and within the international financial community;
- a center for economic and monetary research;
- a prime counterparty for central banks in their financial transactions;
- agent or trustee in connection with international financial operations.

The head office is in Basel, Switzerland, and there are two representative offices: in the China Hong Kong Special Administrative Region and Mexico.

As its customers are central banks and international organizations, BIS does not accept deposits from or provide financial services to, private individuals or corporate entities. BIS strongly advises caution against fraudulent schemes.

BIS:

- Aims at promoting monetary and financial stability;

- Acts as a forum for discussion and cooperation among central banks and the financial community;
- Acts as a bank to central banks and international organizations.

Reading Material

Tencent Holdings Ltd.

Tencent Holdings Ltd. is a Chinese multinational conglomerate holding company established in 1998 and with headquarters in Shenzhen, China. Tencent is run by one of the wealthiest businessmen in China—Ma Huateng, also known as Pony Ma. The company is focused on Internet-related products in the fields of entertainment, AI (artificial intelligence), and technology. Its services include social network, online and mobile games, e-commerce, music, web portals, payment systems, web portals, and other Internet services. The products of the company are offered not only in China but also globally. Moreover, Tencent is the biggest video game company in the world, one of the largest social media companies in the world, and one of the world's most valuable technology companies (Wikipedia, 2020).

The company has a lot of different industries in hands, starting with social networks to movie production. For instance, the new *Men in Black International* and *Terminator: Dark Fate* movies are produced by Tencent Pictures. Furthermore, widely popular App WeChat and messaging service QQ, which combined have over 1 billion users, are also operated by Tencent. Apart from that, Tencent company intensively invests in music services, comic books, e-commerce (Gilbert, 2019).

Unlike many other companies such as Nintendo, Tencent is not just a video games company; as was mentioned above, it is a conglomerate. Therefore, Tencent company can make a bigger investment and take riskier bets, in comparison to other entertainment companies; in addition, the companies failures have less impact on the overall business, which is very important for the multinational companies (Gilbert, 2019).

Warne (2019) highlighted crucial factors that contributed to the success of the Tencent company, which are the following.

- **First-mover advantage**

WeChat's launch in 2011 was incredibly well-timed, since back at that time, global social networks such as Facebook, Twitter, YouTube, or WhatsApp were blocked in China. Thus, the arena of social network and messaging was wide open in China; however, the first-mover advantage was lacking in the global market. Moreover, they lack a first-mover advantage in other industries, particularly in online gaming.

Furthermore, it can be argued that WeChat was not innovative, but an adaptation of the western digital brands. As it can be seen in Figure 2.1, on the "innovation landscape matrix", Tencent's technological competencies together with the business model were existing. As the author (2019) emphasized, the innovation in this case was the fact that it combined all the services on one platform; this is the second success factor, which is discussed further.

		Technical Competencies	
		Existing	New
Business Model	New	Disruptive	Architectural
	Existing	Routine **Tencent 腾讯**	Radical

Figure 2.1   The Tencent Success Story: How It Got There & Risks For the Future
Source: Warne, 2019.

- **The one-stop shop for everything**

In accordance with Warne (2019), the tremendous success of the Tencent company can be attributed to its topline product—WeChat, which is the App for everything in China. It combines the features of different programs such as Facebook, WhatsApp, Youtube, Spotify, Apple Pay, Uber, and many others. Thus, WeChat has become a vital part of the Chinese consumers' life through offering messaging service, e-commerce, and news platform. However, Tencent should seek for some new opportunities to compete with the competing services built by Baidu and Alibaba (Warne, 2019).

Business Tip: Business Lunch

As schedules become more hectic, the business lunch continues to grow in popularity. Make sure to do things right when meeting over lunch with a prospective client or an important associate. The last thing you want is for your encounter to be the final one.

- Avoid extravagance. Pick a quality restaurant noted for its excellent food and reliable services.
- Book a table that is in a quiet corner where business can be discussed without too many noisy disturbances.
- Leave instructions at the counter to usher in your guests to your table.
- You need to stand up when someone arrives and wait for them to be seated before you sit

down.
- If the client has a cocktail, follow his lead. If they order alcohol, you can too, but limit your drinks to one or two light ones. If they don't drink, you don't.
- Enter gracefully, don't be late. People typically have a limited amount of time for lunch.
- Take time to chat. Don't delve into a business until you've placed your order. Instead, make conversation, and try to get beyond the weather. Most people love to talk about themselves, so ask thoughtful questions that aren't too personal, and actively listen to your dining companions' responses.
- Despite all of your preparation, you may make a faux pas during a business lunch—remain calm. A fork could slip out of your hand, or a piece of food could get stuck in your throat. Pardon yourself, smile, and continue the conversation. Your ability to handle a glitch with grace will make a far more profound impression than any minor blunder could.
- The most important people are the ones sitting in front of you. Remember to turn off all cell phones. If you answer a phone call and discuss other business in front of them, the meeting may be over before it began.

Order with care: Ignore your craving for the barbecue pork sandwich or any other potentially messy dish. By sticking to easy-to-eat items, you'll save yourself the embarrassment of sauce dripping down your shirt. Also, don't order the most pricey entrée if you're not paying, and follow the lead of your host when it comes to appetizers, desserts, and other extras.

PART 2

INTERNATIONAL MARKETING

Chapter 3

Introduction of Marketing

Marketing is the process of the planning and executing the conception, pricing, and distribution of ideas, goods, and services to create an exchange that satisfies individual and organizational objectives.

Official definition of marketing by American Marketing Association:

Marketing must not be understood in the old sense of making a sale—"telling and selling" —but in the new sense of discovering and satisfying customer needs.

In marketing, the market is defined as people with the desire and with the ability to buy a specific product.

A market segment is a distinct group of customers within a large market who are similar to one another in some way and whose needs differ from other customers in the large market.

Depending on its goals and resources, a company may choose to focus on only one segment or several. The chosen segment(s) become the organization's target market toward which it directs its efforts.

The marketer's strategic toolbox is called the marketing mix, which consists of the factors that can be manipulated and used together to create a desired response in the marketplace. These factors include the product itself, the price of the product, the place where it is made available, and the promotion that makes it known to consumers.

A need refers to any difference between a consumer's actual state and an ideal or desired state. The particular form of product used to satisfy a need is termed a want, which is shaped by a person's knowledge, culture, and personality. When backed by buying power, wants become demands.

Customer value is a unique combination of benefits received by target buyers, such as quality, price, convenience, on-time delivery, and both before-sale and after-sale services.

There are five alternative concepts under which organizations conduct their marketing activities: the production, product, selling, marketing, and societal marketing concepts.

The central notion of the production concept is that products will sell themselves, so the major concern of business firms is production, not marketing.

Manufacturers that are production-oriented typically focus on increasing production and distribution efficiency while assuming that customers will seek out and buy reasonably priced, well-made products.

The product concept holds that consumers will favor products that offer the best quality, performance, and most innovative features.

Firms that focus on a product orientation tend to develop a narrow view of the market, called marketing myopia. For instance, railroad management once thought users wanted trains rather than transportation and overlooked the growing challenge of airlines, buses, trucks, and automobiles.

The selling orientation means that management emphasizes aggressive sales practices and that marketing is seen strictly as a sales function. But it doesn't mean that consumers get what they want; rather, they are being pushed into buying what is available.

A firm that is selling-oriented is characterized by heavy reliance on promotional activity to sell the products the firm wants to make.

Overly aggressive selling—the "hard sell"—and unscrupulous tactics evolved during the sales-orientation era. As a result, selling developed an unsavory reputation in the eyes of many people. Old habits die hard, and even now some organizations believe that they must use a hard-sell approach to prosper.

In the marketing-orientation stage, companies identify what customers want and tailor all of the activities of the firm to satisfy those needs as efficiently as possible.

The marketing concept holds that achieving organizational goals depends on determining the needs and wants of the target markets and delivering the desired satisfactions more effectively and efficiently than competitors do.

The basic difference between the selling concept and the marketing concept is that selling is internally focused, while marketing is externally focused.

Selling starts with the factory, focuses on the company's existing products, and calls for heavy selling and promotion to obtain profitable sales.

In contrast, marketing starts with a well-defined market, focuses on customer needs, coordinates all the marketing activities affecting customers, and makes profit by creating long-term relationships based on customer value and satisfaction.

In selling the firm attempts to alter consumer demand to fit the firm's supply of the product. In the market, however, the company adjusts its supply to the will of consumer demand.

Companies can be identified as market-focused and customer-driven only when they are finely tuned to the changing customer needs and competitor strategies.

The societal marketing concept holds that an organization should discover and satisfy the needs of its customers in a way that maintains or improves the consumer's and the society's well-being.

A firm that sufficiently extends the breadth and time dimension of its marketing goals to fulfill its social responsibility is practicing the societal marketing concept.

The marketing concept and a company's social responsibility are compatible if management strives over the long run to satisfy the wants of its product-buying customers, meets the societal needs of others affected by the firm's activities, and achieves the company's performance objectives.

Exercises

Exercise 1: Reading comprehension

Choose the best answer for each of the following questions.

1. Which of the following statement is not true about Huawei?
   A. Huawei is one of the main suppliers in China's telecommunication market.
   B. The Chinese government and the Russian government have maintained good diplomatic relations.
   C. Japan was Huawei's first international station.
   D. Huawei's marketing and service network covers the world.
2. Which year did Huawei officially go abroad?
   A. 1996　　　　B. 1997　　　　C. 1998　　　　D. 2000
3. Huawei's product positioning is _____.
   A. Low-end　　B. Middle-end　　C. High-end　　D. Unknown

Exercise 2: Blank filling

Fill each of the blanks with the appropriate word or expression from the box. Change the form of the word or expression when necessary.

> maintain　establish　show　affect　great influence

1. Huawei _____ its leading position in the international communication industry in

nearly 20 years.
2. Russia's telecommunication industry was _____ by the sluggish development of the economy.
3. The politics has a _____ on the economy.
4. The Chinese government and the Russian government have _____ good diplomatic relations.
5. Huawei's annual report _____ that its overseas sales were always over 55%.

Exercise 3: Translate the following sentences into English

1. 1996年，俄罗斯正式成为华为国际化的第一站。
2. 华为的国际化道路越来越广，1997年进入拉丁美洲市场，1998年进入非洲市场，2000年进入亚洲市场。
3. 华为已经用高品质和良好的服务先后在俄罗斯、非洲、北美、欧洲、日本等170多个国家与地区开设业务。

Reading Material

Huawei Goes Global

Huawei founded in 1988, is mainly engaged in the research, development, production, and sales of communication network technology and products, and provides network solutions in the fields of fixed network, mobile network, data communication network, and value-added services for a service provider. Huawei is one of the main suppliers in China's telecommunication market and has successfully entered the global telecommunication market.

As early as 1996, Huawei officially went abroad, taking its low price and fast customer demand response ability as the key to enter the international market, and established its leading position in the international communication industry in nearly 20 years. Huawei's internationalization path basically continues the strategy of "encircling the city in rural areas" and "easy before hard" adopted by Huawei in China's domestic market. From Russia, Africa, Southeast Asia, the Middle East, Europe, North America, and Japan, Huawei has built a global market network and research and development (R&D) platform.

In 1996, Russia officially became the first stop of Huawei's internationalization. At that time, Russia's telecommunication industry was affected by the sluggish development of the economy, and the market demand was very large. There is no uniform technical standard in the industry market. For the purchase of communication equipment, we pay more attention to the cost-effective and value-added services of products. And Russia's joint-stock system reform is beginning. The state has a large share in it, and the politics has a great influence on the economy. The Chinese government and the Russian government have maintained good diplomatic relations, which provides favorable conditions for Chinese enterprises to enter the Russian market.

After that, Huawei's internationalization path has become wider and wider. It entered Latin American market in 1997, African market in 1998, and Asian market in 2000.

After a long and tortuous 10 years, Huawei has successively covered markets in Asia Pacific, Europe, the Middle East, Africa and the Americas, and for the first time in 2005, its overseas sales exceeded domestic sales. Until the end of 2016, Huawei's annual report showed that its overseas sales were always over 55%. At present, Huawei has set up business in more than 170 countries and regions including Russia, Africa, North America, Europe, and Japan with high quality and good service, covering nearly one-third of the world's population, marketing and service network throughout the world.

In addition to establishing the leading brand position in the communication industry, Huawei has promoted its own brand to the height of "outstanding representative" of Chinese brand through consumer products such as smartphones. Different from the low-end low price of other Chinese brands, Huawei is keen to grasp the trend of consumption upgrading, positioning mobile phones as high-end from the beginning, taking the lead in winning the recognition of middle and high-end consumer groups with excellent products, and finally shaping a positive, tall and international corporate brand image, making a perfect demonstration for the brand construction of contemporary Chinese enterprises.

Business Tip: Making a Client Wait

An urgent and unexpected task may lead to unavoidable delays at times. The situation becomes even more critical when one has a client waiting in the office wondering about the appointment that had been fixed well in advance! So, how does one avoid alienating a customer who has been inadvertently placed in such an awkward situation?

- First, take the trouble to make apologies in person. Tell your client how long you are likely to be delayed. If you are away from office, have your secretary or a colleague do this for you.
- Offer refreshments and reading material. This is definitely an occasion to pamper him.
- Don't keep him waiting longer than 15 or 20 minutes. If you can't get away from the urgent task delaying you, explain the situation, apologize, and schedule another meeting.
- Call to express regret for wasting his time. Making amends and restoring goodwill should be your top priority.

Chapter 4

Analysis of Market Environment

4.1 Background of Market Environment

Environmental monitoring—also called environmental scanning—is the process of gathering information regarding a company's eternal environment, analyzing it, and forecasting the impact of whatever trends the analysis suggests.

With disciplined method—marketing intelligence and marketing research—for collecting information, and normally spending more time in the customer and competitor environment, marketers, more than any groups in the company, taking major responsibility for identifying significant changes in the environment.

A company's marketing environment consists of the actors and forces outside marketing that affect marketing management's ability to develop and maintain successful transactions with its target customers. The marketing environment is made up of a microenvironment and a macroenvironment.

The microenvironment (so called because it affects a particular firm) consists of the forces closing to the company that affect its ability to serve its customers—the company, suppliers, marketing intermediaries, customers, competitors, and publics.

The macroenvironment (so called because it affects all firms) consists of the larger societal forces—demographic, economic, natural, technological, political, and cultural forces.

In designing marketing plans, marketing management takes other company groups into account—groups such as top management, finance, research, and development (R&D), purchasing, manufacturing, and accounting.

Under the marketing concept, all functional departments must "think about consumers", and they should work in harmony to provide superior customer value and satisfaction.

A company's corporate culture is the set of shared management attitudes values, and beliefs that influence the practices and norms of behavior for everyone in the organization.

Suppliers, or vendors, provide the raw material, parts, equipment, and other resources that allow a firm to produce goods and services.

Failure to deliver on time, high prices, and availability of needed materials affect both the quantity and timely delivery of the firm's product and have a direct bearing on the product's price tag.

Marketing intermediaries are firms that work the organization to promote, sell, and distribute its goods and services to customers. They include resellers, physical distribution firms, marketing service agencies, and financial intermediaries.

There are five types of customer markets: consumer markets, business markets, reseller markets, governments markets, and international markets.

In marketing any goods or services, there factors need to be considered: people or organizations with demand their purchasing power, and their buying behaviors.

To be successful, a company must provide greater customer value and satisfaction than its competitors. Thus, marketers must do more than simply adapt to the needs of target consumers. They also must gain strategic advantage by positioning their offerings strongly against their competitors' offerings in the minds of consumers.

Publics are groups that have either a current or potential interest in or impact on an organization's ability to achieve its objectives. These groups include stockholders, public agencies, the media, citizen-action groups, communities, and the general public.

The social forces of the environment include the characteristics of the population, its income, and its values. Changes in these can have a dramatic impact on market strategy.

Describing the distribution of the population according to selected characteristics—where people are, their numbers, and who they are, such as their age, ethnicity, income, and occupation—is referred to as demographics.

Marketers keep close track of demographic trends and developments in their markets, both at home and abroad. They track changing age and family structure, geographic population shifts, educational characteristics, and population diversity.

The age distribution of America is changing and successful companies must respond to this change. In recent years, greater marketing attention is being focused on a mature household. People over 50 years old, who represent the fastest-growing age segment in the population, had such households.

A baby boom is the major increase in the annual birthrate of America following World War 2 and lasting until the early 1960s. The "baby boomers" now moving into their prime wage-earning years, have always been a prime target for markets.

In the 1950s, 70 percent of U.S. households consisted of a stay-at-home mother, working father, and one or more children, whereas only 20 percent of today's households do so.

As a result of the shifts in the traditional roles and values of husbands and wives, with husbands assuming more domestic functions such as shopping and childcare, more food and household appliance marketers are targeting husbands.

A major regional shift in the U.S. population toward western and Sunbelt states occurred in the 1980s. In recent decades, people have also moved from areas to major cities and suburbs. So marketers focus on population centers, where about three-fourths of the population live.

Regional marketing is a concept of developing marketing plans to reflect specific area differences in taste preferences, perceived needs, or interests. Such an approach is also referred to as geographical segmentation.

Culture incorporates the set of values, ideas, and attitudes of a homogeneous group of people that are transmitted from one generation to the next.

Ore beliefs and values are passed on from parents to children and are reinforced by schools, churches, businesses, and governments. Secondary beliefs and values are more open to change. Marketers have some chance of changing secondary values, but little chance of changing core values.

Today and for the foreseeable future, in American value consciousness—or the concern for obtaining the best quality, features, and performance for the given price of a product or service—will drive consumer behavior.

As a component of the environment of the environmental scan, the economy pertains to the income, expenditure, and resources that affect the cost of running a business or household.

The natural environment involves the natural resources that needed as inputs by marketers or that are affected by marketing activities.

Scientists today are working on a wide range of technologies that will revolutionize our products and their manufacturing processes. Keeping on top of research and technological developments gives marketers the edge in developing products and strategies that make a difference.

4.2 Relevant Knowledge

It is useful to conceptualize the organization as a system or a whole with interdependent and interrelated parts. The system approach solves problems by diagnosing them within a framework of inputs, transformation processes, outputs, and feedback. Inputs are the labor (human), money (financial), materials, and equipment resources that enter a transformation process. Transformation processes comprise the technologies used to convert inputs into outputs. Outputs are the original inputs as changed by a transformation process, products, and services. Feedback is information about a system's status and performance.

Internally, an organization can be viewed as a resource conversion machine that takes inputs(labor, money, material, and equipment) from the external environment (i.e. the world outside the boundaries of the organization), converts them into useful products, goods, and services, and makes them available to customers as outputs. The organization must continuously monitor and adapt to the environment if it is to survive and prosper. Disturbances in the environment may spell profound threats or new opportunities. The successful organization will identify, appraise, and respond to the various opportunities and threats in its environment.

Reading material

Analyzing Issues in the Environment Using a SWOT Model

Your business will face obstacles to success in addition to those posed by the competition. Half of the battle of overcoming these external obstacles is to understand them. And half of the key to benefiting from "lucky breaks" is being on top of developments and events that can be used to your advantage.

Threats and opportunities (from outside)

Identify, and rank by order of importance, any threats or opportunities your business may face from outside influences. Threats and opportunities come from a variety of sources including:

- The economic outlook of your market's economy—are you starting your business in a healthy economy? If not, can your product still thrive?
- Product innovations—how will changes made to the products of your competitors affect you? What's happening with products that are "complementary" to yours? (If you make toothbrushes, toothpaste would be "complementary products" to you.)
- Technological advancements—what changes in technology will impact you?
- Environment issues—is your product earth-friendly?
- Government regulations—what impact does comply with government regulations have on your business? Is there any pending legislation that may impact you?

- Barriers to market entry—are there high or low barriers to market entry in your field? What would it take for a competitor to start a business in your field? Could a competitor start-up overnight (low barrier) or does your business require special knowledge, expensive machinery, etc. (high barrier)?

Strengths and weaknesses (inside your company)

Identify internal strengths and weaknesses of your company. For example, your education, experience, and reputation in your area of expertise are most likely strengths. A weakness, if you plan to have employees, might be a lack of supervisory experience.

Summarize the main issues in an issues statement

Finally, determine which issues are most sign cant and integrate them into an issues statement. Use your carefully researched issues statement as you set your marketing objectives and strategies.

While there are few barriers to entry to offer public relations counseling to small business owners (a telephone or computer is all that's required), the 30 years combined experience of the partners of widgets public relations is its competitive advantage. No other PR agency in the area widgets serves offers a comparable depth of experience.

A professional manager is being recruited to compensate for the owner's lack of experience and interest in supervising employees. This person should be in place by November.

Business Tip: Learn About the Art of Gifting

The act of gifting is a symbolic way of marking special occasions, impressing another, expressing thanks, and sometimes offering a bribe! Your reason for gifting is your business, but here are some tips on how to do it graciously.

- Ensure that your choice of gift is appropriate for the occasion, and the receiver. For instance, a chocolate cake given to a friend on a diet would be a little thoughtless!
- Sometimes very expensive gifts could embarrass the receiver, especially if he is not in a position to reciprocate with one of similar value. Be sensitive to this issue.
- Certain companies have strict policies about their employees NOT accepting expensive gifts or any gifts from business associates. Take note.

Be careful when considering your choice of gift, by keeping the nationality of the person in mind. Certain items may signify mourning, or be considered a bad omen, and the last thing you need to do is upset a foreign business associate, whom you're trying very hard to impress.

Chapter 5

Market Research

5.1 Pre-knowledge

Do you have the experience that when you go shopping, a person approaches to you and asks you some questions politely, such as what shampoo do you often use to take care of your hair? Do you often change your shampoo brands? Almost everyone has experience. Do you know what job the person does? Yes. He or she is a market researcher.

The first stage in any marketing process is, of course, to make sure that you know your market. You can use one of the specialist market research agencies to carry out their research into the market. Or you can conduct the research yourself. There are several questions anxious to discover answers:

(1) What is the size or potential size of the market for the industry which you are planning?

(2) Who are the potential users of the industry?

(3) What type of goods or services do they require?

Research means studying something by gathering information. Market research means studying places or ways in which a company can sell its products or services. Market research also means studying what customers and prospects need or want from a company and its products market researchers try to find out how customers like the products they have and what the company can do to make things better.

If the company is planning to make a new product or to change a product it is already selling, market researchers ask customers a lot of questions. Answers to these questions are studied to try to improve the company's products and services.

There are different ways to get answers to their questions. One way to get answers is to use a questionnaire. The market research staff also gets information by using surveys and interviews.

A questionnaire is a document with questions written or printed on it. Usually, a questionnaire has a number of questions. People who fill out or answer questionnaires are called respondents. A respondent is a person who answers. Respondents usually write answers to the questions right on the questionnaire forms. Many times respondents can answer questions by marking an X in spaces on the questionnaires. When many people answer the same question in this way, it is possible for the market research staff to compare the answers of all the respondents give the same answer to a question. This tells the market research staff that customers or products to give most customers and prospects what they want. The more people they please, the more units of a product they should sell.

Surveys and interviews are done by talking to respondents in conducting a survey or an interview; the market researcher leads the respondents in answering questions or in giving information that is needed. In surveys and interviews, the respondents are also called subjects. In conducting a survey, market researchers ask just a few questions to many subjects. Sometimes surveys are done on the telephone. The survey takers record information on forms and keep calling or talking to subjects. Sometimes survey takers visit people at their homes or visit places where many people are founded. For example, many market research surveys are taken at railroad stations or airports. In most surveys, there are just a few questions which are designed to get specific information.

Interviews usually take longer than surveys. An interviewer usually talks to the subject for some time. Usually, the interviewer has a few questions to begin with. But when the subject responds, the interviewer asks other questions to find out why the subject does something or likes something. It is said that the interviewer is trying to find out the attitudes and preferences of the subject. Interviews take longer to study attitudes and preferences of customers and prospects than to get specific information on what products they use. But the interviews are important in research because they give the company information on how customers and prospects feel. Respondents and surveys to get the specific information we need about products. But when we want to know about how people really feel, we do interviews.

Questions

1. What are the three purposes of market research?
2. How many ways do you know to conduct market research?

5.2 Theory of Marketing

5.2.1 What is Marketing

Marketing is a set of activities undertaken to stimulate satisfactory exchanges of goods and services. A marketing effort may begin with finding out what products people want, or it may begin with stimulating a new want and then satisfying it. American Marketing Association (AMA) defines marketing as the performance of business activities that direct the flow of goods and services from producer to consumer or user. Marketing activities include such things as marketing research, retailing, sales-force management, advertisement, and transportation.

5.2.2 The Marketing Concept

USA has a long history of advances in production. In recent decades this has been matched by equally impressive advances in marketing. With competition becoming stiffer more and more firms have adopted a new concept—the marketing concept.

The marketing concept is the belief that a whole firm must be coordinated to serve its present and potential customers and to do so at a profit. This means getting to understand what customers really want and following closely the changes in tastes that occur. If a firm is to follow up on this awareness of customer wants in a profitable way, it must be well coordinated in its pursuit of the common goal—customer satisfaction.

5.2.3 Marketing and Utility

The concept of utility (the usefulness of products) is at the heart of the marketing activities. A product has form, place, time, and ownership utility.

Form utility is the usefulness of a product that results from converting raw materials and other inputs into a finished (or more nearly finished) product. Form utility is created by production. Laundry detergent for example, only becomes useful after it is manufactured out of various chemicals and other components.

Place utility is the usefulness of a product that results from a change in its location. Detergent in a loading dock in California must be moved to China, for example, before its usefulness to the Chinese can be realized. The train or truck that transports the detergent eastward creates a place utility for the Chinese.

Time utility is the usefulness of a product that results from its availability when the consumer wants it. Suppose I have a half-used box of detergent in my apartment. The box of detergent on the shelf in Tiankelong Supermarket is not yet fully useful to me. When detergent at my home is being used up, that box is gaining time utility.

Ownership utility is the usefulness of a product that comes about through the passage of legal title to the final user. The full utility of the detergent is realized only when the Chinese actually buy and sell it. In our economy, the legal passage of title is assumed with the exchange of money for a product.

Marketing activities are involved directly in the creation of a product's place, time, and ownership utility. They may also be included in the creation of form utility.

5.2.4 The Target Market

A target market is the group of present and potential customers that a firm aims to please with its goods or services. If a firm is to practice the marketing concept, it must define the characteristics and wants of its target market.

When choosing a target, marketers usually distinguish between industrial products and consumer products. Industrial products are goods or services that will be used by a firm or an institution to produce other goods or services. For example, tables sold to doctors are industrial goods. Manufacturers, hospitals, and lawyers who buy goods and services for their businesses are called industrial buyers.

Consumer products are goods or services that people buy for their own use—to wear, to eat, to look at, or to live in. Such buyers are often called ultimate consumers.

5.2.5 The Industrial Market

Industrial buyers are different from ultimate consumers, and they have the following features:
(1) they have more formal systems for buying;
(2) they have more clearly defined and profit-oriented purchase motion;
(3) they tend to be more concentrated geographically than ultimate consumers.

5.2.6 Government and Institutional Markets

Many of the same products that are sold to businesses are sold to nonprofit institutions as well. These products are a subcategory of industrial products. Nonprofit institutions include federal, state, and local governments, schools and nonprofit hospitals.

5.2.7 The Consumer Market

For firms that produce consumer products, the marketing task can be tricky. This is because the consumer market is so enormous and so diversified.

Notes

[1] Marketing is a set of activities undertaken to stimulate satisfactory exchanges of goods

and services.

营销是指能够引起令人满意的商品或服务交换而进行的一系列活动。

[2] Time utility is the usefulness of a product that results from its availability when the consumer wants it.

（产品的）时间效用指消费者需要一件产品时该产品可供使用而产生的效用。

[3] A target market is that group of present and potential customers a firm aims to please with its goods or services.

目标市场是指公司打算用其产品和服务使他们满意的当前与潜在的消费群。

Questions

1. What is marketing, and why have firms adopted the marketing concept?
2. Why is the marketing task more complex in an economy where are high levels of discretionary income than in one where the people live at the subsistence level?
3. Why there is a demand for industrial goods?
4. Is a product useful to a consumer, if it possesses only form utility?

Reading Material

Business Taboo

Business taboos are defined to be informal values, rules, and regulations that guide business people in transactions. These could be known business regulations, ethics, cultural insights, and best practices. They are sometimes deduced or taken directly from formal business books but also do have cultural influence. It used to be an unwritten rule that you don't discuss specific topics in business, or you don't cross some lines. Those were generally politics, religion, and sexual orientation.

1. Don't pitch every investor in your database

Making a successful investor connection is more like using Match.com and less like kissing a lot of frogs before meeting your prince. Research what individual investors invest in and be sure to heed their criteria and industry preferences. Investors have limited time and focus on specific industries. If you reach out to every investor, you may fail to get to know the ones who can help your company thrive. Pitching to everyone on your list can harm your reputation when you go looking for capital for your next big idea.

2. Avoid cold calling each investor to book an appointment

Always get an intro from someone an investor respect. According to Business 2

Community, only 2 percent of cold calls lead to an appointment. Investors often cite a cold call as reason to filter out those not advanced enough to research and prospect correctly. Additionally, today most people view phone calls as a major interruption.

3. Don't assume your solution solves a big problem

Assume nothing! Be sure your solution solves a big problem. Most businesses aren't worth investing in because the upside is too limited. Investors seek to invest in low-risk, high-growth products, and services that will return a profit.

Your product's solution should be supported by research and the problem must be worth solving. After all, if consumers don't see something as in need of a fix, investors won't either. For example, as people sought ways to use their smartphones to perform tasks, the folks at Nest.com saw a need for a remote control for the homes and invented a suite of products to cost-effectively program temperature and security functions.

4. Steer clear of industry speak

Every industry has its jargon. At its best, such language provides shorthand to let insiders communicate with ease. At its worst, some phrases bastardize the meaning of words and confer an air of truly unwarranted self-importance. Obviously in a medical or technical field, specific terms are necessary for clear communication. Be smart about learning and using those words correctly. I had to master some medical concepts to effectively speak on behalf of my startup.

5. Don't jump into a crowded category

If you're considering launching a startup in a business category with a lot of existing players, be sure your company is differentiated. In the oversaturated cupcake market, Cupcakes by Melissa markets its merchandize with petite size being as its point of difference.

Me-too companies aren't exciting unless there's a big reason for them to succeed though others failed. What sets your idea apart? How will your market different? Be sure this is clear, especially if your product fits into a trendy fad.

6. Shun working without a net

Improve comedy teams might take risks but don't try this with the busy investor crowd. Practice your pitch to the point where you don't need slides, can give it at the drop of a hat, and can modify it instantly based on the interests of an investor. Be sure you can summarize your pitch in five minutes and can also dive into a half-hour presentation. Prepare for any question an investor could ask. The quicker you can give a no-nonsense answer, the more likely an investor will want to move money toward your idea.

7. Don't let your delivery belie your intent

One of the latest areas of market research involves emotion analytics or what a voice tells others about the speaker. Although you may think you are presenting in an earnest, intelligent tone, new technology can analyze your voice and might reveal to you how tired and exasperated your sound.

Want to test and hone your delivery before you face your audience? A new App, Moodies, will record 20 seconds of your speech and provide a critique, letting you work out those pesky voice quirks before presenting to a crowd.

Do you have what it takes to be the next Alexander Graham Bell, Thomas Edison, Elon Musk, or Steve Jobs? You won't know until you try.

8. Avoid gossip or eavesdropping

Gossip and eavesdropping are childish behaviors that have no place in the workplace. If you hear a rumor about someone in the workplace, do not pass it on. People don't always know or remember who starts a rumor, but they always remember who spreads it. If you walk into an area, and it seems your co-workers don't know you are there, make sure to greet them politely to remove any chance that you accidentally eavesdrop on their conversation.

Business Tip: Express Yourself through Your Business Card

Business stationery is the first step in building a corporate identity. It allows a free expression of one's true personality in a smart, "business" sort of way. If you are an artist, or employed "in the media" you can give your imagination free rein. For most other kinds of business, it is best to be conservative and project an image of practicality.

The purpose of a business card is to introduce you. It is also an invitation to establish and retain communication.

- Your card should bear your name, position, and responsibility in the organization, the name of the business, address, a scaled-down logo (if any), and information about how you can be contacted.
- Use a standard sized business card. If your card is too large to fit into a cardholder or wallet, it will end up in the back of a drawer or thrown in a dustbin, and it's of no use to anyone there!
- The standard business card measures 3.5 inches by 2 inches. The most appropriate font size for a business card is 8-10 points for name and business name and 6.5-8 points for address and other information.

Chapter 6

Market Segmentation, Targeting and Positioning

6.1 Introduction

A target market consists of a set of buyers who share common needs or characteristics that the company decides to serve. The firm can adopt one of three market-coverage strategies: undifferentiated marketing, differentiated marketing, and concentrated marketing.

Markets consist of buyers, and buyers differ in one or more ways. They may differ in their wants, resources, locations, buying attitudes, and buying practices. Any of these variables can be used to segment a market.

Because buyers have unique needs and wants, each buyer is potentially a separate market. Ideally, then, a seller might design a separate marketing program for each buyer.

It is best for companies to customize their products and marketing programs for each buyer.

Most sellers face large numbers of smaller buyers and do not find complete segmentation worthwhile. Instead, they look for broad classes of buyers who differ in their product needs or buying responses.

There is no single way to segment a market. A marketer has to try different segmentation variables, alone and in combination, alone and in combination, to find the best way to view the market structure.

Geographic segmentation calls for dividing the market into different geographical units such as nations, states, regions, counties, cities, or neighborhoods.

A company may decide to operate in one or a few geographical areas, or to operate in all areas but pay attention to geographical differences in needs and wants.

Many companies today are "regionalizing" their marketing programs—localizing their products, advertising, promotion, and sales efforts to fit the needs of individual regions, cities, and even neighborhoods. Others are seeking to cultivate as ye untapped territory.

Demographic segmentation consists of dividing the market into groups based on variables such as age, gender, family size, family life cycle, income, occupation, education, religion, race, and nationality. Demographic factors are the most popular cases for segmenting customer groups.

Some companies use age and life-cycle segmentation, offering different products or using different marketing approaches for different age and life-cycle groups.

Gender segmentation has long been used in clothing, hairdressing, cosmetics, and magazines. Recently, other marketers have noticed opportunities for gender segmentation. The automobile industry has begun to use gender segmentation extensively.

Income segmentation has long been used by the marketers of products and services, such as automobiles, boats, clothing, cosmetics, and travel. Many companies target affluent consumers with luxury goods and convenience services.

Psychographic segmentation divides buyers into different groups based on social classes, lifestyle, or personality characteristics. People in the same demographic group may derive different psychographic makeups.

Behavioral segmentation divides buyers into groups based on their knowledge, attitudes, uses, or responses to a product. Many marketers believe that behavior variables are the best starting point for building market segments.

A powerful form of segmentation is to group buyers according to the different benefits that they seek from the product. Benefit segmentation requires finding the major benefit people look for in the product class, the kinds of people who look for each benefit, and the major brands that deliver each benefit.

Markets can be segmented into groups of nonusers, ex-users, potential users, first-time users, and regular users of a product.

A market can also be segmented by consumer loyalty. Consumers can be loyal to brands, stores, and companies. Buyers can be divided into groups according to their degree of loyalty.

Consumer and business marketers use many of the same variables to segment their markets. Business buyers can be segmented geographically or by benefits sought, user status, usage rate, loyalty status, and attitudes. Yet, business marketers also use some additional variables, like operating characteristics, purchasing approaches, situational factors, and personal characters.

The firm has to evaluate the various segments and decide how many and which ones to target. In evaluating different market segments, a firm must look at three factors: segment size and growth, segment structural attractiveness, and company objectives and resources.

The company must first collect and analyze data on current sales, projected sales-growth rates, and expected profit margins for the various segments. It will be interested in segments that have the right size and growth characteristics.

The largest, fastest-growing segments are not always the most attractive ones for every company. Smaller companies may find that they lack the skills and resources needed to serve the larger segments or that these segments are too competitive. Such companies may select segments that are smaller and less attractive, but that are potentially more profitable for them.

Even if a segment has the right size and growth and is structurally attractive, the company must consider its own objectives and resources in relation to that segment.

Some attractive segments could be dismissed quickly because they do not mesh with the company's long-run objectives. Although such segments might be tempting in themselves they might divert the company's attention and energies away from its main goals.

Even if the company possesses the strengths needed to succeed in the segment, it needs to employ skills and resources superior to those of the competitors in order to really win in a market segment. The company should access segments only where it can offer superior value and gain advantages over competitors.

Market segmentation and targeting form the core of modern marketing strategy. Smart targeting helps companies to be more efficient and effective by focusing on the segments that they can satisfy best. Targeting also benefits consumers-companies reach specific groups of consumers with offers carefully tailored to satisfy their needs.

Once a company has decided which segments of the market it will enter, it must decide what "positions" it wants to occupy in those segments.

A product's position is the way the product is defined by consumers on important attributes—the place the product occupies in consumers' minds relative to competing products.

Blue Moon is positioned as a powerful, all-purpose family detergent; Mr. Muscle is positioned as the detergent as a disinfectant; Liby is positioned as the detergent for all temperatures. Volkswagen polo is positioned on economy, Benz on luxury, and Porsche and BMW on performance.

To simplify buying decision-making, consumers organize products into categories—they "position" products services, and companies in their minds. A product's position is the complex set of perceptions, impressions, and feelings that consumers hole for the product compared with competing products.

Marketers do not want to leave their products' positions to chance. They plan positions that will give their products the greatest advantage in selected target markets, and they design marketing mixes to create these planned positions.

The positioning task consists of three steps: identifying a set of possible competitive advantages upon which to build a position, selecting the right competitive advantages, and effectively communicating and delivering the chosen position to the market.

6.2 Relevant Knowledge

6.2.1 Customer's Loyalty

Buyers can be divided into groups according to their degree of loyalty. Some consumers are completely loyal—they buy one brand all the time. Others are somewhat loyal—they are loyal to two or three brands of a given product or favor one brand while sometimes buying others. Still other buyers show no loyalty to any brand. They either want something different each time they buy or always buy a brand on sale.

A company can learn a lot by analyzing loyalty patterns in its market. It should start by studying its own loyal customers. The characteristics of its customers pinpoint the target market for it. By studying its less loyal buyers, the company can detect which brands are most competitive with its own. By looking at customers who are shifting away from its brand, the company can learn about its marketing weaknesses. As for non-loyals, the company may attract them by putting its brand on sale.

Companies need to be careful when using brand loyalty in their segmentation strategies. What appears to be brand-loyal purchase pattern might reflect little more habit, indifference, a low price, or unavailability of other brands. Thus, frequent or regular purchasing may not be the same as brand loyalty.

6.2.2 Realizing the Chosen Position

The company must take strong steps to deliver and communicate the desired position to target consumers. All the company's marketing mix efforts must support the positioning strategies, positioning the company to call for concrete action. If the company decides to build a position on better quality and service, it must first deliver that position. Designing the marketing mix (product, price, place, and promotion) essentially involving working out the tactical details of the positioning strategy.

Once a company has built the desired position, it must take care to maintain the position through consistent performance and communication. It must closely monitor and adapt the position overtime to match changes in consumer needs and competitor's strategies. However, the company should avoid abrupt changes that might confuse the consumers. Instead, a product's position should evolve gradually as it adapts to the ever-changing marketing environment.

6.2.3 Selecting a Brand

Decisions related to branding are critical to the success of marketing efforts. A good brand name can set the product apart from the competition and give rise to positive feelings such as trust, confidence, security, and strength.

To select a brand name, marketers consider a variety of criteria that reflect the following five concerns:

(1) The brand name should imply the benefits delivered by the product.

(2) The brand name should be positive, distinctive, and easy to say and remember.

(3) The name should be consistent with the image of the product or organization.

(4) The name should be legally permissible. This means that the name should not violate the trademark status of another organization's brand.

(5) The brand name for a product to be offered globally should translate well. To speakers of other languages, the brand name should not be offensive or imply something negative about the product. To meet this objective, global marketers sometimes compromise on the first three criteria.

These criteria for choosing a brand imply that marketers need to understand the environment when creating a brand name.

6.2.4 Product Life Cycle

Products pass through four stages in their life in the given market in terms of both sales and profitability.

Introduction: During the introduction stage of the product life cycle, a new product enters the marketplace. Sales start out slowly but begin to climb. Production costs are usually high because the producers lack experience in making the product. Marketing costs tend to be high because sellers must devote resources to educating target markets about what the new product is and how it will benefit them.

Growth: During the growth stage, sales climb rapidly as more and more buyers begin trying the product. Profits also rise as sellers learn to make efficient use of their production facilities and distribution channels. The challenges of this stage include keeping up with demand and fending off competitors who are attracted to the market because of its growth in sales and large profit margins.

Maturity: A product is mature when it becomes familiar to the market and when sales climb more gradually and then plateau. Because many buyers already own the product, sales growth slows and may even begin falling toward the end of this stage.

Decline: Eventually the sales volume for most products begins to fall. There are many reasons for a sales decline. Perhaps new technology has led to a superior alternative. Moreover, needs or values may change so that the product is no longer relevant or appealing. Marketers may respond to the sales decline by seeking ways to keep the product profitable. They can modify products and seek new uses or new markets to forestall decline.

Exercises

Exercise1: Reading comprehension

Choose the best answer for each of the following questions.

1. When did Wal-Mart enter China?
   A. 1996.　　　　B. 1998.　　　　C. 2009.　　　　D. 2013.
2. What does Wal-Mart adhere to in China?
   A. Field procurement.　　　　B. Local procurement.
   C. Imported products.　　　　D. All of the above.
3. Which of the following statements is not true about the article?
   A. Wal-Mart operates a variety of formats and brands in China.
   B. Wal-Mart China has established cooperative relations with more than 7,000 suppliers.
   C. Wal-Mart will not continue to expand its investment in China.
   D. Wal-Mart will continue to upgrade its existing stores.

Exercise 2: Blank filling

Fill each of the blanks with the appropriate word or expression from the box. Change the form of the word or expression when necessary.

> preferential　employee　localization　nationwide　momentum

1. Wal-Mart has about 100,000 _____.
2. Wal-Mart _____ supermarket.
3. Adhering to the current good development _____.
4. Wal-Mart has opened more than 400 stores and about 20 distribution centers in more than 180 cities _____.
5. Wal-Mart China pays attention to the _____ of talents.

Exercise 3: Translate the following sentences into English

1. 目前沃尔玛在中国经营多种业态和品牌，包括购物广场、山姆会员商店、沃尔玛惠选超市等。
2. 沃尔玛在中国的经营始终坚持本地采购。
3. 沃尔玛在中国注重人才本土化，鼓励人才多元化。
4. 秉持着目前良好的发展势头，沃尔玛将持续扩大在华的投资。

Reading Material

Developing Product Positioning and Designing Product

I. Positioning

1.1 Importance of Positioning

No matter what you are marketing, salient positioning is necessary. Positioning is the basis for all of your communications—branding, advertising, promotions, packaging, sales-force, merchandising, and publicity. By having one meaningful, targeted positioning as a guide for all communications, you will convey a consistent image. By conveying a common positioning, each vehicle of communication will reinforce the others for accumulative effect, maximizing the return of your marketing investment. Accordingly, everything you do from a marketing perspective must reinforce one positioning. Otherwise, you will undermine your marketing efforts and confuse the target group as well.

Further, because everything you do should reflect one positioning, the positioning must be correct, or your marketing activities will be ineffective. Worse yet, income positioning could even destroy a successful product. You must look for a positioning that is not only right for your product now but that will also be adaptable years into the future for both the marketplace and the product.

1.2 Develop Product Positioning

Positioning involves creating a favorable perception of the product relative to competing products in the minds of potential buyers. The result—the product's position—is the potential customers' view of the product compared to other alternatives. There are several different types of positioning.

1. Positioning by competitors

Most positioning strategies include positioning a product in comparison to competitors' brands. In some cases, the marketer does this explicitly. In other cases, the comparison with competitors is implied, and attempts are made to convince potential buyers that a product is better than the market leaders on one or more dimensions.

2. Positioning by attributes

Marketers may position a product on the basis of its attributes such product features. For example, an immediate-care facility might advertise that it is open seven days a week and does not require patients to make an appointment, which positions it on the attribute of convenience.

3. Positioning by uses or applications

A product may be positioned for a particular use. Master Card positioned itself as the most useful credit card for everyday transactions—a way to organize one's finances and pay routine expenses.

4. Positioning by users

Marketers may decide to position products as intended for use by a particular group.

5. Positioning by product classes

A product may be positioned relative to other product classes.

Of course, a positioning strategy may include more than one of these dimensions. To select a positioning strategy, marketers consider the product's market share and how the product can deliver better value than competing products. Is the product the market leader or a follower? Perhaps the products are so innovative that there is little, if any, close competition. This information influences the kind of positioning strategy that is most likely to succeed.

A product that is the market leader usually will not position itself directly against smaller share competitors. For products without large market shares, it may be useful to use niche marketing. To position a product using a niche strategy, the marketer looks for a unique market to serve but one so large that it will attract major competitors.

1.3 Designing Products

A product is anything that can be offered to a market for attention, acquisition, use, or consumption and that might satisfy a want or need; it includes physical objects, services, persons, places, organizations, and ideas.

The product planner must build an actual product around the core product. Actual products may have as many as five characteristics: a quality level, features, design, a brand name, and packaging.

The product planner must build an augmented product around the core and actual products by offering additional consumer services and benefits.

Consumers tend to see products as complex bundles of benefits that satisfy their needs. Successful companies add benefits to their offers that not only will satisfy, but also will delight the customer.

Consumer goods are those bought by final consumers for personal consumption,

Marketers usually classify these goods based on consumer shopping habits. Consumer goods include convenience goods, shopping goods, specialty goods, and unsought goods.

Convenience goods are consumer goods and services that the customer usually buys frequently, immediately, and with a minimum of comparison and buying effort. They are usually low priced and widely available.

Industrial goods are those bought by individuals and organizations for further processing or for use in conducting a business.

Shopping goods are consumer goods that the customer, in the process of selection, usually compares or such bases as suitability, quality, price, and style. Consumers spend considerable time and effort in gathering information and making comparison when purchasing shopping goods.

Specialty goods are consumers goods with unique characteristics or brand identification for which a significant group of buyers is willing to make a special purchase effort.

Unsought goods are consumer goods that the consumer either does not know about or knows about but does not normally think of buying. By their very nature, unsought goods require a lot of advertising, personal selling, and other marketing efforts.

Materials and parts are industrial goods that enter the manufacturer's product completely, either through further processing or as components. They fall into two classes: raw materials and manufactured materials and parts.

Capital items are industrial goods that partly enter the finished product. They include two groups: installations and accessory equipment.

Supplies and services are industrial goods that do not enter the finished product at all. Supplies include operating supplies and repair and maintenance items. Business services include maintenance and repair services and business advisory services.

Product quality includes the product's overall durability, reliability, precision, ease of operation and repair, and other valued attributes.

Marketers brand their products to differentiate them from competitors and to help buyers make purchase decisions. A brand is "a name, term, design, symbol, or any other feature that identifies one seller's goods or services as distinct from those of other sellers."

Brand equity includes customers' brand loyalty, name awareness, perceived quality, and brand associations. These components result from buyers' thoughts about the product, the organization, and other variables. Brand equity can be either positive or negative, depending on how consumers perceive the meaning of the brand.

Packaging includes the activities of designing and producing the container or wrapper for a product. Labeling is also part of packaging and consists of printed information appearing on or with the package.

A product lie is a group of products that are closely related because they function in a similar manner, are sold to the same customer groups, are marketed through the same types of outlets, or fall within given price ranges.

Branding has become a major issue in product strategy. Developing a branded product requires a great deal of long-term marketing investment, especially for advertising, promotion, and packaging.

Powerful brand names command strong consumer loyalty. A sufficient number of customers demand these brands and refuse substitutes, even if the substitutes are offered at somewhat lower prices.

Notes

[1] actual product 实际产品
[2] augmented product 附加产品
[3] core product 核心产品
[4] product mix 产品组合
[5] product line 产品线
[6] product extension 产品扩展
[7] brand 品牌
[8] brand extension 品牌扩展
[9] durable goods 耐用品
[10] nondurable goods 非耐用品
[11] consumer goods 消费品
[12] convenience goods 便利品
[13] shopping goods 选购品
[14] specialty goods 特殊品
[15] unsought goods 非必需品
[16] industrial goods 工业用品
[17] capital goods 固定资产
[18] materials and parts 材料与零部件
[19] product features 产品特征
[20] packaging 包装
[21] product design 产品设计
[22] product quality 产品质量
[23] product life cycle 产品生命周期
[24] raw materials 原材料
[25] accessory equipment 附属设备

II. Packaging

Packaging serves several purposes that add value for customers. First, the packaging is functional. Many kinds of products, such as soup, laundry detergent, and lubricating oil, must be carried in some type of container. Besides protecting and containing the product, the package may provide the customer with convenience. Also packaging can provide a degree of safety in that it protects the product from damage in shipping or from tampering.

Packaging can also be used to promote the product. This benefits the customer by providing information and the seller by drawing attention to the product. Colorful, attractive packaging helps a product stand out in the eyes of buyers. Finally, packaging can distinguish products from those of competitors. This is the case with fancy perfume bottles designed to reflect the image of a particular fragrance.

The use of packaging to distinguish a product may be an important part of the marketing mix for reaching certain target markets. To target single people, food marketers might offer smaller or single-serving packages. To target families with children, marketers might use child safety containers for dangerous products like medicine or lye.

In selecting packaging, marketers must consider the costs of various alternatives. Making packaging as attractive, protective, convenient, or safe to use as possible could be prohibitively expensive. Therefore, marketers must determine the costs of various packaging alternatives and select packages that satisfy customer needs at low cost.

One needs to understand how cultural influences are interwoven with the perceived value and importance of market places on a product. A product is more a physical item; it is a bundle of satisfactions the buyer receives. This includes its form, taste, color, odor, and texture; how it functions in use; the package; the confidence or warranty; manufacturer's and retailer's servicing; the confidence or prestige enjoyed by the brand; the manufacture's reputation; the country of origin; and any other symbolic utility received for the possession or use of the goods. In short, the market relates to more than a product's physical form and primary function.

The values and customs within a culture impute much of the importance of other benefits. In other words, a product is the sum of the physical and psychological satisfaction it provides the user.

The meaning and value imputed to the psychological attributes of a product can vary among cultures and are perceived as negative or positive product attributes rather than negative ones, the adaptation of the nonphysical features of a product may be necessary.

When analyzing a product for a second market, the extent of adaptation required depends on cultural differences in product use and perception between the market the product was originally developed for and the new market. The greater these cultural differences are between the two markets, the greater the extent of adaptation that may be necessary.

The problems of adapting a product to sell abroad are similar to those associated with the introduction to a new product at home. Products are not measured solely by their physical specifications. The mature of the new product is in what it does to and for the customers—their habits, tastes, and patterns of life.

Notes

[1] tamper 损坏，干预
[2] lye 碱性洗涤液
[3] impute 把……归因于
[4] adaptation 适应，修改

III. Promotion Tools

Advertising is any paid term of non-personal presentation of ideas, products, or services by an identified sponsor to a targeted audience and delivered primarily through mass media.

Major decisions in advertising include objective setting, budgeting, message strategy, and media strategy. Advertising objective setting depends on the pattern of consumer behavior and information that is involved in the particular product category.

Advertising is used to reach large numbers of consumers who are geographically dispersed. Products can be dramatized through the use of color, sound, and visuals.

It is effective at building awareness, knowledge, and a long-term image for the product. On the other hand, advertising is impersonal, expensive, and not adaptable to individual consumers. It is difficult to measure the effectiveness of advertising campaigns.

Internet ads include banners, sponsors, and rich media. A banner is an ad on a Web page, often using moving images and sounds as well as text. Clicking on a banner usually takes the user to an advertiser's Web site.

Sponsorships, which cost more than simple banner ads at the corner of a Web page, showcase a message much more prominently.

Also popular are rich media ads with video-like images, including flying golf balls and wiggling fingers, which are meant to engage Web surfers.

Informative advertising is used to inform consumers about a new product or feature and to build primary demand.

As most of the target audiences become aware of the product and competition in the category increases, organizations move to persuasive advertising which has the objective of building selective demand for a brand by persuading consumers that it offers them the best value.

When a brand is directly or indirectly compared to a competitor, it is known as comparison advertising is that it provides information that potentially helps consumers make better purchase decisions.

Comparison advertising saves consumers the effort of fining the information from other sources, and helps producers of innovative products to position their products to position their products on the basis of competitive superiority.

For mature products of which everyone is aware, advertisers use reminder advertising. The objective is to remind people about the brand.

Media planning must be coordinated with marketing strategy and with other aspects of advertising strategy.

The strategic aspects of media planning involve four steps: (1) selecting the target audience toward which all subsequent efforts will be directed; (2) specifying media objectives, which typically are stated in terms of reach (What proportion of the target audience must see, read, or hear our advertising message during a specified period?), frequency (How often should the target audience be exposed to the advertisement during this period?), gross rating points or GRPs or effective rating points or ERPs (How much total advertising is necessary during a particular period to accomplish the reach and frequency objectives?); (3) selecting general media categories and specific vehicles within each medium; and (4) buying media.

Cost per thousand (CPM) allows a media planner to compare media based on two variables: audience and cost. CPM is used as a comparative device. The lowest cost per thousand medium is the most efficient, all other variables being equal.

CPM may be computed for a printed page or broadcast time, and the audience base may be either circulation, homes reached, readers, or number of audience members of any kind of demographic or product usage classification.

An organization must decide whether to handle its advertising in-house or whether to hire an advertising agency. Most ad agencies are organized into four major departments: the creative department, the media planning department, the research department, the business or account service department.

The creative department actually produces the ads. The media planning department researches the various media options and purchases the advertising media. The research department studies audience needs and communicates this information to the other departments. The business or account service department meets with clients and understands their needs.

IV. Wal-Mart China Overview

Wal-Mart entered China in 1996 and opened its first Wal-Mart shopping mall and Sam's member store in Shenzhen. Until today, Wal-Mart has been operating in China for more than 20 years with about 100,000 associates.

At present, Wal-Mart operates a variety of formats and brands in China, including shopping malls, Sam's Club, Wal-Mart preferential supermarket, etc. Wal-Mart has opened more than 400 stores and about 20 distribution centers in more than 180 cities nationwide. Wal-Mart has served 7 billion customers since it entered China.

Wal-Mart has about 100,000 local procurement in China. At present, Wal-Mart China has established cooperative relations with more than 7,000 suppliers, and more than 95% of the products it sells are local products.

Wal-Mart China pays attention to the localization of talents and encourages the diversification of talents, especially the cultivation and development of female employees and management. At present, more than 99.9% of Wal-Mart's employees in China are from China, and the general manager of the store is all from China, with about 66% female employees, and nearly 50% of the management team is female. In 2009, the company set up "Wal-Mart China Feminine Leadership Development Committee" to accelerate the career development of women. At the beginning of 2013, Wal-Mart Feminine Leadership Institute was established to better promote the growth and development of women leaders in the company.

Adhering to the current good development momentum, Wal-Mart will continue to expand its investment in China, and in the future, it will work together online and offline to provide better services to customers. At the same time, Wal-Mart will continue to upgrade its existing stores, strengthen food safety, and develop with local suppliers in a win-win way. Wal-Mart hopes to better adapt to the new normal of China's economy, create more jobs, and become an excellent corporate citizen trusted by consumers while developing with China's economy.

Notes

[1] employee *n.* 受雇者，雇工，雇员
[2] format *n.* 总体安排，计划
[3] preferential *adj.* 优先的，优惠的，优待的
[4] nationwide *adj.* 全国性的，遍及全国的，全国范围的
[5] localization *n.* 地方化，局限，定位
[6] diversification *n.* 多样化，变化
[7] current *adj.* 当前的，现在的
[8] momentum *n.* 推进力，动力

Business Tip: Negotiating Tip

Tackle Your Negotiation "Partner"

People often refer to their negotiating partner as "opponent"! This just goes to their attitude towards the process of negotiation. Negotiation is not a fight, but a process of addressing an issue in a creative and civilized manner.

- You may not like your partner. But you have to control your emotions, rather than let your emotions control you. Think of your negotiating partner as someone you need and who needs you in return. This way, you concentrate on the issue at hand.
- This doesn't mean that voicing a critical opinion will cast a negative doubt upon your person. On the contrary, people often appreciate honesty. But then again, it is the way you convey it. Suggest, not accuse.
- During your interaction, try to understand the basic nature of your partner; this will go a long way in the negotiating process.
- You must be confident (or at least appear to be) because most people want to negotiate with someone who they feel will deliver.

Negotiating Don'ts

- Never start the pitch on an aggressive note.
- Don't make demands. Make suggestions.
- Speak in the language of your negotiating partner. Save the jargon for business school.
- Be patient. Persevere.

Chapter 7

The Marketing Mix

7.1 4P's

In carrying out the marketing functions, the firm needs to have a marketing program or strategy. This is known as the marketing mix(the words created by Neil Borden in 1953).

With the development of marketing, many marketing scholars have pointed some theories on the elements of marketing mix. According to E. J. McCarthy's Basic Marketing in 1960, marketing mix contains the following major elements: (a) product, (b) price, (c) place and (d) promotion. These are sometimes referred to as "the 4P's" of marketing which is the base of modern marketing. According to Philip Kotler's Mega Marketing in 1986, marketing mix contains 6P's: (a) product, (b)price, (c)place, (d) promotion, (e) power, and (f) public relations. With the development of cyber marketing/ online marketing, Philip Kotler in the early of 1990's pointed out 4C's which is the new theory on marketing mix: (a) consumer—consumer's wants and needs, (b)cost—cost to satisfy wants and needs, (c) convenience—convenience to buy, and (d) communication—communication with consumers. Here we still adopt McCarthy's 4P's (see Figure 7.1).

7.1.1 Product

The product consists of the items and accessories that the company offers to the consumer. This decision is made during planning. Product planning involves identifying the buyer's needs, working up a preliminary design of the merchandise, checking to see that the product design meets the expectations of buyers, setting on the product's specifications, selecting the brand name for the product, determining the type of packaging to be used, and deciding what services to offer with the product.

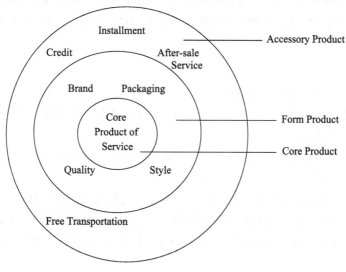

Figure 7.1 Product Layers

7.1.2 Price

The price charged for the product must be high enough to give the company a profit, but low enough to entice the consumer to buy. In settling on a fair price, firms will evaluate their own costs, current pricing laws, what the competition is doing, and the types of discounts and terms of sales that are customary in the industry. On the basis of this information, a price will be agreed upon.

7.1.3 Place

Consumers are accustomed to looking for goods in a particular place. Business needs to have its goods available in the right places. This requires moving the merchandise from where it is produced to where it is desired. Such movement entails transportation, channels of distribution, and storage. The manufacturer needs to have a strategy for taking care of all these matters. Some use middlemen such as wholesalers to move their merchandise to the consumer. Others go directly to the finial buyer's themselves. In any case, the goods must eventually be moved to the right place for purchase.

7.1.4 Promotion

The fourth element in the marketing mix is promotion. The purpose of promotion is to stimulate demand for the company's products. Common promotional techniques include advertising, packaging, branding, personal selling, and sales manuals, enlisting of dealer cooperation in displaying goods at the point of purchase, and coupons and premiums. A firm may not use all of these promotional techniques to move a product, but many will rely on two or three of them because one alone cannot usually do the job.

Notes

[1] mix 英文原意为 things put together，意即混合、结合，如 product mix（产品组合）指一个企业提供给市场的产品项目组合，即经营范围和结构，又叫 product assortment（产品搭配）。

[2] 由于营销组合的四个要素 product、price、place、promotion 的英文首字母都是"p"，所以营销组合又称为 4P。

[3] channels of distribution 分销渠道，也可以解释为销售渠道。在贸易中，可以有不同种类的分销渠道，如 manufacturer（制造商）—consumer（消费者），又如 manufacturer（制造商）—wholesaler（批发商）—retailer（零售商）—consumer（消费者）。

Questions

1. What is the marketing mix?
2. In what way are product planning and marketing research related?
3. Of the 4P's, which do you think is the most important? Why?

7.2 Promotional Mix

It is not enough for a business to have good products sold at attractive prices. To generate sales and profits, the advantages of products have to be communicated to consumers. In marketing, this is commonly known as "promotion". Promotion is all about companies communicating with customers.

A business's total marketing communications programmer is called the "promotional mix" and consists of a blend of advertising, personal selling, sales promotion and public relations tools.

It is helpful to define the four main elements of the promotional mix before considering their strengths and limitations.

7.2.1 Personal Selling

Personal selling is oral communication with potential buyers of a product with the intention of making a sale. It may focus initially on developing a relationship with the potential buyer, but will always ultimately end up with an attempt to "close the sale".

Personal selling is one of the oldest forms of promotion. It involves the use of a sales-force to support a push strategy (encouraging intermediaries to buy the product) or pull strategy (where the role of the sales-force may be limited to supporting retailers and providing after-sale service).

What are the main roles of the sales-force?

Kotler describes six main activities of a sales-force:

(1) prospecting—trying to find new customers;

(2) communicating with existing and potential customers about the product range;

(3) selling—contact with the customer, answering questions and trying to close the sale;

(4) servicing—providing support and service to the customer in the period up to delivery and also post-sale;

(5) information gathering—obtaining information about the market to feedback into the marketing planning process;

(6) allocating—in terms of product shortage, the sales-force may have the power to decide how available stocks are allocated.

What are the advantages of using personal selling as a means of promotion?

- personal selling is a face-to-face activity; customers therefore obtain a relatively high degree of personal attention;
- the sales message can be customized to meet the needs of the customer;
- the two-way nature of the sales process allows the sales team to respond directly and promptly to customer questions and concerns;
- personal selling is a good way of getting across large amounts of technical or other complex product information;
- frequent meetings between sales-force and customer provide an opportunity to build good long-term relationships.

Given that there are many advantages to personal selling, why don't more businesses maintain a direct sales-force? The main disadvantage of personal selling is the cost of employing a sales-force. In addition to the basic pay package, a business needs to provide incentives to achieve sales and the equipment to make sales calls.

In addition, a sales person can only call on one customer at a time. This is not a cost-effective way to reach a large audience.

7.2.2 Public Relations

The institution of public relations defines public relations as follows: the planned and sustained effort to establish and maintain goodwill and mutual understanding between an organization and its publics.

What does it mean by the term in the above definition?

A business may have many publics with which it needs to maintain good relations and build goodwill. For example, consider the relevant "publics" for a publicly-quoted business engaged in medical research:

- employees
- shareholders
- trade unions
- members of the "general public"
- customers
- pressure groups
- the medical profession
- charities funding medical research
- professional research bodies and policy-forming organizations
- the media
- government and politicians

The role of public relations is to:

- identify the relevant publics
- influence the opinions of those publics by reinforcing favorable opinions
    (1) transforming perhaps neutral opinions into positive ones
    (2) changing or neutralizing hostile opinions

7.2.3 Public Relations Techniques

There are many techniques available to influence public opinion, some of which are more appropriate in certain circumstance than others.

(1) Consumer communication. Companies may use customer press releases, trade press releases, promotional videos, consumer exhibitions, competitions and prizes, product launch events, celebrity endorsements and web sites, etc.

(2) Business communication. Business communication includes corporate identity design, company and product videos, direct mailings, and web sites and trade exhibitions.

(3) Internal/employee communication. Internal communication may be realized through in-house newsletters and magazines, intranet, notice boards or employee conferences or emails.

(4) External corporate communication. External communication includes company literature, community involvement programs, trade, local, national and international media relations.

(5) Financial communication. Financial communication includes financial media relations, annual report and accounts, meetings with stock market analysts, fund managers etc., or with shareholders (including the annual general meeting).

Given the wide range of techniques used in public relations, how is it possible to measure the effectiveness of public relations?

It is actually quite difficult to measure whether the key messages have been communicated to the target public. In any event, this could be quite costly since it would involve a large amount of regular research. Instead, the main measures of effectiveness concentrate on the process of public relations, and include:

- monitoring the amount of media coverage obtained (press cuttings agencies play a role in keeping businesses informed of this);
- measuring attendance at meetings, conferences;
- measuring the number of enquiries or orders received in response to specific public relation efforts.

7.2.4 Sales Promotion

A good definition of sales promotion would be as follows: an activity designed to boost the sales of a product or service. It may include an advertising campaign, increased PR activity, a free sample campaign, offering free gifts or trading stamps, arranging demonstrations or exhibitions, setting up competitions with attractive prizes, temporary price reductions, door-to-door calling, telemarketing, and personal letters and other methods.

More than any other element of the promotional mix, sales promotion is about "action". It is about stimulating customers to buy a product. It is not designed to be informative—a role which advertising is much better suited to.

Sales promotion is commonly referred to as "Below the Line" promotion. Sales promotion can be directed at:

- the ultimate consumer;
- the distribution channel, this is usually known as "selling the trade".

7.2.5 Methods of Sales Promotion

There are many consumer sales promotional techniques available, summarized as below.

(1) Price promotions. Price promotions are also commonly known as "discount". These offer either a discount to the normal selling price of a product, or more of the product at the normal price.

Increased sales gained from price promotions are at the expense of a loss in profit, so these promotions must be used with care.

A producer must also guard against the possible negative effect of discounting on a brand's reputation.

(2) Coupons. Coupons are another, very versatile, way of offering a discount. Consider the following examples of the use of coupons:

- on a pack to encourage repeat purchase;
- in coupon books sent out in newspaper allowing customers to redeem the coupon at a retailer;
- a cut-out coupon as part of an advert;
- on the back of till receipts.

The key objective with a coupon promotion is to maximize the redemption rate—this is the proportion of customers actually using the coupon.

One problem with coupons is that they may simply encourage customers to buy what they would have bought anyway. Another problem occurs when retailers do not hold sufficient stocks of the promoted product—causing customer disappointment.

Use of coupon promotions is, therefore, often best for new products or perhaps to encourage sales of existing products that are slowing down.

(3) Gift with purchase. The gift with purchase is a very common promotional technique. It is also known as a "premium promotion" in that the customer gets something in addition to the main purchase. This type of promotion is widely used for:

- subscription-based products;
- consumer luxuries.

(4) Competitions and prizes. Another popular promotion tool is with many variants. Most competition and prize promotions are subject to legal restrictions.

(5) Money refunds. Here, a customer receives a money refund after submitting a proof of purchase to the manufacturer. These schemes are often viewed with some suspicion by customers—particularly if the method of obtaining a refund looks unusual or onerous.

(6) Frequent user/loyalty incentives. Repeat purchases may be stimulated by frequent user incentives. Perhaps the best example of this are the many frequent flyer or user schemes used by airlines, train companies, car hire companies etc.

(7) Point-of-sale displays. Research into customer buying behavior in retail stores suggests that a significant proportion of purchases results from promotions that customers see in the store. Attractive, informative and well-positioned point-of-sale displays are, therefore, very important part of the sales promotional activity in retail outlets.

7.2.6 Push and Pull Strategies

Marketing theory distinguishes between two main kinds of promotional strategy—

"push" and "pull".

(1) Push. A push promotional strategy makes use of a company's sales-force and trade promotion activities to create consumer demand for a product.

The producer promotes the product to wholesalers, the wholesales promote it to retailers, and the retailers remote it to consumers.

A good example to push selling is mobile phones, where the major handsets manufacturers such as Huawei promote their products via retailers. Personal selling and trade companies such as Huawei—for example offering subsidies on the handsets to encourage retailers to sell higher volumes.

Push strategy tries to sell directly to the consumer, bypassing other distribution channels. With this type of strategy, consumer promotions and advertising are the most likely promotional tools (see Figure 7.2).

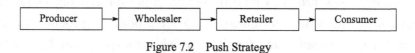

Figure 7.2　Push Strategy

(2) Pull. A pull selling strategy is one that requires high spending on advertising and consumer promotion to build up consumer demand for a product.

If the strategy is successful, consumers will ask their retailers for the product, the retailers will ask the wholesalers, and the wholesalers will ask the producers.

A good example of a pull is the heavy advertising and promotion of children's toys—mainly on television. The demand created from broadcasting of the toys and a major advertising campaign is likely to pull demand from children and encourage retailers to stock toys in the stores for holidays and vacations (see Figure 7.3).

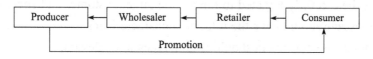

Figure 7.3　Pull Strategy

7.2.7　Advertising

The Institute of Practitioners in Advertising (IPA), the body which represents advertising agencies, defines advertising as: The means of providing the most persuasive possible selling message to the right prospects at the lowest possible cost.

Kotler and Armstrong provide an alternative definition: Advertising is any paid form of non-personal presentation and promotion of ideas, goods and services through mass media such as newspapers, magazines, television or radio by an identified sponsor.

There are five main stages in a well-managed advertising campaign.

Stage 1: Set Advertising Objectives

An advertising objective is a specific communication task to be achieved with a specific target audience during a specified period of time.

Advertising objectives fall into three main categories.

(1) To inform—e.g. tell customers about a new product;

(2) To persuade—e.g. encourage customers to switch to a different brand;

(3) To remind—e.g. remind buyers where to find a product.

Stage 2: Set the Advertising Budget

Marketers should remember that the role of advertising is to create demand for a product. The amount spent on advertising should be relevant to the potential sales impact of the campaign. This, in turn will reflect the characteristics of the product being advertised.

For example, new products tend to need a larger advertising budget to build awareness and to encourage consumers to try the product. A product that is highly differentiated may also need more advertising to help set it apart from the competition—emphasizing the points of difference.

Setting the advertising budget is not easy—how can a business predict the right amount to spend? Which parts of the advertising campaign will work best and which will have relatively less effect? Often businesses use "rules-of-thumb" (e.g. advertising/sales ratio) as a guide to set the budget.

Stage 3: Determine the Key Advertising Messages

Spending a lot on advertising does not guarantee success (witness the infamous John Cleese campaign for Sainsbury's). Research suggests that the clarity of the advertising message is often more important than the amount spent. The advertising message must be carefully targeted to impact the target customer audience. A successful advertising message should have the following characteristics:

(1) Meaningful—customers should find the message relevant;

(2) Distinctive—capture the customers' attention;

(3) Believable—a difficult task, since research suggests most consumers doubt the truth of advertising in general.

Stage 4: Decide Which Advertising Media to Use

There are a variety of advertising media from which to choose. A campaign may use one or more of the media alternatives. The key factors in choosing the right media include:

(1) Reach—what proportion of the target customers will be exposed to the advertising?

(2) Frequency—how many times will the target customer be exposed to the advertising message?

(3) Media Impact—where, if the target customer sees the message—will it have most impact? For example, does an advert promoting holidays for elderly people have more impact on television (if so, when and which channels) or in a national newspaper or perhaps a magazine focused on this segment of the population?

Another key decision in relation to advertising media relates to the timing of the campaign. Some products are particularly suited to seasonal campaign on television (e.g. Christmas hampers) whereas for other products, a regular advertising campaign throughout the year in media such as newspaper and specialist magazines (e.g. cottage holiday in the Lake District) is more appropriate.

Stage 5: Evaluate the Results of the Advertising Campaign

The evaluation of an advertising campaign should focus on two key areas:

(1) The Communication Effects—is the intended message being communicated effectively and to the intended audience?

(2) The Sales Effects—has the campaign generated the intended sales growth? This second area is much more difficult to measure.

7.2.8 Types of Advertising

Advertising is complex because so many diverse advertising try to reach so many different types of audiences.

(1) Brand Advertising: The most visible type of advertising is national consumer advertising. Another name for this is brand advertising, which focuses on the development of a long-term brand identity and image. It tries to develop a distinctive brand image for a product.

(2) Retail Advertising: In contrast, retail advertising is local and focuses on the store where a variety of products can be purchased or where a service is offered. Retail advertising emphasizes price, availability, location and hours of operation.

(3) Political Advertising: Political advertising is used by politicians to persuade people to vote for them and therefore is an important part of the political process in the United States and other democratic that permit candidate advertising. Although it is an important source of communication for votes, some critics are concerned that political advertising tends to focus more on image than on issues.

(4) Directory Advertising: Another type of advertising is called directional because people refer to it to find out how to buy a product or service. The best-known form of directory advertising is the Yellow Pages.

(5) Direct-Response Advertising: Direct-response advertising can use any advertising medium, including direct mail, but the message is different from that of national and retail advertising in that it tries to stimulate a sale directly. The consumer can respond by

telephone or mail and the product is delivered directly to the consumer by mail or some other carrier.

(6) Business-to-Business Advertising: Business-to-business advertising includes messages directed at retailers, wholesalers and professionals such as lawyers and physicians. Business advertising tends to be concentrated in business publications or professional journals.

(7) Institution Advertising: Institutional advertising is also called corporate advertising. The focus of these messages is on establishing a corporate identity or on winning the public over to the organization's point of view.

(8) Public Service Advertising: Public service advertising communicates a message on behalf of some good cause, such as presenting child abuse. These advertising are created for free by advertising professionals and the space and time are donated by the media.

7.2.9 Advertising Media

Advertising have a choice of media, i.e. where they can place their advertisements. The medium chosen will depend upon the target population being aimed for and of course, the cost.

(1) Newspapers. There are various types of newspaper, some with national circulation and some with only local circulation. Some newspapers are read by particular sections of the community and an advertiser needs to keep this in mind when placing his advert. The cost of advertising depends upon the paper circulation, the size of the advert and also where it is placed. A large front-page advertisement in a newspaper with a large circulation could be very expensive.

(2) Magazines. Obviously certain magazines have a particular type of readership.

(3) Radio and TV. Advertising here is very expensive but one of the great advantage of it is that everyone listening or viewing at that time will hear or see it. When someone reads a newspaper or magazine he may not even notice the advertising.

(4) Outdoor Advertising. Advertising is also done by using hoardings, vans, buses, trains, etc. This form of advertising, which mostly uses simple and short message, has the advantage of being seen by large numbers of people.

7.2.10 Roles of Advertising

Advertising can also be explained in terms of the roles it plays in business and in society. Four different roles it plays.

(1) The Marketing Role: Marketing is the strategic process a business used to satisfy consumer needs and wants through goods and services. Marketing also includes a mechanism for communicating this information to the consumer, which is called marketing this information to the promotion.

(2) The Communication Role: Advertising is a form of mass communication. It transmits different types of market information to match buyers and sellers in the marketplace. Advertising both informs and transforms the product by creating an image that goes beyond straight forward facts.

(3) The Economic Role: There are two major schools of thought concerning the effects of advertising on the economy—market power school and market competition school. According to the market power school, advertising is a persuasive communication tool used by marketers to distract consumers' attention from the price of the product. In contrast, the market competition school sees advertising as s source of information that increases consumers' price sensitivity and stimulates competition.

Actually, little is known about the true nature of advertising in the economy. Charles Sand Age, an advertising professor sees the economic role of advertising as "helping society to achieve abundance by informing and persuading members of society with respect to products, services and ideas".

(4) The Societal Role: Advertising also has a number of social roles. It informs us about new and improved products and teaches us how to use those innovations. It helps us compare products and features and make informed consumer decisions. It mirrors fashion and design trends and contributes to our aesthetic sense.

Advertising tends to flourish in societies that enjoy some level of economic abundance. That is, in such societies supply exceeds demand.

Figure 7.4 summarizes the marketing strategies.

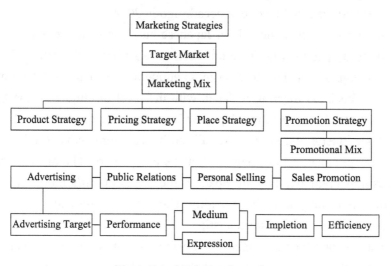

Figure 7.4 Marketing Strategies

Notes

[1] promotional mix 促销组合，它是营销组合的一个重要组成部分。促销活动有利于

克服销售的阻滞现象，争取产品优势，使顾客更加喜爱本企业及其提供的产品。

[2] A business' total marketing communications program is called the "promotional mix" and consists of a blend of advertising, personal selling, sales promotion and public relations tools.

一家企业所有的营销交流活动称为促销组合，促销的基本方法有四种：广告、人员销售、营销推广和公共关系。

[3] Yellow pages 黄页电话号簿，即专载公司、厂商等电话用户的名称及号码，按行业划分排列，并附有分类广告。

Questions

1. What is the marketing mix?
2. In what way are product planning and marketing research related to?

Reading Material

Japanese Business Etiquette

Japanese business etiquette is another misunderstood aspect of doing business in Japan: as with the section on Japanese business culture, maybe it's not surprising that hundreds of thousands of people have also browsed this Japanese business etiquette section since it first went online over a decade ago in 2004.

There has been much written about Japanese business etiquette, but sadly much of it seems written by people who have not been to Japan since the 1970s. Such authors often wrongly suggest that Japanese business etiquette is a mystical art endowing even the most trivial business meeting in Japan with the level of etiquette expected of a tea ceremony in Kyoto. Yet in practice, Japanese business etiquette is not so different from good business etiquette elsewhere: after all, politeness, sensitivity to others, and good manners are the pillars of good business etiquette everywhere. The main difference with Japanese business etiquette, as with Japanese society, is that it's more formal and thus more obvious, especially at a first meeting when the hierarchical exchange of those Japanese business cards is almost ritualistic.

The most obvious facets of Japanese business etiquette, affect personal behavior during and around business meetings, but there are other less obvious things affecting how your company's Japanese subsidiary must behave. Fortunately for foreign company executives doing business in Japan, Japanese businesspeople will not hold them to the same strict standards expected of their Japanese colleagues: within reason, they will tolerate quite severe transgressions, while minor transgressions, which would doom a

Japanese salesperson, might even help to break the corporate ice.

The key personal aspects of Japanese business etiquette to consider, are mostly related to first meetings, especially first meetings with senior Japanese executives. As time passes, the relationship with a Japanese customer strengthens and the formalities will decrease, especially after one or two dinners, lunches, or even offsite meetings at Starbucks. Regardless, I recommend that a foreign executive never assumes he or she has reached the same level of business intimacy with a Japanese senior manager or executive, as he or she might have with executives in US or elsewhere. A since retired president of a Toyota Motors subsidiary told me that Japanese usually do not begin to trust a person in business until having known them for at least 10 years. It happened that at that time I had known him for 10 years and met him many times, but even now, I have no idea about his family life, or even if he has sons and daughters: there are some things that many Japanese businesspeople just don't talk about.

Let's look at some of the key aspects of Japanese business etiquette that affect foreign company executives and subsidiaries in Japan.

Japanese business cards are a must-have. Have double-sided business cards printed, with the Japanese face using the same design elements as the English face. If an executive's original business cards are not English, such as for a German, French, or Italian company executive, I recommend using double-sided English and Japanese business cards for business in Japan.

Business Attire

For Men. Japanese business etiquette has become less formal, but business attire has not changed much since I first wrote this section back in 2004.

From October thru April, most Japanese businessmen, especially senior managers, executives, and salarymen, wear dark navy, charcoal gray, or black suits, with a white shirt and subdued tie.

Do not wear a black suit, white shirt, and black or near-black tie because that is funeral attire.

Japanese businesspeople tend to wear formal coats in the winter months of December thru February, and Burberry-style short raincoats in March and April.

From May thru September, Japanese businessmen swap their dark suits for light gray suits.

Japanese summers are hot and humid, so most Japanese men wear half-sleeve shirts during the summer months. Japan's popular "salaryman Prime-Minister" Koizumi passed the "cool biz" regulation in the early 2000s, which allowed government male employees to forgo ties and unbutton their collars. Private companies followed, thus few

Japanese salarymen (except salespeople) wear ties in summer. Some companies might insist their male employees wear ties to summer meetings, so to avoid embarrassment I recommend wearing a tie to such meetings and then asking if it's acceptable to remove it if the Japanese side are more casual.

Japanese businessmen generally have well-groomed short hairstyles.

Avoid wearing too much aftershave or cologne in a meeting.

Consider that most Japanese companies do not allow male employees to wear beards nor to shave their heads.

For Women. Sadly, little has changed for women in Japanese business since I first wrote this site over a decade ago: in fact, not much has changed since I started business in Japan in December 1991. Successive governments talk of encouraging women in the workforce, but industry's interest often seems more focused on bringing mothers in their late 30s back to pressing photocopier buttons in humdrum office jobs, than in encouraging any real parity for women in the workplace. The idea of promoting women to senior management jobs, even in Japan's internet companies where one might expect faster evolution, still has a long way to go. Many Japanese salarymen, senior managers and executives still don't find it easy to relate to female executives, and it can present problems for such executives from US and Europe.

Each of us, male or female, must make our own decisions about how and to what extent we adjust our image to suit our company's business needs and goals.

Business Tip: Business Etiquette

The business etiquette is the way professional businesspeople — no matter what their job title or type of business — conduct themselves around others with grace and style.

Americans will tell you that they are taught to believe in themselves, put their best foot forward, and stand out from the crowd. In such a big country, survival of the fittest rules.

1. Snapshot of the American workplace

The American working environment has changed drastically. With one eye on costs and the other on retention, employers are increasingly offering part-time or shared jobs, or outsourcing to external contractors. Change is constant as companies are restructured, work teams become "virtual", and flexible work arrangements become the norm.

2. Dress code

Dress codes vary depending on the industry and corporate culture. Men typically wear dark suits, and women dress skirts or pant suits. Many companies have instituted "casual Fridays". For others, smart casual attire is permitted all week, unless a client meeting is scheduled. While this dress code allows for greater comfort, some grumble that it requires them to buy a second "uniform", usually chinos (khaki pants) with an open-necked shirt for men, and casual skirt or pants and top for women. Professional clothes in general are expected to be of good quality but not overly stylish. Women's makeup and jewelry should be scheduled. If in doubt, always err on the side of conservatism. A confident posture, personal hygiene, and good grooming（穿着）are all essential.

3. The bottom line

> **First Impressions**
>
> Remember, "you never get a second chance to make a first impression." You will be judged on your conduct and appearance. Sloppy（邋遢的）manners or inappropriate behaviors may sink a deal or relationship.

The Americans do not feel the need to know the people they do business with. Trust is placed in lawyers and contracts, not in people. Rules are made and applied universally to all. Deals are swayed（支配）by a client's reputation, by profit margins or delivery time — not by the nature of the relationship.

In this "high task" "low relationship" society, everything is systematized. While Latin American employees may rely on the long-term patronage of a patriarchal（家长式的）boss to get ahead, newly appointed Americans are assigned a temporary "mentor" to help them navigate the new organization. Meanwhile, the savvy professional will develop a "network" — a loose-knit group of professional acquaintances who support each other on a reciprocal basis. Job-hunting is still a matter of who you know — 80 percent of jobs are secured through networking contacts.

4. Management style

> **Success Factors in U.S. Business**
> Show energy and enthusiasm.
> Take initiative and responsibility.
> Behave with integrity and consideration for others.
> Be positive, upbeat, and assertive.
> Deliver quality work within the deadline.
> Be visible. Network!

A good manager is expected to set goals, be action-oriented, and deliver results. The command-and-control style manager doesn't cut it here. To describe the preferred

U.S. management style, the analogy of the sports coach is often used. The manager will provide strategy and resource, and then cheerlead（带领大家一起欢呼）from the sidelines as the player "run with the ball". The approach is to empower a subordinate to show initiative, make decisions, and be an independent contributor. "Don't bring me a problem — bring me the solution" is the mantra（常说的话）. The plethora of management books suggests that while great leaders may be born, a good manager can be developed.

Managers are evaluated on developing others, as well as on their own performance. The annual appraisal is an inclusive process, with employees being evaluated against mutually agreed upon goals or objectives.

5. Negotiation

> **If You're Standing Still — You're Moving Backward**
>
> While older societies might rely on precedent for wisdom and direction, the Americans look to the future for their inspiration. They are masters of reinvention, of generating and managing change. They may seem impetuous（冲动的）to outsiders. According to Swiss interculturalist Thomas Zweifel (*Managing Global Teams*), Americans have a "just do it" approach to business. They prefer "learning by doing" to cautious planning. Business is a moving target, so problem-solving and decision-making will provide short-term solutions, and not be etched in stone.

The American negotiating style tends to be a "hard sell"（强行推销）— sometimes characterized as sledgehammer subtlety combined with missionary zeal! A strong pitch about a product's, or individual's strengths may sound boastful but is meant to inspire confidence and trust. It is also consistent with the penchant（倾向）for logical reasoning, directness, and comfort with self-promotion.

American negotiators may have little familiarity with, or patience for, the formal business protocol, indirect communication style, or consensual decision-making practices of other countries (a fact that savvy international negotiators often use to their advantage). Their focus is on the short term and the "big picture": securing the best deal in a timely manner. Their approach is informal, cordial, and straightforward. The U.S. team will reveal its position and expect the other party to engage in a competitive bargaining process. If an impasse（僵局）is reached, American tenacity, creativity, and persuasiveness will come to the fore. Despite the "hard sell" tactics, negotiating partners should not feel pressured into making a decision. The Americans expect their counterparts across the table to be similarly pragmatic and single—minded in trying to secure a favorable deal. The greatest source of frustration for American negotiators is feeling that they are being "strung along"(欺骗), or that their negotiating partners don't have the authority to make the necessary decisions.

> Note: Americans like to walk away from a meeting having secured a verbal agreement: the details will be hammered out later(经过深入讨论得出). Thus, a handshake may "seal the deal", but the agreement isn't in place until the ink on the contract is dry!

Chapter 8

Distribution

8.1 Channels of Distribution

Figure 8.1 shows the channels of distribution. You will notice that goods reach the consumer by one of a number of routes.

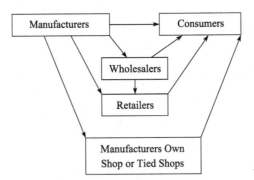

Figure 8.1 Channels of Distribution

In this part, we will deal with retailing.

Retailing is carried on by businesses which sell goods to the final consumer and most retailing is done by shops.

There are many different types of shops and retail outlets.

As the following example shows:

In my family, a weekly housekeeping allowance is ¥500. In a typical week, I would probably use most types of retailing establishments. Look! Every Sunday evening I go to the supermarket and spend about ¥200 on food of various sorts. Almost every morning

I spend ¥20 buying milk and bread from a mobile shop. There is a street market near our institute. I go there every Monday morning and spend about ¥100 on vegetables, fruits and so on. I find it convenient to slip over the local grocery shop where I spend about ¥25 a week. And each week on average, I go to a little restaurant for supper with my husband; it costs about ¥60. From these we know almost every type retail outlets we can touch in our daily life.

8.1.1 Independent Retailer

You will remember that I spent about ¥25 a week buying items from the shop across our block. These are usually owned by small businesses, often sole traders. Since they are small they cannot buy their goods in bulk and therefore cannot obtain them cheaply. Consequently, prices are often higher in small shops than in large supermarkets.

Most people only use the small shop as me for convenience, to buy those items which may have been forgotten.

The small shop is often conveniently placed and it is often open for much longer hours. The pattern for most people is to do the bulk of their shopping in supermarket and obtain smaller or overlooked items in the corner shop.

It is quite easy these days for people to travel to the larger shops. Many families have cars and can spend an hour or so in the local supermarket meeting most of their requirements. This has meant that the small shops still survive and they do so for the following reasons:

(1) They provide a convenient service because they are around residential area;

(2) They often have much more convenient hours of opening;

(3) Small shops, because they know their customers, will often give credit and will put goods on the slate.

8.1.2 Multiple Shop (GB) or Chain Store (U.S.)

It's multiple shop. As the name suggests, these are shops operated by large companies with numerous branches. There are two types of multiples:

(1) The multiple specialist shops which specialize in the sale of a fairly narrow range of goods;

(2) The multiple variety chain stores which sell a variety of goods.

8.1.3 Departmental Store

A department store has been described as a number of shops under one roof, and in fact each department specializes in a particular range of goods.

The big advantage that a departmental store has is that it can offer the shopper the opportunity to do all his/her shopping under one roof and even in many cases have lunch during shopping. Departmental stores offer a variety of credit facilities, for example through the use of account cards.

8.1.4 Cooperative Retail Societies

Most of the shops would be considered to be multiple chain stores. In some large towns they are departmental stores. There have been enormous changes in organization of the cooperative retail societies in the last fifteen years or so, among which are:

(1) Many more experienced and well-paid managers have been recruited so that societies might compete with other retail establishments;

(2) To gain the advantage of large-scale bulk buying many of the local societies have amalgamated.

8.1.5 Supermarkets and Hypermarkets

Supermarkets are usually in the control of multiples, although it is possible for an independent retailer to open a supermarket. The distinguishing feature of a supermarket is its size, not the type of ownership.

A supermarket has floor space of at least 186 square meters. The growth of supermarket in the past ten years or so has been due to a number of factors:

(1) They usually stock a wide range of goods so that once in, the shopper can obtain all requirements;

(2) The goods are on display and are selected by the customer, therefore resulting in less labor being required with a corresponding saving in costs and therefore prices;

(3) Prices are often also low because goods can be bought in bulk at a discount;

(4) Supermarkets stock only goods with quick turnover-goods which sell well.

Supermarkets concentrate on stocking the minimum but never running out. This is a delicate balance and it requires well-thought-out stock keeping methods. This policy, however, saves costs and ensures that the goods are always fresh.

The hypermarkets are very large shops with over 2,500 square meters of floor space. Hypermarkets started in France.

8.1.6 Shopping Mall

A shopping mall is a building or set of buildings that contain stores and have interconnecting walkways may or may not be enclosed. In the United Kingdom and Australia, these are called shopping centers or shopping arcades.

Shopping mall is a newly complex business-style, update of hypermarket, which is combination by shopping, entertainment, dining and tour etc. The feature is the large size in floor, and parking lots with more callings, more stores and multiple services.

8.1.7 Voluntary Retail Chains

An independent retailer cannot obtain the benefit of bulk buying and often has to buy small quantities at high prices from the wholesaler. In order to lower prices many independent retailers have organized themselves into groups, orders for goods are placed through the group and higher discount can be obtained.

Notes

[1] channels of distribution 分销渠道，也译作分配渠道或配销通路，指产品所有权从生产者向消费者或用户转移过程中所经过的各个环节连接起来的通道。从图 8-1 中可以看出，分销渠道有直接渠道（生产者与消费者之间没有任何中间环节）、一层渠道（有一个中间环节）和二层渠道（有两个中间环节）。此外，因小零销商一般不可能直接向大批发商进货，三层渠道（生产者——一级批发商—二级批发商—零售商—消费者）也并不常见。

[2] retailing 零售、零售业，指所有将货物或劳务交付最终消费者用于生活消费的商业活动。不论由哪类企业经营、归谁所有，也不论以何种方式在何处将货物或劳务卖出，只要符合上述概念，均属零售范畴。零售商的主要类型在正文及练习中已有概略介绍。

[3] multiple shop 连锁商店，又称 chain store，是英国用语，可以简称为 multiple，美国常称之为 chain store。

[4] departmental store 百货商店、百货公司，是英国用语，一般称为 department store。

> ## Questions
> 1. What is the difference between a multiple specialist store and a multiple variety chain store?
> 2. What is the distinctive feature of a departmental store?
> 3. Why has the decline of cooperative retail societies been halted?

8.2 Wholesaling

Retailers do not stock large quantities of any one type of goods and this means that they obtain few of the goods direct from the manufacturers.

A wholesaler occupies a place between manufacturer and retailer and is therefore sometimes known as a "middleman". Retailer deals with wholesalers in a number of different ways; in some cases, he places his orders with wholesalers' representatives who visit his shop from time to time. For other goods he will sell well and then place orders. Wholesalers always ask retailers to do cash-and-carry business. As the term "cash-and-carry" suggests he pays for the goods and takes them away on the same day.

Wholesalers have come in for criticism because some argue that they increase costs of goods since they occupy yet another stage in the process of goods reaching the consumer. However, although there has been a decline in the number of wholesalers, as manufacturers deal increasingly with retailers directly, they still play an important part in the process of distribution.

The wholesalers provide service to the manufacturers and retailers. Retailers may wish to order goods at numbers with manufacturers and this would surely be very time-consuming both for the retailers and the manufacturers. By channeling orders through a wholesaler the retailer need to contact only one source for most of his goods.

Figure 8.2 shows the reduction in the number of contacts which results from the presence of a wholesaler.

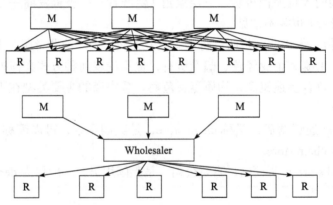

Figure 8.2　How wholesalers save transport and administrative costs?
Note: M—Manufacturers, R—Retailers.

(1) By selling a lot of goods to one source the manufacturer can save:

- transport costs;
- administration costs;
- costs by simplifying paperwork (each order involves paperwork and this of course will be saved if fewer orders are necessary).

(2) As pointed out earlier, the wholesaler stores his goods in warehouses.

They are expensive in terms of rent and labor and these costs are saved by the manufacturer.

(3) The wholesaler can take some of the risk from the manufacturer. Goods sometimes go quickly out of fashion. Often it is the wholesaler who takes this risk, sometimes being left with stock which has gone out of demand.

(4) Wholesalers also help manufacturers and retailers with cash problems.

Manufacturers often want their money quickly back, so that they can buy materials for new batches of goods. If they sold goods direct to small retailers they might have to wait because the small retailers often require some credit, perhaps one month. Wholesalers may assist manufacturers by paying quickly for large supplies but then giving credit to retailers as shown in Figure 8.3.

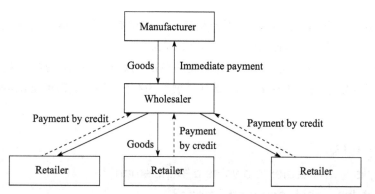

Figure 8.3　How the wholesaler helps both manufacturer and retailer in "cash problems"?

(5) The wholesaler can buy goods from manufactures throughout the year even though demand is "seasonal". Take sales of Christmas cards for example; retailers sell Christmas cards for the Christmas period, but manufacturers produce these all year round and supply them to wholesalers who have the task of storing them for sale at the appropriate time. The wholesaler then plays an important part in smoothing out supply and demand fluctuation. The manufacturer can produce continuously. And the retailer does not need to store goods for long periods. Sometimes the situation is reversed. Supply is seasonal but demand is regular throughout the year. Such as fruit, much of the fruit grown is harvested at a certain time of the year and then stocked. Large quantities are produced and the wholesaler will take these large quantities, selling them to retailers at regular intervals (see Figure 8.4).

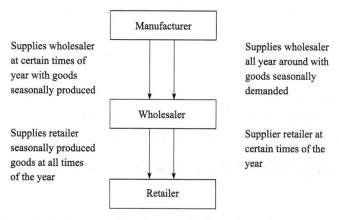

Figure 8.4　How a wholesaler can assist with seasonally demanded and seasonally produced goods?

Notes

[1] wholesaling 批发，就其性质来说，批发是与零售不同的经济活动，其主要区别不在于卖方是谁，也不在于交易量大小，而在于买方的购买目的和用途。凡是不以直接消费为目的，而是为转卖、加工生产而购买货物和劳务的商业活动，都属于批发。

[2] cash-and-carry 现付自运，指以现金交易、货物由顾客自己运走的买卖方式。常用作定语，如 cash-and-carry store/system/wholesaler。

[3] demand 需求，指按一定的价格购买某一商品的数量，不仅指购买某一商品的愿望。为了区别于需要（need），需求有时被称为有效需求（effective demand）。

Questions

1. Why is a wholesaler known as a "middleman"?
2. What does "cash-and-carry" mean?
3. In what way can the wholesaler assist the manufacturer and the retailer in the problems of cash?

Business Tip: Conversational Tip

Good conversation is an art that can add value to your personality every day, provided you keep the following pointers in mind:

- Never thrust your opinion on another person.
- Don't boast. Your importance will be reflected by your actions.
- People will gossip. However, think twice before you speak about anyone.
- Don't be critical or insulting of someone who is not present.
- Avoid talking about salaries and commissions, and promotions you feel should have been rightfully yours.
- Never discuss your sex life or another's, about a colleagues sexual orientation or about office affairs.
- Make a polite excuse if the speaker is rambling, and cutting into your time.
- Avoid interrupting and wait for the other person to finish speaking.
- Listen actively to what people around are talking about.

Participate enthusiastically! Don't overwhelm others with the force of your voice and opinion.

Chapter 9

About E-commerce

9.1 Marketing for E-commerce

The key to E-commerce—particularly on the Web—is to provide compelling content for visitors and to enhance the experience of conducting business online. The quality of a site's content is directly correlated to its success.

Effective E-commerce sites assume the customer's perspective rather than the company's perspective, providing substantial information of value to the visitors rather than providing the online corporate brochures.

The site must be easy to use and navigate; if online sales are offered, the process should be as simple as possible to make it more user-friendly the process should be as easy as possible for the user.

The site should be updated frequently, providing the user with an incentive to return.

Because the Web is a two-way communication medium, customers should be able to provide feedback either using online forms or through an email address; the company should then respond to the feedback.

Partially designed to provide answers to common questions, voice response units (VRUs) at many companies provide callers with a range of options. VRUs have gained in acceptance in the business world.

The Web site should also provide information about a company's products and services. FAQs (frequently asked questions) provide a straightforward approach to questions asked by customers, helping them evaluate whether the product is suitable and potentially educating customers about some of the technical or little understood benefits of the product in question.

Valuable information is the foundation of Web development. The structure of the Web site, which enables customers to locate that information, is at least as important.

If a site is not structured so that users can quickly find what they are looking for, it matters little how much valuable information the site contains. Not surprisingly, sites that are difficult to navigate are often rejected by users.

Designers tend to construct a site in a tree structure, moving from the home page out to all the branching pages.

Using search engines, all pages on the site are indexed. A very focused search may lead the user to a page eight levels into the site, perhaps to the technical specifications for a product.

Some sites even include an index, a table of contents that allows users to quickly locate pages of interest.

Because one cannot predict which page the user will start on, it becomes essential to provide a link to the home page on each page of the site. Providing links to each major topical area on every page is also effective.

In addition to providing sound structure and easy navigability among pages, it is important to include a search engine so users can retrieve information quickly.

Pages on the Web are far more interactive and graphical today than the flat gray pages that predominated in early 1995.

The Web page is a graphical medium and requires design work from professionals.

Multimedia elements can bolster an E-commerce Web site if these elements are properly aligned with business goals and are appropriate for the demographics of the site's audience.

The primary benefit of using interactive technology is the ability to run programs on the client system, programs that may either have entertainment value (an online game) or perform complex operations such as enabling a customer to conduct banking business.

Interactive technology is increasingly being used, not to add entertainment value to a site, but to perform business functions.

Humor and creativity personalize the Web site, but the Web is capable of even more. Genuine interactivity makes the Web a potential groupware platform, and E-commerce sites can use this to effectively create online communities.

Web-based chat groups and discussions called forums can move the Web site beyond being a place to review product specifications. Forums can enable discussions among users or with product managers. Sites can have online salespeople responding to inquiries from users.

The key to establish an online community is in undertaking the needs of the target market and the nature of the information that would be useful to such a market.

Providing quality information on the Web leads to sales. Health-related sites can sponsor an "asks the doctor" feature; a company selling lawnmowers could provide information on quality lawn care.

Companies that build comprehensive sites on given topics can take over Web markets entirely. CD now is a comprehensive music and movie source. Golf Web encompasses the universe of information relating to golf. A comprehensive site can provide market domination for the company who creates it.

Creating an online community is one possibility for E-commerce, but obtaining feedback from users is essential. By responding appropriately to email from customers, companies have an opportunity to cement relationship with these customers.

Designate a person capable of appropriately routing email to read the mail. If not email is being received, post questions on the site or solicit contributions.

If customers respond with email, they deserve the same follow-up attention that telephone calls and letters to the company receive. How, and whether the company responds to email, may determine whether the visitor returns.

Notes

[1] navigate 浏览，搜索
[2] two-way communication medium 双向式交流媒介
[3] feedback 反馈
[4] respond 反应，回应
[5] corporate brochures 公司宣传册
[6] marketing communications materials 营销宣传材料
[7] voice response units(VRUs) 语音应答系统
[8] frequently asked questions(FAQs) 频繁提出的问题
[9] Web design 网页设计
[10] search engine 搜索引擎
[11] retrieve information 信息检索
[12] business goals 经营目标
[13] promotion 促销，推广，提高
[14] publicize 宣传，公布
[15] positioning 定位
[16] three-dimensional(3-D) 三维技术
[17] virtual reality(VR) 虚拟现实

[18] virtual/online community 虚拟社区
[19] interactive technology 交互式技术
[20] information system 信息系统
[21] target market 目标市场
[22] quality information 高质量的信息
[23] newsgroup 新闻组
[24] forum 网络讨论组
[25] mailing list 邮件组
[26] demographics 人口统计
[27] narrow casting 有目标的广告与宣传
[28] customer tracking service 客户跟踪服务
[29] public relation 公共关系

9.2 Relevant Knowledge

9.2.1 Strategies for Promoting the Web Site

Without promotion, there is no question that a Web site will be lost in cyberspace. After all, the only way to find a new Web site is to type in its URL. Unless customers are guessing that the company has a Web site, and guessing correctly what the URL for the home page would be, the chances are minute that anyone will find the corporate Web site. Promotion, then, is not an option; it is requisite for survival on the Web.

Promoting the presence of the company Web site with a variety of methods is important. Coopers & Lybrand Consulting studied methods used to find out about Web sites. Word-of-mouth recommendations were most often mentioned (44%), with traditional media not far behind (39%). Browsing (including search engines) and hotlinks accounted for 32% and 10%, respectively. This study highlights the need for cross-promotion in traditional recommendations. In addition, more links that point to the corporate home page from a variety of locations online (through browsers and hotlinks) to garner more customer traffic to the site must be established.

Once the Web site is in place, complete with the best domain name possible, the Web site must be cross-promoted. Press release that point out the highlights of the site and focus on information of interest to customers such as a package tracking feature or a discussion group should be issued. The most important content on the site and its benefit to customers should be highlighted, and, if possible, a newspaper or trade publication should be prevailed upon to write an article about the site, instead of leaving it to be announced in the next press release.

Beyond issuing press releases and promotional articles, print the Web address in as many places as possible. Anywhere the company's address or phone number appears, the Web address, known as a URL, should also be present, alerting customers to the fact that this company is on the Web (which provides a cutting-edge image). Business cards, brochures, stationery, print and TV advertisements are all potential URL locations. Be sure that business cards and stationery also include email addresses for those who may not have Web access or who want to ask a specific question not addressed by information on the site.

Direct mail using postcards provides an inexpensive way to announce the site to customers. Print postcards that echo the design of the Web page. Provide the URL and a few highlights of what users can find at the site. If the company is offering special incentives at the Web site (such as discounts or a contest), the postcards can also include this information.

9.2.2 Promotion through Search Engines and Catalogs

By widely publishing the company's URL, users can become aware of the site through traditional media. Because the Web itself is so enormous, it is equally, if not more important to promote the Web site on the Web itself.

People navigate the Web by typing keywords into search engines or by browsing through catalogs such as Google! that place Web sites into various categories. Catalogs are created manually, and Web sites must be submitted to Google! for inclusion. In theory, inclusion in search engines is automatic. The Web indexing program for the search engine visits as many sites on the Web as possible, adding keywords to its online index. In practice, however, the Web is growing so quickly that most indexing programs cannot keep pace. As a result, it could be months before the indexing programs arrive at the corporate Web site. Companies cannot afford this delay or leave the promotion of their site to change. Submitting the Web site for inclusion on various engines, then, ensuring the site will be listed when customers and prospects for the company online.

9.2.3 Creating Cross-links

Exchanging links with other sites provides a way to increase the number of hotlinks on the Web. Approach relevant sites and ask whether the corporate Web site can include a link to their site and if they will return the favor by including a link on their Web page.

Frequently, ambitious users construct hot lists that become a clearinghouse for Web sites on a given topic. By seeking out such sites and requesting to be added to the list, traffic to the Web site is increased. Even if the list of vendors includes competitors, adding the corporate site to the listing provides a means for people to reach the Web site and be persuaded of the value of the company's products.

Search the Web for reference to the competitor's site. Doing so can provide ideas for places where one should add links to the corporate site.

Reading Material

Marketing Strategies for E-commerce

I. Effective Content of the Web Site

Compelling content of a Web site is key to success on the Web. By focusing on the customer rather than the company and by using design that considers users with various levels of connectivity, site builders will be able to create a site that adheres to the needs of their audience.

A Web site should provide information wanted or needed by the customer, including information about the company's products and services. FAQs provide a straightforward approach to asking customer's question, helping them evaluate whether the product is suitable, and potentially educating customers about some of the technical or little understood benefits of the product in question. Valuable information is the foundation of Web developing. The structure of the Web site, which enables customers to locate that information, is at least as important. If a site is not structured so that users can quickly find what they are looking for, it matters little how much valuable information the site contains. A site's Web page should contain an intuitive structure. Some sites even include an index, a table of contents that allows users to quickly locate pages of interest. Sites that are difficult to navigate are, not surprisingly, often rejected by users.

In an addition to providing sound structure and easy navigability among pages, include a search engine so users can retrieve information quickly. The larger site, the more diligent designers must be to structure it in a way that enables customers to quickly locate information.

Streamlining the shopping process is very important, too. The goal of E-commerce is to encourage customers to order products. Surprisingly, the ordering process at many sites can be frustrating, using too many forms to accomplish the task. Given the time it may take it page to load, shopping on online can prove to be more time consuming than ordering by telephone. Online ordering systems should make the process of shopping at least as easy as traditional methods. Successful sites typically accept payments using a variety of methods, both online and offline. Offering multiple payment methods, including browser-based encryption for handling credit cards, makes purchasing online convenient for shoppers. Providing an option to arrange for payment offline using fax or telephone accommodates customers who prefer not to input credit card numbers on the Internet.

The Web is graphical medium and requires design work from professionals. Effective E-commerce sites can be created by combining winning designs that make judicious use of graphics with sensitivity to how the design will appear on a variety of browsers. Various techniques should be used to speed graphics loading. Multimedia elements can bolster an E-commerce Web site if these elements are properly aligned with business goals and are appropriate for the demographics of the site's audience. Beyond multimedia are the technologies that add interactive content to make Web pages capable of performing any tasks a normal software program can perform. The primary benefit of using these interactive technologies is the ability to run programs on the client system, programs that may either have entertainment value(an online game) or perform complex operations such as enabling a customer to conduct banking business, use a spreadsheet or draw a map.

II. Promoting the Site in Forums and Mailing Lists

Participating in online forums and mailing lists also gives the company a means to promote its site. Forums are Web-based discussion groups. In a mailing list, only people who subscribe to the list receive the messages that make up the discussion. Participants can then reply either to the sender of a particular message or to the mailing list as a whole.

The signature file of employees who participate in these online discussions provides a means for people to visit the company's Web site if it includes the company's URL and email address. Such participation should be encouraged. If a person contributes appropriately and briefly and refers to specific pages on the Web site to which parties interested in receiving more information than reference, this is viewed as helpful to the group and not as shameless self-promotion. If the content of the site is enticing enough and the contribution to the newsgroup is deftly written, such postings may result in many forum readers visiting the Web site and even bookmaking it.

III. Conducting Online Marketing: One-on-One Marketing

While traditional marketing campaigns can be rather easily adapted for the Web, there are other means that take advantage of the Web's interactivity. An increasing number of sites are varying their content depending on the information they have about the user. In doing so, they effectively use the Web to target specific groups, a practice known as narrow casting. If accomplished successfully, such targeted advertising and promotion reduces the level of noise for the user, who need not be subject to various advertisements that are of no personal interest.

How do Web sites gather information about users? Tools such as Internet profiles I/Code enable Web site developers to gather information from Web users who fill out online forms, and require these forms to be filled out as a part of online registration for using the site. Beware, however, of pushing online registration too heavily. Users may be unwilling to provide information and many choose to go to another site rather than bother filling out even a short survey. Rewards, either in the form of increased access to valuable areas of the site or in the form of an incentive such as a discount or contest entry should be offered to those willing to disclose information on a survey of this nature.

Those unfamiliar with Web server logs may be surprised to realize how much information is automatically collected on each visitor. Servers record the type of browser in use, the computing platform of the user, and the domain from which the user is visiting. Some savvy designers use this information to their advantage when providing Web services. For example, Lombard's investment Web site produces graphs of stock performance. If the user's browser has java capabilities, a java applet interactively crates the graph. If the browser is not java-enabled, Lombard's site creates the graph using a tool that is compatible with any browser. This flexibility enables the company to provide value-added content to all its users, rather than telling users with older or low-end browsers or computing platform that they cannot participate without further investment on the client side. By sensing the user's browser and computing platform automatically, the server spares users from having to be aware of the capabilities of their browsers.

One-to-one works particularly well for Web-based malls, enabling customers to purchase items from a variety of stores with a single transaction. The software is object-oriented, complying with common object request broker architecture (CORBA) standards. One-to-one provided connections to backend systems such as order entry, product management, and shipping.

One-to-one is without question the most interesting and effective E-commerce product on the market. However, it is rather expensive. But for some serious E-commerce sites, this will be money well spent. Some search engines are planning to offer users customized content, hoping to better target advertising. Whatever the method used to generate it, the trend toward creating targeted content continues.

Business Tip: Handshake, Exchange of Business Card and Communication

- It is commonly perceived that the proper way of a handshake is to firmly hold the hand, and two quick pumps. It is also appropriate that during the handshake, you should

establish eye contact and a smile. This is mainly for the purpose of building rapport.
- Another widely known example of business etiquette is the exchange of business card. Just by accepting a business card from a person can establish respect. The proper behavior in this case is that after accepting the business card put it safely on your card case. Carelessly putting it away with your pocket or other personal belongings is very demeaning to the part of the person who gave it.
- Be Clear and Simple: Whether communicating orally or in writing, avoid long, complex sentences, highly technical language, jargon, and colloquialisms. Don't be condescending, but do use simpler words when they are available.

PART 3

PRACTICE OF INTERNATIONAL BUSINESS

Chapter 10

Principles, Structure, and Layout of Business Letters

The major part of the business or commercial activities of the world is conducted by correspondence. Therefore, it is extremely important to be able to write good business letters. The following are the general principles, structure, and layout that go to make up an attractive, well-groomed business letter.

10.1 General Principles of Business Communication

To compose effective correspondences, you must apply the "five C's" principles, they are clarity, conciseness, correctness, courtesy and completeness.

10.1.1 Clarity

A business letter must be clear and easily understood. To avoid ambiguity and confusion, simple and accurate wording is required, short and simple sentence pattern is appropriate. Choose precise, concrete and familiar words, construct effective sentences and paragraphs.

10.1.2 Conciseness

This means increased cost. Wordy expressions and redundancies and the major blunders to overcome. Eliminate wordy expressions, include only relevant material and avoid unnecessary repetition.

10.1.3 Correctness

A business letter should be linguistically correct. Wrong spelling, incorrect grammar and improper punctuation are not allowed. Use the right level of language, check accuracy of figures, facts and words.

10.1.4 Courtesy

The principle of courtesy requires one to be thoughtful and polite. True courtesy needs to use tactful tone and respective expressions. Be sincerely tactful, thoughtful and appreciative, use expressions that show respect, choose nondiscriminatory expressions.

10.1.5 Completeness

A good business letter should be complete, providing all the necessary information and data necessary for a specific issue. At the same time, it answers all questions asked and gives something extra when desirable.

10.2 Structure of Business Letters

Every well-constructed business letter is made up of seven main parts details as follows:

- Letterhead
- Date Line
- Inside Address
- Salutation
- Body of the Letter
- Complimentary Close
- Signature

Some letters may contain more optional parts as shown below:

- Attention Line
- Subject Line
- Reference Notation
- Enclosure Notation
- Carbon Copy Notation
- Postscript

The first impression that a business letter makes depends on its appearance. Any business letter should be clear, brief and businesslike. It should be written on good paper of the right size and kind, often on white paper of good quality in standard size (usually

A4). Don't write confused, overlong or pointed letters and try to be polite, friendly and formal to write concise and purposeful letter.

The typical business letter has three sections: the beginning; the content; the ending.

10.2.1 The Beginning

This part of the letter is made up of writer's address, date, reader's address, attention line, salutation and subject line.

The writer's address should be put at the head of the first page of the letter. However, the printed letterhead, which includes the company's name, address, telephone and fax number, has become more and more popular because it can save you the trouble of typing. And another point must be paid attention, that is, short forms should be avoided. The address like "6HS Man" (meaning "6 High Street Manchester") can not be easily understood by the addressee.

The date is unavoidable and the full date should be given. It is typed at the left margin or right margin, leaving a double line space below the letterhead of your address. There are two styles of giving the date. The first is American style which is in the line of the full name of the month, day of the month in digits followed by a comma and year in digits. Model: September 9, 2020. The second is British style which is sequenced by day of the month in digits, full name of the month and year in digits. Model: 1 April 2020.

The reader's address is followed in the third line below the date. Make sure it is the same as the reader himself writes. Use the courtesy titles such as Mr., Mrs. or Ms.. If you are not sure of the gender of the reader, "Dear Sir or Madam" can be used. Then the titles should be spelled out in full. For example, Sales Manager, President, etc. and then the full name of his company is given.

The attention line is sometimes used to allow the letter directing to a certain person. It is often placed at the second line below the reader's address. But nowadays it is seldom used, for it seems redundant.

The salutation often begins with the word "dear" and follows by the name of the person you are writing to. If the relationship with the addressee is friendly, it is customary to use Dear Mr. ____ / Mrs. ____ / Miss ____ / Ms. ____. If the name of the person you are writing to is not known, you may use Dear Sir/Madam. If the letter is addressed to an organization, you may begin with Dear Sir or Madam. It is often placed at two line spaces below the reader's address.

The subject line makes the reader quickly get the outline of the letter. It is placed one line space below the salutation.

10.2.2 The content

All the letters should follow the same pattern.

First, make clear the purpose, the circumstances and the action of the letter. The first paragraph states the purpose of the letter. What the letter is about. The next paragraph or paragraphs explain the reasons of writing the letter and the last one or ones explain what action should be taken.

Second, please make sure the letter clear and completely readable: don't put more than one idea in a sentence; don't put more than one topic in a paragraph; don't put more than one subject in a letter.

Finally, be natural, human and sympathetic: put yourself in the reader's place to think about him; don't try to intimidate the reader and make him angry; write short, businesslike letters which appeal to the reader's interest and sense of fairness.

10.2.3 The Ending

This part should not be ignored in the same way. Except the usual components such as the close and the signature, it can also include enclosures, copies and postscripts.

The close is placed one line space below the content. It can be divided into formal (Yours very truly, Very truly yours, Respectfully yours), less formal (Sincerely, Sincerely yours, Cordially yours etc.) and informal (with best regards, Best wishes, Cheers etc.).

The signature is put behind the close, leaving three line spaces for the signature before a typed version of the name and title. The writer of the letter can sign for him/herself, or for the company, but the name and title should be typed underneath the signature.

Enclosures are used to enclose something in the letter. It is usually put below the writer's signature. You can choose the short or full form: 2 Encls or 2 Enclosures. For example:

Enclosures: the New Catalogue and the New Price List.

"C.C." stands for "carbon copy", which means a copy of your letter is sent to someone else. It is typed one line space below the signature.

Postscripts may be abbreviates as "P.S.". It is used to add a personal note to a business letter. It is placed under enclosures and "C.C.".

The appearance of your letter is important. The business letter should follow one of the basic styles—block, intended, modified block.

10.3 Layout of Business Letters

10.3.1 Block Style

The style is widely used currently, for it is fast and efficient and reflects the dynamic approach we take in business. Everything starts at the left margin. This saves a certain amount of typing time.

The first paragraph is placed one line space below the salutation and single spacing within paragraphs and double spacing between paragraphs are used.

Johnson-Johnson

1J&J Plaza New Brunswick,
NJ 089333 U.S.A.
Tel: 732-524-0400
E-mail: carrie@jnj.com

May 20, 2020
Soft Health Care Product Corp.
Room 2301 Yili BLD, 35 Nanjing Road,
Shanghai, China
Dear Sir or Madam,
Re: SHAMPOO

 We've received your letter of July 10th inquiring about our JOHNSON'S Baby Shampoo, but unfortunately, the stock of this product is running low due to the heavy demand. But we will inform you as soon as the new supplies come up.

 We sell a wide variety of Baby's Shampoo. All of them are made of the NO MORE TEARS formula. For your reference, we enclose an illustrated catalogue of our shampoos and we hope you will find it interesting.

 We hope that we can close business to our mutual advantage in the future.

Yours faithfully,
Peter Ostwald
(Manager)

Encl.: A copy of catalogue

10.3.2 Indented Style

This style is preferred by many people because of its balanced appearance. The date is ranged right. The close is to the right of center with the signature aligned beneath it. And each paragraph is indented five spaces.

10.3.3 Modified Block Style

This style is the most popular one. Placement of date on the left-hand side of the paper may cause inconvenience when particular letters are required from the files. Because of this, some firms using the blocked style of layout prefer a date position on the right. Single line-spacing gives a letter an appearance of compactness and is usual for both long and short letters, though double line-spacing is preferred by some for very short letters.

Electrolux

St Gangsgatan 143 Stockholm, 105 45 Sweden
Tel: 46-8-738-60000   E-mail: hwlee@electrolux.com

May 20, 2020

Messrs. William & Warner
105 Roller Road
Sydney, Australia
Dear Sir or Madam,

Re: Shipping Advice of Freezers

With reference to your order No. F256 of February 5 for 1,000 sets of Freezers, we're pleased to inform you that goods have been loaded on board S.S. "Peace", which is sailing for your port on April 1st.

We've sent a fax to the above effect this morning. Please insure the goods as contracted and make preparation for taking the delivery. We are now making out the necessary documents for negotiation.

We assure you that our goods will be found satisfactory upon arrival at your port. We also hope that we can close more business with you in the future.

Yours sincerely,
Horis De Wolley
Jenny
(Manager)

(Adapted from: International Business Correspondence & Form Handbook, 邹海峰, 赵耀, Manvel Lunes)

SAMSUNG ELECTRONICS

310 Taepyung-ro 2-ga, Chung-gu
Seoul, 100-102, Korea
Tel: 82-2-3706-1114   E-mail: qsl@samsungcorp.com

May 20, 2020

Shandong Science & Technology Co. Ltd.
21/F Bright Plaza, 138 Jinni Road, Jinan
Shandong Province, China
<u>Attention: Mr. Zhou Jun, Import Dept.</u>
Dear Sir or Madam,
<u>Re: Our Offer for PDA Type Ⅲ -H</u>

Thank you for your interest in our latest Personal Digital Assistant Type Ⅲ -H.

As requested, we offer you 500 sets of PDA at USD140 per set FOB Inchon Incoterms® 2020 for shipment in February, 2020. We require payment by L/C.

Because there is an increasing demand for this product, our price is non-negotiable. We look forward to your reply.

Yours truly,
Samung Eletronics
Lavis Kim
(Manager)

Notes

[1] 商务英语写作的 5C 原则：
- Clarity 清楚性
- Conciseness 简明性
- Correctness 正确性
- Completeness 完整性
- Courtesy 礼貌性

[2] 商务书信一般由以下七个基本部分组成：

(1) Letterhead 信头（发件人），一般包括公司名称、地址、邮编、电话号码、电传号码、传真号码、电子邮件地址，还可以附加公司总经理的姓名。

(2) Date line 发信日期

(3) Inside name and address 封内名称和地址（收件人）

(4) Salutation 称呼

(5) Body of the letter 正文

(6) Complimentary close 结尾敬语

(7) Signature 签名

需要之时，还可以包括以下可选部分：

(1) Attention line 经办人姓名，书信人希望此信直接交给某人或某部门

    e.g.：Attention: Import Dept.

    Attention of the Sales Manager

(2) Subject line 事由或标题

(3) Reference notation 归档或参考行

(4) Enclosure 附件

(5) Carbon copy notation 抄送

(6) Postscript 附言

[3] 商务信函格式主要有三种：平头式、缩行式、改良平头式。

（1）平头式（Block Style）：每行从左边开始取齐。见上面的样本。

（2）缩行式（Indented Style）：每段起始行缩进 5 个字母，日期右上端，签名中间偏右下方。见上面的样本。

（3）改良平头式（Modified Block Style）：基于平头式基础把日期放在右边。见上面的样本。

[4] businesslike *adj.* 商务性质

[5] pointed *adj.* 带有攻击性

[6] concise *adj.* 简洁的；简明的

[7] salutation *n.* 称呼

[8] Manchester 曼彻斯特

[9] sympathetic *adj.* 同情的
[10] intimidate *v.* 威胁，威吓
[11] indentation *n.* (印刷，书写) 缩进，空格

Reading Material

12 Tips for Chinese Business Etiquette and Culture

With increasing globalization comes the need for more and more people to do business with the Chinese. As a result, many in the Dig Mandarin audience seek to improve their business vocabulary. While language is important in bridging an intercontinental relationship, the cultural expectations and etiquette behind the language are even more essential. Developing insights into the Chinese business culture and social etiquette of China will help you avoid miscommunication and potential misunderstandings. When it comes to Chinese business etiquette, there is just one overarching rule: When in China, do as the Chinese do!

Chinese Meeting Etiquette

1. Greetings

In China, the most common ways to greet people in a formal business context are shaking hands or nodding with a smile. In official business meetings, you will be offered a handshake. This handshake must be initiated by your Chinese counterpart.

There are several rules of shaking hands in China:

- It is not appropriate to shake hands with too much or too little strength, as they could infer dominance or disrespect respectively.
- The person with the seniority position should give the hand first. Then the other person is allowed to shake hands with him or her. Otherwise nodding with a smile is more appropriate.
- Shaking hands with both left and right hands is a way to show respect or hospitality. To do so, when one is shaking his right hand with another person, he should also cover his left hand on the handshake.

Chinese people also greet each other in different ways, depending on their relationship. In daily life and formal business context where people meet each other for the first time, "nihao" is a common way to say hello. However, it is important to note that "ninhao" is a more polite expression with the same meaning, and it should be used when the other person is at a seniority position.Besides "很高兴认识你" (hěn gāoxìng rènshi nǐ; Nice to meet you.), you can also say "幸会" (xìng huì; I'm charmed to meet you.) or "久仰" (jiǔyǎng; I've long been looking forward to meeting you.), two proper expressions which will no doubt impress! Chinese people will always appreciate it if you can use some Chinese words, but make sure you know the exact meanings and use in appropriate situations.

2. Addressing

Chinese names are structured in a different order than Western names. Specifically, the family name comes before the given name. For example, if one has "Li" as the family name, and "Qiang" as the given name, his name is structured as "Li Qiang" in Chinese. However, calling someone with his or her full name is not appropriate in China, especially when the other person is more senior. In China, the correct way of addressing people is to add titles after one's family name. There are several examples of how to address people in formal business context:

General rule: [family name] + title

Examples:

- [family name] + 先生 (meaning: Mr. ; Pronounce as "xiansheng")
- [family name] + 小姐 (meaning: Ms. ; Pronounce as "xiaojie")
- [family name] + 女士 (meaning: Ms. ; Pronounce as "nüshi")
- [family name] + 总 (meaning: Boss. ; Pronounce as "zong")
- [family name] + 老板 (meaning: Boss. ; Pronounce as "laoban")
- [family name] + 博士 (meaning: PhD. ; Pronounce as "boshi")

Regarding a courteous address, most people should be addressed with their titles followed by their surname. For example:

- 王经理 (Wáng jīnglǐ; Manager Wang)
- 张教授 (Zhāng jiàoshòu; Prof. Zhang)

If you are not sure about the precise titles, you can also use 先生 (xiānsheng; Sir, Mr.), 小姐 (xiǎo jiě; miss) or 女士 (nǚ shì; madam) instead.

3. Business cards

Exchanging business cards is another key part of introductions. A business card is regarded as an extension of the person, so treat the business card carefully. The polite thing to do is to accept the business card with both hands and look at it carefully as you do so. A business card can also be a cheat sheet for your counterpart's exact rank and title.

4. Contact people

The commonly used channels to contact Chinese clients or business partners are emails, messages, phone call and WeChat. Emails are often used for formal communications, such as sending invitations and business-related documents. Messages and phone calls are more flexible but less formal. Surprisingly, WeChat has been an innovative way of connecting business people. In the article of *Why Should You Do Business in China*, we mentioned the power of the Chinese super App WeChat. With more than 1 billion monthly active users, nearly everyone in China has a WeChat account, including business people. Adding each other as contacts on WeChat is a sufficient way for entrepreneurs to build personal bonds with Chinese people. Furthermore, WeChat sensed the opportunity to expand its business to enterprises, providing professional systems for companies to advertise and manage customers on WeChat.

Chinese Chatting Etiquette

5. Small talk

Chinese people, much like English-speaking people around the world, often open conversations with small talk, which can break the ice. Questions like "你吃了吗?" (Nǐ chī le ma? Have you eaten?) or "你去哪儿了?" (Nǐ qù nǎr ér le? Where have you been?) are common ice breaking pleasantries in Chinese culture. Thus, you don't need to go into details for your answer go into detail in your answer. These questions are just like "How are you?" in English culture.

6. Conversation topics

Dos:

Climate, travel, scenery, and food are all popular and safe topics to use while talking with Chinese people. Talking about your positive impressions of China in such aspects is always welcomed.

Don'ts:

Try to avoid sensitive discussions, it's polite and wise to keep basic respect.

7. Save and give face (给面子 in Mandarin; 俾面 in Cantonese)

"Face" (面子) is one of the key aspects of Chinese culture. A Chinese person always wants to save face, never lose it. In order to "give face", pay attention to elders and rankings.

Be careful when commenting with strong negative statements. For Chinese people, it's impolite to give negative answers directly. The blunt "No" should be replaced by the euphemistic "maybe" or "we'll think about it".

Chinese Dining Etiquette

8. Seat and order

During a Chinese dinner, there is a certain rule in which people must sit down. You can expect more senior business people to be seated first, then just wait for the host to show you your seat.

9. Eating

Don't start eating before others, especially the elders and seniors as rank is very important in Chinese culture.

Don't finish all your food. Otherwise, the Chinese people at the table will think you are still hungry and that they didn't feed you well enough. This could result in them continuing to add food to your plate.

Table manners: *Never* stick your chopsticks straight into your bowl. This action is reserved for funerals, so it is very really offensive to a table of live persons.

Furthermore, never tap your bowl with your chopsticks as this is associated with begging.

10. Invitation

If you invite someone to do an activity or have a meal, you are expected to pay for it. While "going Dutch" is common in the younger generation, the expectation in a business setting is still that the person who gives the invitation pays. If you do invite and pay, try not to show your money in front of your guests.

Chinese Gifts Etiquette

11. Accepting gifts

When you receive a gift, just as when you receive a business card, accept it with two hands. Don't open the gift immediately unless the person who gives it to you requests that you open it right away.

12. Giving gifts

Giving gifts to your Chinese colleagues is a kind of art. What do you give? When do you give? To whom should you give? These are all questions worth discussing. However, for the sake of brevity, I will just give you an overview.

The most important thing is to take cultural taboos seriously to avoid offending others.

Don't s:

Don't give clocks, watches, green hats, or chrysanthemums as gifts.

Gifts should not be too expensive. And if your business counterparts are government officials, make sure you don't give them a reason to mistake your kindness as bribery.

At the end of the day, Chinese business people (especially those in the younger generation) are understanding and respectful of cultural differences. They don't expect foreigners to be fully accustomed to their traditions. However, having a basic grasp of Chinese business etiquette and culture can not only impress your Chinese colleagues, counterparts, and clients but also help you build stronger working relationships with clear and smooth communication.

(Adapted from: https://www.digmandarin.com/chinese-business-culture-etiquette.html)

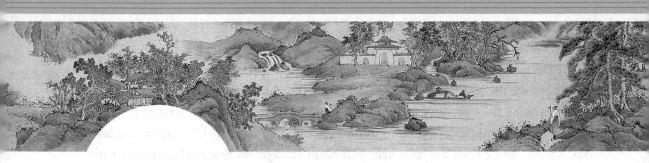

Chapter 11

Establishing Business Relations

11.1 Pre-knowledge

Seeking new clients and establishing business relations with a new company is the first step in foreign trade transactions. It means that you should find your definite partner before you really start doing international business. A business company should have a worldwide business contact with customers in international business field. As is well known, customers are the basis of business development and expansion. In this unit, you will learn how to establish business relations with potential partner.

11.1.1 Channels for Establishing Business Relations

In international business, the importer is usually in one country and the exporter in another. They are separated sometimes by thousands of miles. Usually they can use the following sources to get the information about each other:

(1) banks
(2) trade directory
(3) chambers of commerce both at home and abroad
(4) commercial counselor's office
(5) advertisement
(6) exhibitions and trade fairs
(7) market investigations
(8) self-introduction or introduction from his business connections

(9) a branch office or representative abroad

(10) the internet

11.1.2 Credit Investigation

In international trade, geographic separation, different kinds of legal systems, different trade practice and customs, different kinds of languages, different kinds of currencies, and so on, all causes great risks for buyers and sellers to communicate with the other. So, before starting a concrete transaction, the seller and the buyer should make an investigation into the credit of each other.

In a word, to companies engaged in international trade, business relations are extremely valuable. Therefore, traders must do their utmost to cement their established relations with their existing customers and to develop and revitalized the trade by searching for new connections.

11.2 Correspondence Writing Guide and Specimen Letters

In general, the following contents should be expressed in letters of establishing business relations:

(1) the source of information;

(2) the intention of writing the letter—expressing the strong desire to establish business relations;

(3) the business scope of the firm;

(4) the reference as to the firm's credit standing, such as financial position and integrity;

(5) expectation for cooperation and an early reply.

11.2.1 Sellers Asking to Establish Business Relations

Dongguan Lighting Import & Export Corporation
No.15 Xinji Ave., South Area, Dongguan, Guangdong, China
Tel: +86-769-83456789

March 5, 2020

WALDEMAR INDUSTRIES INC.
1234S. MICHIGAN AVE., CHICAGO, IL60616, U.S.A.
TEL: +1-312-427-5678

Dear Sir or Madam,

  The Commercial Counselor's Office of the Embassy in USA has advised us of your name and address. We take the liberty to introduce ourselves as we understand that your business scope coincides with ours.

We are one of the leading manufacturers of lighting products in Dongguan City, Guangdong Province and have enjoyed an excellent reputation through sixty years' business experience. We specialized in the exporting of lamps, considerable business was done with your country on such items. Now we are desirous of establishing direct business relations with your corporation.

Kindly find enclosed our latest catalogue so that you can have a general idea of our products. We shall be grateful if you will let us know whether you are interested in any of the items. We shall be glad to send you quotations and samples upon receipt of your specific inquiries.

We are looking forward to your early and favorable reply.

Yours sincerely,
Phoebe He
Sales Manager

Encl. a copy of catalogue

11.2.2 Buyers Asking to Establish Business Relations

WALDEMAR INDUSTRIES INC.
1234S. MICHIGAN AVE., CHICAGO, IL60616, U.S.A.
TEL: +1-312-427-5678

March 5, 2020
Re: CHINESE LIGHTING
Dear Sir or Madam,

We owe your name and address to the Chamber of Commerce of Guangdong through whom we understand that you are interested in establishing business relations with Chinese corporation for the purpose of selling lighting of your country.

We take this opportunity to introduce ourselves as one of the important dealers in the line of lighting products in China for many years. We should appreciate your sending us the latest catalogues and price list of your products, and we shall gladly study the sales possibilities in our market.

If your prices are competitive, we trust many transactions can be concluded.

We are anticipating your early reply.

Yours sincerely,
Andy Estes

Notes

[1] lighting 照明设备

[2] Commercial Counselor's Office 商务参赞处

[3] take the liberty to 冒昧地

[4] leading manufacturers 龙头厂商，具有领导地位的制造商

[5] enjoyed an excellent reputation 享有盛誉

[6] specialize in 专营，例：

We specialized in the above business. 我方专营上述业务。

This corporation specializes in importing textiles. 本公司专营纺织品的进口业务。

[7] considerable business 大量的交易

[8] item *n.* 货物、商品，尤指表格中列出的一系列产品。

on such items 就此类产品

[9] establish direct business relations 建立直接的贸易关系。与 enter into direct business relations 意义相同。

例：We are desirous of establishing direct business relations with your corporation. 我们热切希望同贵公司建立贸易关系。

[10] corporation *n.* 公司

关于名称中"公司"的说法，常用的有 corporation（缩写为 Corp.）和 company（缩写为 Co.）。如 General Electric Company——通用电气公司，China National Machinery Import & Export Corporation——中国机械进出口公司。有限公司称作 limited company（简称 Co., Ltd.）。

[11] prospective *adj.* 预期的，未来的，可能的。

prospective client / customer 可能成为客户的人，潜在的客户

[12] your business scope coincides with ours 或 fall (come) within the scope of our business activities 属于我们的经营范围。同样的表达方式还有 textiles are our line，纺织品是我们的经营范围。

[13] general idea 概况

detailed information / full details 详细情况

[14] enclose *v.* 封入，随附。例：

We enclose a copy of our price list. 随函寄上价目单一份。也可表达为：

A copy of price list is enclosed.

Enclosed is a copy of price list.

enclosure *n.* 附件

[15] price list 价目表，价格单（见 Figure 11.1）。

[16] quotation *n.* 报价。常与动词 make、send、give 等连用，后跟介词 for。例：

Please make (send, give) us your lowest quotation for Nike basketball shoes. 请报耐克篮球鞋的最低价。

[17] upon / on receipt of… 一俟收到……即刻……，例：

Upon receipt of your instructions we will send the goods. 一收到你方通知，我方即可发货。

On receipt of your L/C we shall ship the goods without delay. 收到信用证后我方将迅速装船。

[18] specific inquiry 具体的询盘。

inquiry 询盘，也可写作 enquiry。

[19] favorable reply 合意的答复，相当于中文信中的"佳音"。

[20] We owe your name and address to… 承蒙……告知贵公司的名称和地址

owe…to… 把……归功于……

[21] Chamber of Commerce of Beijing 北京商会

[22] for the purpose of 目的或意图。例：

Please send us a collection of specimen for reference purpose. 请寄给我们一组样品作为参考。

They went to America for the purpose of meeting some of their business clients. 他们赴美前去会晤一些商务客户。

[23] take this opportunity to do / for doing… 借此机会……，例：

We like to take this opportunity to express our wish to enter into business relation with you. 我们借此机会表示，我们愿与你方建立业务关系。

[24] in the line of 从事某行业 / 业务

[25] catalogue 目录，目录册

[26] competitive price 有竞争力的价格

[27] conclude a transaction 达成交易

April 25, 2020 Prices are subject to our final confirmation. Please confirm when placing your order. Please refer to the Item Number and specifications in our catalogue.			
Item No.	Description	Price per unit	Shipment
CRT-504	13" Polyresin table lamp	£ 6.58	September
CRT-505	16" Polyresin table lamp	£ 7.00	October
CRT-505	18" Polyresin table lamp	£ 8.50	December
CRT-508	20" Polyresin table lamp	£ 9.00	September
Prices are CIFC 3% London Incoterms® 2020 in Pound Sterling. Packing: 1 piece in a box, 6 boxes to a cardboard carton, and 100 cartons to a container.			
			Hongyuan Lighting Co., Ltd. …
			Sales Manager

Figure 11.1 Sample Price List

Notes

[1] Item Number or Article Number（缩写：Art. No.）产品编号
[2] description 产品描述

11.3 Dialogues

11.3.1 May We Have a Look at Them

(*Mr. Brown and Ms. Perless are at the fair.*)

Brown: Good morning. My name is Bob Brown. I'm from Australia. Here is my card.

Perless: Thank you. I'm pleased to meet you, Mr. Brown. My name is Kathy Perless, the representative of Green Textile Import and Export Corporation.

Brown: Pleased to meet you too, Ms. Perless. This is my first visit to your country. I must say I am very interested in your products. May we have a look at them?

Perless: Certainly. But they are in the showroom.

Brown: Is it far from here?

Perless: Not very far. It's only half an hour's car ride. Are you free now?

Brown: I will be free tomorrow afternoon. Suppose we make it, say three o'clock tomorrow afternoon. Could you manage that?

Perless: Yes. I'll pick you up at your hotel. These are our catalogues and the pamphlets. You can have a look at them first.

Brown: Thank you.

11.3.2 We Wish to Establish Relations with You

(*In the showroom, Mr. Brown and Ms. Perless are discussing the possibility of establishing business relations with each other.*)

Perless: Have you seen our products? On display are most of our products, such as silk, woolen knitwear, cotton piece goods, and garments.

Brown: Oh, yes. I had a look just now. I found some of the exhibits to be fine in quality and beautiful in design. The exhibition has successfully displayed to me what your corporation handles. I've gone over the catalogues and the pamphlets you gave to me yesterday. I've got some idea of your exports. I'm interested in your silk blouses.

Perless: Our silk is known for its good quality. It is one of our traditional exports. Silk blouses are brightly colored and beautifully designed. They've met with great favor overseas and are always in great demand.

Brown: Some of them seem to be of the latest style. Now I've a feeling that we can do a lot of trade in this line. We wish to establish relations with you.

Perless: Your desire coincides with ours.

Brown: Concerning our financial position, credit standing and trade reputation, you may refer to Bank of Hong Kong, or to our local Chamber of Commerce or inquiry agencies.

Perless: Thank you for your information. As you know, our corporation is a state-owned one. We always trade with foreign countries on the basis of equality and mutual benefit. Establishing business relations between us will be to our mutual benefit. I have no doubt that it will bring about closer ties between us.

Brown: That sounds interesting. I'll send a fax home. As soon as I receive a definite answer, I'll make a specific inquiry.

Perless: We'll then make an offer as soon as possible. I hope a lot of business will be conducted between us.

Brown: So do I.

Notes

[1] showroom *n.* 陈列室，展品室
[2] card 名片，常用 business card
[3] representative *n.* 代表，代表人
[4] exhibition hall 展览厅
[5] woolen knitwear 毛织品
[6] fine in quality and beautiful in design 质量上乘，设计美观
[7] brightly colored and beautifully designed 色彩鲜艳，设计美观
[8] meet with great favor 受欢迎
[9] of the latest style 最新式样
　　latest 是 late 的最高级，表示"最晚的，最近的"
　　the latest catalogue 最新目录；the latest price list 最新价目表
[10] financial position, credit standing and trade reputation 财务状况，信用地位，贸易声誉
[11] state-owned 国有
[12] on the basis of equality and mutual benefit 在平等互利的基础上
[13] offer *n.* 发盘，报价

Exercises

Exercise 1: Choose the best answer to complete the following sentences

1. We are looking forward to _____ from you soon.

A. hearing   B. hear   C. heard   D. be heard
2. Your name and address _____ to us by the Commonwealth Bank.
   A. have given   B. have been given C. give   D. given
3. _____ in 1935, this company specializes in the export of cotton piece goods.
   A. Establish   B. Established   C. Establishing   D. To be established
4. We take the pleasure of introducing ourselves _____ an experienced importer _____ the line of dairy products.
   A. of, on   B. as, in   C. for, by   D. be, at
5. _____ please find the catalogues and the latest price list.
   A. Enclose   B. Enclosing   C. Enclosed   D. Enclosure
6. As the goods _____ within the scope of our business activities, please contact us at once.
   A. fall   B. falls   C. fell   D. felling
7. We are a Sino-Korean Joint Venture _____ silk clothes.
   A. deal in   B. dealing in   C. dealt in   D. engage
8. We are sending you by separate cover the samples, _____ you will find them satisfactory.
   A. to hope   B. hoping   C. hopefully   D. hope
9. We hope to enter _____ business relations _____ your firm.
   A. into, with   B. with, into   C. /, at   D. with, at
10. _____ will be appreciated.
   A. You reply our letter early   B. You reply to our letter early
   C. Your early reply our letter   D. Your early reply to our letter

Exercise 2: Translate the following sentences into Chinese

1. We've come to know your name and address from the Commercial Counselor's Office of the Chinese Embassy in London.
2. Having obtained your name and address from the Bank of China, we are writing to you with a view to establishing trade relations with you.
3. We are writing to you in the hope that we can open up business relations with your firm.
4. We enclose herewith a list of goods to supply you at the lowest possible price.
5. By the courtesy of Mr. Black, we are given the name and address of your firm.
6. We have the pleasure of introducing ourselves to you with the hope that we may have a good chance of cooperation with you in your business extension.
7. We are the exporter of long standing and high reputation, engaged in exports of light industrial products.
8. In order to make us familiarized with your products, we shall appreciate your giving

us the technical details of them at your earliest convenience.
9. To give you some ideas of various types of bicycles we are dealing in, we are pleased to send you, under separate cover, by air-mail our latest catalogue and a price list.
10. We have been in the line of chemical fertilizer for many years.

Exercise 3: Translate the following sentences into English

1. 我们的产品质量上乘，价格优惠。
2. 希望早日收到你方答复。
3. 我公司专营轻工业品的进口业务。
4. 我们意欲购买各种形状、质量优良的瓷茶杯。
5. 经当地商会推荐，特致函贵方，希望建立贸易关系。

Exercise 4: Translate the following letter into English in the right format

敬启者：

  我们从中国驻鹿特丹使馆商务处获悉贵公司名字和地址，兹告知我公司专营工业和药物化工原料，并希望同你们建立业务联系。

  为了使你们对我方产品有大概的了解，现附上有关我们公司经营的各种产品的一整套小册子，内有详细规格和包装情况。一俟收到你们的具体询价，我们马上寄样报价。

  盼早日收到你们的回信。

此致　中国化工产品进出口公司

荷兰化工产品进出口公司
李　明　谨上
2020年3月30日

附件：一套公司资料

（注：荷兰化工产品进出口公司
   地址：P.O. BOX 200/3804 New Sharon Road
      Pella, Iowa 50219, Holland
  中国化工产品进出口公司
   地址：67, Tian Mu Shan Road
      Beijing, China）

Exercise 5: Compose a dialogue on the following situation

David Jones, A Canadian businessman, deals in machine tools.

Zhang Ming, deputy manager of China National Machinery & Equipment Import & Export Corporation, wants to have direct contact with a Canadian supplier.

They are discussing the trade possibility.

Reading Material

China Mainland Commodity Imports & Exports
By Daniel Workman

Chapter 12

Inquiries and Offers

12.1 Pre-knowledge

Negotiations usually begin with inquiries and offers, which are among the most important and the busiest work.

An inquiry is to request the potential seller to give the information about the goods he or she intends to purchase, such as the price, terms of payment, shipment, specification, etc. A catalogue, a price list and samples may also be demanded. Inquiries can be made either orally or written. Whichever style is used, they must be short and clear. Enquiry may be roughly classified as general enquiries and specific enquiries. In the general enquiry, the buyer merely asks for price list, catalogues, samples, etc. In a specific enquiry, the buyer has a definite aim of purchasing and asks for offers.

Upon receipt of the inquiry, the seller should give a reply. And the reply is a so-called offer. Simply speaking, an offer is the reply made by a seller to the inquiry by a buyer. It has also been the practice that a seller voluntarily makes an offer without waiting for an inquiry from his customers. It must be communicated to the offeree and it must give an undertaking that all essential terms are clearly definite.

There are two kinds of offers: firm offer and non-firm offer. A firm offer is made when a seller promises to sell goods at a stated price within a stated time.

There are some words in it like "for acceptance within 5 days" "this offer is valid (open, firm, good) for 5 days" or similar qualifying words. It is a contractual obligation. Once it has been accepted unconditionally within the validity, it can't be withdrawn. A non-firm offer is just an indication of price without contractual obligation. E.g.: "We are making an offer for the following, subject to our final confirmation." For these offers, the seller can take them back at will.

12.2 Correspondence Writing Guide and Specimen Letters

12.2.1 Enquiry/Inquiry

A **general enquiry** usually includes the following contents:

(1) Telling addressees the source of information and making a brief self-introduction.

(2) Indicating the intention of writing the letter, i.e. to ask for a catalogue, samples or a price list.

(3) Stating the possibility of placing an order and expectation of an offer.

A **specific enquiry** usually includes the following contents:

(1) Indicating the names and descriptions of the goods inquired for, including specifications, quantity, etc.

(2) Asking whether there is a possibility of giving a special discount and what terms of payment and time of delivery you would expect.

(3) Stating the possibility of placing and order and expectation of an offer.

12.2.2 Offers

A satisfactory offer will include the followings:

(1) Name of commodities, quality, quantity and specification.

(2) Unit price and type of currency.

(3) Packing condition and date of delivery.

(4) Terms of payment and discount.

(5) The terms of validity of the offer.

(6) Indication of what the price covers.

Offers must be prompt and courteous and cover all the information asked for.

12.2.3 Examples

1. General Inquiry

March 11, 2020

Dear Sir or Madam,

We have read your advertisement in www.Alibaba.com and are interested in your table lamps of all sizes.

Please quote us for the supply of the item listed on the enclosed form. We appreciate your sending us some detailed information about FOB Shenzhen, Incoterms® 2020, delivery schedule, terms of payment and discounts for regular purchases. Please also send us some catalogues if available.

We thank you in advance for your kind attention and assure you that your offer will certainly receive our careful consideration.

We hope this will be a good start for our long and mutually beneficial business relations.

Yours sincerely,
Andy Estes

2. Specific Inquiry

March 12, 2020

Dear Sir or Madam,

We have learned from www.alibaba.com that you export lamps to American market.

At present, we are interested in table lamps A001 and A003. We would like you to send us details.

We will highly appreciate it if you could quote us your lowest price, FOB Shenzhen Incoterms® 2020, stating quantity discount on 2,400pcs, terms of payment and the earliest date of shipment.

Should your goods prove satisfactory and price be found competitive, we intend to place a large order with you.

Your early reply will be much appreciated.

Yours sincerely,
Andy Estes

3. Inquiry and Asking for Proforma Invoice

March 12, 2020

Dear Sir or Madam,

We learn from one Indian company of the same trade that you export lightings. We are interested in them. Would you please send us your Proforma Invoice in duplicate, giving us information about prices, specifications, quantity available, time of delivery and payment?

We are one of the largest department stores here. If your price is right, we shall be able to send you regular orders.

Your prompt attention and early reply would be highly appreciated.

Yours Sincerely,
Andy Estes

4. Firm Offer

March 13, 2020

Dear Andy,

We are in receipt of your letter dated March, 12, inquiring for lamps A001 and A003. As requested, are airmailing you, under separate cover, one catalogue and two sample books for our lamps. We hope they will reach you in due course and will help you in making your selection.

In order to start a concrete transaction between us, we take pleasure in making you a special offer as follows:

Art. No.:	A001
	A003
Specifications:	A001 13 INCHES POLY TABLE LAMP
	A003 16 INCHES POLY TABLE LAMP
Quantity:	2,400PCS
Packing:	1 piece in a box and 6 boxes to carton
Price:	A001: USD8.00 per PCS FOB Shenzhen Incoterms® 2020
	A003: USD10.00 per PCS FOB Shenzhen Incoterms® 2020
Shipment:	To be made in three equal monthly installments, beginning from June, 2020
Payment:	By confirmed, irrevocable L/C payable at sight to be opened 30 days before the time of shipment

The above offer is firm subject to your reply reaching here not later than the end of this month.

We trust the above will be acceptable to you and await your early reply.

Yours sincerely,
Phoebe He
Sales Manager

5. Non-Firm Offer

March 13, 2020

Dear Sir or Madam,

We acknowledge with thanks the receipt of your letter dated March 11, 2020, showing your interest in table lamps and extending the wish to place large orders with us.

In reply, we are offering you as follows, subject to our final confirmation:

<u>Art. No.　　Unit Price FOB Shenzhen</u> Incoterms® 2020
A001　　　USD8.00
A002　　　USD8.00
A003　　　USD10.00
A004　　　USD10.00

Shipment: To be effected within one month from receipt of the relevant L/C
Payment: By sight L/C

Under separate cover, we have send you a catalogue and sample book as requested. I am sure you will find that our products are of excellent quality and at favorable prices.

We look forward to receiving your detailed requirements.

Yours faithfully,
Phoebe He
Sales Manager

Notes

[1] table lamp 桌灯，台灯

[2] the enclosed 随函附上的

[3] terms of payment 付款方式

[4] CIF = Cost, Insurance and Freight 成本、保险加运费

[5] discount 折扣。常见的折扣有 cash discount（现金折扣）、quantity discount（数量折扣）等。

[6] delivery schedule 交货期，交货时间表。表示"交货期"的还有 delivery time、time of delivery。

[7] in advance 提前，预先

[8] learn from 从……获知

[9] Proforma Invoice 形式发票。形式发票是交易达成之前开制的一种概略发票。主要用于：供进口商申请进口许可证或申请外汇；代替报价单；形式发票经双方确认后可作为销售确认书等。形式发票样本如图 12-1 所示。

[10] We are in receipt of your letter dated March, 12. 收到你方 3 月 12 日来信。dated 是动词 date 的过去分词，指写信的日期。

[11] as requested 按照要求（请求）

东莞灯具进出口公司
Dongguan Lighting Import & Export Corp.
No.15 Xinji Ave., South Area, Dongguan, Guangdong, China
Tel: +86-769-83456789

形式发票
PROFORMA INVOICE

Contract No.:
March 5, 2020

卖方 Sellers
Dongguan Lighting Import & Export Corp.
No.15 Xinji Ave., South Area,
Dongguan, Guangdong, China
Tel: +86-769-83456789

买方 Buyers
ASD TRADING CO. LTD
130-S, HSK, PUNKIAGSAN-DONG
GYEON, KOREA
Tel: +82-31-74958621

双方同意按以下条款达成交易：
The undersigned Sellers and Buyers have agreed to close the following transactions according to the terms and conditions stipulated below:

订单号：
ORDERNO.: SF2020-160

货号 Art. No.	规格 Description	数量 Quantity	单价 Unit Price	总金额 Total Amount
CRT-504	13" Polyresin table lamp	1,000	£ 6.58	£ 6,580
CRT-505	16" Polyresin table lamp	2,000	£ 7.00	£ 14,000
CRT-505	18" Polyresin table lamp	1,000	£ 8.50	£ 8,500
CRT-508	20" Polyresin table lamp	500	£ 9.00	£ 4,500
TOTAL			FOB SHENZHEN	£ 33,580

1. 交货期：收到定金后 20 天。
   Delivery time: 20 days after receipt of deposit.
2. 包装：纸盒装。
   Packing: In cardboard cases.
3. 付款方式：40% 定金，60% 出货前付清。
   Terms of Payment: 40% by deposit, and 60% by T/T before shipment.

图 12-1　形式发票样本

[12] airmail 航邮

[13] under separate cover 另封，也可说 by separate mail

[14] in due course 在适当的时候，如期地（同 duly）

[15] concrete 具体的

[16] special offer 特别报价

[17] offer 发盘，报盘，报价。常用动词有 make、send、give，后常接介词 for、on。

[18] as follows 如下。这是一个习惯用语，不论前面的主语是单数还是复数，也不论后列的事物是一个或几个，都必须用 as follows。

[19] confirmed, irrevocable L/C payable at sight 保兑的、不可撤销的、凭即期汇票付款的信用证

[20] subject to 以……为条件（为准）。subject to your reply reaching here not later than the end of this month 以你方答复本月底前到达有效；subject to our final confirmation 以我方最终确认为准。

[21] acceptable adj. 可接受的。accept: *v.* 接受； acceptance: *n.* 接受。
[22] place a large order with sb. 向……下一笔大订单
[23] sight L/C 全称：sight letter of credit，即期信用证

12.3　Dialogues

12.3.1　I'd like to Have Your Lowest Quotations

(*At the Guangzhou Trade Fair, a Spanish buyer Henry Jones inquiries about prices at a bed-cover stand.*)

Henry Jones: Good morning. My name is Henry Jones. We are one of the major companies in selling bed-covers in Barcelona, Spain. I'm very interested in your bed cover. I have seen your exhibits and catalogues. They are attractive. Here is a list of requirement. I'd like to have your lowest quotations, CIF Barcelona, Spain.

Salesman: Thank you for your inquiry, Mr. Jones. Will you please tell me the quantity you require so as to enable us to sort out offers?

Henry Jones: OK, I will do that. Could you give me an indication of the price?

Salesman: Here are our latest FOB price sheets. All the prices in the sheets are subject to our final confirmation.

Henry Jones: For how long does your quotation price remain open?

Salesman: It's open for three days. When can you decide the size of your order?

Henry Jones: That will depend on your price. If your price is reasonable and I can get the commission I want, we can place an order immediately.

Salesman: In principle, we don't allow any commission. But if your order is large, we will take it into consideration. From the price sheets, you will find our prices are very competitive. And heavy inquiries witness the quality of our products. You know, the prices of materials have gone up sharply. But the prices of our products haven't changed much.

Henry Jones: I'm very pleased to hear that. How long will it take you to deliver the goods?

Salesman: Usually we deliver the goods within 3 months after receipt of the covering letters of credit.

Henry Jones: Good. I can't make the decision by myself. I will call my head office in Spain and consider the price carefully. If they think the prices are favorable, we can place order right away. I will come back to you tomorrow. All right?

Salesman: Right. See you tomorrow.

12.3.2　I'm Making You An Offer

(*Mr. Zhang from Shandong Native Produce and Animal By-products Import &*

Export Corporation is making a British businessman, Mr. Davidson an offer for cotton.)

Zhang: Mr. Davidson, I received your email inquiring for cotton, 2020 Crop.

Davidson: You got that? Great! Have you worked out on that?

Zhang: Yes, I have. I'm making you an offer.

Davidson: Great! I hope it's a favorable one.

Zhang: For cotton, 2020 Crop, we are offering for 50 metric tons at US $ 600 per metric ton, CIF Liverpool Incoterms® 2020.

Davidson: Can you offer on FOB terms? We have agreements with shipping lines and insurance companies at our end. We can receive good rates from them. We'd like to arrange shipment and insurance by ourselves.

Zhang: OK, that's fine. The price should be lower. We offer US $ 570 per metric ton.

Davidson: As I know, 570 dollars are roughly 20 dollars above the world market. Do you think it possible for you to make a reduction?

Zhang: Mr. Davidson. Considering the quality of our goods, I assure you that this is the best offer you can receive from any other suppliers. I recommend you accept this offer.

Davidson: Well, I'll think about it. I'll discuss it with you again in a few days.

Zhang: That's OK. But this offer is not final. It's subject to the goods being unsold. I hope you'll make a decision soon.

Davidson: I see. I'll talk to you later.

Notes

[1] bed-cover 床罩

[2] Barcelona 巴塞罗那（西班牙港口城市）

[3] sort out 整理好，解决

[4] an indication of the price 参考价格。indication: n. 表示，标示

[5] price sheet 同 price list，价目表、价格单

[6] commission n. 佣金，指按业务活动量给予代理商的报酬，通常以百分率表示。例：
He's on commission. 他以抽取佣金形式获得酬劳。

[7] in principle 原则上

[8] inquire 同 enquire（询问、询盘），后常跟介词 about、for

[9] crop 收获，收成。cotton, 2020 Crop 指 2020 年收成的棉花。

[10] metric ton 吨，通常略写为 M.T. 或 M/T，重量单位，等于 1 000 千克。国际上常用的重量单位还有 long ton（长吨，英国重量单位，等于 1 016 千克），short ton（短吨，美国重量单位，等于 907 千克）。

[11] rate 费率

[12] reduction 减少，削减。这里指减价

[13] recommend 劝告，建议

Exercises

Exercise 1: Choose the best answer to complete the following sentences

1. We can supply 1,000 cases of Pepsi Cola _____ stock _____ present.
   A. in, at B. in, in C. from, at D. from, in
2. We thank you for your letter of March 18 _____ our silk blouses of various styles.
   A. inquiring for B. inquiry for C. inquired for D. inquire for
3. We are enclosing herewith a copy of our illustrated catalogue _____ for in your last letter.
   A. ask B. asks C. asked D. asking
4. We thank you for the inquiry you _____ us.
   A. have made to B. have offered to C. have let D. have informed to
5. You quotation _____ washing machines is too high to be workable.
   A. in B. against C. with D. of
6. As requested _____ your e-mail of October 1, we are enclosing _____ the required quotation sheet.
   A. in, herewith B. for, herewith C. for, in D. on, herewith
7. Please quote us your lowest prices _____ a CIF Singapore basis for embroidered silk blouses _____ prompt shipment.
   A. on, for B. from, for C. on, on D. from, on
8. We are pleased to make you an offer _____ 5,000 dozen of Ladies' Folding Auto Umbrellas _____ USD 35 per dozen CIF London Incoterms® 2020.
   A. for, on B. for, at C. on, for D. on, at
9. We would like to inform you that we have received a large inquiry _____ 800 sets of refrigerators.
   A. of B. with C. at D. for
10. We acknowledge with thanks _____ your fax of March 3.
    A. receipt B. receive C. receipt of D. receiving

Exercise 2: Translate the following sentences into Chinese

1. Please quote us your lowest price CIF Hamburg for 10 M/Ts of walnut meat.
2. We have already made an enquiry for your articles, please make an offer before the end of this month.
3. We refer to our negotiations during the spring Guangzhou fair 2020 and would like to know whether you are now in a position to offer us automatic probes.
4. We are interested in Chinese arts and crafts.
5. At your request, we make you an offer as follows.
6. There is a heavy demand for these products, but the supply is limited. We strongly

recommend you to accept this offer as soon as you can.

7. We are sorry that we are not able to offer you the information you requested in your last letter of February 2.
8. The quotation we offer you at exceptionally low prices is subject to reply by return of post.
9. We hope that our quotation will be a satisfactory one and expect your orders.
10. With reference to your inquiry of July 10, we shall be pleased to supply 50 sets of scanners at the price of USD110 per set.

Exercise 3: Translate the following sentences into English

1. 现寄上我方的第 1234 号询价单一份，请报 FOB 价格。
2. 所报发盘有效期 7 天。
3. 获悉贵公司对我们的产品感兴趣，非常感谢。
4. 恳请惠寄商品目录、价格表和付款方式细则。
5. 我方愿意做如下报价，但以你方 10 日内接受有效。
6. 如果你方报价具有竞争力，我们愿意向你方订货。
7. 一俟收到你方具体询价，我们将告知报价。
8. 鉴于我们长期的贸易关系，特报此盘。
9. 这是我方最新价格单，您会发现我方价格是具有竞争力的。
10. 如果你方订货数量大，价格还可以进一步商量。

Exercise 4: Translate the following letter into English with the right format

敬启者：

　　感谢你方 4 月 27 日询购 AHS20 立体声耳机的传真。你方对此产品感兴趣，我们非常感谢，抱歉因其生产已停止，我方已不能供应此产品，但我们相信我们的新产品 AHS30 将是一种优良的替代品。

　　该产品质量和规格都有很大的改进，而成本的提高却微乎其微，目前非常畅销。我们已用航空快递方式寄出了样品、价格单和产品目录。

　　我们肯定该优良产品将会有很好的销路，令你方完全满意。

此致　美国 ABC 贸易公司

中国电子产品进出口公司
张志明　谨上
2020 年 5 月 25 日

（注：美国 ABC 贸易公司地址：
　　　　No. 356 Fish Rd,
　　　　New York, USA
　　中国电子产品进出口公司地址：
　　　　No. 15, De Sheng Men Street
　　　　Beijing, P. R. China）

Exercise 5: Compose a dialogue on the following situation

Mr. Fisher, an American businessman has come with an inquiry for your pillow cases. He would like to ask for your unit price CIF New York. You just want to make a FOB offer because his order is very small. Other terms are as follows:

Specifications: NJ100.
Quantity: 10 thousand dozens.
Unit price: USD 23 per dozen FOB Shanghai Incoterms® 2020.
Payment: By confirmed and irrevocable letter of credit payable at sight.
Shipment: During July/August 2020.

Reading Material

Incoterms® 2020: Rules and Updates

Chapter 13

Counter-offers

13.1 Pre-knowledge

Counter-offer constitutes the main part of a business negotiation. When a buyer rejects an offer, or finds part of the offer unacceptable, he or she proposes amendments on the terms of the original offer and raises new ones in his counter offer. Each transaction generally follows such procedures as inquiry, offer, counter-offer and confirmation before it is brought to a conclusion.

Price is one of the most important factors. Both sides will bargain with each other till they come to terms at the end. The buyer always wants a lower price so that he may earn some money by reselling the goods at a higher price. While the seller always insists on a higher price in order to gain more profit.

In the course of price negotiation, appropriate trade terms and favorable money of account also should be determined. In addition, commission and discounts could be used as a flexible way of motivating the initiatives of the supplier and expanding sales.

13.1.1 Trade Terms

In last chapter's Reading Material, we introduced the Incoterms® 2020. Among the eleven trade terms, China prefers to accept FOB terms in imports and send Chinese ships for the shipment. On the other hand, China desires CIF for exports because it enables us to cut down the freight cost by making reasonable use of transport facilities and keep in the country the insurance premium, which, more often than not, is in hard currency.

13.1.2 Money of Account

In international trade, as the change of the value of the selected currency may directly affect the financial interest of both parties, the parties concerned would choose the most favorable currency during pricing. As to the currency used in an export trade, there are generally three kinds of currencies—that of the importing country or region, of the exporting country or region, and of a third country or region. And those chiefly used in our foreign trade are US dollar, Euro, Pound Sterling, Swiss Franc, Hong Kong Dollar, Canadian Dollar, Australian Dollar and Japanese yen, etc.

13.1.3 Commission and Discount

Commission is the service fees charged by the agents or brokers for negotiating a sale, based on a percentage of the selling price. Discount is the price deduction allowed by the seller to the buyer. There are cash discount, quantity discount, trade discount, etc. Discount is usually deducted from the payment when the buyer pays for the goods.

13.2 Correspondence Writing Guide and Specimen Letters

A satisfactory counter-offer will include the followings:
(1) Thanking for the offer and mentioning briefly the contents of the offer;
(2) Expressing regret for unable to accept the offer and giving reasons for non-acceptance;
(3) Making an appropriate counter-offer;
(4) Hoping the counter-offer will be accepted and there may be an opportunity to do business together.

A letter of declining should include the followings:
(1) Thank the seller for his offer;
(2) Express regret for unable to accept;
(3) State reasons for non-acceptance;
(4) Suggest that there may be other opportunity to do business together.

13.2.1 Counter-offer

March 15, 2020

Dear Mr. He,

  We have received your offer dd. March 13, 2020, and thanks for your attention to our inquiry.

  We really appreciate the good workmanship and cute designs of your products. However, after careful study, we regret to inform you that your price is too high to come to business and our margin of profit would be quite narrow. It is obviously out of line with the prevailing market. Information indicates that most of other suppliers can supply at a level about 10% lower than yours.

  We do not deny that the quality of yours is slightly better but the difference in price should, in no case, be as large as 10%. It would be very difficult for us to persuade our end-users to accept your price.

  Prices still count much, especially in the initial sale stage. To step up the trade, may we suggest you give 10% discount or 5% commission?

  We hope you will consider our counter most favorably and await your immediate reply.

Yours sincerely,
Andy Estes

13.2.2 Accepting a Counter-offer

March 16, 2020

Dear Ms. Estes,

Re: Table Lamps

  We learn from your letter of March 15, 2020 that our prices for the captioned article is found to be on the high side.

  You mention that other suppliers in China are being offered to you at a price approximately 10% lower than our quotation. We must point out that our goods are of superior quality and creative design which explains why our clients in Europe and America keep buying from us at our price level. Other suppliers do not measure up to ours. So we do hope that you can draw your end-users' attention to the quality, rather than prices only.

  Although it is difficult to comply with your request for our price is quite realistic, we have finally decided to accept your counter-offer with a view to initiating our business with you at an early date. Enclosed is the updated price list.

  As the stock is running low, we hope we can conclude the transaction without further delay. Await your prompt reply.

Yours sincerely,
Phoebe He
Sales Manager

13.2.3 Declining a Counter-offer

March 16, 2020

Dear Sirs,

We acknowledge with thanks receipt of your e-mail of March 15. We learn that our prices are found to be on the high side.

Much as we would like to cooperate with you, we are regretful that we just cannot see our way to entertain your counter offer as our quotation is quite realistic. We must point out that your bids are out of line with the current market price. Other companies in your region are buying freely at our quoted price.

The best we can make a concession is to give you 3% discount if your quantity is over 6,000pcs each.

The market is firm and trending upward. There is very little likelihood of any significant change. In view of the above, we would suggest in your interest that you accept our offer without further delay.

Yours faithfully,
Phoebe He
Sales Manager

Notes

[1] dd. =dated 日期是……天的
[2] good workmanship 良好的工艺
[3] on the high side（价格）偏高
    on the low side（价格）偏低
[4] margin of profit 利润率
[5] prevailing market 现行行市，the prevailing price 现行价格
[6] count 重要
[7] initial sale stage 最初的销售阶段
[8] discount 折扣
[9] commission 佣金
[10] quotation 报价
[11] The market is firm and trending upward. 市场坚挺，有上涨的趋势。
    表示市场状况的说法还有：
    the market is easy 市场疲软
    the market is dull 市场黯淡
    the market is gloomy 市场黯淡

the market is sluggish 市场疲软

the market is steady 市场稳定

the market is quiet 市场清淡

the market is firm 市场趋升

the market is active 市场活跃

the market is strong 市场坚挺

[12] captioned 标题中所列的

[13] in view of 考虑到，鉴于

[14] stock 存货，库存。例：

Your order can be supplied from stock.

你的订单可现货供应。

[15] without further delay 勿再延迟

13.3　Dialogues

13.3.1　We'll Have a Lot of Difficulties in Persuading Our Clients to Buy at This Price, but I'll Have to Try

(*Mr. Martin is a purchaser from America. Ms. Xu Lin is the sales manager of an export company. They are discussing the price of bristles.*)

Martin: Good morning, Ms. Xu. I've come to hear about your offer for bristles.

Xu: Good morning, Mr. Martin. We have the offer ready for you. Let me see. Here it is. 100 cases of Bristles, 57 mm, at 12 Pounds Sterling per Kilogram, CIF European Main Ports Incoterms® 2020, for shipment in June 2020. The offer is valid for five days.

Martin: Why, your price is too high.

Xu: I'm a little surprised to hear you say that. It is much lower than last year's contract price.

Martin: We admit your offer is lower than last year's, but it is much higher than the prevailing level. It compares very unfavorable with those of other origins, Japan, for instance.

Xu: That is due to the freight rate. Our price is lower on FOB basis. Of course if you tackle from the CIF angle, that's quite another pair of shoes. So what is really high is the freight, not the Bristle.

Martin: But the users must consider the landed price.

Xu: We are sure our FOB price is lower than that you may possibly obtain from Japan. What's more, it's the quality that counts. Everyone in the trade knows that our bristles are of superior quality to those from Japan.

Martin: I agree that yours are of better quality. But there's competition from synthetic products, too. You can't very well ignore that.

Xu: There's practically no substitute for bristles for certain uses. That's why demand for natural bristles keeps rising in spite of cheaper synthetic ones. To be frank with you, if it were not for the friendly relationship between us, we would hardly be willing to make you a firm offer at this price.

Martin: Well, we'll have a lot of difficulties in persuading our clients to buy at this price. But I'll have to try, I suppose.

13.3.2 How about Meeting Each Other Halfway

(At the Guangzhou Trade Fair, the Spanish buyer Henry Jones, comes to the bed-cover stand again. This time, he wants to talk about the price of the bed-covers.)

Jones: Good morning. I am Henry Jones. I came to you yesterday for inquiry about your bed-covers.

Salesman: Oh, Mr. Jones. Nice to see you again.

Jones: Nice to see you too. Yesterday afternoon, I called my head office in Spain, they are very interested in your bed-covers.

Salesman: Good.

Jones: But, there's one problem.

Salesman: What' that?

Jones: Price. The price in your price sheet is much too high. We can in no way sell your bed-covers in our market at your prices. As a matter of fact, bed-cover retail prices here show a downward trend. To make the business possible, I would suggest that you allow us a special discount of, say 6%, so as to enable us to continue our business with you.

Salesman: Oh sorry. We'll never be able to bring down our price to your level. You know, our price is closely calculated and the margin of profit is very small.

Jones: I think it unwise for either of us to insist on his own price. How about meeting each other halfway? I only ask you to make a concession of 3% on your quotation. That's reasonable, isn't it?

Salesman: To tell you plainly, the price we quoted you yesterday is really the lowest and we cannot stand any cuts.

Jones: To reduce your cost, I'm prepared to place you a large order of 2,500 dozens. This is certainly a big contract, and in view of our future relations I feel sure you'll try your best to help me settle the price problem, otherwise my home office will complain about me. That wouldn't be very good!

Salesman: You certainly have a way of talking me into it. But the best we can do would be a reduction of 2%. That'll definitely be our rock-bottom price.

Jones: All right. I accept the 2% discount. You're very helpful. Now we've come to an agreement on the price for an order of 2,500 dozens of bed-covers.

Salesman: I'm glad we have brought this transaction to a successful conclusion and hope this will be the forerunner of other business in the future.

13.3.3 We Have No Choice but to Give Up the Deal This Time

(*Mr. Zhang, from Shandong Native Produce and Animal By-products Import & Export Corporation, receives a call from the English businessman, Mr. Davidson. Now, they are talking about the price of the cotton.*)

Davidson: Mr. Zhang, we've studied your quotation for our order of 50 metric ton of cotton at US$570 per metric ton. But we find it on the high side. I don't think it's possible to come to an agreement at this price.

Zhang: Well, Mr. Davidson. Different quality will cause different prices. Our cotton is of superior quality. When you take this into consideration, you may find our price favorable. I can assure you that you can not find a price lower than ours.

Davidson: Do you think so? But in fact, some suppliers from India would offer US$ 540 for the same quality. And geographically, India is much closer to us than China. We don't need to pay as much in shipping and insurance, either. However, in view of our long-standing relationship, we would prefer to do business with you.

Zhang: I'm glad to hear that. Anyhow, let's have your counter-offer first.

Davidson: I'm afraid a price of US$550 per metric ton is quite reasonable.

Zhang: What? No, no, we'll never reduce our price to that extent. That's impossible.

Davidson: Mr. Zhang, our counter-offer is based on the world market.

Zhang: But that's really too low for us to accept. To show our goodwill to a customer like you, the best we can do is to cut our offer by 5 dollars and make it US$ 565.

Davidson: There is still a wide gap.

Zhang: I'm sorry, but this is the best we can do for you. As an expert in cotton business, you know our cotton is worth much more than your counter-offer.

Davidson: Thanks for you compliment, however, if you insist on your own price, we have no choice but to give up the deal this time. I hope we'll cooperate in other opportunities in the future.

Zhang: All right. Should there be anything I can help with in the future, please don't hesitate to tell me.

Davidson: I will. Keep in touch.

Zhang: Keep in touch.

Notes

[1] bristle *n.* 猪鬃

[2] Pound Sterling 英镑

[3] European Main Ports 欧洲主要港口，缩写为 EMP，按照航运工会统一规定 EMP 包括意大利的热那亚（Genoa）、法国的马赛（Marseilles）、比利时的安特卫普（Antwerp）、荷兰的鹿特丹（Rotterdam）、英国的伦敦（London）、德国的汉堡（Hamburg）、丹麦的哥本哈根（Copenhagen）等港口（见表 13-1）

[4] freight rate 运费率、运价，freight 运费

[5] Tackle from the CIF angle 从成本加保险费、运费这一角度来计算货价

[6] That's quite another pair of shoes. 那完全是另外一回事。

[7] landed price 到岸价

[8] It's the quality that counts. 重要的是质量。

[9] synthetic products 人造制品

[10] retail price 零售价，wholesale price 批发价

[11] margin of profit 利润。margin 利润，盈利；a narrow margin of profit 微利；marrow（或 small, thin, tight）margin 薄利，利润有 gross margin（毛利）、net margin（净利）

[12] How about meeting each other halfway? 双方都各让一半怎么样？

[13] concession *n.* 优惠，折让

[14] To tell you plainly…坦白说，plainly *adv.* 坦白地，明白地

[15] dozen *n.* 打，缩写为 doz.，一打为 12 个。国际贸易中常用的数量表达方式还有：

　　件：piece

　　双：pair

　　套：set

　　罗：gross，缩写为 gr.，1 罗 =12 打

　　令：ream、rm，纸张计量单位，1 令为 500 张

[16] talk s b. into sth. 说服某人做某事

[17] rock-bottom price 底价，最低价格

　　lowest price 最低价格

　　moderate price 公道价格

　　reasonable price 合理价格

　　favorable price 优惠价格

　　competitive price 竞争性价格

　　attractive price 具有吸引力的价格

　　best price 最好价格（可以是最低或是最高价格，取决于是买方还是卖方）

[18] forerunner *n.* 预兆

[19] counter-offer 还价，还盘

[20] Should there be anything I can help with in the future, please don't hesitate to tell

me. 倒装句，正常语序为：If there should be anything I can help with in the future, please don't hesitate to tell me.

表 13-1　世界主要港口按航线划分中英文对照表

Exercises

Exercise 1: Choose the best answer to complete the following sentences

1. We are sorry to say it is not possible _____ us to meet the price you requested.
   A. for　　　　　　B. of　　　　　　C. with　　　　　　D. to
2. In reference to your letter, we cannot _____ a better offer than the one we suggested to you.
   A. take　　　　　　B. make　　　　　　C. receive　　　　　　D. get
3. We are aware _____ the fact that your goods are among the best on the market.
   A. for　　　　　　B. of　　　　　　C. in　　　　　　D. to
4. We regret that it is not possible to accept the _____ price you offer.
   A. reducing　　　B. having reduced　　C. reducing　　　D. reduced
5. We _____ allow you a 3% quantity discount if your order exceeds 2,000 dozens.
   A. are prepared　　B. are prepared to　　C. will be prepared　D. will prepare
6. Only _____ reducing the price by 6% _____ come to business.
   A. by, we can　　B. in, we can　　C. on, can we　　D. by, can we
7. Our goods are _____ those from other suppliers in every aspect.
   A. superior to　　B. superior than　　C. more superior to　D. more superior than
8. The buyer made a bid _____ RMB ￥3,000 per ton _____ wheat.
   A. at, in　　　　　B. on, in　　　　　C. at, for　　　　　D. on, for
9. Prices of raw materials _____ steeply since we made our contract on Sep. 7.
   A. rose　　　　　B. have risen　　　C. have raise　　　D. to have risen
10. We hope that upon reconsideration you will be able to _____ our offer.
    A. receive　　　　B. make　　　　　C. accept　　　　D. decline

Exercise 2: Translate the following sentences into Chinese

1. There is not any room for our price to go down.
2. It is regrettable that we cannot entertain your counter-offer.
3. We are most anxious that you will do your utmost to reduce the price.

4. As the wholesale price of leather is rising, it is certain, we believe, that you will not be able to buy the items we mentioned at the same price during next few months.

5. If you agree to buy 200 cases more of our products, we could conclude the deal at the price of USD122 per case FOB Xingang, China Incoterms® 2020.

6. To help you sell our products, as an exception, we'll give you a special discount of 2%.

7. In order to close this deal, we shall further reduce our price by 5%.

8. In view of the goods in great demand, we would advise in your interest that you accept our offer without delay.

9. Much to our regret, as your price is out of line with the market level, it is difficult for us to accept it.

10. Our products are modestly priced.

Exercise 3: Translate the following letter into English with the right format

敬启者：

  感谢你方4月9日对我方毛织内衣的还盘。经仔细考虑，很抱歉我方不能接受。我方4月3日信中报价对我方盈利甚微，实际上低于竞争者的价格。

  生产中所用的羊毛经特殊专利法处理，以防缩水，增强耐力。我公司是本国最大的毛织内衣供应商，这一事实本身说明我方产品的价值。

  我们会高兴听到你方回复，并慎重考虑能达成交易的任何建议。

此致 德国纺织品进出口公司

中国纺织品进出口公司
徐明威 谨上
2020年5月26日

（注：德国纺织品进出口公司地址：
    Garstedter Feldstr. 24
    D 22850 Norderstedt
    Germany
 中国纺织品进出口公司地址：
    No. 456, Da Wang Rd. Chaoyang Street
    Beijing, P. R. China）

Exercise 4: Translate the following sentences orally

1. I dare say that the price we offer compares favorably with any quotations you can obtain elsewhere.

2. What we give you is a good price. We don't think it could be put any better. Take it or

leave it, it's up to you.
3. Isn't it possible to give us a little more discount?
4. If possible we'd like to ask for reduction of USD 5.50 per M/T.
5. We can accept the goods only at a reduction of 20% off the contract price.
6. If your order is large enough, we are ready to reduce our prices by 5%.
7. 请你们以美元报布鲁塞尔成本加保险费加运费价。
8. 如果你方提价 2%，交易才有可能。
9. 如果你们答应提前交货，我们可接受你方价格。
10. 价格太高，我无法推销。

Exercise 5: Compose a dialogue on the following situation

You get an offer of tin foil sheets reading:

Commodity: Tin Foil Sheets.

Price: USD120 per long ton CFR New York Incoterms® 2020.

Quantity: 60 long tons.

Payment: By irrevocable L/C payable at sight.

You ask for an 8% reduction in the price. But the sellers refuse to consider any reduction, but give you a 2% commission. Finally, you conclude the business.

Reading Material

Pricing Strategies and Price Clauses in Sales Contract

Pricing

Proper pricing is a critical element in selling a product or service internationally. Even for the experienced exporter, pricing is much problematic.

As in the domestic market, the price at which a product or service is sold directly determines a firm's revenues. It is essential that a firm's market research include an evaluation of all of the variables that may affect the price.

The traditional components for determining proper pricing are costs, market demand, and competition. These categories are the same for domestic and foreign sales and must be evaluated in view of the firm's objectives in entering the foreign market. An analysis of each component from an export perspective may result in export prices different from domestic prices.

Foreign market objectives

An important aspect of a company's pricing analysis involves determining market objectives. Is the company attempting to penetrate a new market? Looking for long-term market growth? Looking for an outlet for surplus production or outmoded products? For example, many firms view the foreign market as a secondary market and consequently have lower expectations regarding the market share and sales volume. Pricing decisions are naturally affected by this view.

Firms also may have to tailor their marketing and pricing objectives for particular foreign markets. For example, marketing objectives for selling products to a developing nation where per capita income may be one tenth of that in the United States are necessarily different from the objectives for selling products to Europe or Japan.

Costs

The computation of the actual cost of producing a product and bringing it to the market or providing a service is the core element in determining whether exporting is financially viable. Many new exporters calculate their export price by the cost-plus method alone. In the cost-plus method of calculation, the exporter starts with the domestic manufacturing cost and adds administration, research and development, overhead, freight forwarding, distributor margins, customs charges, and profit. The net effect of this pricing approach may be that the export price escalates into an uncompetitive range.

A more competitive method of pricing for market entry is what is termed as marginal cost pricing. This method considers the direct, out-of-pocket expenses of producing and selling products for export as a floor beneath which prices cannot be set without incurring a loss. For example, export products may have to be modified for the export market to accommodate different sizes, electrical systems, or labels. Changes of this nature may increase costs. On the other hand, the export product may be a stripped-down version of the domestic product and therefore costs less. Or, if additional products can be produced without increasing fixed costs, the incremental cost of producing additional products for export should be lower than the earlier average production costs for the domestic market.

In addition to production costs, overhead, and research and development, other costs should be allocated to domestic and export products in proportion to the benefit derived from those expenditures. Additional costs often associated with export sales include:

(1) Market research and credit checks;
(2) Business travel;
(3) International postage, cable, and telephone rates;
(4) Translation costs;
(5) Commissions, training charges, and other costs involving foreign representatives;
(6) Consultants and freight forwarders;
(7) Product modification and special packaging.

After the actual cost of the export product has been calculated, the exporter should formulate an approximate consumer price for the foreign market.

Market demand

As in the domestic market, demand in foreign market is a key to setting prices. What will the market fear for a specific product or service?

For most consumer goods, per capita income is a good gauge of a market's ability to pay. Per capita income for most of the industrialized nations is comparable to that of the United States. For the rest of the world, it is much lower. Some products may create such a strong demand—chic goods such as "Levis", for example—that even low per capita income will not affect their selling prices. However, in most markets with lower per capita income, simplifying the product to reduce selling price may be an answer. The firm must also keep in mind that currency valuations alter the affordability of their goods. Thus, pricing should accommodate wild fluctuations in currency and the relative strength of the dollar, if possible. The firm should also consider who the customers will be. For example, if the firm's main customers in a developing country are expatriates or the upper class, a high price may work even though the average per capita income is low.

Competition

In the domestic market, few companies are free to set prices without carefully evaluating their competitors' pricing policies. This point is also true in exporting, and it is much more complicated by the need to evaluate the competitors' price in each export market that the export intends to enter.

Where a particular foreign market is being serviced by many competitors, the exporter may have little choice but to match the going price or even go below it to establish a market share. If the exporter's product or service is new to a particular foreign market, it may actually be possible to set a higher price than it is normally charged domestically.

Pricing summary

Determine the objective in the foreign market.

Compute the actual cost of the export product.

Compute the final consumer price.

Evaluate market demand and competition.

Consider modifying the product to reduce the export price.

(资料来源：张军，等. 国际贸易英语政策、组织与实务 [M]. 北京：中国水利水电出版社, 2006.)

Price Clauses in Sales Contract

The following statements are examples for price clauses in sales contract:

1. The price shall be US$ 200 per unit FOB New York Incoterms® 2020.

2. Unit Price: At US$ 16 per dozen CIF New York Incoterms® 2020.

Total amount: US$ 160,000 (SAY US Dollar ONE HUNDRED SIXTY THOUSAND ONLY).

3. At CAD 15 per case CIPC2 Montreal Incoterms® 2020.

4. At USD 2.1 million per set FOB Hamburg Incoterms® 2020.

5. The price specified above is based on freight rates on the goods between the warehouse of the buyer and the factory of the seller. If such freight rates increase or decrease, the price specified shall be adjusted accordingly.

6. The seller shall have the right to increase the price of the goods specified in this contract at any time. If the buyer refuses to accept the price increase specified by the seller, the buyer may cancel this agreement. Unless this contract is so canceled, the increased price shall be charged for all goods shipped thereafter.

Questions

1. When we decide the price of an export product, what factors do we need to consider?
2. How many foreign market objectives does the text mention? What are they?
3. Many new exporters calculate their export price by the cost-plus method. Is it good enough? Why?
4. What does export costs of products include?
5. What is the reasonable pricing strategy in a country with lower per capita income?
6. To establish a market share in a foreign market serviced by many competitors, what pricing option should the exporter select?
7. If the exporter's product or service is new to a particular foreign market, what pricing option should he select?

Chapter 14

Shipment

14.1 Pre-knowledge

Packing is of particular importance in foreign trade because goods have to travel long distances before arriving at destination. The seller should ensure that packing effectively protect the goods from damage and sustain a long distance of transportation.

Packing can be divided into transport packing (usually known as outer packing) and sales packing (usually known as inner packing). Sales packing is designed mainly to promote sales which must be attractive to the customers' and helpful to sales.

Shipment is an important part in international business. It refers to the carriage of the goods from the seller to the buyer, and it is realized by transportation—by sea or by air, by road or by rail. With the expansion of international trade, the container service has become popular. As far as foreign trade is concerned, shipment is mostly made by sea. So this unit mainly introduces the shipment by sea.

Shipment is complicated. Negotiation about it involves time of delivery, port of loading and destination, means of transportation, shipping documents, partial shipments and transshipment, name of ship, shipping advice, etc.

14.1.1 Parties of Shipment

There are three parties involved in most movements of goods, the consignor—who sends the goods, the carrier—who carries them and the consignee—who receives them at the destination.

14.1.2 Partial Shipments and Transshipment

Generally, partial shipments and transshipment are favorable to the seller, which puts the seller in a better position to perform the relevant contract. According to the relevant stipulations of the UCP, transportation documents which appear on their faces to indicate that shipment has been made on the same means of conveyance and for the same journey, if they indicate the same destination, will not be regarded as covering partial shipments. If transshipment is necessary in case of no direct or suitable ship available for shipment, clause can be stipulated in sales contract, i.e. partial shipments and transshipment are allowed.

14.1.3 Shipping Advice

The seller should arrange to send shipping advice to the buyer immediately after the shipment finishes and he receives the signed bills of lading from the ship company. The shipping advice contains the time of shipment, the ports of loading and destination, means of transportation, partial shipment, transshipment, name of ship, date of effecting shipment and arrival, contract number, etc.

14.1.4 Shipping Documents

Shipping documents refer to Bill of Lading, Insurance Policy, Letter of Credit, and Commercial Invoice, Packing List, along with the export Bill of Exchange. Although other documents like Invoice, Certificate of Origin, and Certificates of Inspection will be sent along with the draft, they are not indispensable documents. Shipping documents only include documents of the ownership, but not all export documents. When negotiating payment of goods, the shipping documents should be given by the seller to the bank. And sometimes, when sending the shipping advice to the buyer, the copies or duplicates of these documents should be given, too.

14.1.5 B/L (Bill of Lading)

Bill of Lading (B/L) is issued by the captain or carrier to testify that the captioned goods have been received or shipped on delivery to a certain place of destination. Since it represents title to the goods, it plays a very important role in international trade.

There are several kinds of B/L:

- On board B/L (or Shipped B/L) and Received for Shipment B/L
- Clean B/L and Unclean (or Foul) B/L
- Straight B/L, Blank B/L and Order B/L
- Direct B/L, Transshipment B/L and Through B/L
- Original B/L and Copy B/L
- Advanced B/L
- Antedated B/L
- Stale B/L

14.2 Correspondence Writing Guide and Specimen Letters

The following are the typical writing steps concerning packing:

(1) Pleasant opening/ To inform the receiver that you would like to discuss about packing.

(2) To expresses the detailed requests such as packing materials and packing cost.

(3) To express the wish that the receiver can accept the package requirements and early reply.

The following are the typical writing steps for the replies concerning packing:

(1) Express appreciation for receiving letter and your main idea.

(2) Write your opinions or solutions to the package.

(3) Express the hope to confirm your proposal and pleasant ending.

The following are the typical writing steps concerning shipment:

(1) Stating that the covering letter of credit has been opened.

(2) Explain the necessity and reason for immediate shipment.

(3) Advise the impacts of delay in shipment and hope for an early shipment.

The following are the typical writing steps for the replies concerning shipment:

(1) Notify the buyer that the goods under the contract have been shipped by/via something on a certain date.

(2) Inform the buyer what documents have been sent.

(3) Hope the goods will arrive or reach in sound condition.

(4) Appreciate the concluded business and expect to receive further orders.

14.2.1 Buyer's Requirements for Packing

March 23, 2020

Dear Phoebe,

We thank you for your letter of March 22 enclosing Sales Confirmation No. SC2020-102. We find that the packing clause in it is not clear enough after going through the contract. In order to avoid future trouble, we would like to make clear in advance our packing requirements as follows:

The item under the contract should be packed in international standard color boxes, 6 color boxes to a corrugated brown carton. On the outer packing please mark our initials BI in a triangle, under which the port of destination and sales confirmation No. SC2020-102 should be stenciled. In addition, marks like FRAGILE, HANDLE WITH CARE, MADE IN CHINA, should also be indicated.

We hope that the above requirements could be met and paid special attention.

Best regards,
Andy Estes

14.2.2 A Reply to the above Packing Requirements

March 24, 2020

Dear Andy,

We have received your letter of March 23 concerning the details of packing and shipping marks. We will make sure to meet all the requirements. Packing of 2,400PCS A001 and A003 each under S/C No. SC2020-102 will be packed as you required.

We will stencil the shipping mark on the outer packing as follows:

 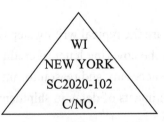

Please let us know whether you are satisfied with the above design of shipping marks. Shipment could be made within 30 days after the receipt of your L/C.

Best regards,
Phoebe He
Sales Manager

14.2.3 Urging Shipment

April 25, 2020

Dear Sirs,

<u>Re: S/C No. SC2020-102</u>

We should like to draw your attention to the captioned Sales Confirmation No. SC2020-102 covering 2,400PCS A001 and A003 each for which we sent to you on April 5 an irrevocable L/C expiration date May 30. Up to the present moment no news has come from you about the shipment.

As the season is rapidly approaching, our buyers are in urgent need of the goods. We shall much appreciate it if you effect shipment as soon as possible, thus enabling the goods to arrive here in time to catch the brisk demand at the start of the season.

We trust you will see to it that the order is shipped within the stipulate time, as any delay would cause us no little inconvenience and financial loss.

Your close cooperation will be highly appreciated.

Yours faithfully,
Andy Estes

14.2.4 Requesting Partial Shipments

April 26, 2020

Dear Sir or Madam,

We feel regretful to inform you that our factory has suffered a flood. It is impossible for us to ship 2,400PCS A001 and A003 each ordered by one lot by the end of May, 2020.

We request you to allow us partial shipment, that is 2,000PCS A001 and A003 each within the contracted time and the remaining 400PCS each in June, 2020. We will request you to extend the validity of your L/C to June 30, 2020. Though this is a case of Force Majeure, we are make every effort to recover our production.

We will appreciate it if you would kindly understand the situation and accept our request. Look forward to your early reply.

Sincerely yours,
Phoebe He
Sales Manager

14.2.5　Suggesting Transshipment

Dear Sirs,

　　We have received the L/C No. 6688 you established through Citibank, New York on April 5, covering Contract No. SC2020-102. We find that the port of destination should be New York and transshipment is not allowed.

　　However, we are advised by the shipping company that because direct vessels sailing for New York are few and the shipping space has been fully booked up to the end of May. Under this circumstance, we regret being unable to meet your requirement. We suggest you to make transshipment via Los Angeles. In this case, you must bear the additional transshipment charges.

　　In order to make sure that the goods will be duly delivered, which is to our mutual benefit, we request that you amend the L/C to allow transshipment.

　　Please take the above into consideration and let us know your decision as soon as possible.

Yours sincerely,

14.2.6　Shipping Instruction

Dear Sirs,

Re: Your Sales Confirmation No. SC2020-102

　　Thank you for informing us that the items under SC2020-102 are now ready for shipment. Since the purchase is made on an FOB basis, you are to load the goods at Shenzhen on the ship appointed by us.

　　Please arrange to send the consignment to Shenzhen for shipment by S.S. Victory due to sail for New York on May 15 from May 10 to 14 inclusive. All cartons should be clearly marked and numbered as shown in our official order. For further instructions, please contact our forwarding agent, ABC Co., Ltd., New York.

　　We await your shipping advice. Invoices, Packing List and other necessary documents should be sent to us at the same time.

Yours truly,

14.2.7 Shipping Advice

Dear Sirs,

Re: Your L/C No.6688 covering Sales Confirmation No. SC2020-102

We are glad to inform you that the above captioned goods have been shipped on May10 per S.S. "Victory" scheduled to arrive at your port on June 20.

To facilitate your taking delivery of the goods when they duly arrive at your port, we are sending you under cover one set of the following shipping documents, which comprise:

- Commercial Invoice No. BI123 in duplicate
- Packing List No. 234 in triplicate
- Non-negotiable Bill of Lading No. YGMG20234567
- Certificate of Origin No. 20200510
- Survey Report No. 678
- Insurance Policy No. 457

We trust the above shipment will reach you in sound condition and expect to receive your further orders before long. All your future correspondence will get our careful attention.

Yours sincerely,

Notes

[1] types of packing:
　　transportation packing/outer packing 外包装
　　packing for sales/inner packing 内包装
　　neutral packing 中性包装

[2] packing marks:
　　shipping mark 运输标志，也称为"唛头"
　　identification mark 识别标志
　　indicative mark 指示性标志
　　warning mark 警示性标志

[3] indicative marks 常见的指示性标志有：
　　handle with care 小心轻放
　　this side up 此端向上

keep dry / keep away from moisture 保持干燥 / 远离湿气
keep away from heat 远离热源
use no hooks 请勿用钩
fragile 当心破碎

[4] different types of packing：
polyethylene bag 聚乙烯塑料袋，kraft paper bag 牛皮纸袋
carton 纸箱，corrugated carton 瓦楞纸箱
corrugated brown carton 棕色瓦楞纸箱，俗称"黄盒"
wooden case 木箱，crate 板条箱
fiber board case 纤维板箱，veneer case/plywood case 胶合板箱
bag 袋，gunny bag 麻袋，sack 布袋，bale 捆包
tin 听，can 罐，bottle 瓶
iron drum 铁桶，barrel 鼓形桶

[5] 常见的包装表达法有：
（1）in…用某物包装，用某种形式装货，例如：
in wooden cases 木箱包装
in cartons 纸箱包装
in poly bag 塑料袋包装
（2）in…of…each 或 in…, each containing…用某物包装，每件装多少，例如：
in cartons of 20 dozen each/in cartons, each containing 20 dozen 用纸板箱装，每箱装 20 打
（3）in…of…each, …to…用某物包装，每件装多少，若干装于一大件中，例如：
用盒装，每打装一盒，100 盒装一木箱 in boxes of a dozen each, 100 boxes to a wooden case

[6] expiration date 过期日期
[7] effect shipment 装运
[8] stipulated time 规定的时间
[9] be highly appreciated 非常感谢
[10] force majeure 不可抗力
[11] recover our production 恢复生产
[12] Citibank 花旗银行
[13] transshipment 转运
[14] instruction 这里指 shipping instruction，装运指示
[15] lot *n.* 批，组，群。例：
We propose to have the goods in two equal lots. And please inform us whether you agree or not.
我方建议货物分两批均装，请告知同意与否。

[16] shipping company 船公司，航运公司
[17] vessel *n.* 船，船舶
[18] liner *n.* 班轮
[19] tramp *n.* 不定期船
[20] shipping space 舱位。预订舱位用动词 book、reserve
[21] via 经由
[22] S.S. =steamship 轮船，也可写作"S/S"或"s.s."
　　 M.V. motor vessel 机动船
[23] duplicate 副本。in duplicate：一式两份，in triplicate：一式三份
[24] take delivery of 接收
[25] commercial invoice 商业发票，样本如注释［31］中的图 14-1 所示。
[26] Packing List 装箱单。主要用于说明货物的包装情况，如品名、数量、包装方式、毛重、体积，视产品类别的需要还可以加上其他详细说明，如净重等。装箱单样式与发票相仿，只是不需要注明货物价值。样本见注释［31］中的图 14-2。
[27] non-negotiable 不可转让的，非流通的
[28] Bill of Lading 简称"B/L"，提单，船公司或船代签发的货物收据，样本如注释［31］中的图 14-3 所示。
[29] Certificate of Origin 原产地证，一般原产地证和普惠制原产地证样本如注释［31］中的图 14-4 和图 14-5 所示。
　　 新版原产地证书（22 种）如表 14-1 所示，新版金伯利进程国际证书（1 种）如表 14-2 所示。

表 14-1　新版原产地证书　　　　表 14-2　新版金伯利进程国际证书

[30] Survey Report 检验报告，如品质证书（Certificate of Quality）和数量证书（Certificate of Quantity）
[31] 相关单据样本如下所示：
　　 图 14-1：商业发票样本
　　 图 14-2：装箱单样本
　　 图 14-3：海运提单样本
　　 图 14-4：一般原产地证样本
　　 图 14-5：普惠制原产地证 FORM A 样本
　　 图 14-6：品质检验证书样本
　　 图 14-7：健康证书样本
　　 图 14-8：植物检疫证书样本
[32] Insurance Policy 保险单（见图 15-2）

Issuer: DONGGUAN LIGHTING IMPORT & EXPORT CORPORATION NO.15 XINJI AVE., SOUTH AREA, DONGGUAN, GUANGDONG, CHINA	商业发票 **COMMERCIAL INVOICE**	
To: WALDEMAR INDUSTRIES INC. 1234S. MICHIGAN AVE., CHICAGO, IL60616, U.S.A.	No.: BI123	Date MAY 10, 2020
Shipment details: SEA FREIGHT FROM SHENZHEN, CHINA TO NEW YORK, USA	S/C No.: SC2020-102	L/C NO. 6688
	Country of origin: CHINA	

Marks & Nos.	Description of goods POLYRESIN TABLE LAMPS	Quantity	Unit Price	Amount FOB SHENZHEN, CHINA
WI NEW YORK SC2020-102 C/NO.1-800	ITEM NO. A001 A003	2,400PCS 2,400PCS	USD8.00 USD10.00	USD19,200.00 USD24,000.00
		4,800PCS		USD43,200.00

SAY TOTAL: SAY U.S. DOLLARS FORTY-THREE THOUSAND TWO HUNDRED ONLY.

GOODS ARE TOTAL PACKED IN 800CARTONS.
TOTAL NET WEIGHT: 8,400.00KGS
TOTAL GROSS WEIGHT: 9,600.00 KGS

AS PER S/C NO. SC2020-102 DATED MARCH 22, 2020.

东莞灯饰进出口公司（章）
Dongguan Lighting Import & Export Corporation

何菲（章）

图 14-1 商业发票样本

Dongguan Lighting Import & Export Corporation

No.15 Xinji Ave., South Area, Dongguan, Guangdong, China
Tel: +86-769-83456789   Fax: +86-769-83456788

PACKING LIST

To:	Invoice No.:	123
WALDEMAR INDUSTRIES INC.	Invoice Date:	May10, 2020
1234S. MICHIGAN AVE., CHICAGO, L60616	S/C No.:	SC2020-102
TEL: +1-312-427-5678		
FAX: +1-312-427-5679	L/C No.:	6688

Transport details   Date of Shipment: May10th, 2020

From: (3) SHENZHEN, CHINA   To: NEW YORK   BY VESSEL

Marks & Nos	C/No., Package	Quantity Description of goods	G. Weight	N. Weight	Measurement
WI NEW YORK SC2020-102 C/NO. 1-800	1-400 400Ctns	13" polyresin table lamp ITEM NO. A001 1pk/color box, 6box/ctn	@12Kgs 4,800.00	@10Kgs 4,000.00	@(60*50*40CM) 48CBM
	401-800 400Ctns	16" polyresin table lamp ITEM NO. A003 1pk/color box, 6box/ctn	@12Kgs 4,800.00	@11Kgs 4,400.00	@(60*55*50CM) 66CBM
TOTAL	800CTNS	4,800PCS	9,600.00KGS	8,400.00KGS	114CBM

SAY TOTAL: SAY EIGHT HUNDRED CARTONS ONLY.

WE HEREBY STATE THAT THE EACH CARTON HAS BEEN MARKED THE LABEL "MADE IN CHINA" AS REQUESTED.

东莞灯饰进出口公司（章）
Dongguan Lighting Import & Export Corporation

何菲（章）

图 14-2 装箱单样本

Shipper③ DONGGUAN LIGHTING IMPORT & EXPORT CORPORATION NO.15 XINJI AVE., SOUTH AREA, DONGGUAN, GUANGDONG, CHINA		B/L NO. YGMG 20234567① ***ORIGINAL*** 中国对外贸易运输总公司② CHINA NATIONAL FOREIGN TRADE TRANSPORT CORPORATION **OCEAN BILL OF LADING**
Consignee or order④ TO ORDER OF THE SHIPPER		SHIPPED on board in apparent good order and condition (unless otherwise indicated) the goods or packages specified herein and to be discharged or the mentioned port of discharge of as near there as the vessel may safely get and be always afloat. THE WEIGHT, measure, marks and numbers quality, contents and value, being particulars furnished by the Shipper, are not checked by the Carrier on loading. THE SHIPPER, Consignee and the Holder of this Bill of Lading hereby expressly accept and agree to all printed, written or stamped provisions, exceptions and conditions of this Bill of Loading, including those on the back hereof. IN WITNESS where of the number of original Bill of Loading stated below have been signed, one of which being accomplished, the other(s) to be void.
Notify address⑤ WALDEMAR INDUSTRIES INC. 1234S. MICHIGAN AVE., CHICAGO, IL60616, U.S.A.		
Pre-carriage by⑥	Port of loading⑦ SHENZHEN	
Vessel⑧ VICTORY V.501	Port of transshipment⑨ LOS ANGELES	
Port of discharge⑩ NEW YORK	Final destination⑪ NEW YORK	

Container Seal No. or marks and Nos.⑫	Number and kind of packages⑬	Designation of goods⑭	Gross weight (kgs)⑮	Measurement (m³)⑯
WI NEW YORK SC2020-102 C/NO.1-800 2×40'HQ*FCL, CFS/CFS CN.:12345678910	800CARTONS	POLYRESIN TABLE LAMPS	9600.00KGS	114.00CBM

TOTAL NUMBER OF CONTAINERS OR PACKAGES (IN WORDS)⑰ SAY EIGHT HUNDRED (800) CARTONS ONLY.			Freight and charge⑱ FREIGHT TO COLLECT
Ex. rate	Prepaid at	Fright payable at DESTINATION	Place and date of issue⑲ SHENZHEN MAY 10, 2020
	Total Prepaid	Number of original B/L⑳ THREE	Signed by **AN-ASIA SHIPPING CO., LTD. SHENZHEN BRANCH** On Behalf of the Carrier: **CHINA NATIONAL FOREIGN TRADE TRANSPORT CORPORATION** 王五(章)

图 14-3 海运提单样本

1. Exporter DONGGUAN LIGHTING IMPORT & EXPORT CORPORATION NO.15 XINJI AVE., SOUTH AREA, DONGGUAN, GUANGDONG, CHINA	Certificate No. 20200510 **CERTIFICATE OF ORIGIN** **OF** **THE PEOPLE'S REPUBLIC OF CHINA**
2. Consignee WALDEMAR INDUSTRIES INC. 1234S. MICHIGAN AVE., CHICAGO, IL60616, U.S.A.	
3. Means of transport and route SEA FREIGHT FROM SHENZHEN, CHINA TO NEW YORK, USA	5. For certifying authority use only
4. Country / region of destination NEW YORK, U.S.A.	

6. Marks and numbers	7. Number and kind of packages; description of goods	8. H.S. Code	9. Quantity	10. Number and date of invoice
WI NEW YORK SC2020-102 C/NO.1-800	EIGHT HUNDRED (800) CARTONS OF POLYRESIN TABLE LAMPS *** *** *** *** *** *** *** *** ******	9405200090	4,800PCS	BI123 May 10, 2020

11. Declaration by the exporter The undersigned hereby declares that the above details and statements are correct, that all the goods were produced in China and that they comply with the Rules of Origin of the People's Republic of China. SHENZHEN, CHINA, MAY 10, 2020 何蕊（手签） 东莞灯饰进出口公司（章） Dongguan Lighting Import & Export Corporation Place and date, signature and stamp of authorized signatory	12. Certification It is hereby certified that the declaration by the exporter is correct. 中华人民共和国 深圳 ORIGIN 海关（章） SHENZHEN, CHINA, MAY 10, 2020 李四（手签） Place and date, signature and stamp of certifying authority

图 14-4　一般原产地证样本

1. Goods consigned from (Exporter's business name address country) BEIJING LIGHT INDUSTRIAL PRODUCTS IMP. AND EXP. CORP. NO.123 GUANGHUA ROAD, BEIJING CHINA		Reference No. TZG113333410890093 **GENERALIZED SYSTEM OF PREFERENCES**		
2. Goods consigned to (Consignee's name, address, country) IWATANI CANDLE CO., LTD. 1320-5 NISHIACHI-CHO KURASHIKI CITY, OKAYAMA, JAPAN		**CERTIFICATE OF ORIGIN** (Combined declaration and certificate) **FORM A** issued in **THE PEOPLE'S REPUBLIC OF CHINA** (country)		
3. Means of transport and route SEA FREIGHT FROM XINGANG, TIANJIN TO YOKOHAMA		4. For official use		
5. item number	6. Marks & Nos of packages	7. Number of kind of packages; Description of goods	8. Origin criterion	9. Gross weight & other Quantity	10. Number and date of Invoice
1	IWATANI ZLP11E0318 YOKOHAMA NO. 1-40	FORTY (40) CARTONS OF CANDLE HOLDERS *** *** ****** ****** ****** ****** ***	"P"	G.W.500KGS 2400PCS	SEP250415 15 APR., 2020
11. Certification It is hereby certified, on the basis of control carried out, that the declaration by the exporter is correct. [BEIJING CUSTOMS ORIGIN seal] 李四 (手签) BEIJING 15 APR., 2020 Place and date, signature and stamp of certifying authority		12. Declaration by the exporter The undersigned hereby declares that the above details and statements are correct; that all goods were produced in CHINA (Country) and that they comply with the origin requirements specified for those goods in the Generalized System of Preferences for goods exported to <u>JAPAN</u> (importing country)		
		北京轻工业品进出口公司（章） **BEIJING LIGHT IND. PRODUCTS I/E CORP.**	张三 (手签)	
		BEIJING 15 APR., 2020 Place and date, signature of authorized signatory		

图 14-5　普惠制原产地证 FORM A 样本

(Adapted from www.pocib.com)

ENTRY-EXIT INSPECTION AND QUARANTINE

正本 ORIGINAL

编号No.: 1010000002

QUALITY INSPECTION CERTIFICATE

发货人 Consignor	Russia Yisi Import and Export Trade Company
收货人 Consignee	South Africa Xinyuan Import and Export Trading Company

品名 Description of Goods	CANNED TOMATO PASTE	标记及号码 Mark & No.	XINYUANCO 0001 Capetown 1/1,000
报检数量/重量 Quantity/Weight Declared	-1,000-箱S/-13,200-KGS(N.W.)		
包装种类及数量 Number and Type of Packages	-1,000-/纸箱S		
运输工具 Means of Conveyance	COSCO NAPOL		

检验结果：
RESULTS OF INSPECTION:

IN ACCORDANCE WITH THE RELEVANT STANDARD, THE REPRESENTATIVE SAMPLE WERE DRAWN AT RONDOM AND INSPECTED WITH RESULTS AS FOLLOWS:
　　　OF NORMAL QUALITY
THE QUALITY OF THE GOODS IS IN CONFORMITY WITH THE RELEVANT REQUIREMENTS.

印章 Official Stamp

签证地点 Place of Issue　St.Petersburg, Russia　　签证日期 Date of Issue Jul.24, 2018

授权签字人 Authorized Officer　GUODAYE　　签　名 Signature 郭达业

我们已尽所知和最大能力实施上述检验，不能因为我们签发本证书而免除卖方和其他方面根据合同和法律所承担的产品质量和其他责任。All inspections are carried out conscientiously to the best of our knowledge and ability. This certificate does not in any respect absolve the seller and other related parties from his contractual and legal obligations especially when product quality is concerned.

图 14-6　品质检验证书样本

ENTRY-EXIT INSPECTION AND QUARANTINE

正本 ORIGINAL

编号No.: 1020000002

健 康 证 书
HEALTH CERTIFICATE

发货人名称及地址 Name and Address of Consignor	Russia Yisi Import and Export Trade Company
收货人名称及地址 Name and Address of Consignee	South Africa Xinyuan Import and Export Trading Company
品名 Description of Goods	CANNED TOMATO PASTE
加工种类或状态 State or Type of Processing	
报检数量/重量 Quantity/Weight Declared	-1,000-箱S/-13,200-KGS(N.W.)
包装种类及数量 Number and Type of Packages	-1,000-/纸箱
贮藏和运输温度 Temperature during Storage and Transport	
加工厂名称、地址及编号(如果适用) Name, Address and approval No. of the approved Establishment (if applicable)	

标记及号码 Mark & No.:
XINYUANCO
0001
Capetown
1/1,000

启运地 Place of Despatch	St.Petersburg PORT, Russia
到达国家及地点 Country and Place of Destination	Capetown PORT, South Africa
运输工具 Means of Conveyance	COSCO NAPOL
发货日期 Date of Despatch	Jul.25, 2018

检验结果:
RESULTS OF INSPECTION:

WE HEREBY STATE THAT THE PRODUCTS ARE FIT FOR HUMAN CONSUMPTION AND HAVE NOT BEEN TREATED WITH CHEMICAL PRESERVATIVES OR OTHER FOREIGN SUBSTANCE INJURIOUS TO HEALTH.

THE PRODUCTS HAVE BEEN PREPARED, PROCESSED AND PACKED IN A SANITARY MANNER UNDER INSPECTOR'S SUPERVISION AND THE PRODUCTS ARE IN GOOD CONDITION.

I AM FAMILIAR WITH THE PROCESS OF MANUFACTURE AND HAVE NO REASON TO DOUBT THE MANUFACTURER'S DECLARATION.

印章 Official Stamp

签证地点 Place of Issue: St.Petersburg, Russia
签证日期 Date of Issue: Jul.24, 2018
授权签字人 Authorized Officer: GUODAYE
签名 Signature: 郭达业

我们已尽所知和最大能力实施上述检验,不能因为我们签发本证书而免除卖方或其他方面根据合同和法律所承担的产品质量和其他责任。All inspections are carried out conscientiously to the best of our knowledge and ability. This certificate does not in any respect absolve the seller and other related parties from his contractual and legal obligations especially when product quality is concerned.

图 14-7 健康证书样本

(Adapted from www.pocib.com)

ENTRY-EXIT INSPECTION AND QUARANTINE

正 本
ORIGINAL

编号No.: 1040000002

植 物 检 疫 证 书
PHYTOSANITARY CERTIFICATE

发货人名称及地址 Name and Address of Consignor	Russia Yisi Import and Export Trade Company
收货人名称及地址 Name and Address of Consignee	Russia Yisi Import and Export Trade Company

品名 Description of Goods	CANNED TOMATO PASTE	植物学名 Botanical Name of Plants	
报检数量 Quantity Declared	-1,000-箱S/-13,200-KGS(N.W.)	标记及号码 Mark & No.	XINYUANCO 0001 Capetown 1/1,000
包装种类及数量 Number and Type of Packages	-1,000-/纸箱S		
产地 Place of Origin	Russia		
到达口岸 Port of Destination	Capetown		
运输工具 Means of Conveyance	COSCO NAPOL	检验日期 Date of Inspection	Jul.24,2018

兹证明上述植物、植物产品或其他检疫物已经按照规定程序进行检查和/或检验，被认为不带有输入国或地区规定的检疫性有害生物，并且基本不带有其他的有害生物，因而符合输入国或地区现行的植物检疫要求。

This is to certify that the plants, plant products or other regulated articles described above have been inspected and/or tested according to appropriate procedures and are considered to be free from quarantine pests specified by the importing country/region, and practically free from other injurious pests; and that they are considered to conform with the current phytosanitary requirements of the importing country/region.

杀虫和/或灭菌处理 DISINFESTATION AND/OR DESINFECTION TREATMENT

日期 Date	********	药剂及浓度 Chemical and Concentration	********
处理方法 Treatment	********	持续时间及温度 Duration and Temperature	********

附加声明 ADDITIONAL DECLARATION

印章 Official Stamp	签证地点 Place of Issue St.Petersburg, Russia	签证日期 Date of Issue	Jul.24, 2018
	授权签字人 Authorized Officer GUODAYE	签 名 Signature	郭达业

我们已尽所知和最大能力实施上述检验，不能因为我们签发本证书而免除卖方或其他方面根据合同和法律所承担的产品质量和其他责任。All inspections are carried out conscientiously to the best of our knowledge and ability. This certificate does not in any respect absolve the seller and other related parties from his contractual and legal obligations especially when product quality is concerned.

图 14-8　植物检疫证书样本

(Adapted from:www.pocib.com)

14.3 Dialogues

14.3.1 Is It Possible to Effect Shipment during September

(*Mr. Allen is afraid to miss the selling season. He is urging his supplier, Ms. Lin to advance shipment.*)

Allen: Now we have settled the terms of payment. Let's talk about the shipment. Is it possible to effect shipment during September?

Lin: I don't think we can.

Allen: Then when is the earliest we can expect shipment?

Lin: By the middle of October, I think.

Allen: That's too late. You see, November is the season for this commodity in our market, and our Customs formalities are rather complicated.

Lin: I understand.

Allen: Besides, the flow through the marketing channels takes at least ten days. Thus, after shipment it will be four to five weeks altogether before the goods can reach our retailers. Therefore, the goods must be shipped before October; otherwise we won't be in time for the selling season.

Lin: But our factories are fully committed at the moment.

Allen: Mr. Brown, a timely delivery means a lot to us. If we miss the season, it'll cause no profit.

Lin: I see your point. However, we have done more business this year than any of the previous years. I am very sorry to say that we cannot advance the time of delivery.

Allen: That's too bad, but I sincerely hope you will give our request your special consideration.

Lin: You may take it from me that the last thing we want to do is to disappoint an old customer like you. But the fact remains that our manufacturers have a heavy backlog on their hands.

Allen: Can't you find some way to get round your producers for an earlier delivery? Make a special effort, please.

Lin: All right. We'll get in touch with our producers and see what they have to say.

14.3.2 It Will Be Better to Take the Goods to Tianjin First, and then Ship It to London by Freighter

(*Mr. Li from China National Light Industrial Products Imp. & Exp. Corp. is discussing about the port of shipment with his customer, an English businessmen, Mr.*

Palmer.)

Li: Hello, I'd like to speak to Mr. Palmer.

Palmer: Hello, this is he. Who's speaking?

Li: I'm Li Liang of China National Light Industrial Products Imp. & Exp. Corp.. I've got something to talk to you.

Palmer: What is it about? Is there something wrong?

Li: Nothing serious. It's about the port of shipment. In my opinion, it will be better to take the goods to Tianjin first, and then ship it to London from Tianjin by freighter.

Palmer: Is there enough time? In addition, there will be risk of losing goods, and more importantly the procedure is too tedious.

Li: At present, freight transportation of exporting to European ports has been greatly improved. We have transported before, and we have not had any trouble. Besides, there are more ships sailing to London every month. If shipment were effected from Tianjin, you could receive the goods earlier. Please do not worry. We will take care of the procedure.

Palmer: How much will the extra freight charge be?

Li: It does not need any additional charges.

Palmer: Really, if so, we will proceed as what you mentioned.

Li: OK, after loading, we will inform you of the name of the vessel, date of departure and the number of the bill of lading.

Palmer: Fine.

Notes

[1] selling season 销售季节
[2] Customs formalities 海关手续
[3] marketing channel 销售渠道
[4] timely *adj.* 及时的
[5] backlog 积压而未交付的订货。例：
   We have a large backlog.
   我们积压的订货很多。
[6] get round 说服
[7] freighter *n.* 货船；ship by freighter 用货船装运
[8] tedious *adj.* 烦琐的
[9] extra freight charge 额外运费。这里的 freight 是 "运输、货运" 的意思。freight 除了这个意思，还有 "运费" 的意思，如 cost, freight and insurance：成本、运费加保险费

[10] load v. 装货，把货物装上船；to load cargo into a ship：装货上船：port of loading，装运港

Exercises

Exercise 1: Choose the best answer to complete the following sentences

1. Sometimes transshipment and partial shipment are _____.
   A. permission   B. permitting   C. permitted   D. permit
2. We are _____ of the goods we ordered with you, but so far we have not received any news from you about their dispatch.
   A. urgent in need   B. bad in need   C. in badly need   D. in urgent need
3. Any _____ shipment will put us in great trouble.
   A. delay with   B. delay to   C. delay on   D. delay in
4. We must insist on immediate delivery, _____ we shall cancel the order in accordance with the contract stipulations.
   A. otherwise   B. however   C. likewise   D. but
5. _____ any changes in the date of delivery, please let us know in advance.
   A. There should be   B. Should there be   C. There would be   D. Would there be
6. For the goods under S/C No.325, we have _____ space on S.S. Shanghai due to arrive in London around May 1.
   A. booked   B. hired   C. retained   D. bought
7. Shipment will be _____ in January.
   A. started   B. done   C. effected   D. left
8. Goods will be shipped within two months on _____ of your order.
   A. receiving   B. receipt   C. being received   D. received
9. The letter of credit stipulates that the bill of lading _____ be made out to order.
   A. should   B. would   C. could   D. had to
10. The date of sailing is March 5. We enclose herewith one set of shipping documents covering this consignment _____:
    A. as follow   B. as following   C. as follows   D. as followed

Exercise 2: Translate the following sentences into Chinese

1. Generally, shipment can be effected within 30 days after receipt of your L/C.
2. We will try our best to advance shipment, but we cannot commit ourselves.
3. The shipment time is February or March at our option and the goods will be shipped in one lot.

4. Owing to heavy commitments, we cannot advance shipment of your order.
5. We find it impossible to ask our end-users to accept the delayed delivery.
6. Shipment is to be made during April to June in three equal lots.
7. We would inform you that the above goods were already shipped out on May 18.
8. We take pleasure in notifying you that the goods under S/C No. 456 have been dispatched per M/V "Yunnan" sailing on May 15, 2020 for Hong Kong.
9. We hope the goods would arrive in time for the new year rush.
10. In case you fail to effect delivery within the stipulated time, we should have to lodge a claim against you for the loss and reserve the right to cancel the contract.

Exercise 3: Translate the following sentences into English

1. 按合约规定，上述货物将分三批装运。
2. 见信后请即刻传真确切装运日期。
3. 因我方用户急需此批货物，请你方保证早日交货。
4. 请装运下列货物，交货期不晚于5月31日。
5. 我们迫不得已要求你方同意转船运输。

Exercise 4: Complete the following letter with proper words

> enclosed   copy   advise   partial shipment   remaining   appreciate   glad

Dear Sirs,

We are _____ to inform you that we have shipped, in _____ of your Order No. 5216, 10 sets of safety pin machines（安全别针机）per S.S. "Qinggong" which sailed yesterday. please find a full set of _____ shipping documents.

Regarding the _____ 20 sets, we will try to hurry shipment and will _____ you as soon as it is effected.

We _____ the business you have been able to secure for us and assure you that all your further inquiries and orders will continue to receive our most careful attention.

Yours faithfully,

Exercise 5: Compose a dialogue on the following situation

You and your customer are discussing about the date of shipment. You think the shipment may be effected in April, but the buyer wants you to advance shipment as he is in urgent need.

Finally, you agree that shipment will be effected in two lots, and the first lot will be shipped in March, and the second in April.

Reading Material

Part One: 10 Largest Container Shipping Companies in the World[2019]

Ulrica Carlson & Jörgen Fredrikson

1. Evergreen Marine Corporation.
2. NYK.
3. Maersk.
4. Hapag-Lloyd.
5. MSC.
6. APL.
7. CSCL.
8. COSCO.
9. Hanjin.
10. CMA CGM.

It won't be a stretch to say that the container ships form the backbone of world commerce. These ships enable the movement of a vast amount of goods to be through the ocean at a quickly and cheaply.

Container ships are cargo ships that move their load in truck-size standardized containers of freight. They revolutionized the way goods are transported across the globe.

Largest Container Shipping Companies in the World

Following are some of the largest container shipping companies in the world.

1. Evergreen Marine Corporation

Evergreen Marine Corporation is a container shipping and transportation company from Taiwan. It has its headquarters in Luzhu District, Taoyuan City, China Taiwan. Evergreen corporation mostly operates between the trading routes from the Far East to North America, Central America as well as the Caribbean. It also operates from the far East to northern Europe and the Mediterranean. Other routes include Europe to the eastern coast of America, the Far East to Australia, Mauritius, South Africa, Asia, and South America. Evergreen Marine Corporation has more than 150 ships in its fleet. Over the world, it operates on 240 ports spread over 80 countries. It is the fifth largest company of its type. Founded in 1968, the company presently employees more than 3000 people. The ships from this company are usually painted green with the word evergreen written in block capitals in white. The company belongs to the evergreen group of shipping transportation and other acquainted industries in Taiwan. The current chairman of the corporation is Chang, Cheng-Yung. In 2018, it had a revenue of 4.26 billion dollars. Some of its divisions include Uniglory Marine Corp., Evergreen UK Ltd. and Italia Marittima S.p.A.

2. NYK

It is a Japanese shipping company. It stands for Nippon Yusen Kabushiki Kaisha. NYK is considered one of the largest and oldest shipping company in the world. It was founded on September 29, 1885. At the moment, it is 135 years old. Its headquarters are in Tokyo, Japan. The company has more than 800 ships. These ships include container ships, tankers, woodchip carriers, bulk carriers, reefer vessels, LNG carriers as well as cruise ships. Yasumi Kudo is the chairman of the company with Tadaaki Naito as its president. The company employs more than 33,000 people. It has a net income of about 400 million dollars. Most of the ships in the company are named after flowers, stars, constellations, old Japanese provinces etc. In the first half of the 20th century, most of the merchant ships in Japan belonged to the Nippon Yusen Kabushiki Kaisha. Their ocean routes included those to Vancouver in Canada, Seattle, Hawaii and San Francisco in the United States of America, India and the Indian Ocean, Europe, Australia, and New Zealand. Locally, there are 78 home seaports out of which 38 seaports are open to foreign trade. The most important of these are Yokohama, Kobe, and Osaka.

3. Maersk

Maersk is a business industry which is involved in activities like transport, logistics, and several energy sectors. It is from Denmark. Its full name is A. P. Moller-Maersk Group. The company has its headquarters in Copenhagen, Denmark. The company is one of the largest shipping companies in the whole world and also quite often considered as the largest operator of container ships and supply vessels. It employs more than 88,000 people and has nearly a thousand subsidiaries spread across 130 countries. Some of the key people in the company are Søren Skou who is the CEO of the group and Claus V. Hemmingsen who is the Vice CEO. This company is 116 years old. It was founded in 1904 by Peter Mærsk Møller and his son Arnold Peder Møller. In 2016, the company split into two separate divisions namely transport and logistics & energy. It is thought to have as many as 786 vessels that it operates. In 2017, the company had a revenue of 35 billion dollars. The logo of the company is a square with a blue background with a seven-pointed white star on it. It was given by P. M. Møller who was a very religious Christian.

4. Hapag-Lloyd

Hapag-Lloyd AG is an international transportation company based in Germany. It was formed in 1970 by the merging of two companies namely Hamburg America Line (HAPAG) and Norddeutscher Lloyd (NDL) or North German Lloyd (NGL). Hamburg America Line (HAPAG) was founded in 1847 while Norddeutscher Lloyd (NDL) was formed in 1856. The headquarters of the company are in Hamburg, Germany. Some of the key people in the company are Rolf Habben Jansen who is the CEO, Nicolás Burr that is the CFO, Anthony James Firmin, the COO etc. The company employs more than 13,000 people. It also has more than 130 ships which cater to over 5 million containers all over the world. Hapag-Lloyd AG is one of the most renowned shipping and transportation companies in the whole world. In terms of capacity, it ranks number 5 in the world. It operates on trade routes across South America, Transatlantic, the Middle East, trans-pacific trades etc. Some of the other services that the company provides are international cruises and private jet services to the customers. Some of the current, as well as former cruise ships of the company, are MS Europa, MS Europa 2, MS Bremen, MS Columbus etc.

5. MSC

The Mediterranean Shipping Company which is of an abbreviated as the MSC is one of the largest container shipping companies in the whole world. It is a Swiss company which has its headquarters in Geneva, Switzerland. MSC has about 471 container vessels which makes it the second largest shipping company in terms of the number of container vessels. It operates more than 480 offices spread across more than 150 countries over the world. MSC also employees more than 24,000 people. It operates on more than 200 different trade routes with over 315 ports. The company operates in almost all of the major parts of the world. The most important port of the company is Antwerp in Belgium. MSC launched the world's largest container ship called the MSC Oscar in January 2015. It has a capacity of 19,224 twenty-foot equivalent units or TEU. A TEU is a unit used to measure the capacity of any container ship. The whole company has a capacity of more than 2,435,000 twenty-foot equivalent units. Some of the most important ships of the company are MSC Oscar, MSC Beatrice, MSC Bruxelles, MSC Camille, MSC Geneva, MSC Sabrina, MSC Chicago, MSC Leigh, MSC Zoe etc.

6. APL

The American President Lines or the APL is a transportation and shipping company. The company along with its parent company called the CMA CGM is the world's third largest container shipping company. This company is more than 170 years old. It has its headquarters in Singapore and Rockville, Maryland in the United States of America. The company was originally a subsidiary of another company known as the Neptune Orient Lines or NOL. The NOL is an international transportation and logistics company which is based in France. Founded in 1848, APL's current chief executive officer of the company is Nicolas Sartini. The company employees more than 5,000 people and also has a revenue of over 4.6 billion dollars. The company mainly operates in North America and Asia. It provides more than 80 weekly services the main of which is container shipping. APL also has a container ship fleet which has more than 153 container vessels. It operates at 10 different strategic points around the world. These include Dutch harbor in Alaska, the United States, Kobe and Yokohama in Japan, Ho Chi Minh City in Vietnam, Laem Chabang in Thailand, Qingdao in China Mainland, Nhava Sheva in India and Kaohsiung in China Taiwan.

7. CSCL

China Shipping Container Lines Co., Ltd was the Chinese Marine shipping company based in Shanghai. It was founded in 1997. CSCL does not work independently today but is a subsidiary of a company called COSCO. In 2013 the container shipping market became crippled because of various factors such as weak global GDP, sluggish global trade growth, muted demand for container shipping etc. All of this cost a downfall of the container shipping industry. This also led to financial instability when it came to shipping businesses. Hence the company merged with a Chinese government-owned company called COSCO in 2015 and now is a subsidiary of it. The two companies together now one of the largest container shipping companies in the whole world. The aim to expand their capacity to more than 2 million TEU which would make than the third largest container shipping company in the world. The company has several ports all around the world with 30 ports being situated in south China and north China itself. It has experienced rapid growth in recent years and aims to grow even more in the future. Thus, the company seems to have a bright future in the container shipping industry.

8. COSCO

China Ocean Shipping (Group) Company often abbreviated as COSCO is a Chinese transportation and logistics company. The company has its headquarters in Ocean Plaza which is situated in the Xicheng District in Beijing. The company has 1,114 ships, which include a fleet of ships with the capacity of 1,580,000 twenty-foot equivalent units (TEU), dry bulk vessels and a tanker fleet which contains over 120 vessels. It operates across 40 countries all over the world. The company operates at around 1,000 different ports all over the world. COSCO is also the fourth largest shipping company in the world in terms of the number of vessels. The company expects to increase the number of ships and its fleet by 400 very soon as it has bought a rival company from Hong Kong for 6.3 billion dollars. China Ocean Shipping (Group) Company was founded on April 27, 1961. Today, it is 59 years ago. COSCO also has several subsidiary companies.

The number of subsidiaries that the company is estimated to be more than 300. Most of them operate in China, Japan, and Singapore. These subsidiary companies mainly deal with businesses such as shipbuilding, ship repairing, container manufacturing, terminal operations, trade, finance, information technology, and even real estate.

9. Hanjin

Hanjin Shipping Co., Ltd. is a former Republic of Korean logistics and container transport company. It was one of the biggest shipping companies of Republic of Korea and one of the top 10 shipping and logistics companies in the world in terms of shipping capacity. It has its headquarters in Republic of Korea. Founded on 16 May 1977 the company rose quickly before going bankrupt. Hanjin was declared as dysfunctional on 17 February 2017. It had a fleet of nearly 60 ships. This list included container ships, LNG carriers, and bulk. It transported and more than a hundred million tonnes of cargo every year. Hanjin also operated around the world and head offices in many different countries and regions. It has a capacity of 3.7 million TEU. The company also has several dockyards. It on a total of 14 dockyards which span across countries and regions such as Republic of Korea, the United States of America, Japan, Spain, China Taiwan, Vietnam, and Belgium. The company also has several subsidiaries of its own. The company was also the first ever to introduce a class carrier ship with a capacity of 10,000 TEU which travel from Asia to Europe. On 17 February 2017 Republic of Korean courts declared the company as bankrupt. The shipping terminals of the country were internationally distributed.

10. CMA CGM

The CMA CGM is a container shipping and transportation company based in France. It is France's leading company of its kind. It is also one of the largest worldwide shipping groups. CMA CGM has a total of 200 different shipping routes with more than 420 ports spread across 150 countries. Its headquarters are based in Marseille France. Its North American headquarters are based in Norfolk, Virginia in the United States of America. It was founded by Jacques Saadé in 1978. Jacques Saadé is also one of the key people in the company as its chairman. Rodolphe Saadé is the CEO of the company. It employs more than 29,000 people. In 2018, the company had a revenue of 21.1 billion dollars. The shipping containers for this company are painted in dark blue with the words CMA CGM painted in white. The CMA CGM also runs a foundation called the CMA CGM Corporate Foundation for Children which was started in 2005. Its main objective is to improve the well-being of children. Etiquettes to improve the everyday lives of sick children, promoting equal opportunities for underprivileged children and to encourage the personal development of differently abled children. As you have guessed the world has moved a great deal from the revolutionary clipper ships of the yore to modern container ships but the fascination for the largest and fastest remains the same in both seafarers and the general public.

(Adapted from: https://www.maritimemanual.com/largest-container-shipping-companies/)

Part Two: Top 50 World Container Ports

Part Three: China Railway Express—Freight Network Facilitates Trade between China and Europe

Chapter 15

Insurance

15.1 Pre-knowledge

In international trade, during cargo transportation from the port of shipment to port of destination, there are a lot of risks, which, if occur, will involve traders in financial losses. Although these risks can not be avoided, they can be transferred to insurance company by covering the goods for various risks or insurance clause with the insurer.

Insurance is the trader's protection against losses or damage caused by dangers during the transportation. It is provided to cover almost any kind of occurrence that may result in loss. But as far as foreign trade is concerned, that mainly concerns is the Marine Insurance, for a large percentage of trade in and out a country goes by sea.

The terms of insurance in a contract usually contains the insurance to be covered by whom, against certain kinds of risks, for certain amount of money, and as per what kind of clause it is to be executed. The following sentence pattern is usually used: to be covered by…, against…, for…, and as per…it is to be executed…

15.1.1 Who Will Cover the Insurance

Under the terms of FOB and CFR, the importer is responsible for insurance up to the port of destination. Under the terms of CIF, it is the exporter who issues the goods.

15.1.2 Ocean Marine Insurance Coverage

Under China Insurance Clause (CIC) issued by People's Insurance Company of China (PICC), there are three kinds of risks:

(1) Basic risks, including:

- FPA (Free from Particular Average)（平安险）;
- WPA (With Particular Average)（水渍险）;
- AR (All Risks)（一切险）.

(2) General additional risks, including:

- TPND (theft, pilferage, and non-delivery)（偷窃提货不着险）;
- FWRD (Fresh Water and/or Rain Damage)（淡水雨淋险）;
- Shortage Risk（短量险）;
- Intermixture and Contamination（混杂、玷污险）;
- Leakage（渗漏险）;
- Clash and Breakage（碰损破碎险）;
- Risk of Odor（串味险）;
- Hook Damage（钩损险）;
- Breakage of Packing（包装破损险）;
- Risk of Rust（锈损险）.

(3) Special additional risks, such as:

- SRCC (Strike, Riot, and Civil Commotion)（罢工、暴动、民变险）;
- War Risk（战争险）;
- Import Duty（进口关税险）;
- Rejection（拒收险）;
- Failure to Delivery（交货不到险）;
- On Deck（舱面险）;
- Aflatoxin（黄曲霉素险）.

The additional risks cannot be covered individually. Before the additional risks are covered, the basic risks must be covered first. The insured can choose the right coverage based on the nature of their different goods.

15.1.3 Insurance Value

The insurance value is calculated as: CIF value + a reasonable profit on sale of goods. "A reasonable profit on sale of goods" is usually a percentage of the total amount and this percentage is usually 10%. For example:

Insurance is to be effected for 110% of the CIF invoice value against All Risks.

Sometimes, buyers may request insurance to cover more than 110%. In this case, the extra premium will be for the buyer's account.

15.1.4 Insurance Clause

In international trade, there are two kinds of insurance clauses: CIC issued by PICC, and ICC (Institute Cargo Clause) issued by Institute of London Underwriters.

The ICC includes the following types: ICC (A), ICC (B), ICC (C), Institute War Clauses-cargo, Institute Strikes Clauses-cargo, Malicious Damage Clauses.

15.1.5 Insurance Policy

An insurance policy is issued when goods are insured, but it is also usual to use a "Certificate of Insurance" which is used as evidence of insurance. A policy is a contract, a legal document, and principally it serves as evidence of insurance of the agreement between the insurer and the insured.

As a title document, insurance policy can be transferred, the same as the ocean B/L.

There are some other insurance documents: Cover Note, Open Cover, and Combined Certificate.

15.2 Correspondence Writing Guide and Specimen Letters

The writing guide for letters between seller and buyer regarding insurance is as follows:

(1) Openings: provide information of the consignment to be insured.

(2) Body: express what you ask the reader to do in terms of cover, insurance value and policy or let the reader know whether you will grant what they require you to do.

(3) Closings: make it clear how to settle the extra fees.

15.2.1 Asking for Insurance Arrangement

April 28, 2020

Dear Sirs,

<u>Re: Contract No. SC2020-102 for polyresin table lamps</u>

We wish to refer you to our Order No. SC2020-102 for 2,400pcs each A001 and A003 of polyresin table lamps, from which you will see that this order was placed on a FOB basis.

As we now desire to have the shipment insured at your end, we shall be much pleased if you kindly arrange to insure the same on our behalf against F.P.A. as per and subject to OCEAN MARINE CARGO CLAUSES (2009) OF PICC for 110% of the invoice value, i.e. US $47,520, the rate of the cover is 1%. We shall refund the premium $475.2 to you upon receipt of your debit note or, if you like, you may draw on us at sight for the same.

Yours sincerely,

15.2.2 Reply to an Insurance Application

April 30, 2020

Dear Sirs,

<u>Re: Contract No. SC2020-102 for polyresin table lamps</u>

We thank you for your letter of April 28 requesting us to effect insurance on the captioned shipment for your account.

We are pleased to confirm having covered the above shipment with the People's Insurance Co. of China against F.P.A. for US $47,520. The policy will be sent to you in a day or two together with our debit note for the premium.

This cargo will be shipped on s/s "Victory", sailing on or about the May 15 2020.

Yours sincerely,

15.2.3 Covering Insurance for the Sellers

April 30, 2020

Dear Sirs,

<u>Re: Contract No. SC2020-100 for polyresin table lamps</u>

We wish to refer you to contract No. SC2020-100 for 2,400pcs A002 polyresin table lamps, from which you will see that this order was placed on a CIF basis Incoterms® 2020. You have to cover insurance on the captioned goods for 110% of the invoice value against F.P.A. as per and subject to OCEAN MARINE CARGO CLAUSES (2009) OF PICC.

The cargo will be on board S.S. PRINCESS No. 815, sailing on May 10 from Shenzhen to New York.

We hope you will cover the consignment and let us have the policy as soon as it is ready. We are awaiting your early reply.

Yours sincerely,

Notes

[1] insurance *n.* 保险。insurance company 保险公司

insure *v.* 给……保险，投保，承保。insure 后可跟：

for us 为我方

with an insurance company 有保险公司

for the sum of US$ 10,000 总金额 10 000 美元

at the rate of… 保险费率为……

with/against FPA/WPA/AR/breakage…

for the buyer's account 由买方负担保险费

on behalf of the buyer 代买方办理

insurer *n.* 保险公司

insured *n.* 被保险人，投保者

[2] coverage *n.* 保险范围，承保险别，投保条款

[3] with regard to 关于

[4] in the absence of 没有，在没有……的情况下

[5] on condition that 如果……，在……条件下

[6] extra premium 额外保险费

[7] serve your purpose 使你达到目的。serve *v.* 帮助达到；当作

[8] for invoice value plus 10%=for 110% of the invoice value 发票金额加成 10%

[9] policy 指保险单（insurance policy），货物运输保险投保单样本和保险单样本如图 15-1 和图 15-2 所示

货 物 运 输 险 投 保 单
APPLICATION FOR CARGO TRANSPORTATION INSURANCE

投保单号：MI0001931

注意：请您在保险人明确说明本投保单及适用保险条款后，如实填写本投保单，您所填写的材料将构成签订保险合同的要约，成为保险人核保并签发保险单的依据。除双方另有约定外，保险人签发保险单且投保人向保险人缴清保险费后，保险人开始按约定的险种承保货物运输保险。

投保人 Applicant	RIQING EXPORT AND IMPORT COMPANY				
投保人地址 Applicant's Add	P.O.BOX 1589, NAGOYA, JAPAN			邮编 Code	197-0804
联系人 Contact	CHUANBEN	电话 Tel.	81-3-932-3588	电子邮箱 E-mail	
被保险人 Insured	RIQING EXPORT AND IMPORT COMPANY			电话 Tel.	
贸易合同号 Contract No.	contract01	信用证号 L/C No.	002/0000398	发票号 Invoice No.	IV0000066

标记 Marks & Nos.	包装及数量 Packing & quantity	保险货物项目 Description of goods
RIQINGCO CONTRACT01 NAGOYA 1/1,000	1,000　　　CARTONS	CANNED LITCHIS

装载运输工具：TBA
Name of the Carrier

起运日期 Departure Date：2018-08-29　　　赔付地点 Claims Payable At：JAPAN

航行路线：自 SHANGHAI,CHINA　经 _____　到达（目的地）NAGOYA, JAPAN
Route　From　　　　　　　　Via　　　　　To(destination)

包装方式：_____
运输方式：_____

承保条件　投保人可根据投保意向选择投保险别及条款，并划 √ 确认，但保险人承保的险别及适用条款以保险人最终确定并在保险单上列明的险种、条款为准。

Conditions:
进出口海洋运输：[√]一切险　[ ]水渍险　[ ]平安险　（《海洋运输货物保险条款》）
　　　　　　　　[ ]ICC(A)　[ ]ICC(B)　[ ]ICC(C)　（《伦敦协会条款》）
进出口航空运输：[ ]航空运输险　[ ]航空运输一切险　（《航空运输货物保险条款》）
进出口陆上运输：[ ]陆运险　[ ]陆运一切险　（《陆上运输货物保险条款》）

特殊附加险：　[√]战争险　[√]罢工险

特别约定 Special Conditions：
1、加成　Value Plus About　110　　%
2、CIF金额　CIF value _____　　　3、保险金额　Insured Value _____
4、费率(‰)　Rate _____　　　　　5、保险费　Premium _____

投保人声明：
1. 本人填写本投保单之前，保险人已经就本投保单及适用的保险条款的内容，尤其是关于保险人免除责任的条款及投保人和被保险人义务的条款向本人作了明确说明，本人对该保险条款及保险条件已完全了解，并同意接受保险条款的约束。
2. 本投保单所填事项内容均属事实，同意以本投保单作为保险人签发保险单的依据。
3. 保险合同自保险单签发之日起成立。

投保人签字(盖章)：RIQING EXPORT AND IMPORT COMPANY　　　日期 2018-08-29

图 15-1　货物运输保险投保单样本

中保财产保险有限公司	
The People's Insurance (Property) Company of China, Ltd	
Invoice No. BI123	Policy No. 457

海洋货物运输保险单
MARINE CARGO TRANSPORTATION INSURANCE POLICY

Insured: Dongguan Lighting Import & Export Corporation
No.15 Xinji Ave., South Area, Dongguan, Guangdong, China

中保财产保险有限公司（以下简称本公司）根据被保险人的要求，及其所缴付约定的保险费，按照本保险单承担险别和背面所载条款与下列特别条款承保下列货物运输保险，特签发本保险单。

This policy of insurance witnesses that the People's Insurance (Property) Company of China, Ltd. (hereinafter called "The Company"), at the request of the Insured and in consideration of the agreed premium paid by the Insured, undertakes to insure the undermentioned goods in transportation subject to conditions of the Policy as per the Clauses printed overleaf and other special clauses attached hereon.

货物标记 Marks of Goods	包装单位 Packing Unit	保险货物项目 Descriptions of Goods	保险金额 Amount Insured
WI NEW YORK SC2020-102 C/NO.1-800	800 CARTONS	POLYRESIN TABLE LAMPS	USD47,520

总保险金额：
Total Amount Insured: SAY US DOLLARS FORTY-SEVEN THOUSAND FIVE HUNDRED AND TWENTY ONLY.

保费 Premium AS ARRANGED	开航日期 Slg. on or abt. MAY 15, 2020	载运输工具 Per conveyance S.S. VICTORY V.501

承保险别
Conditions
COVERING F.P.A AS PER AND SUBJECT TO OCEAN MARINE CARGO CLAUSES OF THE PEOPLE'S INSURANCE COMPANY OF CHINA DATED 10/1/2009.

起运港 From SHENZHEN	中转港 VIA LOS ANGELES	目的港 To NEW YORK

所保货物，如发生本保险单项下可能引起索赔的损失或损坏，应立即通知本公司下述代理人查勘。如有索赔，应向本公司提交保险单正本（本保险单共有2份正本）及有关文件。如一份正本已用于索赔，其余正本则自动失效。

In the event of loss or damage which may result in acclaim under this Policy, immediate notice must be given to the Company's Agent as mentioned hereunder. Claims, if any, one of the Original Policy which has been issued in two original (s) together with the relevant documents shall be surrendered to the Company. If one of the Original Policy has been accomplished, the others to be void.

赔款偿付地点
Claim payable at NEW YORK

日期 DATE MAY 10, 2020	中保财产保险有限公司深圳分公司 The People's Insurance (Property) Company of China, Ltd. Shenzhen Branch 王天华

图 15-2 保险单样本

[10] a note for the premium 费用通知，premium 这里指保险费
[11] debit note 借记单

15.3 Dialogues

15.3.1 I Prefer CFR Terms

(*Mr. Wilson finds one problem in the draft contract, now he is discussing it with his supplier, Mr. Ma.*)

Ma: Is there anything not clear in the draft contract? Or have you any comments on them?

Wilson: Oh, yes. I do find a few points to be clarified. I think it's better to have a good understanding of the terms and conditions before signing a contract so that no friction would ever grow from misunderstanding.

Ma: That's right. All the terms should meet with common understanding. They should be definite and unambiguous.

Wilson: I'm glad we are of the same mind. Now let's go over these points one by one.
Ma: Please.
Wilson: May I ask, according to your usual CIF terms, what does "I" exactly cover?

Ma: As our usual practice, "I" covers WPA, for 110% of the invoice value. If coverage against other risks is required, such as breakage, leakage, TPND, and hook, the extra premium involved would be for the buyer's account.

Wilson: I see. Then what about your CFR price? How much will you take off?

Ma: Roughly speaking, the difference between CIF and CFR is about 3%. Of course, the premium varies with the range of insurance.

Wilson: Frankly speaking, we have an open policy with the ×× Insurance Co. All we have to do when a shipment is made is to advise them the particulars. Furthermore, we usually receive quite a handsome premium rebate at regular intervals from our underwriters. That's why I prefer CFR terms.

Ma: OK, we will figure out the CFR price for you. CIF or CFR, you can choose either of them.

Wilson: Fine.

15.3.2 I Have Some Insurance Issues to Discuss with You.

(*Mr. Stan is discussing the insurance issues with Miss Liu.*)

Stan: Miss Liu, I have some insurance issues to discuss with you.

Liu: Sure.

Stan: Now, suppose we order goods from you, how will the goods be insured?

Liu: According to our usual practice, we will insure the goods against WPA for 110% of their CIF value.

Stan: Does it cover any damage caused by natural disasters and accidents?

Liu: Generally speaking, it does.

Stan: How about theft, pilferage, breakage, and rain water damage?

Liu: I'm afraid not. I mean you don't need that. They are not delicate goods. They are not likely to get these kinds of damage.

Stan: You are probably right. On the other hand, what about the strike insurance? If there is a strike, what will happen when the goods are shipped?

Liu: We only cover WPA for the goods. If you prefer, we can insure against Strike Risk on your behalf, but the extra premium is for your account.

Stan: I see. Could you tell me a general sum of money for Strike Risk?

Liu: Well, the premium rate of Strike Risk is 0.03%.

Stan: I see. I think I will need to discuss with my boss before I tell you our final decision.

Liu: Sure. You can send us an e-mail or fax, if you have any questions about it.

Stan: OK. See you.

Notes

[1] draft contract 合同草案

[2] clarify 阐明，澄清

[3] friction 摩擦

[4] meet with common understanding 达成共识

[5] unambiguous 不含糊的，明确的

[6] take off 原意是"拿掉，脱衣，减弱"的意思，这里是"降低，降价"的意思。例：

How much will you take off?

你方会降价多少？

[7] open policy 预约保单。have an open policy with 与……订有预约保单。它是由保险公司与被保险人双方签订预约保险合同，承保一定时期内发运的一切货物或某几项货物。凡属于预约保险单的保险范围内的进出口货物，一经起运，即自动按预约保单所列条件承保。它适用于经常有进出口货物的单位，既可防止漏保，又可消除逐笔投保的麻烦。

[8] particulars 具体细节

[9] underwriter 保险商

[10] rebate *n.* 回扣
[11] at regular intervals 每隔一定时间，定期
[12] issue *n.* 问题
[13] delicate goods 精致货物

Exercises

Exercise 1: Choose the best answer to complete the following sentences

1. Insurance is to be covered _____ All Risks and War Risk.
   A. for   B. on   C. against   D. to
2. _____ is the general practice that the insurance is covered in the same currency as in the letter of credit.
   A. This   B. That   C. It   D. As
3. Please make sure that insurance is covered against FWRD in addition _____ WPA.
   A. with   B. against   C. to   D. by
4. If broader coverage is required, the extra premium should _____ the buyers' account.
   A. for   B. be for   C. be to   D. to
5. I have received your e-mail of June 4 _____ many thanks.
   A. with   B. in   C. on   D. for
6. Please effect insurance _____ All Risks _____ the amount of 10,000 Yuan _____ our order No. 506.
   A. for, for, on   B. against, on, for   C. against, for, on   D. with, for, for
7. We are now replying to your letter of March 2 _____ insurance. Which of the following is NOT right?
   A. in regard to   B. with regard to   C. regarding   D. as regard
8. Please let us know your premium _____ which you cover insurance against All Risks.
   A. with   B. for   C. against   D. at
9. We do not wish to have any risks of _____ the only steamer available this month.
   A. to miss   B. missing   C. to lose   D. losing
10. Since the premium varies with the scope of _____ , should additional risks be covered?
    A. assurance   B. insurance   C. business   D. enterprises

Exercise 2: Translate the following sentences into Chinese

1. For FOB and CFR sales, insurance is to be covered by buyers, while for CIF sales,

insurance is to be covered by sellers.

2. The coverage is to be from warehouse to warehouse and come to effect from May 10.
3. Please insure for us these products for the invoice value plus 10%.
4. They are not delicate goods that can be damaged on the voyage. FPA will be good enough.
5. We shall effect insurance of the goods for 110% of their CIF value.
6. We have insured the shipment for 130% of the invoice value, but the premium for the difference between 130% and 110% should be for your account.
7. I have some glassware to be shipped to China Hong Kong. What risks should I cover?
8. Please insure for me against all risks 200 pieces of high-quality furniture valued US$20,000.
9. Please let us know the premium of Breakage.
10. We can insure the porcelain vases on your behalf, but at a rather high premium and all the additional premium will be for your account.

Exercise 3: Translate the following sentences into English

1. 请将此货物投保一切险和战争险。
2. 我们将200吨大米按发票金额的110%投保一切险。
3. 随函寄上提单和保险单。
4. 额外保险费由买方负担。
5. 如你方愿意投保破碎险，我们可代为办理。

Exercise 4: Complete the following letter with proper words

| with regard to   FPA   cover   under   against   SRCC   upon   theft |

Dear Sirs,

Thank you for your letter of December 6 and your Order No. 367.

On going through the stipulations of your order, we regret to find that in addition to _____ and War Risk, you require insurance to _____ TPND and _____ which were agreed _____ by both parties during our negotiations at the Beijing International Fair.

_____ the ordinary circumstances, no loss or _____ of such merchandise as mild steel flat bars is likely to occur during transportation or after arriving at its destination. Therefore, it is our practice to cover FPA for such commodity. Since you desire to have your shipment insured _____ TPND, we can arrange such insurance at your cost.

_____ SRCC, we wish to state that the People's Insurance Company of China, from now on, accept this special coverage, and will fall in with the usual international practice.

We hope you will take the above into consideration and give us a new order soon.

Yours faithfully,

Exercise 5: Compose a dialogue on the following situation

You have a batch of porcelain wares to be shipped from Shanghai to New York, but you have no idea about what risks to be covered.

Mr. Zhang, a representative from the People's Insurance Company of China, explains the different kinds of coverage to you, and finally your effect the insurance on your porcelain wares.

Reading Material

Institute Cargo Clauses 2009

Chapter 16

Terms of Payment

16.1 Pre-knowledge

Payment plays an important role in foreign trade. It is often more complicated than payment in home trade. Both the sellers and buyers face risks in transaction. For the sellers, there is the risk that the importer fails to pay or he might not pay in full for the goods. On the other hand, the buyers may face the risk that the goods will be delayed in delivery and they might only receive them a long time after paying for them. It is even possible that the wrong goods might be sent. So, each party will seek the terms of payment favorable to themselves.

As both parties concern this highly, they negotiate it very carefully until the definite word is fixed.

16.1.1 Bill of Exchange

It is seldom to pay the transaction with cash, but mostly with the instruments of bill of exchange (or draft), promissory note and check, especially with the bill of exchange.

A bill of exchange or a draft is defined as "an unconditional written order drawn or issued by the drawer to the drawee requiring the drawee to pay a certain amount of money to someone, or the ordered one, or the holder at sight, or at a fixed time in the future or at the time state".

16.1.2 Terms of Payment

In general, there are three basic methods of payment in international trade: remittance, collection and letter of credit (L/C).

Remittance means the buyer sends the payment through a bank or other forms to the seller initiatively. It is widely used for payment in advance and business on open account. It is divided into three forms: mail transfer (M/T), telegraphic transfer (T/T) and demand draft (D/D). The most widely used one is T/T.

Collection means the exporter issues the bill of exchange and entrusts the bank to collect the payment of the goods. It has two forms, i.e., documents against payment (D/P) and documents against acceptance (D/A). And, D/P can be divided into two kinds: D/P at sight and D/P after sight according to the time of effecting payment.

Remittance and collection are based on commercial credit. They are based on the sellers' credit when dispatch the goods first, pay the money after and the buyers' credit when pay the money first, send the goods after respectively.

The most generally used method of payment in international trade is the letter of credit, which is a reliable and safe method of payment, facilitating trade with unknown buyers and giving protection to both sellers and buyers.

16.1.3 L/C

A letter of credit (L/C) is a written promise made by a bank that it will make payment for the goods shipped. Different from the former two methods of payment, it is based on banker's credit.

According to the express of the nature of letter of credit given in the Uniform Customs and Practice for Documentary Credit of International Chamber of Commerce Publication No. 600(UCP 600), we can have many kinds of L/C from different points of views:

- Revocable L/C and Irrevocable L/C;
- Clean L/C and Documentary L/C;
- Sight L/C and Usance L/C (or Time L/C);
- Transferable L/C and Non-transferable L/C;
- Confirmed L/C and Unconfirmed L/C.

Among these L/Cs, it is the confirmed and irrevocable L/C used most widely in Chinese foreign trade.

Generally speaking, as to the sellers' benefit, L/C is better than D/P, D/P at sight is better than D/P after sight, whereas D/P is better than D/A. In international trade, payment by collection is accepted only when the financial standing of the importer is sound or the exporter has the confidence that the importer will be good for payment.

16.2 Correspondence Writing Guide and Specimen Letters

1. Exporter urging establishment of L/C

(1) Opening: Refer to the contract number or order number and inform the buyer that the goods are ready for dispatch.

(2) Politely push the buyer to open the L/C without delay.

(3) Express expectations and ask the buyers to take immediate action.

2. Advising the seller of the establishment of the L/C

Usually makes clear the details such as the L/C No., letter of credit amount, the opening bank, opening date and the validity of the L/C.

3. Amendment to L/C

(1) Express appreciation to the buyer for opening the L/C.

(2) State your suggestions to amend the L/C and explain the reasons.

(3) Expect to receive an early amendment.

16.2.1 Asking for Easier Terms of Payment

March 15, 2020

Dear Sirs,

    We are pleased that the businesses between us have proved to be very smooth and successful.

    Our past purchase of table lamps from you has been paid, as a rule, by confirmed, irrevocable letter of credit. On this basis, it has indeed cost us a great deal. From the moment we open the credit till the time our buyers pay us, our funds are tied up for about five months. We believe we have proved trustworthy business partners to each other after these years of satisfactory cooperation. So we should think that we deserve some easier terms of payment, say, documents against payment.

    Your kindness in giving priority to the consideration of the above request and giving us an early favorable reply will be highly appreciated.

Yours faithfully,

16.2.2 Accepting Payment by D/P

March 16, 2020

Dear Sirs,

 Thank you for your letter of March 15, 2020.

 We have carefully studied your proposal for payment by D/A for a trial order of lamps. Now we regret being unable to meet your request.

 As our usual practices go, we require payment by confirmed and irrevocable letter of credit. However, in consideration of our friendly relations, we are, as an exceptional case, prepared to accept D/P at sight.

 We sincerely hope that the above payment will be acceptable to you and expect to receive your trial order in due course.

 Looking forward to your early reply.

Sincerely yours,

16.2.3 Payment by L/C

March 16, 2020

Dear Sirs,

 We have received your letter of March 15, 2020 and appreciate your intention to push the sales of our products in your country.

 Although we have confidence in your integrity and ability, we wish to re-mention that our usual terms of payment by sight L/C remain unchanged in all trade with new clients. Therefore, we regret being unable to accept your D/P or D/A terms. Maybe after several smooth and satisfactory transactions, we can consider other easier terms.

 We are sorry to hear about the difficulties you are having. Our products are well-known in America and competitive in price, which will help you a lot to stand firmly in your market.

 We look forward to your first order at an early date.

Sincerely yours,

16.2.4 Urging Establishment of L/C

March 28, 2020

Dear Sirs,

<u>Re: Sales Confirmation No. SC2020-102</u>

The goods under the captioned S/C covering 2,400PCS A001 and A003 each have already for shipment. The date of delivery is approaching, but we still have not received your covering Letter of Credit to date. Please do your utmost to rush the L/C, so that we can effect shipment within the stipulated time.

In order to avoid subsequent amendments, please make sure that the L/C stipulations are in exact accordance to the terms of the Sales Confirmation. Moreover, we wish to call your attention to the fact that the contract is concluded on FOB SHENZHEN basis; therefore, your responsibility is to dispatch the vessel to the loading port in time.

We are looking forward to your L/C soon.

Sincerely yours,

16.2.5 Advice of Establishment of L/C

April 5, 2020

Dear Sirs,

<u>Re: Sales Confirmation No. SC2020-102</u>

Thanks for your letter of March 28, 2020 in connection with the above Sales Confirmation. We are very sorry to learn that you have not received the L/C.

In reply, we are pleased to tell you that we have established with the Citibank, New York branch the confirmed, irrevocable Letter of Credit No.6688 in your favor for the amount of USD43, 200 payable by sight draft accompanied by a full set of the shipping documents. The expiry date is May 30, 2020.

Please do your utmost to get all the goods ready and arrange shipment on the designated vessel within the time limit upon receipt of the L/C.

Thank you in advance for your cooperation.

Sincerely yours,

16.2.6　Asking for Amendment to L/C

March 28, 2020

Dear Sirs,

Re: Irrevocable Letter of Credit No. 6688

　　We have today received the captioned L/C No.6688 covering Sales Confirmation No. SC2020-102. But we regret to say that after checking the L/C clauses, we have found some discrepancies between your L/C stipulations and the terms and conditions of our sales confirmation. Therefore, please make the following amendments of L/C without the least delay:

　　1. The amount both in figures and in words should respectively be USD43, 200 and SAY U.S. DOLLARS FORTY-THREE THOUSAND TWO HUNDRED ONLY.

　　2. Draft to be at sight, instead of at 30 days after sight.

　　3. "CIF NEW YORK" should read "FOB SHENZHEN".

　　4. The port of shipment should be SHENZHEN instead of HONG KONG.

　　5. Allow partial shipment and transshipment and delete the clause "by direct steamer".

　　6. Amend the date of expiry and place to read June 30, 2020 in Dongguan, China.

　　Since the shipment date is approaching, please see to it that your amendments reach us by April 6, 2020. Otherwise, shipment will be further delayed.

Yours faithfully,

16.2.7　Reply to the Request of Amendment to L/C

March 29, 2020

Dear Sirs,

Re: Irrevocable Letter of Credit No. 6688

　　Thanks for your letter asking for amendment to L/C No. 6688.

　　We feel very sorry for the discrepancies between the L/C clauses and the term & conditions of Sales Confirmation No. SC2020-102.

　　We wish to inform you that we have submitted an application to the issuing bank requesting for the L/C amendment in accordance with your instructions in your letter of March 28, 2020. You may rest assured that Citibank, New York branch will send the amendment notification to you ASAP.

　　Please keep us posted of the arrival of the L/C amendment.

Yours faithfully,

16.2.8　Asking for Extension of L/C

> March 28, 2020
>
> Dear Sirs,
>
> Re: Irrevocable Letter of Credit No. 6688
>
> Thank you for your letter of Credit No.6688 covering 2,400 pieces A001 and A003 each.
>
> We regret to tell you that we are unable to get the goods ready before the latest date of shipment May 30, 2020 because our factory has suffered a tornado and flood. Therefore, we have to request you to extend the date of shipment and validity of the L/C to June 15 and June 30, 2020 respectively.
>
> Your compliance with our request will be highly appreciated.
>
> Yours sincerely,

Notes

[1] as a rule 通常

[2] confirmed, irrevocable letter of credit 保兑的、不可撤销信用证

保兑信用证：由另一银行保证对符合信用证条款规定的单据履行付款义务，开证行与保兑行都负第一性的付款责任，这种信用证对出口商最有利；不可撤销信用证：信用证一经开出，在有效期内，未经受益人及有关当事人的同意，开证行不得片面修改和撤销。只要受益人提供的单据符合信用证规定，开证行必须履行付款义务，这种信用证对出口商较有保障，在国际贸易中使用广泛。

[3] open the credit 开立信用证。credit=letter of credit：信用证，开立信用证还可以用动词 establish。

[4] tie up 冻结资金

[5] trustworthy adj. 值得信赖的

[6] deserve vt. 应该得到，vi. 应受赏（罚）

[7] easier terms of payment 易于接受的支付方式，easier adj.（价格、发盘等）易于接受的

[8] give priority to 优先考虑

[9] trial order 试订单。试订，一般数量较小，主要是为了使产品，特别是新产品进入市场，或是新客户初次订货。

[10] usual practices 通常做法，惯例

[11] in consideration of sth 由于，考虑到，等于短语 considering sth.
[12] as an exceptional case 作为破例，exceptional *adj.* 特殊的，例外的
[13] D/P at sight 即期付款交单
[14] push the sales of 推销
[15] integrity *n.* 信誉，资信
[16] do your utmost 尽力而为
[17] amendments 修改
[18] call your attention 引起注意
[19] dispatch the vessel 派船
[20] in your favor 以你方为抬头
[21] draft 汇票
[22] discrepancies 差异，不符点

信用证最常见的修改事项如下：

（1）更换受益人名称和地址。

Beneficiary name and address changed to read ____ instead of previously stipulated.

（2）延长装船日期及信用证有效期。例：

Shipment and validity date extended to April 20, 2020 and May 5, 2020 respectively.

（3）金额与货物的增减。

Increase (Decrease) L/C amount by ____ to ____ and quantity of commodities increase (decrease) by ____ to ____.

（4）修改价格条件，CIF 改为 FOB。

Price term amended to be FOB basis instead of CIF.

（5）要求通知银行加以保兑。

Please add your confirmation to this L/C. This confirmation charges, if any, are for applicant's /beneficiary's account.

（6）更改装货港或卸货港。

Shipment from _____ to _____ instead of previously stipulated.

（7）保险种类的修改。

Insurance covering Institute Cargo Clause (A) instead of Cargo Clause (B).

（8）准予分批装运。

Partial shipment allowed.

（9）准予转运。

Transshipment allowed.

（10）保险费改由出口商承担。

Insurance premium to be paid by beneficiary.

（11）所有银行费用由卖方负担。

All banking charges are for beneficiary's account.

（12）修改为可转让信用证。

This credit is transferable.

（13）删除某条款。

Delete the clause "××".

[23] tornado 龙卷风

[24] flood 洪水

[25] 单据样本如下：

 图 16-1：汇票样本

 图 16-2：不可撤销信用证开证申请书样本

 图 16-3：SWIFT 信用证样本

 图 16-4：信用证通知书样本

 图 16-5：信用证修改通知书样本

 图 16-6：不可撤销即期信用证样本

 图 16-7：不可撤销、保兑信用证样本

 （Mainly adapted from www.pocib.com）

BILL OF EXCHANGE

凭　　　　　　　　　　　　　　　　　　　　　　　信用证 第　　　号

Drawn under　CITI BANK, NEW YORK BRANCH　　**L/C No.**　6688

日期

Dated　ARIL 5, 2020　　支取 Payable with interest @　% per annum 按年息　付款

号码　　　　　　　　汇票金额　　　　　　　　　　东莞　　年　　月　　日

No.　BI123　　**Exchange for**　USD43,200.00　　Dongguan　JUNE 10, 2020

见票　　　　　　　　日后（本汇票之副本未付）付交

At　**********************　sight of this **FIRST** of Exchange (Second of exchange　金额

being unpaid) **Pay to the order of**　BANK OF CHINA, DONGGUAN BRANCH　**The sum**

SAY U. S. DOLLARS FORTY-THREE THOUSAND TWO HUNDRED ONLY.

款已收讫

Value received

此致

To:

CITI BANK, NEW YORK BRANCH

399 PARK AVENUE, NEW YORK, NY, USA

东莞灯饰进出口公司（章）
Dongguan Lighting Import & Export Corporation

何菲（章）

图 16-1　汇票样本

IRREVOCABLE DOCUMENTARY CREDIT APPLICATION

TO: Date:

Please issue an irrevocable documentary credit as follows:

Applicant (full name and address)	L/C No. Ex Card No. Contract No.	
	Date and place of expiry of the credit	
Beneficiary (full name and address)	Advising bank	
Partial shipments ☐ allowed ☐ not allowed	Transshipment ☐ allowed ☒ not allowed	☐ Issue by airmail With brief advice by teletransmission ☐ Issue by express delivery ☐ Issue by teletransmission (which shall be the operative instrument)
Loading on board/dispatch taking in change at/from not later than for transportation to	Amount (both in figures and words) SAY	

Description of goods	Credit available with
	☐ by sight payment ☐ by acceptance ☐ by negotiation
	☐ by deferred payment at
	   against the documents detailed herein
	☐ and beneficiary's draft for ____ % of the invoice value
	   at	

Packing:	☐ FOB ☐ CFR ☐ CIF or other terms	

Documents required: (marks with ×)
1. ( ) Signed Commercial Invoice in copies indicating L/C No. and Contract No.
2. ( ) Full set of clean on board ocean Bills of Landing made out to ____ and blank endorsed, marked "freight [ ] to collect/ [ ] prepaid [ ] showing freight amount" notifying
3. ( ) Air Waybills showing "freight [ ] to collect/ [ ] prepaid [ ] including freight amount" and consigned to
4. ( ) Memorandum issued by ____ consigned to
5. ( ) Insurance Policy/Certificate in copes for ____ % of the invoice value showing claims payable in China in currency of the draft, blank endorsed, covering ([ ] Ocean Marine Transportation / [ ] Air Transportation /[ ] Over Land Transportation) All Risks, War Risks.
6. ( ) Parking List/Weight Memo in copies issued by indicating the quantity/gross and the weights of each packing and packing condition as called by the L/C.
7. ( ) Certificate of Quantity/Weight in copies issued by an independent surveyor at loading port, indicating the actual surveyed quantity/weight of shipped goods as well as the packing condition.
8. ( ) Certificate of Quality in copies issued by [ ] manufacturer / [ ] public recognized surveyor / [ ]
9. ( ) Beneficiary's Certificate certified copy of cable dispatched to the accountees within hours after shipment advising [ ] name of vessel / [ ] flight No. / [ ] wagon No. , date, quantity, weight and value of shipment.
10. ( ) Beneficiary's Certifying that extra copies of the documents have been dispatched according to the contract terms.
11. ( ) Shipping Co's Certificate attesting that the carrying vessel is chartered or booked by accountee or their shipping agents.
12. ( ) Other documents, if any:

Additional instructions:
1. ( ) All banking charges outside the opening bank are for beneficiary's account.
2. ( ) Documents must be presented with days after the date of issuance of the transport documents but with the validity of this credit.
3. ( ) Third party as shipper is not acceptable. Short Form / Blank Back B/L is not acceptable.
4. ( ) Both quantity and amount ____ % more or less are allowed.
5. ( ) Prepaid freight drawn in excess of L/C amount is acceptable against presentation of original charges voucher issued by shipping Co. / Air Line / or it's agent.
6. ( ) All documents to be forwarded in one cover, unless otherwise stated above.
7. ( ) Other terms, if any:

Account No. : _____ with _____ (name of bank)	
Transacted by: Telephone No.: Fax No.: E-mail:	(Applicant: name, signature of authorized person) (with seal)

图 16-2　不可撤销信用证开证申请书样本

MT700-------------------ISSUE OF A DOCUMENTARY CREDIT-------------------------	
SEQUENCE OF TOTAL	*27: 1/1
FORM OF DOC. CREDIT	*40A: IRREVOCABLE
DOC. CREDIT NUMBER	*20: 6688
DATE OF ISSUE	31C: 200405
EXPIRY	*31D: DATE200530 PLACE CHINA
APPLICANT	*50: WALDEMAR INDUSTRIES INC. 1234S. MICHIGAN AVE., CHICAGO, IL60616, U.S.A. TEL: +1-312-427-5678
BENEFICIARY	*59: DONGGUAN LIGHTING IMPORT & EXPORT CORPORATION No.15 XINJI AVE., SOUTH AREA, DONGGUAN, GUANGDONG, CHINA TEL: +86-769-83456789
AMOUNT	*32B: CURRENCY USD AMOUNT 43200,00
AVAILABLE WITH/BY	*41D: ANY BANK IN CHINA BY NEGOTIATION
DRAFT AT …	42C: AT SIGHT
DRAWEE	*42D: OURSELVES
PARTIAL SHIPMENT	43P: ALLOWED
TRANSSHIPMENT	43T: ALLOWED
LOADING IN CHARGE	44A: SHENZHEN PORT
FOR TRANSPORT TO….	44B: NEW YORK PORT
LATEST DATE OF SHIP.	44C: 200530
DESCRIPT. OF GOODS	45A: POLYRESIN TABLE LAMPS AS PER S/C NO. SC2020-102 FOB SHENZHEN PORT, INCOTERMS 2020
DOCUMENTS REQUIRED	46A: +COMMERCIAL INVOICE IN DUPLICATE ALL STAMPED AND SIGNED BY BENEFICIARY CERTIFYING THAT THE GOODS ARE OF CHINESE ORIGIN. +FULL SET OF CLEAN ON BOARD BILL OF LADING MADE OUT TO ORDER OF SHIPPER AND BLANK ENDORSED, MARKED FREIGHT TO COLLECT AND NOTIFY APPLICANT. +PACKING LIST IN TRIPLICATE SHOWING PACKING DETAILS SUCH AS CARTON NO.S AND CONTENTS. +CERTIFICATE STAMPED AND SIGNED BY BENEFICIARY STATING THAT THE ORIGIAL INVOICE AND PACKING LIST HAVE BEEN DISPATCHED TO THE APPLICANT BY COURIER SERVISE 2 DAYS BEFORE SHIPMENT. +MANUALLY SIGNED COMMERCIAL INVOICE IN DUPLICATE ALL STAMPED AND SIGNED BY BENEFICIARY CERTIFYING THAT THE GOODS ARE OF CHINESE ORIGIN. +FULL SET OF CLEAN ON BOARD BILL OF LADING MADE OUT TO ORDER OF SHIPPER AND BLANK ENDORSED, MARKED FREIGHT TO COLLECT AND NOTIFY APPLICANT. +PACKING LIST IN TRIPLICATE SHOWING PACKING DETAILS SUCH AS CARTON NO.S AND CONTENTS. +CERTIFICATE OF QUALITY ISSUED BY CIQ, STATING THAT THE GOODS ARE UP TO UL STANDARDS +CERTIFICATE OF ORIGIN ISSUED BY CUSTOMS
ADDITIONAL COND.	47A: +INSURANCE COVERED BY THE APPLICANT. +A USD50,00 DISCREPANCY FEE, FOR BENEFICIARY'S ACCOUNT, WILL BE DEDUCTED FROM THE REIMBURSEMENT CLAIM FOR EACH PRESENTATION OF DISCREPANT DOCUMENTS UNDER THIS CREDIT.
PRESENTATION PERIOD	48: WITHIN 15 DAYS AFTER THE DATE OF SHIPMENT BUT WITHIN THE VALIDITY OF THE CREDIT.
CONFIRMATION	*49: WITHOUT
INSTRUCTION	78: ON RECEIPT OF DOCUMENTS CONFIRMING TO THE TERMS OF THIS DOCUMENTARY CREDIT, WE UNDERTAKE TO REIMBURSE YOU IN THE CURRENCY OF THE CREDIT IN ACCORDANCE WITH YOUR INSTRUCTIONS, WHICH SHOULD INCLUDE YOUR UID NUMBER AND THE ABA CODE OF THE RECEIVING BANK.

图 16-3　SWIFT 信用证样本

ADDRESS: 170 People Avenue, Shanghai China
FAX: 86-21-5289××××

信 用 证 通 知 书
Notification of Documentary Credit

Date:20190729 日期

To: 致: SHANGHAI MINHUA IMP. & EXP. CO., LTD. RM. 9021 UNION BUILDING, 　　1202 ZHONGSHAN ROAD(N), 　　SHANGHAI, P.R. CHINA	WHEN CORRESPONDING PLEASE QUOTE OUR REF. NO.	AD94001A40576
Issuing Bank 开证行 THE FUKUOKA CITY BANK, LTD. INTERNATIONAL DIVISION, JAPAN	Transmitted to us through 转递行 REF NO.	
L/C NO. 信用证号 FJD-MHLC07	DATED 开证日期 20190729	Amount 金额 USD108,000	EXPIRY PLACE 有 效 地 SHANGHAI, CHINA
EXPIRY DATE 有效期 20190830	TENOR 期限	CHARGE 未付费用	CHARGE BY 费用承担人 BENEFICIARY
RECEIVED VIA 来证方式 SWIFT	AVAILABLE 是否生效 VALID	TEST/SIGN 印押是否相符 YES	CONFIRM 我行是否保兑 NO

Dear Sirs, 敬启者:
We have pleasure in advising you that we have received from the a/m bank a(n) **Letter of Credit**, contents of which are as per attached sheet(s).
This advice and the attached sheet(s) must accompany the relative documents when presented for negotiation.
兹通知贵司,我行收自上述银行信用证一份,现随附通知。贵司交单时,请将本通知书及信用证一并提示。

Remarks 备注
Please note that this advice does not constitute our confirmation of the above L/C nor does it convey any engagement or obligation on our part.
本通知书不构成我行对此信用证之保兑及其他任何责任。

This L/C consists of __TWO__ sheet(s), including the covering letter and attachment(s).
本信用证连同面函及附件共 __2__ 纸。

If you find any terms and conditions in the L/C which you are unable to comply with and or any error(s), it is suggested that you contact applicant directly for necessary amendment(s) of as to avoid any difficulties which may arise when documents are presented.
如本信用证中有无法办到的条款和/或错误,请与开证申请人联系,进行必要的修改,以排除交单时可能发生的问题。

This L/C is advised subject to ICC UCP publication No.600.
本信用证之通知系遵循国际商会跟单信用证统一惯例第 600 号出版物办理。

此证如有任何问题或疑虑,请与结算业务部审证科联络,电话: 86-21-5289××××。

Yours faithfully,
FOR **BANK OF CHINA** 中国银行

图 16-4　信用证通知书样本

东京三菱银行

THE BANK of TOKYO-MITSUBISHI, LTD.

2-10-22 Kayato Bldg 4F, Akebonocho Tachikawa Shi, Tokyo
FAX:81-3-932-××××

修 改 通 知 书
NOTIFICATION OF AMENDMENT

Date:170519 日期

TO 致: Tokyo Sakura Furniture Co., Ltd. Jingshen 56rd, Kobe, Japan	WHEN CORRESPOND NG PLEASE QUOTE OUT REF NO.	AD94001A40576
ISSUING BANK 开证行 Banque Nationale de Paris	TRANSMITTED TO US THROUGH 转递行 REF NO.	

L/C NO. 信用证号 002/0000095	DATED 开证日期 20170516	AMOUNT 金额 USD	EXPIRY PLACE 有效地 JAPAN
EXPIRY DATE 有效期 20170616	TENOR 期限 SIGHT	CHARGE 未付费用	CHARGE BY 费用承担人 BENEFICIARY
RECEIVED VIA 修改方式 SWIFT	AVAILABLE 修改是否生效 VALID	TEST/SIGN 印押是否相符 YES	CONFIRM 我行是否保兑修改 NO
AMEND NO 修改次数 1	AMEND DATE 修改日期 20170518	INCREASE AMT 增额	DECREASE AMT 减额

DEAR SIRS 敬启者:
WE HAVE PLEASURE IN ADVISING YOU THAT WE HAVE RECEIVED FROM THE A/M BANK A(N) AMENDMENT TO THE CAPTIONED L/C, CONTENTS OF WHICH ARE AS PER ATTACHED SHEET(S).
兹通知贵公司,我行收自上述银行收到修改一份,内容见附件。
THIS AMENDMENT SHOULD BE ATTACHED TO THE CAPTIONED L/C ADVISED BY US, OTNER WISE, THE BENEFICIARY WILL BE RESPONSIBLE FOR ANY CONSEQUENCES ARISING THERFORM.
本修改须附于有关信用证,否则,贵公司须对因此而产生的后果承担责任。

REMARK 备注:

THIS AMENDMENT CONSISTS OF ___ SHEET(S), INCLUDING THE COVERING LETTER AND ATTACHMENT(S).
本修改连同面函及附件共___纸。
KINDLY TAKE NOTE THAT THE PARTIAL ACCEPTANCE OF THE AMENDMENT IS NOT ALLOWED.
本修改不能部分接受。
THIS AMENDMENT IS ADVISED SUBJECT TO LCC UCP PUBLICATION NO. 600.
本修改之通知系遵循国际商会跟单信用证统一惯例第600号出版物办理。

此证如有任何问题及疑虑,请与结算业务部审证科联络,电话: 81-3-932-××××

YOURS FAITHFULL,
FOR 东京三菱银行

图 16-5 信用证修改通知书样本

Commercial Development Bank

Commercial Center Building   Date: 10th August 2020
Kuala Lumpur, Malaysia

To: Samata International Trading Co., Ltd.   **Transmitted through:** Commercial Trust
International Commercial Building   Bank, Jakarta, Indonesia
Jakarta, Indonesia

Irrevocable Letter of Credit
NO. MISC 957-321

We hereby issue in your favor this Irrevocable Documentary Letter of Credit for the amounts not exceeding USD500,000 (say five hundred thousand US Dollars only) available by your draft(s) at sight, drawn in duplicate accompanied by the following documents:

1. Commercial invoice in duplicate;

2. Full set of clean "On Board" ocean Bills of Lading made out to order and indorsed blank marked "Freight Prepaid" and notify accountee;

3. Insurance policy in duplicate covering all risks plus 10% of the invoice value.

Shipment: from Indonesia to Malaysia not later than 10th October, 2020.

Partial shipments are allowed. Tran-shipments are allowed.

Covering shipment of: Materials semiconductors type- Ⅱ X10 in cases.

Special instructions:

1. Documents have to be presented within 15 days after the date of issuance of the bill of lading or other shipping documents.

2. Draft(s) drawn must be inscribed with the number and date of this credit.

3. Draft(s) drawn under this credit must be presented for negotiation in Indonesia on or before 25th October, 2020.

Undertaking clause:

We hereby engage with the drawers, endorsers and bona-fide holders of the draft(s) drawn under and in compliance with the terms of the credit that such draft(s) shall be duly honored on due presentation and delivery of documents as specified if drawn and negotiated within the validity date of this credit.

This credit is subject to Uniform Customs and Practice 600.

Commercial Development Bank
Authorized Signature
_____

图 16-6 不可撤销即期信用证样本

Irrevocable Confirmed Documentary Credit

Korean Export & Importer Bank, Seoul, Korea

To: The Trade Bank, San Francisco, California USA

We hereby issue our irrevocable documentary credit No.12345

Date of issue: June 15, 2020   **Date of expiry:** August 10, 2020

Place of expiry: USA

Applicant: Korean Electronic Importer Seoul, Korea

Beneficiary: American Electronics Exporter San Jose, California USA

Amount: USD15,000.00 Say: Fifteen Thousand US Dollars only

Credit available with: The Trade Bank Drafts payable at sight

Drawee: Korean Export & Importer, Bank, Seoul, Korea

Transshipment: Prohibited   **Partial Shipment:** Allowed

Loading on board San Francisco International Airport, for transportation to Kimpo Airport, Seoul, Korea

Latest date of shipment: July 20, 2020

Description of goods: DRAM chips Model Number MP164Ft12 per proforma invoice dated May 28, 2020

Quantity: 3,000 units

Unit price: USD5.00 per unit

Total amount: USD15,000.00

Price terms: EXW Incoterms® 2020

Country of origin: U. S. A./Singapore /Philippines

Documents required:

1. Signed commercial invoice in triplicate;

2. Airway Bill consigned to Korea Export & Import Bank marked "freight collect" and notify the applicant;

3. Packing list in triplicate.

Additional conditions: Notify party on commercial invoice and Airway Bill must show Korean Electronic Importer, Seoul, Korea.

Air freight should be effected by Emery Airfreight.

Charges: All banking commissions and changes, including reimbursement charges and postage outside Korea are for account of the beneficiary.

Period for Presentation: Documents must be presented within 14 days after the date of shipment.

Confirmation instructions: Confirmed

Reimbursement bank: Korean Export & Importer Bank, Los Angeles, CA USA

Instructions to the paying / accepting /negotiating bank: The amount of each negotiation (draft) must be endorsed on the reverse side of this credit by the negotiation bank.

All documents must be forwarded directly by courier service in one lot to Korean Export & Importer Bank, Seoul, Korea.

If documents are presented with discrepancies, a discrepancy fee of USD40.00 or equivalent should be deducted from the reimbursement claim.

This credit is subject to UCP 600, by International Chamber of Commerce, and engages us in accordance with the terms thereof.

Korean Export & Importer Bank, Seoul, Korea

Signature

图 16-7　不可撤销、保兑信用证样本

16.3 Dialogues

16.3.1 We Only Accept Payment by Irrevocable Letter of Credit Payable Against Shipping Documents

(Mr. Liu insists on payment by L/C, but his customer Mr. White asks him to bend a little.)

White: Well, we've settled the question of price, quality and quantity. Now what about the terms of payment?

Liu: We only accept payment by irrevocable letter of credit payable against shipping documents.

White: I see. Could you make an exception and accept D/A or D/P?

Liu: I'm afraid not. We insist on a letter of credit.

White: To tell you the truth, a letter of credit would increase the cost of my imports. When I open a letter of credit with a bank, I have to pay a deposit. That'll tie up my money and increase my cost.

Liu: Oh sorry. I cannot be of any help in this respect. You'd better consult your bank and see if they will reduce the required deposit to a minimum. Besides, Chinese toys have enjoyed a good reputation in your market and will be selling well. The quick turnover will not only free cost on L/C, but also benefit you a lot.

White: Your words sound okay, but we still feel that to pay by L/C is not reasonable. There are still bank charges in connection with the credit. It would help me greatly if you would accept D/A or D/P. You can draw on me just as if there were a letter of credit. It makes no great difference to you, but it does to me.

Liu: Well, Mr. White, you must be aware that an irrevocable letter of credit gives the exporter the additional protection of the banker's guarantee. Especially for the time being, the world market is quite unsteady. To protect ourselves, we insist on payment by L/C. I hope to have your understanding.

White: To meet you half way, what do you say if 50% by L/C and the balance by D/P?

Liu: I'm very sorry, Mr. White. But I'm afraid I can't promise you even that. As I've said, we require payment by L/C, and we can't accept any other terms of payment.

White: It seems I have no alternative but to accept your terms of payment. Can you deliver the goods before May so that they can catch up with the sales season before the Children's Day?

Mr. Liu: In this case, you'd better open the L/C before 10th of April since we need time to get the goods ready and book the shipping space.

White: OK. I'll have the L/C opened as soon as I get home.

Liu: That'll be fine. The earlier we get your L/C, the sooner shipment can be made.

16.3.2 Do You Think You Could Accept a Time L/C

(Mr. Smith, a businessman from Canada, is talking about the terms of payment with Miss. Chen, who is working at Textiles Import & Export Corporation. Finally, both of them agree the goods are paid by confirmed, irrevocable and time L/C and arrange the details of payment.)

Smith: What mode of payment do you wish to employ?

Chen: Confirmed, irrevocable letter of credit, of course.

Smith: We are old friends, and you should have faith in us. Is the wording of "confirmed" necessary for the letter of credit?

Chen: Yes, It is. This is the normal term of payment in international business, by which payment is assured.

Smith: Is it at sight or after sight?

Chen: It's at sight. So long as the documents are in full conformity with the contract, you are kindly requested to pay for the shipment immediately after your receipt of all the necessary shipping documents.

Smith: Do you think you could accept a time L/C and allow us to delay payment, say 60 days after sight? To tell you frankly, we have some trouble in receiving payment recently.

Chen: As you know, we always demand payment by sight L/C for our exports. And it is quite usual in international trade. But in view of our good relationship and encourage more orders for the future, we could consider your request.

Smith: Thank you. You are of great help.

Chen: Then let's arrange details of payment. Could you send the L/C 30 days before shipment?

Smith: No problem. I'll arrange for the L/C to be opened in your favor as soon as I return. What we are worrying about is that you cannot effect shipment on time. We are in urgent need this time.

Chen: You can rest assure of that. We'll make the necessary preparations and effect shipment in the prescribed time after we get the L/C.

Smith: That's great. By the way, what about the term of validity?

Chen: The L/C should be valid for 15 days after the date of shipment.

Smith: Fine.

Notes

[1] irrevocable letter of credit payable against shipping documents 不可撤销的、凭装运单据付款的信用证付款方式

[2] deposit *n.* 押金，定金

[3] turnover *n.* 周转
[4] in connection with 有关于……，和……有关系的
[5] draw on sb. 向……开出汇票。例：
   You can draw on me.
   你可以向我方开出汇票。
[6] banker *n.* 银行
[7] 50% by L/C and the balance by D/P 50% 采用信用证，剩余部分采用付款交单
[8] at sight 即期，after sight 远期
[9] be conformity with 和……一致
[10] You can rest assure of that 这个你尽管放心
[11] in the prescribed time 在规定时间

Exercises

Exercise 1: Choose the best answer to complete the following sentences

1. Documentary credit seeks _____ from the bank.
   A. guarantee   B. no guarantee   C. no protection   D. insurance
2. It is our usual practice to require sight L/C. We can't make an _____ with this transaction.
   A. example   B. exception   C. experience   D. excellence
3. In compliance _____ your request, we exceptionally accept delivery against D/P at sight.
   A. for   B. with   C. as   D. to
4. Our usual terms of payment are by irrevocable sight L/C, reaching us one month _____ shipment, remaining valid _____ negotiation in China _____ .
   A. before, on, to allow transshipment and partial shipments
   B. after, in, and allow transshipment and partial shipments
   C. before, for, allowing transshipment and partial shipments
   D. after, with, and allow transshipment and partial shipments
5. The letter of credit is to be established through Bank of China, payable _____ draft drawn at 30 days' sight.
   A. with   B. by   C. for   D. to
6. We will draw _____ you payable _____ 60 days' sight _____ USD 42,000 _____ your last shipment.
   A. for, on, for, on   B. on, at, for, with   C. for, for, for, for   D. on, at, for, against
7. Having some difficulties in opening the L/C, our buyers request you to book their orders _____ D/A basis.

A. for B. by C. against D. on

8. The covering L/C must be confirmed by _____.
   A. the bank to accept us
   B. a bank acceptable to us
   C. the bank acceptable for us
   D. a bank acceptable by us

9. We regret _____ unable to consider your request for payment on D/A basis, the reason _____ that we generally accept payment by L/C _____ sight.
   A. being, being, at   B. for, for, at   C. being, for, for   D. for, being, for

10. We are writing to inform you that L/C No. 101 _____ our order No. 555 has been opened _____ the Bank of China.
    A. for, by
    B. covering, with
    C. covering, through
    D. for, through

Exercise 2: Translate the following sentences into Chinese

1. Advanced payment of 25% of the contract value shall be paid within 30 days of the date of signing the contract.
2. The payment shall be made by five annual installments of 20% each.
3. We propose paying by T/T when the shipment is ready.
4. You are requested to extend the validity of the L/C to August 31.
5. For this purchase, we propose to pay in Euros.
6. Please note that easier terms of payment will not only help conclude this transaction, but also bring about lasting satisfaction to both of us.
7. The buyers insist on payment by collection for such a small volume of business.
8. We proposed to pay by 30 days after the date of draft.
9. D/P or D/A is only accepted if the amount involved for each transaction is less than £1,000.
10. For exports, we usually adopt irrevocable letters of credit available by seller's documentary drafts at sight.

Exercise 3: Translate the following sentences into English

1. 以信用证方式支付是世界各国进出口贸易中通常使用的支付方法。
2. 我们希望在付款条件方面你们能通融一些。
3. 我们将开立以你方为受益人的信用证，以美元结算。
4. 我们希望的付款方式是保兑的、不可撤销的信用证。
5. 请务必于下月初开出信用证，准许分批装运和转运。

Exercise 4: Translate the following letter into English in the right format

敬启者，

我方已仔细阅读了你方钻机的规格和价目表，现拟订购该货物，附上我方第243号订单。

因我方急需新货，如蒙落实订单并尽快发运，将不胜感激。

以往我们交易均以即期信用证付款。现建议：当你方货物准备装船及完成订舱时，请以传真方式通知我方，我方即可以电汇方式全额付款。

我方提出此请求，希望能节省开立信用证的费用。相信此安排不会对你方造成太大影响，但能增加我方销量，故希望你方同意我方请求。

希望尽快收到你方回复。

此致　丹麦 ABC 贸易公司

中国电子产品进出口公司
韩卫军　谨上
2020 年 4 月 25 日

（注：丹麦 ABC 贸易公司地址：
　　　121Hook Norton Road
　　　Great Roll right, OX7 5SD
　　　Copenhagen, Denmark
中国电子产品进出口公司地址：
　　　N0. 34, Da Tun Dong Rd. Chaoyang Street
　　　Beijing, P. R. China）

附件：第 243 号订单

Exercise 5: Blank filling for amendments to the L/C

During the course of fulfilling a contract, the sellers, on receiving the relevant L/C, should first of all check the clauses in the L/C whether in full conformity with the terms stated in the contract. If some unforeseen special clauses to which the sellers don't agree are found in the L/C, the sellers should send an advice to the buyers, asking them to make amendments. Now check the following L/C with the given contract, and then complete the following letter asking for amendments to the L/C.

LONDON BANK

Irrevocable Documentary Credit No. LST150

Date and place of issue: 15 September, 2020
Date and place of expiry: 15 December, 2020, London
Applicant: London Imp. Co., Ltd
Beneficiary: South Export Corp., Guangzhou
Advising bank: Bank of China, Guangzhou branch
Amount: GBP 10,000 (SAY STERLING POUND TEN THOUSAND ONLY).
Partial shipments and transshipment are prohibited.

Shipment from China port to London, latest 30 November, 2020

Credit available against presentation of the following documents and of your draft at sight for 90% of the invoice value:

—Signed commercial invoice in quadruplicate.

—Full set of clean on board ocean Bills of Lading made out to order of London Bank marked freight prepaid.

—Insurance certificate of policy endorsed in blank for full invoice value plus 10%, covering All Risks and War Risk.

Covering 5 M/T Fresh Shrimps, first grade, at GBP 2,000 per M/T CIF London Incoterms® 2020 as per Contract No. 245B.

245B 号合同主要条款：

买方：伦敦食品进口有限公司

卖方：广州南方出口公司

5 吨一级冻虾每吨 2,200 英镑 CIF 伦敦 Incoterms® 2020，2020 年 11 月 30 日前自中国港口用直达轮运往伦敦。保险由卖方按发票金额 110% 投保一切险和战争险。凭不可撤销的即期信用证支付。

Dear Sirs,

We are very pleased to receive your L/C No. LST150 opened through London Bank against our S/C No. 245B. After checking it carefully, we regret to find some discrepancies between the L/C and the S/C and would request you to amend the L/C as follows:

(1)
(2)
(3)
(4)
(5)
(6)

We hope you will send us your amendment advice without any delay so as to enable us to effect shipment in time.

Yours faithfully,

Exercise 6: Write a letter in English asking for amendments to the following letter of credit by checking it with the given contract terms

HUA CHIAO COMMERCIAL BANK LTD.

88-89 Des Voeux Road, Central, China Hong Kong

Irrevocable Documentary Credit No. F-07567

Date and place of issue: 2020/03/18 China Hong Kong

Date and place of expiry: 2020/11/30 China Hong Kong
Applicant: J. Brown & Co., 175 Queen's Way, Hong Kong, China
Beneficiary: Liaoning Textiles I/E Corp., Dalian, China
Advising Bank: Bank of China, Liaoning Branch, Dalian, China
Amount: USD26,700. (SAY UNITED STATES DOLLAR TWENTY-SIX THOUSAND SEVEN HUNDRED ONLY).
Partial Shipments and transshipment are prohibited.
Shipment from Dalian, China to Hong Kong, China, latest 2020/11/30
Credit available against presentation of the documents detailed herein and of your draft at 90 days' sight for full invoice value.

— Signed commercial invoice in quadruplicate.

— Full set of clean on board ocean Bills of Lading made out to order of HUA CHIAO COMMERCIAL BANK LTD. Marked freight prepaid.

— Insurance certificate or policy endorsed in blank for full invoice value plus 10%, coving All Risks and War Risk.

- Covering 50 doz. woolen sweaters, S105, @USD 120 per doz.
  CFR China Hong Kong Incoterms® 2020
- 60 doz. woolen sweaters, M107, @USD 150 per doz.
  CFR China Hong Kong Incoterms® 2020
- 70 doz. woolen sweaters, L109, @ USD 180 per doz.
  CFR China Hong Kong Incoterms® 2020

As per Contract No. 28KG063

销售合同主要条款如下：
合同号码：28KG603
卖方：辽宁纺织品进出口公司
买方：J. Brown& Co., 175 Queen's Way, Hong Kong, China
商品名称及数量：羊毛衫　　S105　　50 打
　　　　　　　　　　　　　M107　　60 打
　　　　　　　　　　　　　L109　　70 打
单价：S105　每打成本加运费，中国香港　120 美元
　　　M107　每打成本加运费，中国香港　150 美元
　　　L109　每打成本加运费，中国香港　180 美元
金额：27,600 美元
交货期：2020 年 11 月，不允许分批装运，可转运。
付款条件不可撤销见单后 90 天付款的信用证，效期为装运后 15 天在中国内地到期。

Exercise 7: Write a letter in English asking for amendments to the following letter of credit by checking it with the given contract terms

Copenhagen Bank

Date: 4 January, 2020

To: Bank of China, Beijing

We hereby open our Irrevocable Letter of Credit NO.112235 in favor of China Trading Corporation for account of Copenhagen Import Company up to an amount of GBP1,455,00 (SAY Pounds Sterling One Thousand Four Hundred And Fifty-five Only) for 100% of the invoice value relative to the shipment of:

150 metric tons of Writing Paper Type 501 at GBP97 per m/t CIF Copenhagen as per your S/C No. PO5476 from Copenhagen to China port. Drafts to be drawn at sight on our bank and accompanied by the following documents marked "X":

(X) Commercial Invoice in triplicate

(X) Bill of Lading in triplicate made out to our order quoting L/C No. 112235, marked FREIGHT COLLECT

⋮

(X) One original Marine Insurance Policy or Certificate for All Risks and War Risk, covering 110% of the invoice value, with claims payable in Copenhagen in the currency of draft(s) partial shipments and transshipment are prohibited.

Shipment must be effected not later than 31 March, 2020

This L/C is valid at our counter until 15 April 2020.

附：PO5476 号合同主要条款：

卖方：中国贸易公司

买方：哥本哈根进口公司

商品名称：写字纸

规格：501 型

数量：150,000 千克

单价：CIF 哥本哈根每 1,000 千克 97 英镑

总值：14,550 英镑

装运期：2020 年 3 月 31 日前自中国港口至哥本哈根

保险：由卖方按发票金额的 110% 保一切险和战争险

支付：不可撤销的即期信用证，于装运前 1 个月一到卖方，并于上述装运期后 15 天内在中国议付有效

Exercise 8: Compose a dialogue on the following situation

Mr. John, a businessman from America, has ordered a total of USD 25,000 worth of the sweaters.

Mr. Lin is a salesman from China National Textiles Imp. & Exp. Corp.. Now they have settled everything except the terms of payment. Mr. John suggests D/A or D/P terms. Mr. Lin tries to talk him into accepting payment by L/C, while Mr. John states his difficulties if demanded payment by L/C.

Reading Material

Letter of Credit and Terms of Payment in Sales Contract

I. Documentary Credit

Cash payment in international trade is rarely adopted; instead, non-cash payment is commonly used. Payment by credit transfers the importer's obligation of payment to the bank, which ensures that the exporter can get payment safely and promptly while the importer gets the shipping documents on time.

As we know, a buyer and a seller live far apart, international business is carried out beyond each other's control and mutual trust is hard to establish. The seller is unwilling to ship the goods without receiving payment, while the buyer is reluctant to part with his money without actually controlling the goods. In case the credit worthiness becomes the major bottleneck, the problems of the buyer and the seller are solved by the intervention of a third party—the bank.

A contract often stipulates that payment is made by documentary credit agreed upon by both the buyer and the seller, who both wish for the superior credit standing of a large financial institution to stand between them. A documentary credit often referred to as L/C is, in essence, a letter addressed to the seller, written and signed by a bank, as a written engagement acting on behalf of a customer. If the seller conforms exactly to the specific conditions set forth in the letter of credit, the bank promises that the drafts by the beneficiary, up to a total of the stated amount, will be honored. In most commercial transactions, the conditions will state that the seller is to submit the required documents usually relative to the shipment of specified goods. Only when the documents presented are exactly as specified, will the bank pay.

Documentary credit is the product of international business and the creation of merchants and bankers and they have gone a long way, hand in hand, with the development and settlement of credit and money. Development of world business has always been an immense impetus to the evolution of documentary credits. Technological advance in banking, transportation and telecommunications have made it possible for the worldwide acceptance of credit operations. The objective of documentary credit is to facilitate international payment by making use of the financial expertise and credit reputation of the banks. It differs from other methods of payment in the credit and offers both the buyer and the seller a means of security. This bilateral security is the unique and characteristic feature of the documentary credit.

II. Operation of a Documentary L/C

Now let's see how a documentary letter of credit operates.

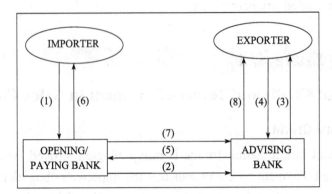

(1) The importer applies to his bank to open an L/C in favor of the exporter for the amount of the purchase.

(2) The importer's bank opens an L/C and sends it to its correspondent bank in the exporter's country, giving instructions about the amount of the credit, the beneficiary, the currency, the documents required and other special instruction. The importer's bank is called the opening bank because it opens the L/C.

(3) The exporter's bank receives the L/C from the opening bank and passes it on to the exporter. This is the advising bank because it advises the exporter and forwards the L/C to him. If this is a confirmed L/C, the exporter's bank has to add its confirmation, becoming the confirming bank.

(4) The exporter completes the shipment and prepares the draft (sight draft) and all shipping documents. He sends them to the advising bank for negotiation of payment, i.e. asking for payment. The advising bank now helps the exporter to make arrangement to get payment.

(5) The draft and shipping documents are now sent by the advising bank to the opening bank for payment.

(6) The opening bank receives the draft and shipping documents and gives them to the importer.

(7) The opening bank which is now called the paying bank remits the money to the advising bank.

(8) The advising bank receives the money and gives it to the exporter.

III. Urging Establishment of L/C

When a transaction is concluded, the importer, as a rule, is under obligation to establish a letter of credit with his bank within the time stipulated in the sales contract. It is the usual practice in export trade that the L/C is to be established and to reach the exporter one month prior to the date of shipment so as to give the exporter ample time to make preparations for shipment, such as making the goods ready and booking shipping space. For prompt shipment, it is advisable that the letter of credit be transmitted by telex or fax immediately after the transaction is concluded.

However, there may be circumstances where the importer fails to establish the letter of credit, or the letter of credit does not reach the exporter in time; then a letter, usually a telex or cable has to be sent to the importer to urge him to expedite the L/C or to ascertain its whereabouts.

Messages urging establishment of letter of credit must be written with tact. Their aim is to persuade the buyer to co-operate more closely and in fact to fulfill his obligations; otherwise they will give defence to the importer and bring about unhappy consequences.

Ⅳ. L/C Amendment and Extension

The exporter, on receiving the relevant L/C, should first of all make a thorough examination to see whether the clauses set forth in the L/C are in full conformity with the terms stated in the sales contract. If some unforeseen special clauses to which the exporter does not agree are found in the L/C, the exporter should send an advice to the importer, asking him to make amendment. Sometimes an unexpected situation with regard to supply, shipping, etc. may arise. In this case, an amendment to the original L/C will also be required.

Not only can the seller ask for amendment to an L/C, the importer can likewise ask for amendment if he finds something in the L/C needs to be altered. The usual procedure is that the importer should first obtain consent from the exporter and then instruct the opening bank to amend the L/C.

Sometimes the exporter may fail to get the goods ready for shipment in time or the importer may request that the shipment be postponed for one reason or another; then the exporter will have to ask for extension of the expiry date as well as the date of shipment of the L/C.

Ⅴ. Terms of Payment in Sales Contract

There are several examples of terms of payment in sales contract as follows:

1. Within 15 days from the date of this Agreement, the Buyer shall establish an irrevocable L/C with a first-rate bank in compliance with the terms and conditions set forth in this contract.

2. All the payments shall be made in US currency by the Buyer to the Seller by T/T to the Seller's designated accounts with the bank in United States.

3. The Buyer, on receipt from the Seller of the shipping advice, shall open an irrevocable letter of credit with the Bank of China, in favor of the Seller for the total value of shipment 25-30 days prior to the date of delivery. The L/C shall be available

against the Seller's draft drawn at sight on the issuing bank for 100% invoice value accompanied by the shipping documents specified in payment clause mentioned in sales contract. The L/C shall be valid until the 20 day after the shipment is effected.

4. The Seller may present the sight draft together with the shipping documents through the Seller's Bank to the Buyer for collection after shipment. Since D/P (Documents against Payment) is agreed on, the collecting bank will deliver the documents against receipt of payment.

5. The Buyer shall open a 100% confirmed, irrevocable and negotiable letter of credit in favor of the seller within 5 calendar days from the date of the agreement through the issuing bank. The letter of credit shall be drawn against draft at sight upon presentation of the following documents:

   a. Full set of the Seller's commercial invoice.
   b. Full set of clean, blank, endorsed bill of lading.
   c. Inspection certificate of quality and quantity.

6. The Buyer shall send a confirmed, irrevocable, and transferable letter of credit to be drawn by sight draft to the Seller before Nov.20, 2007. The letter of credit remains valid until 15 days after the above mentioned delivery and will expire on Dec. 30th, 2007. Meanwhile, a deposit of 10% of the total price should be paid by the Buyer immediately after signing the contract.

7. The Buyer shall open through a bank acceptable to the Seller an irrevocable sight L/C to reach the Seller 45 days before the date of delivery, valid for negotiation in China until the 15 day after the latest shipment date.

8. The payment is made by D/P after 60 days' sight. The Buyer shall duly accept the documentary draft drawn by the Seller at 60 days' sight upon first presentation and make payment on its maturity. The shipping documents are to be delivered against payment only.

Questions

1. By the payment of L/C, who will be responsible for the payment?
2. What is an L/C?
3. Under what conditions, the bank will effect payment?
4. Where is an L/C different from other methods of payment?
5. Describe the operation of a documentary L/C.
6. In export trade, when should the L/C reach the seller? If it is demanded for prompt shipment, what should the buyer do so as to make sure the L/C reach the seller in time?
7. If the letter of credit does not reach the seller in time, what should the seller do? Keep waiting?
8. Under what conditions, the L/C should be amended?

Chapter 17

Complaints, Claims, and Settlement

17.1 Pre-knowledge

During the execution of the contract, both parties should strictly perform the contract. If either party fails to do it, it will cause problems and sometimes economic losses for the other party. In this case, the party suffering the loss has the right to claim damages or take other remedial actions against the other party under the claim terms of the contract.

If a customer is not satisfied the execution of the order, he will complain. In doing so he should refer clearly to the items in question, by referring to the order or sales contract or confirmation number. He should then specify the nature of his complaint, and finally state what action he wants his supplier to take.

Replies to complaints should always be courteous: even if the sellers think that the complaint unfounded, they should not say so until they have good and reliable grounds on which to repudiate the claim. All complaints should be treated as serious matters and thoroughly investigated.

On receiving the complaint and claims, the sellers will make investigations, and if the complaint is justified, they will at once apologize to the buyers and suggest a solution. The compensation usually include: (1) claim for damages; (2) request for replacement; (3) request a reduction or discount; (4) request refund of payment and compensation for losses.

It is normal for one party to make a complaint or claim against the other in international trade. Although the parties to a sales contract are the seller and the buyer, the claim-settlement procedures may include other parties such as shipping companies (carrier) and insurance companies.

The seller is held responsible for the following:
(1) Non-fulfilment of a contract
(2) Discrepancies in specification
(3) Inferior, defective quality or damaged goods
(4) not in conformity with the sample
(5) Wrong quantity
(6) Improper packing
(7) Non-delivery or part-delivery
(8) Delay in delivery/shipment of goods

The buyer is held responsible for the following:
(1) Delay in payment
(2) Refuse to open an L/C
(3) Delay in opening L/C
(4) Not in conformity with the invoice value

The carrier is held responsible for the following:
(1) Short-landed
(2) Goods missing
(3) Rough handling

The insurer is held responsible for the following:
(1) Goods suffering losses or damages in transit because of the risks insured against.
(2) Other reasons stipulated in the policy according to which, the insured is entitled to ask for compensation.

17.2　Correspondence Writing Guide and Specimen Letters

The claim from the buyer is usually about the quality, quantity, date of delivery or packing. The seller may make a claim against the buyer for the problems involved in payment. All claims should be treated as serious matters and thoroughly investigated. A letter of complaint or claim, whether made by the buyer or by the seller, should be written calmly and tactfully in order to get a satisfactory settlement. Claims letters always express the regret about the loss with the clear and complete evidence. Give your proposals and hope for an early reply and settlement. Settlement letters always make clear explanation or promise to take actions. Both claim and settlement letters should express to maintain a good business relationship.

1. When making a claim, refer to the following points

(1) Beginning with the statement of the problems, make clear what your claim is and give the facts. The most important rule is to avoid rudeness or sarcasm.

(2) Mention the order or sales contract/confirmation number, date of delivery, and the goods complained or claimed about.

(3) State your reasons for being dissatisfied and ask for an explanation.

(4) Refer to the inconvenience or losses caused. State possible action or suggest a solution.

2. When dealing with a complaint or claim, the following is the guide to arranging your letter

(1) The reply to complaint or claim should be written calmly, politely, tactfully and timely. Express the regret for the losses.

(2) After receiving the complaint, you should investigate the case. Briefly explain the reason fully, honestly and reassuringly any favorable facts.

(3) Suggest the solution or rejecting the request.

(4) End your letter with assurance and desire for future development.

17.2.1 Claim for Inferior Quality

June 20, 2020

Dear Sirs,

Re: Shipment of Table Lamps under Sales Confirmation No. SC2020-102

The above shipment of Item No. A001 and A003 under SC2020-102 have arrived at New York on June 20, 2020.

Much to our regret, we are sorry to inform you that the quality of these polyresin table lamps is not in accordance with the standard we expected. We enclose one copy of inspection certificate No.620 from a local surveyor. The certificate proves that the above-mentioned goods are inferior in quality. Such goods are quite unsuited to sell in market. Under such circumstances, we would like you to refund the money we have paid for this shipment.

We are looking forward to your settlement at an early date.

Yours sincerely,

17.2.2　Claim for Damaged Goods

June 20, 2020

Dear Sirs,

　　Re: Shipment of Table Lamps under Sales Confirmation No. SC2020-102

　　We received the goods shipped by S.S. Victory covering 400 cartons A001 and A003 each.

　　Unfortunately, it was found upon examination that 10 cartons of A003 are broken which we could not sell to our customers. The survey report showed that it was due to improper packing. We presumed that the damage was made because the inner foams and outer cartons are not strong enough.

　　We require you to send us replacement for the damaged 10 cartons at once. The package should be reinforced for future deliveries.

　　Your early settlement will be highly appreciated.

Sincerely yours,

17.2.3　Claim for Wrong Goods

June 20, 2020

Dear Sirs,

　　Re: Table Lamps under Sales Confirmation No. SC2020-102

　　We have taken the delivery of the captioned goods which arrived on S.S. Victory on June 20, 2020.

　　Unfortunately, when we open the carton No.401, 402, 403, 404 we found they contained polyresin candleholders which were not what we had ordered. We presume that a mistake was made in assembling the order. As we are in urgent need of these items to complete deliveries to our customers, we have to lodge a claim against you to make immediate arrangement to dispatch the correct items at once.

　　Meanwhile, we are holding the mentioned 4 cartons at your disposal, please let us know what you wish to do with them.

Yours faithfully,

17.2.4 Complaining about Short Delivery

> June 20, 2020
>
> Dear Sirs,
>
> <u>Re: Table Lamps under Sales Confirmation No. SC2020-102</u>
>
> I am writing to inform you that the captioned consignment arrived today.
>
> The quantity of A001 we ordered is 2,400PCS (400 cartons), but the consignment arrived here contained only 350 cartons of A001 which is 50 cartons short. This error put us in a difficult position, as we had to make some emergency purchases to fulfill our commitments to all our customers.
>
> This caused us considerable inconvenience. Please make up the shortfall immediately and to ensure that such errors do not happen again. Otherwise, we may have to look elsewhere for our supplies.
>
> Yours sincerely,

17.2.5 Accepting a Claim

> June 21, 2020
>
> Dear Sirs,
>
> <u>Re: A Reply to the Claim on Damage Packages</u>
>
> We are sorry to learn from your letter of June 20, 2020, informing us that 10 cartons of A003 were broken due to improper packing.
>
> Upon receipt of your letter, we have given this matter our immediate attention and investigation. We found that the present damage was indeed made in imperfectness packing.
>
> We have arranged for 10 cartons of A003 with reinforced package (with full foam inside and 5 layers corrugated carton outside) to be dispatched to you within 3 days. The relative documents will be mailed to you as soon as they are ready.
>
> We apologize for the trouble and inconvenience caused to you.
>
> Yours sincerely,

17.2.6 Declining a Claim

June 22, 2020

Dear Sirs,

<u>Re: A Reply to the Claim on Inferior Quality</u>

Thank you for your letter of June 20, 2020, with inspection certificate, claiming for inferior quality on the consignment of table lamps shipped per s. s. "Victory".

We immediately looked into the matter and we are convinced that the quality of our goods did tally with contract. We, on our part, really cannot account for the reason of your claim. We entrusted the SHENZHEN CUSTOMS of the People's Republic of China to inspect the quality of A001 and A003 in our warehouse which is among the same lot as the order dispatched to you. Inspection certificates issued by SHENZHEN CUSTOMS prove our goods are completely up to the said quality.

For this reason, we regret that we can't accept your request for refunding the money.

Sincerely yours,

Notes

[1] inferior, defective quality or damaged goods 货物质量低劣、有缺陷或损坏
[2] improper packing 包装不当
[3] imperfectness packing 包装不当，包装缺陷
[4] rough handling 野蛮装卸
[5] inferior quality 质量低劣
[6] inspection certificate 检验证书
[7] refund the money 退款
[8] settlement 解决
[9] foam 泡沫
[10] full foam 全泡沫 / 保丽龙
[11] 5 layers corrugated carton 5 层瓦楞纸箱
[12] candleholders 烛台
[13] lodge a claim against sb. 向某人提出索赔
[14] considerable inconvenience 极大的不便
[15] tally with contract 符合合同规定

[16] account for the reason 说明原因
[17] SHENZHEN CUSTOMS 深圳海关

17.3 Dialogues

17.3.1 10 Cartons of the Lamps' Shades are Water-stained

(Andy, Phoebe and Mr. Zhang are discussing the settlement of claim for water-stained shades.)

Andy: Hi, Mr. Zhang, the table lamps arrived yesterday. Here's a survey report issued by a well-known public surveyor here.

Phoebe: (reading) 50 cartons of the lamps' shades are water-stained. Oh, no. How can that be?

Andy: That's the question I want to ask.

Phoebe: You know the goods were inspected by SHENZHEN CUSTOMS before shipment. They were carefully packed and shipped in excellent condition.

Andy: Yes, we have got the clean B/L and survey report issued by SHENZHEN CUSTOMS.

Phoebe: They may be stained by rain or sea water during transit.

Andy: We don't know yet. We'll present a claim to the underwriters through your company as the consignment was insured at you end covered against the risk of FPA (free from particular average) and fresh water and rain damage.

Phoebe: OK. I will get in touch with PICC.

(Mr. Zhang from PICC, SHENZHEN BRANCH, comes to settle the claim.)

Mr. Zhang: I am Mr. Zhang of the People's Insurance Company of China. I come to settle the claim.

Phoebe: Thank you for coming Mr. Zhang, this is our survey report, which shows the stain is caused by fresh water. The log book shows there was a storm during transit. Probably, the rain came into cartons during the storm.

Mr. Zhang: If that's the case, we're prepared to meet your claim for the loss. But first we'll carry out a thorough investigation to verify that it is within the scope of coverage.

Phoebe: That's understood.

Mr. Zhang: After the settlement we will immediately seek recourse from the ship owners. We hope you will give us necessary documentary support at that time.

Phoebe: No problem.

17.3.2 Breakage of Packing

(*Andy and Phoebe are discussing the settlement of broken packages.*)

Andy: Phoebe, we would like to have you help fix the trouble concerning the breakage of the packing.

Phoebe: Yes, of course. Could you be more specific?

Andy: I'm just coming to that. When the goods arrived in June 20th this year, it was found that 10 packages were broken, the glass font of A003 were broken.

Phoebe: Just a minute. How many pieces were broken?

Andy: 60 PCS A003 were broken.

Phoebe: Have you found the cause of the breakage?

Andy: Apparently it was due to improper packing.

Phoebe: Our company has always attached great importance to the packing and never before has such a thing occurred.

Andy: I'm unwilling to lodge a claim, but the damage was unbearable.

Phoebe: I suppose this breakage took place the route.

Andy: I'm sorry to say that it was not the route. We had it examined by authoritative cargo handling experts and they said it was obviously damaged prior to it being loaded onto the ship.

Phoebe: I'm sorry that such incident took place. If your claim is well grounded, we'll certainly settle it according to the contract. We will arrange for 10 cartons of A003 with reinforced package to be dispatched to you within 3 days.

Andy: I'm very glad to hear you say so. Is a letter of confirmation needed?

Phoebe: Yes, send it to us as early as you can.

Andy: OK, we'll do that.

Notes

[1] shades 灯罩
[2] underwriters 保险商（尤指船只）
[3] fresh water and rain damage 淡水雨淋险
[4] specific 明确的，具体的，详细的
[5] glass font 对话中特指台灯的玻璃"肚"

Exercises

Exercise 1: Choose the best answer to complete the following sentences

1. You can lodge a claim with the insurance company who will _____ the loss

insured.

   A. compensate
   B. compensate for
   C. compensate to you
   D. compensate you

2. As arranged, we have effected insurance _____ the goods _____ 110% of the invoice value _____ FPA.

   A. of, at, with
   B. for, in, against
   C. on, for, against
   D. to, at, over

3. We _____ improper package of this kind of fragile items resulted in the breakage.

   A. presume
   B. resume
   C. preserve
   D. propose

4. We have just received the survey report from Beijing Customs _____ the broken cartons being due to rough handling.

   A. evidence
   B. evidenced
   C. evidencing
   D. to evidence

5. We have already _____ a claim against the insurance company for EUR300 for damage in transit.

   A. raised
   B. arisen
   C. risen
   D. praised

6. The goods under Contract No.102 arrived at the destination _____ .

   A. in a good condition
   B. in good conditions
   C. in good condition
   D. in the good condition

7. The buyers shall lodge any claim on this consignment _____ the sellers for _____ 30 days _____ arrival of the goods.

   A. on, for, on
   B. on, for, upon
   C. against, for, after
   D. against, within, after

8. The survey report has revealed the fact that the damage is _____ to improper packing.

   A. contributable
   B. attributive
   C. attribution
   D. attributable

9. We suggest that this article _____ packed _____ color boxes of 6 pieces each, 10 color boxes _____ a brown carton.

   A. is, with, in
   B. is, in, in
   C. be, with, in
   D. be, in, to

10. Please return the wrongly delivered goods to us for _____ .

    A. replacement
    B. replace
    C. correction
    D. service

Exercise 2: Translate the following sentences into Chinese

1. We are regret to inform you that quality of the shipment for Order No.123 has been found not in conformity with the agreed specification.
2. After checking up the sample of the delivery, we agreed to compensate you for the loss caused by improper packing.
3. As the shipping company is liable for the damage, your claim should be referred to them for settlement.
4. They received a claim from their customer for smartphones.

5. Please send back to us the damaged and defective at our expense.
6. We hereby lodge a claim against you for Euro1,000 for the damage to our ordered goods.
7. It is quite clear that you should be held responsible for the damage to the goods as a result of rough handling at the port of destination.
8. We can assure you that such a thing will not happen again in future deliveries.
9. To make up for your loss, we agree to allow you a reduction of 10% off the invoice value, which we hope will compensate you for your loss to some extent.
10. On examination we found that the goods do not agree with the original samples.

Exercise 3: Translate the following sentences into English

1. 国际贸易中经常发生索赔现象。
2. 我们现在向贵司提出索赔。
3. 买方对货物提出索赔10,000美元。
4. 你方索赔须有充分的证据。
5. 由于货物在运输途中受损,我们已经向保险商提出索赔2,000欧元。

Exercise 4: Write a letter with the information given below

Suppose you ordered 1,000 cartons of green tea from FUJIAN International Trading company at the Canton Fair. When the cargo arrived at the port of destination (Los Angeles) on May 10th, you found 50 cartons were moldy and in there were even small bugs crawling. Suppose you are the buyer, write a letter to claim for compensation for USD5,000.

Reading Material

RAPEX 2018 Annual Report—2,257 Dangerous Products Alerts and 4,050 Follow-up Actions

The European Commission's RAPEX 2018 Annual Report shows a stabilization in the number of dangerous product reports and follow-up actions for national authorities.

The European Commission (EC) has released its RAPEX 2018 Annual Report. The EC's RAPEX 2018 Annual Report notes stabilization in the number of notifications and member state follow-up actions. However, market surveillance authorities need to improve monitoring for products sold online.

Key Messages

1. The stabilization of the European information exchange system on dangerous products is confirmed with just over 2,000 alerts and 4,000 follow-up actions last year.

2. The report again highlights the need for national authorities to improve

surveillance of online offers.

16% of notifications are related to products sold on the internet; national authorities should further develop tools and specialize in the monitoring of products sold online.

To support unsafe product detection online, a Product Safety Pledge has been signed by the four major online market places (Alibaba, eBay, Amazon, and Rakuten France) allowing national authorities to contact them directly and ask them to remove products identified as unsafe from their platforms.

3. The RAPEX website has been updated to make it useful to users, consumers, companies and national authorities. Amongst other updates, the RAPEX website has been renamed "Safety Gate" and is now available in 25 European languages.

4. A cooperation agreement on the exchange of information on unsafe products has been signed with Canada.

Results

In 2018, 2,257 alerts were sent through the Rapid Alert System with 4,050 follow-up actions.

Toys represent the largest group of products reported to RAPEX, followed by "motor vehicles", and "clothing, textiles and fashion items".

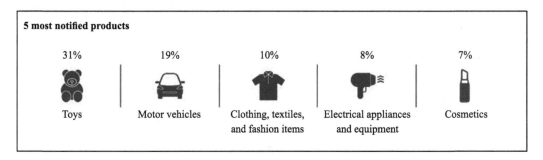

Regarding the risks, the main risk notified in 2018 is "chemical", ahead of "injuries" and "choking".

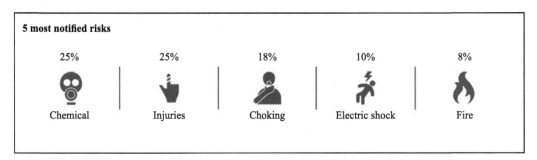

In 2018, a new type of toy, named squeezable or squishy toy, has been notified several times in the RAPEX.

The reported risks for these squishy toys relate to small parts (choking risks) and dangerous chemical substances such as N,N-dimethylformamide, N,N-dimethylaminoethanol, cyclohexanone and triethylenediamine, which pose a risk to the eyes, or cause mucous membrane irritation and liver damage. There are no harmonized standards to check these chemical substances, but the requirements for the assessment of dangerous chemical substances is mentioned in the Toy Safety Directive 2009/48/EC.

In a drive to ensure maximum circulation, to increase awareness of product recalls and to promote product safety among clients, SGS will soon launch a Product Recalls on-line, searchable, database of all unsafe product notifications compiled by official authorities operating in the European Union (RAPEX and RASFF) and United States (CPSC and FDA). Additionally, SGS Product Recall Trends (www.sgs.com/en/publications/product-recall-trends) provides a quarterly overview of the top recalled product categories and products, and the main associated risks, in EU and USA.

Products Recalls and Product Recall Trends are distributed in the Safe Guards emailing.

(Adapted from: 2018 results of the Rapid Alert System; the Directorate-General for Justice and Consumers; https://www.sgs.com/en/news/2019/06/safeguards-08719-rapex-2018-annual-report-2257-dangerous-products-alerts-and-4050-follow-up-actions)

Chapter 18

Conclusion of Business

18.1 Pre-knowledge

Going through inquiry and quotation and many a round of offer and counter-offers, both parties come to an agreement. Maybe the buyer places an order to the seller, or the seller sends a sales confirmation to the buyer. The business is concluded.

18.1.1 Acceptance

If the offeree is interested in the offer or accept the offer, he may send out an acceptance. An acceptance is the assent to the terms of an offer. In accordance with the usual practice in international trade, an acceptance should confirm the following conditions: (1) the acceptance should be given by the offeree; (2) the acceptance should accept all of the contents of the previous offer unconditionally (otherwise it is not an acceptance but a counter-offer); (3) the acceptance should be given within the validity of the previous firm offer; (4) the acceptance should be given in the form of expression or some kinds of action which should reach the offerer.

18.1.2 Order

An order is a written notification of purchase from the buyer to the seller, demanding the seller to supply the goods and services in accordance with the order. It is not legally binding upon either party until the seller has confirmed it. Nowadays, many companies prefer official printed order forms, which save time and ensure that no information may be ignored.

18.1.3 Confirmation

Confirmation is a contract in simple form. It has Sales Confirmation(S/C) form and Purchase Confirmation form. Usually it just gives out the important terms concisely. This kind of contract is widely used in the business of small amount and with lots of shipment. And it can also be used for the business under the form of agency and exclusive sales agreement. Confirmation has the legal effectiveness as contract does. So it has the binding force to the both parties legally.

18.2 Correspondence Writing Guide and Specimen Letters

The essential qualities of an order are accuracy and clarity. An order or order letter should:
(1) include full details of description, quantities, prices, etc.;
(2) state mode of packing, port of destination and time of shipment;
(3) confirm the terms of payment as agreed upon in preliminary negotiations.
Confirmation of the first order should include:
(1) express pleasure in receiving the order;
(2) add a favorable comment on the goods ordered;
(3) include an assurance of prompt and careful attention;
(4) draw attention to other products likely to be of interest;
(5) hope for further orders.

18.2.1　Placing an Order

March 20, 2020

Dear Sirs,

　　We acknowledge with thanks the receipt of your letter dated March 5 in which you enclosed your price list and catalogue. We find both your prices and qualities are satisfactory. We are pleased to place a trial order with you. Enclosed please find our Order No. 123.

　　We would like to stress that is a trial order. Please note that the quality of your delivery should be in accordance with that of the samples. We expect to find a good market for the goods and hope to place further orders with you in the near future.

　　Please send us your Sales Confirmation in duplicate.

Yours sincerely,
Andy Estes

Encl. Order No. 123

18.2.2　Acceptance of Order

March 22, 2020

Dear Sirs,

Re: Your Order No. 7325

　　We are pleased to confirm the above order from you and are sending you our Sales Confirmation No. SC2020-102 in duplicate. Please countersign and return one copy to us for our file.

　　It is understood that a letter of credit in our favor covering the above-mentioned goods will be established immediately. The stipulations in the relevant credit should strictly conform to the terms stated in our Sales Confirmation in order to avoid subsequent amendments. We shall effect shipment without delay upon receipt of your credit.

　　We appreciate your cooperation and look forward to receiving your further order.

Yours sincerely,

Encl.: Sales Confirmation No. SC2020-102

18.2.3 Counter-signature

March 22, 2020

Dear Sirs,

We have received your Sales Confirmation No. SC2020-102. Enclosed please find the duplicate with our counter-signature.

The relative L/C in your favor has been established with the Citibank, New York branch. We trust it will reach you in due course.

Please see to it that the shipment is effected within the contracted time. Thanks for your cooperation in advance.

Yours sincerely,

18.2.4 Contract

March 22, 2020

Dear Sirs,

We hereby confirm having sold to you the under-mentioned goods, subject to the terms stated below:

Quantity: 2,400 pcs A001 POLY TABLE LAMP
           2,400 pcs A003 POLY TABLE LAMP

Price: A001: USD8.00/PCS FOB Shenzhen Incoterms® 2020
       A003: USD10.00/PCS FOB Shenzhen Incoterms® 2020

Packing: 1pk/color box, 6box/ctn

Port of shipment: Shenzhen

Time of shipment: In May 2020, transshipment not allowed.

Payment: By confirmed, irrevocable L/C payable at sight to be opened 30 days before the time of shipment.

Insurance: to be covered by the buyer for 110% of invoice value against F.P.A. as per and subject to OCEAN MARINE CARGO CLAUSES (2009) OF PICC.

Remarks: Kindly sign and return one copy each of the original and duplicate hereof as evidence of your acceptance.

Notes

[1] order *n.* 订单

　　first order 首笔订单，第一笔订单

　　trial order 试订单

　　fresh/new order 新订单

　　duplicate order 重复订单（与上一订单数量等条款相同）

　　repeat order 续订单（与上一订单商品相同，但有些条款不同）

　　与 order 相关的常用动词有：

　　to accept/entertain an order 接受订单

　　to decline/refuse an order 拒绝订单

　　to fulfill/perform/carry out an order 执行订单

　　to complete/finish an order 完成订单

　　place an order with sb. for sth. 向某人订购某物

[2] in accordance with 与……一致，依照

[3] countersign *v.* 会签，附署（指在一个文件需要两个人签字的情况下，一个人签署后，须由另一个人签署）

[4] for our file 以便我方存档

[5] in our favor 以我方为受益人

[6] relevant *adj.* 有关的

[7] conform to 符合，遵照

[8] see to it that = make certain of something 注意，确保

[9] contracted time 合同规定的时间

[10] hereby [公文、布告等用语] 特此，因此，兹，例：

　　We hereby confirm having sold to you the under-mentioned goods.

　　兹确认向你方出售下列货物。

[11] original *n.* 正本 duplicate 副本

[12] hereof = of this 在本文件中，本文的

[13] FPA 平安险，全称是 free from particular average

Dongguan Lighting Import & Export Corporation

No.15 Xinji Ave., South Area, Dongguan, Guangdong, China
Tel: +86-769-83456789 Fax: +86-769-83456788

销 售 确 认 书
SALES CONFIRMATION

合同号
Contract No. SC2020-102
Your Reference order No. 123
日期
Date: March 22, 2020

The Seller:

DONGGUAN LIGHTING IMPORT & EXPORT CORPORATION
No.15 XINJI AVE., SOUTH AREA, DONGGUAN, GUANGDONG, CHINA
Tel: +86-769-**83456789**
Fax: +86-769-**83456788**

The Buyer:

WALDEMAR INDUSTRIES INC.
1234S. MICHIGAN AVE., CHICAGO, IL60616, U.S.A.
TEL: +1-312-427-5678
FAX: +1-312-427-5679

下列要求双方同意按以下条款达成交易:
The undersigned Seller and Buyer have agreed to close the following transactions according to the terms and conditions stipulated below:

1. 货号 Art No. or Item No.	2. 品名及规格 Name of Commodity & Specification	3. 数量 Quantity	4. 单价 Unit Price FOB Shenzhen	5. 金额 Total Amount
A001	13 inches polyresin table lamp with round bell shade	2,400PCS	@USD8.00/PC	USD19,200
A003	16 inches polyresin table lamp with crackle glass font, with round bell shade	2,400PCS	@USD10.00/PC	USD24,000
	总计 TOTAL	4,800PCS		USD43,200

总计
TOTAL : SAY U.S. DOLLARS FORTY-THREE THOUSAND TWO HUNDRED ONLY.

6. 包装
   Packing: 1pk/color box, 6box/ctn
7. 唛头
   Shipping Marks: To be designated by the Sellers.
8. 保险
   Insurance: To be covered by the Buyers for the full invoice value plus 10% against F.P.A. as per and subject to OCEAN MARINE CARGO CLAUSES (2009) OF PICC.
9. 装船港口
   Port of shipment: SHENZHEN
10. 目的港口
    Port of Destination: NEW YORK
11. 装船期限
    Time of Shipment: In May 2020, transshipment not allowed.
12. 付款条件
    Terms of Payment: By confirmed, irrevocable L/C payable at sight to be opened 30 days before the time of shipment.

The Seller:
Dongguan Lighting Import & Export Corporation

Date: March 22, 2020

The Buyer:
WALDEMAR INDUSTRIES INC.

Date: March 22, 2020

图 18-1 销售确认书样本

售货合同
SALES CONTRACT

合同编号：
No：
签订时间：
Date：
合同页号：
Page：

卖方：
THE SELLERS：
地址 Address：
传真 Fax：
电子信箱 E-mail：

买方：
THE BUYERS：
地址 Address：
传真 Fax：
电子信箱 E-mail：

The Sellers agree to sell and the Buyers agree to buy the undermentioned goods according to the terms and conditions as stipulated below：

1. 商品名称及规格 Name of Commodity & Specifications	数量 Quantity	单价 Unit Price	总值 Total Value
总计 Total			

2. 包装
   Packing

3. 唛头
   Shipping Marks：To be designated by the Sellers/Buyers.

4. 保险
   Insurance：To be covered by the Buyers/Sellers for the full invoice value plus 10% against _____.
   Should the Buyers desire to cover for any other extra risks besides aforementioned or amount exceeding the aforementioned limit, the Sellers' approval must be obtained beforehand and all the additional premiums thus incurred shall be for the Buyers' account.

5. 装船港口：
   Port of shipment：

6. 目的港：
   Port of Destination：

7. 装船期限和分批：
   Time and Lots of Shipment：

8. 付款条件：
   Terms of Payment：

9. 检验：
   Inspection：The Inspection Certificate of Quality issued by _____ shall be taken as the basis for the shipping quality.

10. 不可抗力：由于人力不可抗拒事故，使卖方不能在合同期限内交货或者不能交货，卖方不负责任。但是卖方应立即以电报、电传或传真通知买方，如果买方提出要求，卖方应以挂号函向买方提供由中国国际经济贸易促进委员会或有关机关所出具的证明，证明上述事故的存在。
    Force Majeure：The Sellers shall not be held responsible if they, owing to Force Majeure, fail to make delivery within the time stipulated in this Contract or even cannot deliver the goods. However in such a case, the Sellers shall inform the Buyers immediately by cable, telex or fax. The Sellers shall send to the Buyers by registered letter, at the request of the Buyers, a certificate attesting the existence of such a cause or causes issued by the China International Economic and Trade Arbitration Commission or by a competent Authority.

11. 异议索赔：如果卖方不能在合同规定期限内把整批或分批的货物装上船，除非人力不可抗拒原因或者取得买方同意而重新修改合同规定外，买方有权在合同到期后撤销未履行部分的合同，如果货到目的口岸买方对品质有异议，可以凭卖方认可的检验机构出具的检验报告，在货到口岸 30 日内向卖方提出，卖方将根据实际情况考虑理赔或不理赔，一切损失凡由于自然原因或属于船方或保险公司责任范围内者，卖方概不受理。
    如果买方不能在合同规定期限内将信用证开到或开来的信用证不符合合同规定而在接到卖方通知后不能按期办妥修正，卖方可以撤销合同或延期交货，并有权提出赔偿要求。
    Discrepancy and Claim: In case the Sellers fail to ship the whole lot or part of the goods within the time stipulated in this Contract, the Buyers shall have the right to cancel the part of the Contract which has not been performed after the expiration date stipulated in the Contract unless there exists a Force Majeure cause or the contract stipulation has been modified with the Buyers' consent. In case the Buyers have objection on the quality of the goods after arrival of the goods at the port of destination, claim may be lodged against the Sellers within 30 days after arrival of the goods at the port of destination being supported by Inspection Certificate issued by surveyor recognized by the Sellers. The Sellers shall then consider the claim in the light of the actual circumstances. For the loss or losses due to natural causes, or causes falling within the responsibilities of the Ship Owners or the Underwriters, the Sellers shall not consider any claim for compensation.
    In case the Letter of Credit does not reach the Sellers within the time stipulated in the Contract, or the Letter of Credit opened by the Buyers does not tally with the Contract terms and the Buyers fail to amend thereafter its terms within the time limit after receipt of notification by the Sellers, the Sellers shall have the right to cancel the Contract or to put off the shipment of the goods and shall have also the right to lodge claims for compensation.

12. 仲裁：一切因执行本合同所发生或与本合同有关之争执，由双方通过友好方式协商解决，如协商不能解决时，应提交中国国际经济贸易仲裁委员会，按照仲裁委员会所制定之条例仲裁，此仲裁会设于中国北京。由仲裁会所做出之决定为双方处理争执之最后依据，双方均应接受。仲裁费用除另有决定外，应由败诉一方负担。
    Arbitration: All disputes in connection with this Contract or the execution thereof shall be settled amicably by negotiation. In case no settlement can be reached, the case under dispute may then be submitted to the China International Economic and Trade Arbitration Commission for arbitration. The arbitration shall take place in Beijing, China and shall be executed in accordance with the rules of the said Commission and the decision made by the Commission shall be accepted as final and binding upon both parties for settling the disputes. The fees for arbitration shall be borne by the losing party unless otherwise awarded.

13. 法律适用：本合同之签订地或发生争议时货物所在地在中华人民共和国境内或被诉人为中国法人的，适用中华人民共和国法律，除此规定外，适用《联合国国际货物销售公约》。本合同使用的 FOB、CFR、CIF、DDP 术语根据国际商会《ICOTERMS 2020》。
    Law application : It will be governed by the law of the People's republic of China under the circumstances that the contract is signed or the goods while the disputes arising are in the People's Republic of China or the defendant is Chinese legal person, otherwise it is governed by United Nations Convention on Contract for the International Sale of Goods. The terms in the contract are based on INCOTERMS 2020 of the International Chamber of Commerce.

14. 文字：本合同中、英文两种文字具有同等法律效力，在文字解释上，若有异议，以中方解释为准。
    Versions: This contract is made out in both Chinese and English of which version is equally effective. Conflicts between these two languages arising therefrom, if any, shall be subject to Chinese version.

15. 附加条款（本合同上述条款与本附加条款有抵触时，以本附加条款为准）。
    Addition Clauses (conflicts between contract clause hereabove and this additional clause, if any, it is subject to this additional clause).

16. 本合同共____份，自双方代表签字（盖章）之日起生效。
    This condition is in ____ copies, effective since being signed/sealed by both parties.

卖方代表人：
Representative of the sellers：
签字：
Authorized signature：

买方代表人：
Representative of the buyers：
签字：
Authorized signature：

图 18-2　销售合同样本

18.3 Dialogues

18.3.1 We'd Like to Place a New Order with You Immediately

(*Mr. Mason, an import manager from a European company, bought some tool kits from Hope Tool Enterprise, and he is very satisfied with the products. Now he is placing repeat order with Ms. Liu, the salesman of Hope Tool Enterprise.*)

Mason: How are you doing, Ms. Liu?

Liu: Fine, thank you. And you?

Mason: I'm fine, too. Thanks. I'm very happy to inform you that your products are selling very well in our market. We'd like to place a new order with you immediately.

Liu: I'm glad to hear that. We'll do our best to meet your requirements.

Mason: To meet the heavy demand, our order will be much bigger than the last one. Please give us your best offer for 5,000 sets.

Liu: That will be USD 3.50 per set FOB China port Incoterms® 2020.

Mason: It is almost the same price as we had last time.

Liu: You are right. However, actually it is much cheaper than last time.

Mason: Why did you say so?

Liu: The situation has been changed a lot since your last order. As you may know, US dollar has been devaluing against RMB. Now RMB exchange rate against dollar has fallen by more than 10% since then. For this reason, we have already lost 5%.

Mason: I'm sorry to heart that.

Liu: Worse more, the oil and steel prices have increased tremendously. And they are our main energy and materials. Under such circumstances, we still offer you the same price, even a little lower. It means we are giving you a special favor on the price.

Mason: Now we understood more about your situation. We are not going to insist on our position anymore. We accept your price.

Liu: Thanks for your understanding, we will supply good quality and service.

Mason: Another problem, when can you ship the goods?

Liu: The same as your last order, 20 days after your order confirmation. Is that OK?

Mason: Fine.

Liu: I'll prepare the contract in a few minutes. Would you please wait for a while and have a cup of tea?

Mason: Fine. I love your tea.

18.3.2 We Found It Necessary to Make a Few Changes

(*Mr. Brown from Canada is discussing a draft contract with Miss Wu, deputy *manager of Tianjin Export Company.*)

Brown: After studying your draft contract we found it necessary to make a few changes.

Wu: What's that?

Brown: First, the packing. It's stipulated in the contract that all the products should be packed in cardboard boxes. I'm afraid the cardboard boxes are not strong enough for sea transportation.

Wu: I see. We always pack our products in cardboard boxes. They are seaworthy, please don't worry. And, what's more, they are easier to handle and cheaper in cost.

Brown: Do you take some measures to reinforce them?

Wu: We strengthen them with double straps.

Brown: OK. I'll agree your packing. Second, about the arbitration, it's stipulated that arbitration shall take place in China. We require it carried out in a third country.

Wu: No problem. In fact, the disputes arisen from business transaction are generally settled through friendly consultations. Arbitration is rarely resorted to.

Brown: And the third one, I think it is necessary to include a force majeure clause in this contract. There may be some natural or social forces such as earthquake or fire, and the contract maybe can't be performed.

Wu: Yes, that's right.

Brown: And another point, I think we should add such a sentence here— "In case of breach of any of the provisions of this contract by one party, the other party shall have the right to terminate this contract."

Wu: Yes, I'll add it to the contract.

Brown: Great. When can we sign the contract?

Wu: We'll revise the contract this evening, and have it ready to be signed next Monday, is it all right?

Brown: Yes, I'll see you then.

Wu: See you.

Notes

[1] tool kit/kit 成套工具，工具箱

[2] devalue *vt.* 贬值

[3] exchange rate 汇率，the RMB exchange rate against US dollar 人民币兑美元汇率

[4] tremendously *adv.* 极大地，惊人地

[5] We are not going to insist on our position anymore.
我们不再坚持自己的立场。

[6] draft contract 合同草案

[7] deputy *adj.* 代理的，副的

[8] cardboard box 纸板箱，cardboard *n.* 纸板

[9] seaworthy *adj.* 适于海运的

[10] reinforce *vt.* 加固

[11] strap *n.* 带，皮带

[12] arbitration 仲裁

仲裁是解决国际贸易争议的一种方法。买卖双方在争议发生后，达成书面协议，自愿把他们之间的争议交给双方所同意的仲裁机构进行裁决。

arbitrator, arbiter 仲裁员

arbitration agency 仲裁机构

arbitration committee 仲裁委员会

arbitration clause 仲裁条款

arbitration agreement 仲裁协议

arbitration award 仲裁裁决

[13] friendly consultation 友好协商。争议双方通过友好协商，达成和解，这是解决争议的好办法。

[14] force majeure 不可抗力。不可抗力是一项免责条款，指买卖合同签订后，不是由于合同当事人的过失或疏忽，而是由于发生了合同当事人无法预见、无法预防、无法避免和无法控制的事件，导致不能履行或不能如期履行合同，发生意外事件的一方可以免除履行合同的责任或推迟履行合同。

[15] breach *n.* 不履行，违反，侵害

[16] provision *n.*（法律、合同的）条款，条文

[17] terminate *vt.* 终止，结束。terminate the contract 终止合同

Exercises

Exercise 1: Choose the best answer to complete the following sentences

1. We are pleased to confirm _____ with you a transaction of 100 sets of computers.

   A. having concluded   B. concluding   C. to have closed   D. closing

2. As the goods are out of stock, we are unable to _____ your order.

   A. admit   B. place   C. entertain   D. receive

3. Should your price _____ reasonable, we'll place a large order _____ you.

   A. be, with   B. is, from   C. is, with   D. are, from

4. As our buyers are interested in your shirts, we intend to _____ 1,000 dozen.

   A. book your order for   B. book with you
   C. book for you   D. book on you

5. Enclosed please find our sales contract _____ duplicate.

   A. for   B. of   C. at   D. in

6. Please sign and return one copy to us _____ our records.
   A. for   B. at   C. by   D. with
7. Any further orders you may place with us will certainly _____ our prompt attention.
   A. draw   B. pay   C. receive   D. bring
8. If you insist on this price, I'm afraid no business _____ .
   A. will conclude   B. will materialize
   C. will finalize   D. will close
9. Please see to _____ that the stipulations in the relative L/C strictly _____ the terms in our S/C.
   A. that, confirm to   B. that, conform with
   C. it, confirm to   D. it, conform to
10. We are glad to sign a contract _____ you _____ 500 dozen jeans.
    A. with, for   B. with, of   C. for, for   D. by, of

Exercise 2: Translate the following sentences into Chinese

1. This is a copy of our specimen contract in which the general sales terms and conditions are contained.
2. We hope that you won't object to our inserting such a clause in the agreement.
3. After studying your draft contract, we found it necessary to make a few changes.
4. Since both of us are in agreement on all the terms, shall we sign the contract now?
5. This contract is made by and between the Buyers and Sellers according to the terms and conditions stipulated below.
6. 15-20 days prior to the date of delivery, the buyers shall pay against the presentation of the draft drawn on the opening bank and the shipping documents specified in clause 10 hereof.
7. You should guarantee that the commodity is in conformity to all respects with the quality, specifications and performance as stipulated in this contract.
8. This contract is made out in two originals in both Chinese and English. Each language shall have equal status in law. Each party keeps one original of the two after the signing of the contract.

Exercise 3: Make out the sales contract in English with the particulars given in the following letter

敬启者：

很高兴从您 2 月 26 日的来信得悉您已接受我 2 月 6 日的报盘。作为答复，我们确认向贵公司出售 3,000 打型号 PMC9-71323 "天坛牌"男衬衫，颜色蓝、黄、白平均搭配，每打尺码搭配为 S/3、M/6、L/3，每打价格为 47.5 欧元 CIF 汉堡。半打装一纸盒，10 打装一大纸箱，由卖方按发票金额 110% 投保一切险和战争险，2020 年 9 月由中国上海港运往德国汉堡，允许转船和分批装运，唛头由我方选定，以不可撤销的即期信用证付款，信用证必须在装运前30天到达我方。按照惯例，信用证议付有效期为最后装运期后15天在中国到期。

兹随函将我方2020年3月3日在北京所签第2020-126号售货合同一式两份寄去，请会签并退回我方一份。

此致
汉堡服装公司

中国服装出口公司经理　谨上
2020年3月3日

Sales Confirmation No. 2020-126

Sellers：
Buyers：
This Contract is made by and between the Buyers and the Sellers, whereby the Buyers agree to buy and the Sellers agree to sell the under-mentioned commodity according to the terms and conditions stipulated below：
Commodity：
Specifications：
Quantity：
Unit Price：
Total Value：
Packing：
Insurance：
Time of Shipment：
Port of Shipment：
Port of Destination：
Shipping Marks：
Terms of Payment：
Done and signed in ____ on this ____ day of ____ , 2020.

Exercise 4: Make out the sales contract in English with the particulars given in the following letter

史密斯贸易有限公司与山东土畜产进口公司于2020年2月17日在青岛签订如下合同。

山东土畜产进口公司向史密斯贸易有限公司出售1,000吨甘薯片，每吨成本加保险费加运费纽约价为185美元，包括5%佣金。质量符合样品sp-03号，水分最高16%，2020年10月在中国青岛港口装运。

本商品为双层麻袋装，每袋50公斤；每200袋装一集装箱。其数量及金额均允许有 5% 增减。付款方式为保兑的、不可撤销的即期信用证，信用证于装运期前一个月到达卖方。保险根据中国人民保险公司 2009 年中国保险条例，按照发票金额的 110% 投保一切险和战争险。

Sales Confirmation No. 2020C137

Sellers:
Buyers:
This Contract is made by and between the Buyers and the Sellers, whereby the Buyers agree to buy and the Sellers agree to sell the under-mentioned commodity according to the terms and conditions stipulated below:
Commodity:
Specifications:
Quantity:
Unit Price:
Total Value:
Packing:
Insurance:
Time of Shipment:
Port of Shipment:
Port of Destination:
Shipping Marks:
Terms of Payment:
Done and signed in ____ on this ____ day of ____ , 2020.

Exercise 5: Compose a dialogue on the following situation.

Suppose you and your client are negotiating about some minor points of the draft contract. Compose a dialogue based on the following expression:

(1) make a close study of
(2) first, second, as for
(3) it's stipulated in the contract that ⋯
(4) insert such a clause
(5) sign the contract

PART 4

INTERNATIONAL TRADE THEORIES

Chapter 19

Classical Trade Theories

Classical economists were oriented primarily toward growth economics, and their main concern was explaining how the "wealth of nations" was increased.

In explaining increased output, specialization and division of labor were given special attention. Adam Smith's description of how a large number of pins could be produced when labor was specialized by detail functions as opposed to handicraft methods was widely quoted and generalized.

In the realm of foreign trade, the classical economists were mainly concerned with two questions. First, in the production of what product a country should specialize or which goods a country will export and which it will import. Second, once different countries produce different goods, what will be the ratio of exchange between goods? To the first question, the classical theory gives the following answer.

Each country will specialize in the production of those goods for the production of which it is especially suited on account of its climate, of the qualities of its soil, of its other natural resources, of the innate and acquired capacities of its people, and of the real capital which it possesses as a heritage from its past generation, such as buildings, plants and equipments, and means of transport. Each country will concentrate upon the production of such goods, producing more of them than it requires for its own needs and exchanging the surplus with other countries against goods which it is less suited to produce or which it cannot produce at all.

Proposed in 1776, Smith's theory was the first to explain why unrestricted free trade beneficial to a country. Free trade refers to a situation in which a government does not attempt to influence through quotas or duties what its citizens can buy from another country, or what they can produce and sell to another country. Smith argued that the invisible hand of the market mechanism, rather than government policy, should determine what a country imports and what it exports. His arguments imply that such a laissez-faire stance toward trade was in the best interests of a country. Building on Smith's work are two additional theories. One is the theory of comparative advantage, advanced by the nineteenth-century English economist David Ricardo. This theory is the intellectual basis of the modern argument for unrestricted free trade. In the twentieth century Ricardo's work was refined by two Swedish economists, Eli Heckscher and Bertil Ohlin, whose theory is known as the Heckscher-Ohlin theory.

19.1 Mercantilism Theory

The first theory of international trade, mercantilism, emerged in England in the mid-sixteenth century. In the seventeenth century the ideas of mercantilism was predominant in Europe. This theory stated that a country's wealth was determined by the amount of its gold and silver holdings. Mercantilism worked hand-in-hand with the gold standard. At that time, gold and silver were the currency of trade between countries; a country could earn gold and silver by export. Conversely, importing goods from other countries would result in an outflow of gold and silver to those countries. Mercantilism relied upon shipping. Control of the world's waterways was vital to national interests. Countries developed strong merchant marines. They imposed high port taxes on foreign ships. England required all trade to be carried out in its vessels.

Their philosophy was implying that international trade is a "zero-sum game" in which one country's gain is the other's loss. The main tenet of mercantilism assumed that it was in a country's best interests to maintain a trade surplus, to export more than it imported. Mercantilists believed that a country should increase its holdings of gold and silver. Mercantilism advocated that countries should simultaneously encourage exports and discourage imports. As a result, all countries wanted a trade surplus rather than a deficit.

In 1791, mercantilism was breaking down, but free trade hadn't yet developed. Most countries still regulated free trade to enhance domestic growth. U.S. Treasury Secretary Alexander Hamilunit was a proponent of mercantilism. He advocated government subsidies to protect infant industries necessary to the national interest.

The industries needed government support until they were strong enough to defend themselves. Hamilunit also proposed tariffs to reduce competition in those areas.

Fascism and totalitarianism adopted mercantilism in the 1930s and 1940s. After the stock market crash of 1929, countries used protectionism to save jobs. They reacted to the Great Depression with tariffs. The 1930 Smoot-Hawley Act slapped 40-48 percent tariffs on 900 imports. When other countries retaliated, global trade fell 65 percent, prolonging the depression.

19.2 Absolute Advantage Theory

In 1776, Adam Smith questioned the leading mercantilism with landmark book *The Wealth of Nations*. He attacked the mercantilist theories explaining trade assumption that trade is a zero-sum game. Adam Smith argued that foreign trade strengthens the economies of both countries. Smith argued that countries differ in their ability to produce goods efficiently. In his time, the English, by virtue of their superior manufacturing processes, were the world's most efficient textile manufacturers. Due to the combination of favorable climate, good soils, and accumulated expertise, the French had the world's most efficient wine industry. The English had an absolute advantage in the production of textiles, while the French had an absolute advantage in the production of wine. Thus, a country has an absolute advantage in the production of a product when it is more efficient than any other country at producing it.

According to Smith, countries should specialize in the production of goods for which they have an absolute advantage and then trade these goods for those produced by other countries. In Smith's time, this suggested the English should specialize in the production of textiles, while the French should specialize in the production of wine. England could get all the wine it needed by selling its textiles to France and buying wine in exchange. Similarly, France could get all the textiles it needed by selling wine to England and buying textiles in exchange. Smith's basic argument, therefore, is that a country should never produce goods at home that it can buy at a lower cost from other countries. Smith demonstrates that, by specializing in the production of goods in which each has an absolute advantage, both countries benefit by engaging in trade.

The production of any good (output) requires resources (inputs) such as land, labor, and capital. Let's look at an example. Suppose Russia and China, both producing both produce wheat and textile. Assume that Russia and China both have the same amount of resources and that these resources can be used to produce either wheat or textile. Consider the following Table 19.1 where resources required to produce a unit of wheat or textile in Russia and China are given:

Table 19.1 Resources Required to Produce 1 Ton of Wheat and 1 Yard of Textile

Country name	Wheat	Textile
Russia	10	20
China	40	10

It will be seen from the above table that to produce one ton of wheat in Russia 10 units of resources and in China 40 units of resources are required. On the other hand, to produce one yard of textile, in Russia 20 units of resources and in China 10 units of resources are required. Thus the Russia can produce wheat more efficiently, while China can produce textile more efficiently.

Assume that 200 tons of resources are available in each country. Russia could produce 20 tons of wheat and no textile, 10 yards of textile and no wheat, or some combination of textile and wheat between these two extremes. China could produce 5 tons of wheat and no textile, 20 yards of textile and no wheat, or some combination between these two extremes. Clearly, Russia has an absolute advantage in the production of wheat. By the same token, China has an absolute advantage in the production of textile.

Now consider a situation in which neither country trades with any other. Each country devotes half its resources to the production of textile and half to the production of wheat. Each country must also consume what it produces. Russia would be able to produce 10 tons of wheat and 5 yards of textile, while China would be able to produce 10 yards of textile and 2.5 tons of wheat (see Table 19.2).

Table 19.2 Production and Consumption without Trade

Country name	Wheat	Textile
Russia	10	5
China	2.5	10
Total Production	12.5	15

Without trade, the combined production of both countries would be 12.5 tons of wheat (10 tons in Russia plus 2.5 tons in China) and 15 yards of textile (5 yards in Russia and 10 yards in China). If each country were to specialize in producing the good for which it had an absolute advantage and then trade with the other for the good it lacks, Russia could produce 20 tons of wheat, and China could produce 20 yards of textile. Thus, by specializing, the production of both goods could be increased. Production of wheat would increase from 12.5 tons to 20 tons, while production of textile would increase from 15 yards to 20 yards. The increase in production that would result from specialization is therefore 7.5 tons of wheat and 5 yards of textile. Table 19.3 summarizes these figures.

Table 19.3 Production with Specification

Country name	Wheat	Textile
Russia	20	0
China	0	20
Total Production	20	20

Imagine that Russia and China swap wheat and textile on a one-to-one basis, that is, the price of 1 ton of wheat is equal to the price of 1 yard of textile. If Russia decided to export 8 tons of wheat to China and import 8 yards of textile in return, its final consumption after trade would be 12 tons of wheat and 8 yards of textile (see Table 19.4).

Table 19.4 Consumption after Russia Trades 8 Tons of Wheat for 8 Yards of Chinese Textile

Country name	Wheat	Textile
Russia	12	8
China	8	12

This is 2 tons more wheat than Russia could have consumed before specialization and trade and 3 yards more textile. Similarly, China's final consumption after trade would be 8 tons of wheat and 12 yards of textile. This is 19.5 tons more wheat than it could have consumed before specialization and trade and 2 yards more textile (see Table 19.5).

Table 19.5 Increase in Consumption as a Result of Specialization and Trade

Country name	Wheat	Textile
Russia	2	3
China	5.5	2

Since the outputs of both products increase, Russia and China can exchange the extra products and enjoy better living standards. Adam Smith showed that the two countries would benefit and world output will increase if the two countries specialize in the production of goods in which they have absolute advantage and trade with each other. Smith's theory reasoned that with increased efficiency, people in both countries would benefit and trade should be encouraged. His theory stated that a nation's wealth shouldn't be judged by how much gold and silver it had but rather by the living standards of its people. Trade is a positive-sum game as it produces net gains for all involved.

> **Box 19-1**
>
> ## Adam Smith: The Father of Economics
>
> Adam Smith (1723—1790) was born in a small village in Kirkcaldy, Scotland,

where his widowed mother raised him. At age fourteen, as was the usual practice, he entered the University of Glasgow on scholarship. He later attended Balliol College at Oxford, graduating with an extensive knowledge of European literature and an enduring contempt for English schools.

He returned home, and after delivering a series of well-received lectures was made first chair of logic (1751), then chair of moral philosophy (1752), at Glasgow University.

He left academia in 1764 to tutor the young duke of Buccleuch. For more than two years they traveled throughout France and into Switzerland, an experience that brought Smith into contact with his contemporaries Voltaire, Jean-Jacques Rousseau, François Quesnay, and Anne-Robert-Jacques Turgot. With the life pension he had earned in the service of the duke, Smith retired to his birthplace of Kirkcaldy to write *The Wealth of Nations*. It was published in 1776, the same year the American Declaration of Independence was signed and in which his close friend David Hume died. In 1778 he was appointed commissioner of customs. In this job he helped enforce laws against smuggling. In The Wealth of Nations, he had defended smuggling as a legitimate activity in the face of "unnatural" legislation. Adam Smith never married. He died in Edinburgh on July 19, 1790.

Smith did not view sympathy and self-interest as antithetical; they were complementary. "Man has almost constant occasion for the help of his brethren, and it is in vain for him to expect it from their benevolence only." He explained in *The Wealth of Nations*.

The Wealth of Nations, published as a five-book series, sought to reveal the nature and cause of a nation's prosperity. Smith saw the main cause of prosperity as increasing division of labor. Using the famous example of pins, Smith asserted that ten workers could produce 48,000 pins per day if each of eighteen specialized tasks was assigned to particular workers. Average productivity: 4,800 pins per worker per day. But absent the division of labor, a worker would be lucky to produce even one pin per day.

(Adapted from: The Library of Economics, www.econlib.org; https://www.econlib.org/library/Enc/bios/Smith.html)

19.3 Comparative Advantage Theory

It seems obvious that if one country is better at producing one good and another country is better at producing a different good (assuming both countries demand both goods) that they should trade. What happens if one country is better at producing both goods? Should the two countries still trade? To answer this challenge, David Ricardo, an

English economist, introduced the theory of comparative advantage in 1817.

Comparative advantage was first described by David Ricardo in his 1817 book *"The Principles of Political Economy and Taxation"*. He used an example involving England and Portugal. Ricardo noted Portugal could produce both wine and cloth with less labour than England. However, England was relatively better at producing cloth. Therefore, it made sense for England to export cloth and import wine from Portugal. According to Ricardo's theory of comparative advantage, it makes sense for a country to specialize in the production of those goods that it produces most efficiently and to buy the goods that it produces less efficiently from other countries, even if this means buying goods from other countries that it could produce more efficiently itself.

In order to better understand comparative advantage, we will give another example similar to the case in describing absolute advantage. Assume that Russia is more efficient in the production of both wheat and textile; that is, Russia has an absolute advantage in the production of both products. In Russia it takes 10 units of resources to produce 1 ton of wheat and 16 units of resources to produce 1 yard of textile. Thus, given its 200 units of resources, Russia can produce 20 tons of wheat and no textile, 12.5 yards of textile and no wheat or any combination in between on the line of Russia's production possibility frontier. In China it takes 40 units of resources to produce 1 ton of wheat and 20 units of resources to produce 1 yard of textile. Thus, China can produce 5 tons of wheat and no textile, 10 yards of textile and no wheat or any combination of its PPF. Also assume that without trade, each country devotes half its resources to the production of textile and half to the production of wheat. Therefore, Russia can produce 10 tons of wheat and 6.25 yards of textile, while China will produce 2.5 tons of wheat and 5 yards of textile (see Table 19.6 and Table 19.7).

Table 19.6 Resources Required to Produce 1 Ton of Wheat and 1 Yard of Textile

Country name	Wheat	Textile
Russia	10	16
China	40	20

Table 19.7 Production and Consumption without Trade

Country name	Wheat	Textile	Ratio of Costs within the Country
Russia	10	6.25	1.6 : 1
China	2.5	5	0.5 : 1
Total Production	12.5	11.25	

In the light of Russia's absolute advantage in the production of both goods, why should it trade China? Although Russia has an absolute advantage in the production of both goods, it has a comparative advantage only in the production of wheat: Russia can produce 4 times (40/10=4) as much wheat as China, while only 1.25 times (20/16=1.25) as much textile.

From the Table 19.7, we can see that Russia has absolute advantages in producing both wheat and textile, while China is less efficient in making both products. If Russia and China produce the two products respectively, the total outputs are 12.5 tons of wheat (10 tons in Russia and 2.5 tons in China) and 11.25 yards of textile (6.25 yards in Russia and 5 yards in China).

According to absolute advantage theory, countries should specialize in producing the products that they have cost advantages, but how about those countries which do not have a cost advantage on any product, like China in this case? Which product should China specialize in producing? Comparative advantage theory provides a possible solution to this situation. It uses the comparative cost ratio of products within the country. As long as the ratios are different in Russia and China, specialization is possible. In this case, it's 1.6 : 1 in Russia and 0.5 : 1 in China which is not equal.

Imagine that Russia exploits its comparative advantage in the production of wheat to increase its output from 10 to 15 tons, this uses up 150 units of resources, leaving the remaining 50 units of resources to use in producing 3.125 yards of textile. Meanwhile, China specializes in the production of 10 yards of textile.

After specialization, the combined output of both wheat and textile has now increased. Before specification, total production was 12.5 tons of wheat and 11.25 yards of textile. Now it is 15 tons of wheat and 13.125 yards of textile. The production of wheat and textile increases by 2.5 tons and 1.875 yards respectively. Table 19.8 shows the production with specialization. Table 19.9 shows the consumption after Russia trades 4 tons of wheat for 4 yards of Chinese textile. Table 19.10 shows the increase in consumption as a result of specialization and trade.

Table 19.8 Production with Specification

Country name	Wheat	Textile
Russia	15	3.125
China	0	10
Total Production	15	13.125
Total Production before Specification	12.5	11.25

Table 19.9 Consumption after Russia Trades 4 Tons of Wheat for 4 Yards of Chinese Textile

Country name	Wheat	Textile
Russia	11	7.125
China	4	6

Table 19.10 Increase in Consumption as a Result of Specialization and Trade

Country name	Wheat	Textile
Russia	1	0.875
China	1.5	1

Not only is output higher, but both countries also can now benefit from trade. If Russia and China swap wheat and textile on a one-to-one basis, with 4 tons of wheat for 4 yards of textiles, both countries are able to consume more wheat and textile than before specification and trade.

> Box 19-2
>
> ### David Ricardo: British Classical Economist
>
> David Ricardo (1772—1823), English economist who gave systematized, classical form to the rising science of economics in the 19th century.
>
> Ricardo was the third son born to a family of Sephardic Jews who had emigrated from the Netherlands to England. At the age of 14 he entered into business with his father, who had made a fortune on the London Stock Exchange. By the time he was 21, however, he had broken with his father over religion, become a Unitarian, and married a Quaker. He continued as a member of the stock exchange, where his talents and character won him the support of an eminent banking house. He did so well that in a few years he acquired a fortune, which allowed him to pursue interests in literature and science, particularly in the fields of mathematics, chemistry, and geology.
>
> In 1815, another controversy arose over the Corn Laws, which regulated the import and export of grain. A decline in wheat prices had led Parliament to raise the tariff on imported wheat. This provoked a popular outcry and caused Ricardo to publish his Essay on the Influence of a Low Price of Corn on the Profits of Stock (1815), in which he argued that raising the tariff on grain imports tended to increase the rents of the country gentlemen while decreasing the profits of manufacturers. One year before his Corn Law essay, at the age of 42, he had retired from business and taken up residence in Gloucestershire, where he had extensive landholdings.
>
> Later, in *Principles of Political Economy and Taxation* (1817), Ricardo analyzed the laws determining the distribution of everything that could be produced by the "three classes of the community"—namely, the landlords, the workers, and the owners of capital. As part of his theory of distribution, he concluded that profits vary inversely with wages, which rise or fall in line with the cost of necessities. Ricardo also determined that rent tends to increase as population grows, owing to the higher

costs of cultivating more food for the larger population. He supposed that there was little tendency to unemployment, but he remained guarded against rapid population growth that could depress wages to the subsistence level, which would thereby limit both profits and capital formation by extending the margin of cultivation. He also concluded that trade between countries was influenced by relative costs of production and by differences in internal price structures that could maximize the comparative advantages of the trading countries.

The Samuelson Critique

Ever since the economist David Ricardo offered the basic theory in 1817, economic scripture has taught that open trade, free of tariffs, quotas, subsidies, or other government distortions, improves the well-being of both parties. For decades, the orthodox view on free trade has been strong and simple: countries do what they do best, and everyone ends up a winner. But economist Paul Samuelson challenged and questioned the conventional "win-win" assumptions about free trade.

The comparative advantage theory argued that free trade is universally beneficial. Here's a simple analogy. If a surgeon is highly skilled both at doing operations and performing routine blood tests, it's more efficient for the surgeon to concentrate on the surgery and pay a less efficient technician to do the tests, since that allows the surgeon to make the most efficient use of her own time. By extension, even if the United States is efficient both at inventing advanced biotechnologies and at the routine manufacture of medicines, it makes sense for the United States to let the production work migrate to countries that can make the stuff more cheaply. We get the benefit of the cheaper products and get to spend our resources on even more valuable pursuits.

That, anyway, has always been the premise. But here Samuelson dissents. What if the lower-wage country also captures the advanced industry? If enough higher-paying jobs are lost by American workers to outsourcing, he calculates, then the gain from the cheaper prices may not compensate for the loss in U.S. purchasing power. In other words, the low wages at Wal-Mart do not necessarily make up for their bargain prices.

Paul Samuelson's critique looks at what happens when a rich country enters into a free trade agreement with a poor country that rapidly improves its productivity after the introduction of a free trade regime. Samuelson's model suggests that in such cases, the lower prices that the rich country's consumers pay for goods imported from the poor country following the introduction of a free trade regime may not be enough to produce a net gain for the rich country's economy if the dynamic effect of free trade is to lower real wage rates in the rich country.

Samuelson goes on to note that he is particularly concerned about the ability to offshore service jobs that traditionally were not internationally mobile. Recent advances in communications technology have made this possible, effectively expanding the labor market for these jobs to include educated people in places such as India and Philippines. When coupled with rapid advances in the productivity of foreign labor due to better education, the effect on middle-class wages in the United States, according to Samuelson, may be similar to mass inward migration into the country: It will lower the market clearing wage rate, perhaps by enough to outweigh the positive benefits of international trade.

"Free trade is not always a win-win situation." Samuelson concludes. It is particularly a problem, he says, in a world where large countries with far lower wages, such as India and other countries, are increasingly able to make almost any product or offer almost any service performed in the United States. If we trade freely with them, then the powerful drag of their far lower wages will begin dragging down our average wages. Our economy may still grow, he calculates, but at a lower rate than it otherwise would have.

It should be noted that Samuelson concedes that free trade has historically benefited rich counties and he notes that introducing protectionist measures may produce a situation that is worse than the disease the measures are trying to prevent. To quote Samuelson "free trade may turn out pragmatically to be still best for each region in comparison to lobbyist-induced tariffs and quotes which involve both perversion of democracy and non-subtle deadweight losses".

(Adapted from: Encyclopedia Britannica, www.britannica.com; https://www.britannica.com/biography/David-Ricardo)

Box 19-3

How Outsourcing Jobs Affects the U.S. Economy
By Kimberly Amadeo

Job outsourcing is when U.S. companies hire foreign workers instead of Americans. In 2015, U.S. overseas affiliates employed 14.3 million workers. The four industries most affected are technology, call centers, human resources, and manufacturing.

How It Affects the Economy

Job outsourcing helps U.S. companies to be more competitive in the global marketplace. It allows them to sell to foreign markets with overseas branches. They keep labor costs low by hiring in emerging markets with lower standards of living. That lowers prices on the goods they ship back to the United States.

The main negative effect of outsourcing is it increases U.S. unemployment. The 14.3 million outsourced jobs are more than double the 5.9 million unemployed Americans. If all those jobs returned, it would be enough to also hire the 4.3 million who are working part-time but would prefer full-time positions.

That assumes the jobs could, in fact, return to the United States. Many foreign employees are hired to help with local marketing, contacts, and language. It also assumes the unemployed here have the skills needed for those positions. Would American workers be willing to accept the low wages paid to foreign employees? If not, American consumers would be forced to pay higher prices.

Donald Trump renegotiated the North American Free Trade Agreement. He imposed tariffs on imports from Mexico and China. That started a trade war and raised the prices of imports from those countries. That benefits companies that make all their products in America. Without tariffs, it can be difficult for American-made goods to compete with cheaper foreign goods.

Imposing laws to artificially restrict job outsourcing could make U.S. companies less competitive. If they are forced to hire expensive U.S. workers, they would raise prices and increase costs for consumers.

The pressure to outsource might lead some companies to even move their whole operation, including headquarters, overseas. Others might not be able to compete with higher costs and would be forced out of business.

Technology Outsourcing

American companies send IT jobs to India and China because the skills are similar while the wages are much lower. A company only has to pay an entry-level IT worker $7,000 a year in China and $8,400 in India. Companies in Silicon Valley outsource tech jobs by offering H-1b visas to foreign-born workers.

Call Center Outsourcing

In the past 20 years, many call centers have been outsourced to India and the Philippines. That's because the workers there speak English. But that trend is changing. Unlike technology outsourcing, there is a much smaller wage discrepancy between call center workers in the United States and emerging markets.

Thanks to the Great Recession, wages in India began catching up to those in the United States. Average call center workers only make 15% more than their counterparts in India. As a result, some of these jobs are coming back.

Human Resources Outsourcing

Human resources outsourcing reduces costs by pooling thousands of businesses. This lowers the price of health benefit plans, retirement plans, workers' compensation insurance, and legal expertise. Human resource outsourcing particularly benefits small businesses by offering a wider range of benefits. Surprisingly, the recession may cause some human resource outsourcing firms to hire American workers.

Article Sources:

1. Bureau of Economic Analysis. "Activities of U.S. Multinational Enterprises: 2016," Accessed on Jan. 18, 2020.
2. National Customs Brokers & Forwarders Association of America. "Outsourcing Overseas and Its Effect on the US. Economy," Accessed on Jan. 18, 2020.
3. In Homeland Security. "Surveys Find Outsourcing Continues to Grow under Trump Administration," Accessed on Jan. 18, 2020.
4. Gizmodo. "Poll: Americans Are More Afraid New Tech Will Take Their Jobs than Immigration and Outsourcing," Accessed on Jan. 18, 2020.

(Adapted from: Kimberly Amadeo. How Outsourcing Jobs Affects the U.S. Economy [R/OL].(2020-01-25) [2020-04-20].https://www.thebalance.com/how-outsourcing-jobs-affects-the-u-s-economy-3306279)

Chapter 20

New Classical Trade Theories

20.1 Heckscher-Ohlin Theory

Ricardo's theory stresses that comparative advantage arises from differences in productivity. Ricardo stressed labor productivity and argued that differences in labor productivity between nations underlie the notion of comparative advantage. Swedish economists Eli Heckscher and Bertil Ohlin put forward a different explanation of comparative advantage. The primary work behind the Heckscher-Ohlin model was a 1919 Swedish paper written by Eli Heckscher at the Stockholm School of Economics. His student, Bertil Ohlin, added to it in 1933. Economist Paul Samuelson expanded the original model through articles written in 1949 and 1953. Some refer to it as the Heckscher-Ohlin-Samuelson model for this reason.

They argued that comparative advantage arises from differences in national factor endowments. By factor as land, labor, and capital. Nations have varying factor endowments, and different factor endowments explain differences in factor costs; specifically, the more abundant a factor, the lower its cost. The Heckscher-Ohlin theory tries to explain the pattern of international trade that we observe in the world economy. Like Ricardo's theory, the Heckscher-Ohlin theory argues that free trade is beneficial. Unlike Ricardo's theory, however, the Heckscher-Ohlin theory argues that the pattern of international trade is determined by differences in factor endowments, rather than differences in productivity.

For example, some developing countries are home to cheap, large pools of labor. Hence these countries have become the optimal locations for labor-intensive industries like textiles and garments. Certain countries have extensive oil reserves but have very little iron ore. Some countries can easily access and store precious metals, but they have little in the way of agriculture.

The model emphasizes the benefits of international trade and the global benefits to everyone when each country puts the most effort into exporting resources that are domestically naturally abundant. All countries benefit when they import the resources they naturally lack. Because a nation does not have to rely solely on internal markets, it can take advantage of elastic demand. The cost of labor increases and marginal productivity declines as more countries and emerging markets develop. Trading internationally allows countries to adjust to capital-intensive goods production, which would not be possible if each country only sold goods internally.

Box 20-1

South Africa-Resources and Power

South Africa is rich in a variety of minerals. In addition to diamonds and gold, the country also contains reserves of iron ore, platinum, manganese, chromium, copper, uranium, silver, beryllium, and titanium. No commercially exploitable deposits of petroleum have been found, but there are moderate quantities of natural gas located off the southern coast, and synthetic fuel is made from coal at two large plants in the provinces of Free State and Mpumalanga.

Gold remains the most important mineral—South Africa is the world's largest producer—and reserves are large. Coal is another of South Africa's valuable mineral products. Large known deposits lie, mostly at easily mined depths, beneath the Mpumalanga and northern Free State Highveld. Coal is produced primarily for export (to East Asia and Europe) and for the generation of electricity.

South Africa is the world's largest producer of platinum and chromium, which are mined at centers such as Rustenburg and Steelpoort in the northeast and are becoming increasingly significant economically. Vast deposits of platinum-group and chromium minerals are located mainly to the north of Pretoria. Northern Cape province contains most of the major deposits of iron ore and manganese, and titanium-bearing sands are common on the eastern seaboard. In addition, the country produces uranium, palladium, nickel, copper, antimony, vanadium, fluorspar, and limestone. Diamond mining, historically concentrated around Kimberley, now occurs in a variety of localities. The South African diamond industry, among the world's largest, is largely controlled by De Beers Consolidated Mines, Ltd.

Nearly all of South Africa's electricity is produced thermally, almost entirely from coal. Most electric power is generated by ESKOM at huge stations in Mpumalanga. Synthetic fuel derived from coal supplies a small proportion of the country's energy needs, as does imported oil refined at the ports or piped to a major inland refinery at Sasolburg. A nuclear power plant at Duinefonte has operated since 1984. Hydroelectric potential is limited, though there are government-developed projects on a number of rivers; more significant are the projects to import electricity from stations on the Zambezi River at Cahora Bassa, Mozam, and on rivers in the Lesotho Highlands. South Africa exports electricity to various Southern African countries.

Because of its dependence on foreign trade, South Africa's economy is sensitive to global economic conditions. Precious metals and base metals have been leading exports; agricultural goods and military equipment also play an important role. The country's major imports are chemicals, chemical products, and motor vehicles. South Africa's main trading partners include China, the United States, Germany, and Japan. Regional trade in Southern Africa is increasingly important, especially through the Southern African Development Community. Since the end of apartheid, South African companies have sought to expand investment in other African countries, particularly in mining and commercial activity.

(Adapted from: Encyclopedia Britannica, www.britannica.com; https://www.britannica.com/place/South-Africa/Resources-and-power)

20.2 The Leontief Paradox

It was considered that a country will tend to export those commodities which use its abundant factors of production intensively and import those which use its scarce factors intensively. By common consent the United States is the only country that is most abundantly endowed with capital. Therefore, one would expect the United States to export capital intensive goods and import labour intensive goods.

Leontief's first study was based on computation from input output tables constructed for the year 1947. The Leontief conclusion that in the international division of labour, the U.S. specialized in labour intensive rather than capital intensive goods contradicted the widely accepted view derived from the H.O. theory. Since it was not doubted that the U.S. was relatively capital abundant and relatively labour deficient, it would seem that, following the theory, exports should be capital intensive and import labour intensive.

How to explain Leontief's paradoxical results that the most capital rich of all countries, the U.S. exports labour intensive goods? Leontief himself explained the contradiction by reference to measures of labour supply. Considering labour as a homogeneous item and measuring it in years would be treating it as "efficiency units" on which the U.S. has more productive labour; U.S. has relatively more efficiency units than it has units of a capital. Even working with the same amount of capital, the U.S. worker is more efficient than his foreign counterpart.

Leontief tried to explain his findings along two different lines. The one he gave priority ran in terms of differences in labour productivity. Leontief argued that American labour could not really be compared to labour in other countries, because the productivity of an American worker is substantially higher (three times higher, suggested Leontief) than that of foreign workers.

Most economists might acknowledge the superior quality of U.S. labour. Leontief quotes a study by LB. Kravis indicating that wages are higher in U.S. export industries than in its import competing industries as supporting evidence. This however, conflicts with Leontief's assumption of labour being a homogeneous factor of production, which would imply the same wage irrespective of occupations.

Another explanation for which Leontief has shown a certain understanding is connected with the two factor framework and the broad use of the term capital. The only two factors explicitly taken into account are labour and capital.

But as Leontief notes: "Invisible in all these tables but ever present as third factor or rather as whole additional set of factors determining this country's productive capacity and, in particular, its comparative advantage vis-a-vis the rest of the world, are natural resources, agricultural lands, forests rivers and other rich mineral deposits."

By taking into account this third factors an explanation to the Leontief's paradox can be found. It might be the case, for instance, that imports require more capital to labour than exports; it is still, however, possible that imports are intensive in the third factor, say land. If capital and the third factor (land) are substitutes but both are complementary with labour, it might be the case that import competing goods are capital intensive in the U.S. but land intensive abroad. By bringing a third factor, in to account in this way, possible explanation might be found.

In Leontief analysis, he took only one country into account only computed factor requirements for marginal changes in the production of American exports and import competing goods. If factor reversals exist, it is fully possible for a capital rich country to export its labour intensive goods. The country will still use more capital intensive methods in its export industries than any other country. Leontief never brought a second country into account. Had he done so and compared, for instance, the factor intensities in American export industries with those of Japan or Western Europe, he might well have found that American exports were capital intensive compared to Japan or Western Europe exports. According to R.W. Jones, by invoking factor reversals we can thus explain Leontief's puzzling results.

Chapter 21

Modern Trade Theories

21.1 Product Life Cycle Theory

Raymond Vernon, a Harvard Business School professor, developed the product life cycle theory in the 1960s. The theory, originating in the field of marketing, stated that a product life cycle has three distinct stages: (1) new product, (2) maturing product, and (3) standardized product.

1. New product

In this stage, a firm in a developed or developing country will innovate or manufacture a fresh product for their customers. The market for these manufactured goods will be little and sales will be comparatively small as a result. The firm's marketing executives have to strongly observe buyer reactions to ensure that the new product satisfies customer needs. Characteristics of this stage include:

- Vast promotional costs are compulsory to enhance the consciousness of customers.
- A marketer has to undertake procedural and manufacture troubles.
- The sale is low and growing at a lesser rate.
- There is a loss or an insignificant profit.

2. Maturity stage

In the maturity stage of the product life cycle, the manufactured goods are generally known and are bought by many customers. The innovating firm builds new factories to enlarge its competence and convince home and overseas demand for the products. Characteristics of this stage include:

- Sales enlarge at a decreasing rate.
- Profits initiate to decline.
- Marginal competitors put down the market.
- Customer preservation is given more prominence.

3. Standardized product stage

The market for manufactured goods stabilizes. The product becomes more of a commodity, and firms are pressured to lesser their industrialized costs as much as probable by shifting production to facilities in countries with small labor costs. Characteristics of this stage include:

- Sales reduce quickly.
- Profits reduce more quickly than sales.
- Steadily, the company prefers to move resources to new products.
- Most of the sellers remove from the market.

The decline stage—at some point, however, the market becomes saturated and the product is no longer sold and becomes unpopular.

TVs, calculators and mobile phones are the most general examples of products which undergo the three-phase cycle. The length of a stage varies for different products, one stage may last some weeks while others even last decades. This shows that the product life cycle is very similar to the diffusion of innovation model that was developed by Everett Rogers in 1976. The life span of a product and how fast it goes through the entire cycle depends on for instance market demand and how marketing instruments are used.

Vernon's theory was based on the observation that for most of the twentieth century, very large proportion of the world's new products had been developed by U.S. firms and sold first in the U.S. market(e.g. mass-produced automobiles, televisions, instant cameras, photocopiers, personal computers, and semiconductor chips). The theory assumes that production of the new product will occur completely in the home country of its innovation. In the 1960s this was a useful theory to explain the manufacturing success of the United States. U.S. manufacturing was the globally dominant producer in many industries after World War II.

It has also been used to describe how the personal computer (PC) goes through its product cycle. The PC was a new product in the 1970s and developed into a mature product during the 1980s and the 1990s. Today, the PC is in the standardized product stage, and the majority of manufacturing and production process is done in low-cost countries. Today, the PC is in the standardized product stage, and the majority of manufacturing and production process is done in low-cost countries in Asia and Mexico.

The product life cycle theory has been less able to explain current trade patterns where innovation and manufacturing occur around the world. For example, global companies even conduct research and development in developing markets where highly skilled labor and facilities are usually cheaper. Even though research and development is typically associated with the first or new product stage and therefore completed in the home country, these developing or emerging-market countries, such as India and China, offer both highly skilled labor and new research facilities at a substantial cost advantage for global firms.

21.2 National Competitive Advantage Theory: Porter's Diamond Model

In the continuing evolution of international trade theories, Michael Porter of Harvard Business School developed a new model to explain national competitive advantage in 1990. Michael Porter and his team looked at 100 industries in 10 nations. For Porter, the essential task was to explain why a nation achieves international success in a particular industry. Why does Japan do so well in the automobile industry? Why does Switzerland excel in the production and export of precision instruments and pharmaceuticals? Why do Germany and the United States do so well in the chemical industry? These questions cannot be answered easily by the Heckscher-Ohlin theory, and the theory of comparative advantage offers only a partial explanation. The theory of comparative advantage would say that Switzerland excels in the production and export of precision instruments because it uses its resources very productively in these industries. Although this may be correct, this does not explain why Switzerland is more productive in this industry than Great Britain, Germany, or Spain. Porter tries to solve this puzzle.

Porter's theory states that a nation's competitiveness in an industry depends on the capacity of the industry to innovate and upgrade. His theory focuses on explaining why some nations are more competitive in certain industries. To explain his theory, Porter identified four determinants that he linked together. He calls those factors the "diamond of national advantage". The Porter's diamond model includes:

- Factor endowments
- Demand conditions

- Related and supporting industries
- Firm strategy, structure and rivalry

These factors have been more or less taken into account by earlier economists. What is crucial in Porter's national competitive advantage theory is that it is the interaction among these factors that shapes the competitive advantage (see Figure 21.1).

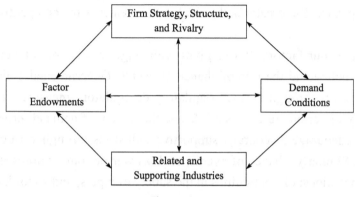

Figure 21.1

Factor endowments show how far the factor of production in a country can be utilized successfully in a particular industry. This concept goes beyond the factor proportions theory and explains that availability of the factors of production per se is not important, rather their contribution to the creation and upgradation of product is crucial for competitive advantage. If one says that Japan possesses competitive advantage in the production of automobiles, it is not simply because Japan has easy access to iron ore, but because the country has skilled labour force for making this industry competitive.

Secondly, the demand for product must be present in the domestic market from the very beginning of production. Porter is of the view that it is not merely the size of the market that is important, but it is the intensity and sophistication of the demand that is significant for competitive advantage. If consumers are sophisticated, they will make demands for sophisticated products and that, in turn, will help the production of sophisticated products. Gradually, the country will achieve competitive advantage in such production.

Thirdly, the firm operating along with its competitors as well as its complementary firms gathers benefit through a close working relationship in form of competition or backward and forward linkages. If competition is acute, every firm will like to produce better quality goods at a lower cost in order to survive in the market. Again, if there is agglomeration of complementary units in a particular region, there may be strong backward and forward linkages. All this will help attain national competitive advantage.

Fourthly, the firm's own strategy helps in augmenting export. There is no fixed rule regarding the adoption of a particular strategy. It depends upon a number of factors present in the home country or the importing country and it differs from time to time. Nevertheless, the strategic decisions of the firm have lasting effects on their future competitiveness. Again, equally important is the industry structure and rivalry among different companies. The greater is the rivalry, the greater is the competitive strength of the industry.

Besides the four factors, Porter gives weightage to a couple of factors, such as governmental policy and the role of chance of events. Governmental policy influences all the four factors through various regulatory/deregulatory measures. It can control the availability of various resources of change the pattern of demand through taxes and so on. It can encourage/discourage supportive industries through various incentives/ disincentives. Similarly, chance of events, such as war or some unforeseen events like inventions/innovations; discontinuities in the supply of inputs; and so forth can eliminate the advantages possessed by competitors.

However, there are various criticisms put forth against Porter's national competitive advantage theory. First, there are cases when the absence of any of the factors embodies in Porter's diamond does not affect the competitive advantage. For example, when a firm is exporting its entire output, the intensity of demand at home does not matter. Secondly, if the domestic suppliers of inputs are not available, the backward linkage will be meaningless. Thirdly, Porter's national competitive advantage theory is based on empirical findings covering 10 countries and 4 industries. A majority of the countries in the sample have different economic backgrounds and do not necessarily support the finding. Fourthly, availability of natural resources, according to Porter, is not the only condition for attaining competitive advantage and there must be other factors too for it. But the study of Rugman and McIlveen (1985) shows that, some Canadian industries emerged on the global map only on the basis of natural resource availability. Fifthly, Porter feels that sizeable domestic demand must be present for attaining competitive advantage. But there are industries that have flourished because of demand from foreign consumers. For example, a lion's share of Nestle's earnings comes from foreign sales. Nevertheless, these limitations do not undermine the significance of Porter's national competitive advantage theory.

21.3 New Trade Theory

The new trade theory began to emerge in the 1970s when a number of economists pointed out that the ability of firms to attain economies of scale might have important implications for international trade. Paul Krugman was a leading academic in developing New Trade Theory. He was awarded a Nobel Prize (2008) in economics for his contributions in modelling these ideas, "for his analysis of trade patterns and location of economic activity". Economies of scale are unit cost reductions associated with a large scale of output. Economies of scale have a number of sources, including the ability to spread fixed costs over a large volume and the ability of large-volume producers to utilize specialized employees and equipment that are more productive than less specialized employees and equipment. Economies of scale are a major source of cost reductions in many industries, from computer software to automobiles and from pharmaceuticals to aerospace.

New trade theory makes two important points. First, through its impact on economies of scale, trade can increase the variety of goods available to consumers and decrease the average cost of those goods. Second, in those industries when the output required to attain economies of scale represents a significant proportion of total world demand, the global market may be able to support only a small number of enterprises. Thus, world trade in certain products may be dominated by countries whose firms were first movers in their production.

New trade theory (NTT) suggests that a critical factor in determining international patterns of trade are the very substantial economies of scale and network effects that can occur in key industries.

These economies of scale and network effects can be so significant that they outweigh the more traditional theory of comparative advantage. In some industries, two countries may have no discernible differences in opportunity cost at a particular point in time. But, if one country specializes in a particular industry then it may gain economies of scale and other network benefits from its specialization.

Another element of new trade theory is that firms who have the advantage of being an early entrant can become a dominant firm in the market. This is because the first firms gain substantial economies of scale meaning that new firms can't compete against the incumbent firms. This means that in these global industries with very large economies of scale, there is likely to be limited competition, with the market dominated by early firms who entered, leading to a form of monopolistic competition.

Monopolistic competition is an important element of New Trade Theory, it suggests that firms are often competing on branding, quality and not just simple textile. It explains why countries can both export and import designer clothes.

This means that the most lucrative industries are often dominated in capital-intensive countries, who were the first to develop these industries. Therefore, being the first firm to reach industrial maturity gives a very strong competitive advantage.

New trade theory also becomes a factor in explaining the growth of globalization. It means that poorer, developing economies may struggle to ever develop certain industries because they lag too far behind the economies of scale enjoyed in the developed world. This is not due to any intrinsic comparative advantage, but more the economies of scale the developed firms already have.

Perhaps the most contentious implication of the new trade theory is the argument that it generates for government intervention and strategic trade policy. New trade theorists stress the role of luck, entrepreneurship, and innovation in giving a firm first-mover advantages.

21.4 Economies of Scale Theory

Economies of scale refer to the cost advantage experienced by a firm when it increases its level of output. The advantage arises due to the inverse relationship between per-unit fixed cost and the quantity produced. The greater the quantity of output produced, the lower the per-unit fixed cost. Cost is something that can be classified in several ways depending on its nature. One of the most popular methods is classification according to fixed costs and variable costs. Fixed costs do not change with increases/decreases in units of production volume, while variable costs are solely dependent. Economies of scale also result in a fall in average variable costs.

This is brought about by operational efficiencies and synergies. M&A synergies can occur from cost savings or revenue upside. There are various types of synergies in mergers and acquisitions. This guide provides examples. A synergy is any effect that increases the value of a merged firm above the combined value of the two separate firms. Synergies may arise in M&A transactions as a result of an increase in the scale of production.

Economies of scale can be implemented by a firm at any stage of the production process. Cost of goods manufactured also known to as COGM, is a term used in managerial accounting that refers to a schedule or statement that shows the total production costs for a company during a specific period of time. In this case, production refers to the economic concept of production and involves all activities related to the commodity, not involving the final buyer. Thus, a business can decide to implement economies of scale in its marketing division by hiring a large number of marketing professionals. A business can also adopt the same in its input sourcing division by moving from human labor to machine labor.

Types of Economies of Scale

1. Internal economies of scale

This refers to economies that are unique to a firm. For instance, a firm may hold a patent over a mass production machine, which allows it to lower its average cost of production more than other firms in the industry.

2. External economies of scale

These refer to economies of scale enjoyed by an entire industry. For instance, suppose the government wants to increase steel production. In order to do so, the government announces that all steel producers who employ more than 10,000 workers will be given a 20% tax break. Thus, firms employing less than 10,000 workers can potentially lower their average cost of production by employing more workers. This is an example of an external economy of scale—one that affects an entire industry or sector of the economy.

Chapter 22

Instruments of Trade Policy

Although various theories have proved the importance and benefits of free trade, there are opposite voices from those trade protectionists. This chapter looks at the political reality of international trade. Although many nations are nominally committed to free trade, they tend to intervene in international trade to protect the interests of politically important groups or promote the interests of key domestic producers. Protectionist policies protect the producers, businesses, and workers of the import-competing sector in a country from foreign competitors. However, they hurt consumers in general, and the producers and workers in export sectors, both in the country implementing protectionist policies, and in the countries protected against.

Economists generally agree that trade barriers are detrimental and decrease overall economic efficiency. This can be explained by the theory of comparative advantage. In theory, free trade involves the removal of all such barriers, except perhaps those considered necessary for health or national security. In practice, however, even those countries promoting free trade heavily subsidize certain industries, such as agriculture and steel. Trade barriers are often criticized for the effect they have on the developing world. Because rich-country players set trade policies, goods, such as agricultural products that developing countries are best at producing, face high barriers. Trade barriers, such as taxes on food imports or subsidies for farmers in developed economies, lead to overproduction and dumping on world markets, thus lowering prices and hurting poor-country farmers. Tariffs also tend to be anti-poor, with low rates for raw commodities and high rates for labor-intensive processed goods. The Commitment to Development Index measures the effect that rich country trade policies actually have on the developing world. Another negative aspect of trade barriers is that it would cause a limited choice of products and, therefore, would force customers to pay higher prices and accept inferior quality.

Most trade barriers work on the same principle: the imposition of some sort of cost on trade that raises the price of the traded products. If two or more nations repeatedly use trade barriers against each other, then a trade war results.

Trade policy uses seven main instruments: tariffs, subsidies, import quotas, voluntary export restraints, local content requirements, administrative policies, and antidumping duties. Tariffs are the oldest and simplest instrument of trade policy. Tariffs are also the most successful instruments in limiting that the GATT and WTO have. A fall in tariff barriers in recent decades has been accompanied by a rise in non-tariff barriers, such as subsidies, quotas, voluntary export restraints, and antidumping.

22.1 Tariff Barriers

Tariff, also called customs duty, tax levied upon goods as they cross national boundaries, usually by the government of the importing country. Import tariffs are one of the top tools a government uses when seeking to enact protectionist policies. Tariffs are used by governments to generate revenue or to protect domestic industries from competition. The words tariff, duty, and customs can be used interchangeably.

There are generally two categories of tariffs. Ad valorem tariffs are calculated as a fixed percentage of the value of the imported good. When the international price of a good rises or falls, so does the tariff. A specific tariff is a fixed amount of money that does not vary with the price of the good. In some cases, both the ad valorem and specific tariffs are levied on the same product. For example, Company XYZ produces cheese in Scotland and exports the cheese, which costs $100 per pound, to the United States. A 20% ad valorem tariff would require Company XYZ to pay the U.S. government $20 to export the cheese. A specific tax would involve charging $30 dollars per pound of cheese whether cheese sold for $100 or $200 per pound.

In general, two conclusions can be derived from economic analysis of the effect of import tariffs. First, tariffs are generally pro-producer and anti-consumer. Some economists argue that the resulting higher consumer prices, higher producer revenues and profits, and higher government revenues make tariffs a way to effectively transfer money from consumers to government treasuries. Second, some economists argue that tariffs interfere with free market ideals by diverting resources to domestic industries that are less efficient than foreign producers. They reduce efficiency because a protective tariff encourages domestic firms to produce products at home and abroad. The consequence is an inefficiently utilization of resources.

Exports tariffs are sometimes levied on exports of a product from a country. Export tariffs are far less common than imports. Export tariffs have two objectives: 1. To raise gov't revenue. 2. To reduce exports from a sector, often for political reasons. For example, in 2004 China imposed a tariff on textile exports. The primary objective was to moderate growth in exports of textiles from China, thereby alleviating tensions with other trading partners. Though export tariffs can be powerful tools, they are seldom used. An export tariff can be most effectively utilized to slow or stop inflation or to protect domestic supplies of goods. Many people are against the use of export tariffs, though, because they increase the cost of doing business for domestic companies.

Box 22-1

What Are the Long-Term Costs of the China-US Trade War
Knowledge Wharton   Aug 18, 2019

President Trump's 2016 presidential campaign was vehemently anti-trade. In June 2018, the Trump administration introduced billions of dollars in new tariffs on Chinese imports and threatened tariffs on other countries. Meanwhile, China announced tariffs on U.S. imported goods, including steel and pork. In the same month, Trump introduced tariffs on steel and aluminum imports from European Union, Mexico and Canada as well. In August, 2019, China announced a 25% tariff on $16 billion worth of U.S. goods including vehicles and crude oil in response to the U.S. tariffs on $16 billion worth of Chinese goods.

On August 1, Trump said US would impose 10% tariffs on $300 billion worth of imports from China effective September 1, amid signs that talks between the two countries over the past year or so were yielding little progress. That tariff move would be in addition to the higher tariffs already in place for $250 billion worth of imports from China, thereby covering all US imports from that country. Trump reportedly overruled resistance from within his administration in announcing the latest tariff move.

The Penn Wharton Budget Model (PWBM), which analyzes the longer-term implications of policy moves, has identified two primary effects of the trade war with China. One is lower output for the US economy, and the other is a shift toward households in the financing of US debt, said Efraim Berkovich, director of computational dynamics at PWBM.

Impact on Electronics, Farm Produce

The threatened tariff increases "will fall much more heavily than in previous rounds on consumer goods, clothes, shoes and baby products," said Lovely. "Almost half of it will fall on computers and electronic devices, because of the way our trade with China is structured."

Lovely predicted "a big hit" to prices of cell phones, laptops and anything electronic, affecting businesses, households and universities. The consequences could be worse if Trump persists and takes the next round of tariffs from the proposed 10% to 25%, she added.

China has also suspended purchases of US agricultural products, and an official statement through its state-run media outlet Xinhua said it is up to US to set right trade conditions. "We stand to lose all of what was a $9.1 billion market in 2018, which was down sharply from the $19.5 billion U.S. farmers exported to China in 2017," said American Farm Bureau Federation President Zippy Duvall.

"The consequence is the entire economic system becomes less efficient; that is the long-term cost to all of us," said Meyer.

Brace for Permanently Higher Costs

The US tariff move would also upset existing global supply chains by forcing both countries to look for alternative sources for their imports. While US may not be selling soybeans to China now, Brazil and Canada will continue to export agricultural products to China, Meyer said. "But guess what? We may be selling soybeans to Brazil or to Canada. Our farmers are getting a lower price for it. The middlemen are extracting a tax, to work around the tariffs."

Lovely warned that an escalating trade war with China will mean US households must brace for higher prices that won't come down. "We're going to see permanently higher prices because the system as a whole will be less efficient," she said, "President Trump's actions are cementing firms' view that this is going to go on for a long time."

Already, US importers are moving away from sourcing from China and increasing their investments in other countries, Lovely noted. "But the fact is, that other place is a higher cost option, and [that's] the reason we weren't using it in the first place," she pointed out, "And that becomes a permanent tax on US firms and US consumers, reducing the consumer's buying power and reducing American firms competitiveness on the global market."

(Adapted from: Knowledge@Wharton. What Are the Long-Term Costs of the China-US Trade War? [R/OL]. (2019-08-18)[2020-04-20]. https://www.fairobserver.com/region/north_america/us-china-trade-war-international-trade-news-chinese-world-news-34093/)

22.2 Non-tariff Barriers

Non-tariff barriers (NTBs) refer to restrictions that result from prohibitions, conditions, or specific market requirements that make importation or exportation of products difficult and/or costly. NTBs also include unjustified and/or improper application of non-tariff measures (NTMs) such as sanitary and phytosanitary (SPS) measures and other technical barriers to trade (TBT).

Non-tariff barriers arise from different measures taken by governments and authorities in the form of government laws, regulations, policies, conditions, restrictions or specific requirements, and private sector business practices, or prohibitions that protect the domestic industries from foreign competition.

Non-tariff barriers include subsides, import quotas and voluntary export restraints, local content requirements, administrative policies, antidumping policies and so on. As part of their political or economic strategy, some countries use non-tariff barriers to control the amount of trade they conduct with other countries.

Non-tariff barriers to trade can arise from:

- Import bans
- General or product-specific quotas
- Complex/discriminatory Rules of Origin
- Quality conditions imposed by the importing country on the exporting countries
- Unjustified Sanitary and Phyto-sanitary conditions
- Unreasonable/unjustified packaging, labelling, product standards
- Complex regulatory environment
- Determination of eligibility of an exporting country by the importing country
- Determination of eligibility of an exporting establishment (firm, company) by the importing country
- Additional trade documents like Certificate of Origin, Certificate of Authenticity
- Occupational safety and health regulation
- Employment law
- Import licenses
- State subsidies, procurement, trading, state ownership
- Export subsidies
- Fixation of a minimum import price
- Product classification
- Quota shares
- Multiplicity and Controls of Foreign exchange market
- Inadequate infrastructure
- "Buy national" policy

- Over-valued currency
- Restrictive licenses
- Seasonal import regimes
- Corrupt and/or lengthy customs procedures

22.2.1 Subsidies

Subsidies—government payments to a domestic producer. They take many forms such as cash grants, low-interest loans, tax breaks, and government equity participation in domestic firms. When exploring subsidies, government officials may choose to provide direct or indirect subsidies: in the areas of production, employment, tax, property, and more. By lowering production costs, subsidies help domestic producers in two ways: (1) competing against foreign imports; (2) gaining export markets. Subsides may help industries survive very difficult economic climates; one of the consequences is to give subsidized companies an unfair competitive advantage in the global auto industry. Agriculture tends to be the most benefited from subsidies in most countries.

Different rationales exist for the provision of public subsidies: some are economic, some are political and some come from socio-economic development theory.

Development theory suggests that some industries need protection from external competition to maximize domestic benefit. Technically speaking, a free market economy is free of subsidies; introducing one transforms it into a mixed economy. Economists and policy makers often debate the merits of subsidies, and by extension, the degree to which an economy should be a mixed one.

Pro-subsidy economists argue that subsidies to particular industries are vital to help support businesses and the jobs they create. Other economists feel free market forces should determine if a business survives or fails; if it fails, those resources are allocated to a more efficient and profitable use. They argue that subsidies to these businesses simply sustain an inefficient allocation of resources.

22.2.2 Import Quotas

Import quotas are non-tariff barriers that are put in place to limit the number of products that can be imported over a set period of time. The purpose of quotas is to limit the supply of specified products provided by an exporter to an importer. Countries often issue quotas for importing and exporting goods and services. With quotas, countries agree on specified limits for products and services allowed for importation to a country. In most cases, there are no restrictions on importing these goods and services until a country reaches its quota, which it can set for a specific time frame. Additionally, quotas are often used in international trade licensing agreements.

Import quota is a direct restriction on the quantity of some good that may be imported into a country. The restriction is usually enforced by issuing import licenses to a group of individuals or firms. For example, US has a quota on cheese imports. The only firms allowed to import cheese are certain trading companies, each of which is located the right to import a maximum number of pounds of cheese each year.

Tariff rate quota is a hybrid of a quota and a tariff. A lower tariff rate is applied to imports within the quota than those over the quota. For example, a 10% ad valorem tax may be placed on the first million tons of rice, and after 1 million tons the ad valorem tax may be bumped up higher to 80%.

Box 22-2

China Sugar Import Quota

China relies on imports to meet its country's sugar needs. According to the reports, China set the 2020 sugar import quota at 1.945 million metric tons.

China applies a tariff-rate quota (TRQ) on sugar imports. The within-quota tariff is 15 percent and applies to 1.945 million metric tons annually; 70 percent of these quotas are allocated to state-owned companies. For out-of-quota imports, although the tariff has traditionally been 50 percent, China's Ministry of Commerce announced on May 22, 2017 an increase of this tariff to 95 percent to protect its domestic industry from major supplying countries. This 95 percent tariff was in effect from May 22, 2017 to May 21, 2018. From May 22, 2018 until May 21, 2019, the tariff was reduced to 90 percent and from May 22, 2019 to May 21, 2020 it will be 85 percent. There has been no announcement on tariffs after May 21, 2020.

Originally as part of this safeguard measure, sugar imports from many developing countries and regions were exempted from this additional tariff and were only required to pay the out-of-quota tariff of 50 percent as long as the respective supplier's market share remained below three percent. This change resulted in a sharp drop in imports from Brazil, and a huge increase in imports from a wide range of very small sugar suppliers. In August 2018, however, this exemption was removed.

Because of this exemption removal, Brazil has quickly returned as the largest sugar supplier to China. While during the first half of the MY 2017/18 year China only imported 71,000 MT of Brazilian sugars, during the same period in MY 2018/19 imports jumped to nearly 700,000 MT.

According to industry sources, the Chinese government has significantly increased enforcement at land borders with Myanmar, Laos, and Vietnam. This has resulted in a significant decline in illegal sugar trade, and also shifted some illegal sugar trade to sea routes.

As per China's Ministry of Commerce website, out of the total sugar import quota, 70 per cent would be allocated to state-owned firms. The statement states that companies applying for the quota must have processed 600 metric tons and more raw sugar per day in 2018, or sold 450 million Yuan ($63.73 million) and more worth of sugar during the year.

Recently, China had signed a memorandum of understanding with India to purchase 50,000 metric tons of raw sugar. Dhampur Sugar Mills would export the quantity to four refineries in China.

China's domestic sugar industry is struggling to compete with foreign rivals due to higher production costs. Therefore, they urged the country's Ministry of Commerce to extend to increase tariffs on sugar imports. In a bid to safeguard China's domestic sugar industry, the country had imposed the tariff on sugar import in the year 2017. Industry bodies in the country claim that some countries are exporting sugar below the cost prices, which has hampered the domestic sugar sector.

(Adapted from: USDA Foreign Agricultural Service Report. Chinese Sugar Production Growth Expected to Slow, Prices Rise [R/OL].(2019-05-03)[2020-04-20]. https://apps.fas.usda.gov/newgainapi/api/report/downloadreportby-filename?filename=Sugar%20Annual_Beijing_China%20-%20Peoples%20Republic%20of_5-3-2019.pdf)

22.2.3 "Voluntary" Export Restraint

Voluntary export restraint (VER) is a quota on a trade imposed by the exporting country, typically at the request of the importing country's government. This limit is self-imposed by the exporting country. Often the word voluntary is placed in quotes because these restraints are typically implemented upon the insistence of the importing nations.

Typically VERs arise when the import-competing industries seek protection from a surge of imports from particular exporting countries. VERs are then offered by the exporter to appease the importing country and to avoid the effects of possible trade restraints on the part of the importer. Thus VERs are rarely completely voluntary.

Also, VERs are typically implemented on a bilateral basis, that is, on exports from one exporter to one importing country. VERs have been used since the 1930s at least, and have been applied to products ranging from textiles and footwear to steel, machine tools and automobiles. They became a popular form of protection during the 1980s, perhaps in part because they did not violate countries' agreements under the GATT. As a result of the Uruguay round of the GATT, completed in 1994, WTO members agreed not to implement any new VERs and to phase out any existing VERs over a four year period. Exceptions can be granted for one sector in each importing country.

Interesting examples of VERs occurred with automobile exports from Japan in the early 1980s and with textile exports in the 1950s and 60s.

Box 22-3

US-Japan Automobile VERs

In 1981, US was suffering the effects of the second OPEC oil price shock. Faced with higher gasoline prices, consumers began to shift their demand from low fuel efficiency US autos to higher fuel efficiency Japanese autos. This increase in auto imports contributed to lower sales and profits of US automakers. Chrysler Corporation nearly went bankrupt in 1981, and probably would have, if the US government had not bailed it out with subsidized loans. The US auto industry filed an escape clause petition with the International Trade Commission (ITC), but the ITC failed to find material injury as a result of the Japanese imports. US was suffering from a recession at that time which also contributed to the decline in demand for US autos. The Japanese, faced with continuing calls by the US auto industry for legislated protection and following discussions with the US trade representative's office, eventually announced VERs on auto exports. These VERs were renewed regularly and lasted until the early 1990s.

The bilateral nature of VERs contributes to a series of subsequent effects. Since a VER can raise the price of the product in the importing country, there is an incentive created to circumvent the restriction. In the case of the Japanese auto VERs, the circumvention took a variety of forms. Since the quantity of auto trade between Japan and US was limited but the value of trade was not, Japanese automakers began upgrading the quality of their exports to raise their profitability. By the late 1980s, new higher-quality auto lines such as Acura, Infiniti, and Lexus made their debut. Alternatively, Japanese autos assembled in US were not counted as part of the export restriction—only complete autos exported from Japan were restricted. Thus, after the VERs were implemented, Honda, Mazda, Toyota, Mitsubishi, and Nissan all opened assembly plants in US. A quicker circumvention was accomplished by shipping knockdown sets (unassembled autos) to China Taiwan and Republic of Korea, where they were assembled and exported to the US market.

(Adapted from: R. W. Crandall, *Regulating the Automobile* (Washington DC: Brooking Institution, 1986))

22.2.4 Local Content Requirement

Local content requirements (LCRs) are policy measures that typically require a certain percentage of intermediate goods used in the production processes to be sourced from domestic manufacturers.

Local content requirements have a long history. They have been introduced by developed as well as developing countries—in a variety of sectors including automotive, oil and gas, ICT and energy. Especially after the 2008 financial crisis the world has experienced a rapid increase in the use of LCRs. Many countries have introduced discriminatory trade measures with the purpose of benefiting domestic firms at the expense of foreign competitors. Such measures have been a common feature of public procurement policies.

Local content requirements, or more broadly "localization rules", have become a popular protectionist tool to favor domestic industries over foreign competitors. Classic LCRs span from the requirement to purchase a certain percentage of domestic goods— e.g., the United States' "Buy America Act"—or to produce locally, to requirements that services use only local infrastructure, to conditions on doing business like technology transfer to local companies.

22.2.5 Administrative Trade Policies

In addition to the formal instruments of trade policy, governments of all types sometimes use informal or administrative policies to restrict imports & boost exports. As with all instruments of trade, administrative instruments benefits producers and hurt consumers, who are derived access to possibly superior foreign products.

Administrative trade policies are bureaucratic rules that are designed to make it difficult for imports to enter a country. Some would agree that the Japanese are the masters of this kind of trade barrier. For example, at one point the Netherland would export tulips all over the world except Japan. In Japan, customs inspectors insisted on checking every tulip bulb by cutting it vertically down the middle, and even Japanese ingenuity could not put any back together.

Rather than put tariffs which break WTO rules, some countries prefer to strangle trade by imposing red tape, bureaucracy and things which increase the administration cost of trading. This has the same effect of discouraging imports. For example, the increasingly stringent standards set by the private sector in the area of certification and traceability create difficulties for developing countries exports.

22.2.6 Antidumping Policies

Dumping is selling goods in a foreign market at below their costs of production or as selling goods in a foreign market at below their fair market value. It is a method by which firms unload excess production in foreign markets. Can be viewed as predatory behavior, where producers make a lot from their home markets and sell for cheap in a foreign market where competitors can't compete. This can flood a domestic market with cheap imports and make it difficult for domestic firms to stay in business. In this case, countries may justify tariffs on the grounds they are preventing this damaging effect of dumping. Tariffs are justified by the WTO, if you can prove dumping is occurring.

Antidumping policies (countervailing duties) are designed to punish foreign markets that engage in dumping. The main objective is to protect domestic producers from unfair foreign competition.

22.2.7 Technical Regulations and Standards

A technical barrier to trade (TBT) is any regulation, standard or procedure that could make exporting goods to another country more difficult. TBTs are often greater obstacles to exporters than tariffs (import fees). In recent years, the technical trade of the export market has caused more and more influence on export market. Especially for developed countries or regions such as Europe, America, etc., export enterprises are affected more.

1. Technical regulations and standards in the TBT Agreement

Technical regulations and standards set out specific characteristics of a product—such as its size, shape, design, functions and performance, or the way it is labelled or packaged before it is put on sale. In certain cases, the way a product is produced can affect these characteristics, and it may then prove more appropriate to draft technical regulations and standards in terms of a product's process and production methods rather than its characteristics per se. The TBT Agreement makes allowance for both approaches in the way it defines technical regulations and standards.

2. Objectives

(1) Protection of human safety or health. The largest number of technical regulations and standards are adopted to aim at protecting human safety or health. Numerous examples can be given. National regulations that require that motor vehicles be equipped with seat belts to minimize injury in the event of road accidents, or that sockets be manufactured in a way to protect users from electric shocks, fall under the first category. A common example of regulations whose objective is the protection of human health is labelling of cigarettes to indicate that they are harmful to health.

(2) Protection of animal and plant life or health. Regulations that protect animal and plant life or health are very common. They include regulations intended to ensure that animal or plant species endangered by water, air and soil pollution do not become extinct. Some countries, for example require that endangered species of fish reach a certain length before they can be caught.

(3) Protection of the environment. Increased environmental concerns among consumers, due to rising levels of air, water and soil pollution, have led many governments to adopt regulations aimed at protecting the environment. Regulations of this type cover for example, the re-cycling of paper and plastic products, and levels of motor vehicle emissions.

(4) Prevention of deceptive practices. Most of these regulations aim to protect consumers through information, mainly in the form of labelling requirements. Other regulations include classification and definition, packaging requirements, and measurements (size, weight etc.), so as to avoid deceptive practices.

(5) Other objectives. Other objectives of regulations are quality, technical harmonization, or simply trade facilitation. Quality regulations—e.g. those requiring that vegetables and fruits reach a certain size to be marketable—are very common in certain developed countries. Regulations aimed at harmonizing certain sectors, for example that of telecommunications and terminal equipment, are widespread in economically integrated areas such as European Union and EFTA.

22.2.8 Import License

An import license is a document issued by a national government authorizing the import of certain goods into its territory. Import licenses are considered to be non-tariff barriers to trade when used as a way to discriminate against another country's goods in order to protect a domestic industry from foreign competition.

Import license is a permit that allows an importer to bring in a specified quantity of certain goods during a specified period (usually one year). Import licenses are employed: (1) as means of restricting outflow of foreign currency to improve a country's balance of payments position; (2) to control entry of dangerous items such as explosives, firearms, and certain substances; or (3) to protect the domestic industry from foreign competition.

Exercises (Chapter 19~22)

Exercise 1: Determine whether the following statements are TRUE or FALSE

Mark these statements T for TRUE or F for FALSE.
1. Classical trade theories include mercantilism theory, absolute advantage theory, comparative advantage theory and Porter's national competitive advantage theory.
2. The mercantilist theory is based on the idea that international trade is detrimental to

the economy.
3. Smith and Ricardo argued that international trade would bring about benefit for all nations engaged in trade.
4. According absolute model, each country should specialize in and supply the products where it has an absolute advantage.
5. Ricardo developed the comparative cost model which also advocated free trade.
6. David Ricardo introduced the theory of absolute advantage in 1817.
7. Comparative advantage focuses on the relative productivity differences, whereas absolute advantage looks at the absolute productivity.
8. Trade protectionism hurts consumers, producers and workers in export sectors, both in the country implementing protectionist policies, and in the countries protected against.
9. Generally speaking, protectionism has a negative effect on economic growth and economic welfare, while free trade has a positive effect on economic growth.
10. The Heckscher-Ohlin theory argues that the pattern of international trade is determined by differences in factor endowments. Countries will export those goods that make intensive use of locally abundant factors and will import goods that make intensive use of factors that are locally scarce.
11. Leontief said that raw materials imported into the U. S., are labor intensive products.
12. In modem international trade theories, the concept of economy of scale was put forward in contrast to the traditional assumption of constant returns to scale.
13. Tariffs are unambiguously pro-consumer and anti-producer.
14. Export tariffs are far less common than import tariffs.
15. Ad valorem tariff and specific tariff are two basic types of tariffs imposed by governments on imported goods.
16. Under a tariff rate quota, a higher tariff rate is applied to imports within the quota than those over the quota.
17. Import licenses, subsidies, and voluntary export restraints are all non-tariff barriers to trade.
18. Unlike other trade policies, local content regulations tend to benefit consumers and not producers.
19. Local content regulations provide protection for a domestic producer of parts by limiting foreign competition.
20. Antidumping policies are designed to punish foreign firms that are engaged in dumping.

Exercise 2: Choose the best answer for the following sentences
1. What term refers to a situation in which a government does not attempt to restrict

what its citizens can buy or sell to another country?
   A. Tariffs   B. Import quotas   C. Free trade   D. Subsidies
2. Which of the following is NOT one of the main instruments of trade policy?
   A. Tariffs   B. Credit portfolios
   C. Local content requirements   D. Administrative policies
3. Specific tariffs are _____.
   A. levied as a proportion of the value of the imported good
   B. government payment to domestic producers
   C. in the form of manufacturing or production requirements of goods
   D. levied as a fixed charge for each unit of a good imported
4. Tariffs do not benefit _____.
   A. consumers   B. domestic producers
   C. governments   D. domestic firms
5. Import tariffs _____.
   A. reduce the price of foreign goods
   B. create efficient utilization of resources
   C. reduce the overall efficiency of the world economy
   D. are unambiguously pro-consumer and anti-producer
6. By lowering production costs, _____ help domestic producers compete against foreign imports.
   A. subsidies   B. duties   C. quotas   D. tariffs
7. Which of the following is a consequence of subsidies?
   A. Subsidies make domestic producers vulnerable to foreign competition.
   B. Subsidies lead to lowered production.
   C. Subsidies protect inefficient domestic producers.
   D. Subsidies produce revenue for the government.
8. _____ is a direct restriction on the quantity of some good that may be imported into a country.
   A. Import tariff   B. Import quota   C. Import subsidy   D. Ad valorem tariff
9. _____ is the process of applying a lower tariff rate to imports within the import quota than those over the quota.
   A. Tariff rate quota   B. WTO promotes   C. Free trade   D. Tariff effects
10. _____ is levied as a proportion of the value of the imported good.
    A. Ad valorem tariffs   B. Expanding Trade Agreements WTO
    C. Agreeing to a VER   D. Specific tariffs

Exercise 3: Translate the following sentences into Chinese

1. Mercantilism is the first theory of international trade that emerged in England in

the mid-16th century. It is an economic philosophy advocating that countries should simultaneously encourage exports and discourage imports.
2. Free trade refers to a situation in which a government does not attempt to influence through quotas or duties what its citizens can buy from another country, or what they can produce and sell to another country.
3. According to Ricardo's theory of comparative advantage, it makes sense for a country to specialize in the production of those goods that it produces most efficiently and to buy the goods that it produces less efficiently from other countries, even if it means buying goods from other countries that it could produce more efficiently itself.
4. Unlike Ricardo's theory, however, the Heckscher-Ohlin theory argues that the pattern of international trade is determined by differences in factor endowments, rather than differences in productivity.
5. Generally, there are four stages to the product life cycle, from the product's development to its decline in value and eventual retirement from the market: Introduction, Growth, Maturity and Decline.
6. Comparative advantage is the ability of a country or firm to produce a particular good or service more efficiently than other goods or services, such that its resources are most efficiently employed in this activity.
7. The English had an absolute advantage in the production of textile, while the French had an absolute advantage in the production of wine. Thus, a country has an absolute advantage in the production of a product when it is more efficient than any other country at producing it.
8. New trade theory argues that through its impact on economies of scale, trade can increase the variety of goods available to consumers and decrease the average cost of those goods.
9. EU ever imposed tariff rates on many agricultural markets. The aim is to increase prices for domestic European farmers in order to increase their income.
10. Protectionism is the imposition of barriers to restrict imports. Commonly used protectionist devices include tariffs, quantitative restrictions (quotas), import licenses, requirements that governments only buy domestically produced goods, and health and safety standards.

Exercise 4: Translate the following sentences into English
1. 17世纪，重商主义者的思想在欧洲占主导地位。
2. 亚当·斯密在1776年的《国富论》中提出绝对优势理论。
3. 大卫·李嘉图是经济理论发展史上最重要的人物之一。
4. 迈克尔·波特提出了国家竞争优势理论，解释了为什么特定的国家在特定的产业中取得了国际上的成功。

5. 关税主要针对进口商品征收，从而提高进口商品的国内价格，并可用于保护国内生产者免受外国竞争。
6. 关税有两种基本类型：从价税和从量税。
7. "购买国货"规定要求各国政府优先考虑国内生产商生产的产品。
8. 非洲香蕉生产商敦促欧盟维持拉美关税。
9. "倾销"是指公司以低于"公平市场价格"的价格出售产品。这可能会使国内市场充斥着廉价的进口商品，使国内企业难以继续经营下去。
10. 针对美国可再生能源产品的补贴，中国启动世界贸易组织（WTO）争端解决机制。

Exercise 5: Critical thinking and discussion questions

1. What is trade protectionism and its function during the international trade?
2. Whose interest should be the paramount concern of government trade policy—the interests of producers (businesses and their employees) or those of consumers?
3. Explain what subsidy is and its various forms.
4. List major types of non-tariff barriers in international trade.
5. Mercantilism is a bankrupt theory that has no place in the modern world. Discuss.

PART 5

INTRODUCTION OF COUNTRIES ON THE BELT AND ROAD

PART 5 selects some countries on the Belt and Road to briefly introduce their general information, economic profile, relations with China and business etiquette and taboos. The selected countries include 4 countries on the Silk Road Economic Belt, 7 countries on the 21st Century Maritime Road, and 2 American countries, which is totaled 13 countries. These countries either trade heavily with China or invest heavily with China. China generally ranks top positions in their trading partners. In addition, China has invested numerous large projects in these countries through foreign investment or foreign aid. All of these suggest that these countries are closely tied with China, and need us to learn more about.

Chapter 23

Countries on the Silk Road Economic Belt

23.1 Kyrgyzstan

23.1.1 General Information

Kyrgyzstan is a landlocked country located in Central Asia, with the area of 199,900 square kilometers. It is further from the sea than any other country in the world. The land itself is largely made up of mountains, valleys, and basins. It is bordered by Uzbekistan, Tajikistan, Kazakhstan, and China.

The largest city and as well as the capital of Kyrgyzstan is Bishkek, with a population. The second-largest city is Osh, in the south of the country.

Many business and political affairs are carried out in Russian. Until recently, Kyrgyz remained a language spoken at home and was rarely used during meetings or other events. However, most parliamentary meetings today are conducted in Kyrgyz, with simultaneous interpretation available for those not speaking Kyrgyz.

The currency of Kyrgyzstan is som.

23.1.2 Economic Profile

In 2018, the GDP of Kyrgyzstan is 8.09 billion USD and the GDP growth rate is 3.5%. The GDP per capita is 1,087.2 USD. Exports account for about 33% of GDP and imports account for about 68% of GDP. The net inflow of Foreign Direct

Investment (FDI) is 144 million USD.

Kyrgyzstan's economy is highly dependent on the exports of gold and other precious metals and stones (34% of total exports). Other exports include: oil, gas and other mineral products (15% of total exports), textiles (12%), vegetables (9%) and transport equipment (8%). Main export partners are: Switzerland (33% of total exports), Kazakhstan (24%), Russia (13%) and Uzbekistan (11%). Others include: China, Turkey, Turkmenistan and Afghanistan.

Kyrgyzstan main imports are: fuel and other mineral products (22% of total imports); transport equipment (13%); machinery (12%); chemicals and related products (9%); food, alcoholic and non-alcoholic beverages, vinegar and tobacco (8%); nonprecious metals (7.7%) and textiles (7%). Main import partners are: Russia (33% of total imports), China (23%) and Kazakhstan (10%). Others include: United States, Japan and Germany.

The time required to start a business has been shortened from 21 days in 2000 to 10 days in 2018. The business environment has been continually improved in recent years.

23.1.3 Trade Agreements

On April 15, 1994, Commonwealth of Independent States (CIS) member states (Azerbaijan, Armenia, Belarus, Kazakhstan, the Kyrgyzstan, Moldova, Russia, Tajikistan, Turkmenistan, Ukraine, and Uzbekistan) agreed to establish a free-trade zone. According to the agreement, imports of goods produced within the CIS having respective certificates of origin are not subject to any customs or value-added taxes in the Kyrgyzstan. However, this exemption does not cover excise goods (such as alcohol and tobacco); furniture; video, television and computer equipment and any accessories to such electronic equipment. Russia, Belarus, Kazakhstan, Kyrgyzstan and Tajikistan have also signed a customs agreement.

In June 2004, the Kyrgyzstan signed a Trade and Investment Framework Agreement (TIFA) with the United States, Kazakhstan, Tajikistan, Turkmenistan, and Uzbekistan. The objective of the TIFA is to provide a forum for addressing trade issues and enhancing trade and investment between the United States and Central Asia. The TIFA also provides a platform to address regional trade issues that hamper intra-regional trade, economic development and investment. The TIFA creates a United States-Central Asia Council on Trade and Investment, which is designed to consider a wide range of issues that include, but are not limited to, intellectual property, labor, environmental issues and enhancing the participation of small-sized and medium-sized enterprises in trade and investment.

The Kyrgyzstan has bilateral investment treaties with the United States, Armenia,

Azerbaijan, Belarus, China, Finland, France, Georgia, Germany, India, Indonesia, Iran, Kazakhstan, the Republic of Korea, Lithuania, Malaysia, Moldova, Mongolia, Pakistan, Sweden, Switzerland, Tajikistan, Turkey, United Kingdom, Ukraine and Uzbekistan.

The Kyrgyzstan has also signed double-taxation treaties with 27 countries including Armenia, Austria, Belarus, Canada, China, Finland, Germany, India, Iran, Kazakhstan, Lithuania, Malaysia, Moldova, Mongolia, Pakistan, Poland, Russia, Switzerland, Tajikistan, Turkey, Ukraine, and Uzbekistan. The U.S.-U.S.S.R. treaty on double taxation, which was signed in 1973, remains in effect between the U.S. and the Kyrgyzstan.

In August 2015, the Kyrgyzstan formally joined the Eurasian Economic Union (EAEU). However, most of the technical regulations, including taxes, tariffs, inspections, and standards, will not be fully implemented for many years to come. Several aspects of the agreement, including levels of taxation on various goods, have not been decided. Uniform implementation of EAEU customs requirements has been uneven across the union and within the Kyrgyzstan itself. Customs inspectors are unable or unwilling to make informed decisions regarding requirements or clearances. Widespread corruption, extending even to the judicial system, affects nearly all aspects of doing business, including customs clearance, registration, employment of locals and foreigners, and payment of taxes.

23.1.4 Relation with China

Since 2012, China has become the largest source of foreign direct investments into the economy of Kyrgyzstan; for 2006-2017, the cumulative gross of Chinese FDI inflow was equal to USD2.3 billion. For this period, Chinese FDI constituted 25%-50% of total FDI to Kyrgyzstan, which is equivalent to 2%-7% of the country's GDP.

Key Chinese FDI sectors are geological explorations, the mining industry and the production of refined petroleum products. Mining-related FDI (geological explorations and the mining industry) concentrate on the development of gold deposits in Kyrgyzstan. Chinese companies operate some 10 medium-sized mines producing gold-copper concentrate which is exported for refining to China. According to official statistics, there are no major Chinese agricultural investment projects in Kyrgyzstan while a plan has been announced by the governments of China and Kyrgyzstan to build the agro-industrial park Iskra Asia near Bishkek to produce meat, fish and animal feed both for the domestic market and exports to China.

At least some of the Chinese investors are state-owned enterprises (e.g. gold producer Full Gold Mining was established by the state corporation Linbao Gold). They operate FDI projects as foreign enterprises or as joint ventures with the Kyrgyz state (e.g. state-owned gold producer Kyrgyzaltyn) and private companies with the majority of shares owned by the Chinese partners.

Chinese companies have built two oil refineries in the northern part of Kyrgyzstan near Bishkek. Zhongda China Petrol Company is the largest such enterprise in this sector in Kyrgyzstan. There are no oil deposits nearby (either in Kyrgyzstan, or in neighboring countries) to supply these refineries through a pipeline. One, rather scarce, source of raw materials is domestic crude oil produced in the south of Kyrgyzstan. Another, more important, source of raw materials is imports of crude oil and semi-processed oil products from Kazakhstan. These raw materials also get to the refineries by rail. Due to the relatively high raw material and transportation costs, the refineries seem to lack competitive advantages on the domestic market in comparison to Russian oil products imported to Kyrgyzstan on beneficial terms. As a result, the refineries are reported to work below one-third of their capacity and mostly export their produce to Tajikistan and Afghanistan where the prices for oil products are higher than in Kyrgyzstan.

Chinese FDI in other sectors of the Kyrgyz economy (e.g. retail trade, construction materials production, food processing) are relatively minor. In 2009, China Eximbank financed the construction of a large cement plant in southern Kyrgyzstan. Later, however, this plant was sold to Kazakh investors.

23.2 Uzbekistan

23.2.1 General Information

The Republic of Uzbekistan declared independent on 31 August 1991, after the disintegration of the Soviet Union. Total area of its territory is about 448,978 square kilometers.

Uzbekistan is landlocked country and borders with all the Central Asian countries—Kazakhstan, Tajikistan, Kyrgyzstan, and Turkmenistan. The capital of the Republic of Uzbekistan is Tashkent.

The official language of Uzbekistan is Uzbek. People in autonomous Republic of Karakalpakstan speak Karakalpak. Moreover, many people speak Russian.

The currency of Uzbekistan is Uzbek som (UZS).

23.2.2 Economic Profile

In 2019, total GDP of Uzbekistan is 328.436 billion USD. GDP per capita is equal to 7,134 USD. Exports and imports in Uzbekistan kept increasing for the last two decades. In 2018, Uzbekistan exported 14.7 billion USD and imported 19.5 billion USD.

Uzbekistan mostly exports precious metals (gold, silver), which account for 45% of total exports. The rest parts of the exports are: textiles 15% (pure cotton yarn, T-shirts, etc.); metals 10% (refined copper, copper wire, raw zinc, etc.); mineral products 9% (petroleum gas, etc.); vegetable products 7% (grapes, pitted fruits, nuts, other fruits, tomatoes, etc.); chemical products 4% (radioactive chemicals, etc.); transportation 2% (cars, vehicle parts, tractors, buses); and others (foodstuffs, machines, etc.).

Main product types that Uzbekistan imports are: machines 25% (large construction vehicles, textile fiber machinery, heating machinery, agricultural machinery, etc.); metals 14% (coated flat-rolled iron, iron pipes, hot-rolled iron, semi-finished iron, iron structures); transportation 12% (cars, vehicle parts, tractors, buses); chemical products 10% (packaged medicaments, etc.); mineral products 7% (refined petroleum, cruel petroleum, etc.); vegetable products 5% (wheat, tea, potatoes); and other products (textiles, wood products, foodstuffs, instruments, paper goods, etc.).

Uzbekistan exports a lot of different products to many countries. According to the data of 2017, almost half of the Uzbek exports value is dedicated to Switzerland due to the reason that Uzbekistan exports gold there. Second and third largest importers from Uzbekistan are China and Russia with 17% and 12%, respectively. Uzbekistan also exports to Turkey, Kazakhstan, Kyrgyzstan and other countries.

The largest exporters to Uzbekistan are also China and Russia with 24% and 23%, respectively. Imports from Republic of Korea and Kazakhstan compose 11% for each. Uzbekistan also imports from Turkey (6%), India and European countries.

FDI inflows in Uzbekistan considerably increased for the past two decades, but experienced significant fluctuations. As it can be seen from Figure 23.1, in the beginning of 2000s, FDI inflows composed about 70 million-100 million USD, with the sharp increase to 705.2 million USD in 2007. There can be observed even sharper increase in the period of 2009-2010, when the inflow of FDI doubled to 1.636 billion USD. However, in 2012 and 2015 there were considerable shrinks to 563 million USD and 66.5 million USD, respectively. With a significant increase by 25 times in 2016, FDI inflow reached its peak in 2017 with approximately 1.8 billion USD. In 2018, it jumped down by almost 3 times and composed 624.7 million USD.

The main part of FDI (almost 60%) flows to mining industry (oil and gas). Considerable parts go to manufacturing, information and transportation industries—13%, 10% and 9%, respectively. The remaining part is divided between the other industries, such as health, electricity and gas supply, water usage and etc. Uzbekistan keeps FDI relationship mainly with China, USA, Turkey, Republic of Korea, Germany,

Russia, and Japan. The major investors in each industry are shown in Figure 23.2.

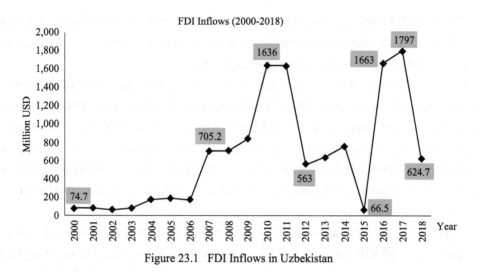

Figure 23.1　FDI Inflows in Uzbekistan

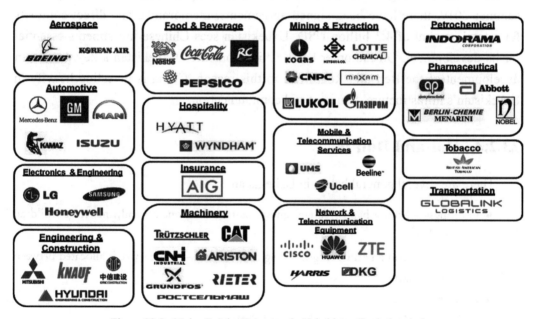

Figure 23.2　Major Foreign Investors in Uzbekistan (by industries)

　　There are pros and cons for Uzbekistan to attract FDI. The positive factors include stable macroeconomy, large domestic market with a population of 33 million, cheap labor force, rich natural resources, sound business environment (ranked 12th among the easiest countries to start a business), and strategic position between China and Europe due to the New Silk Road. However, there are several places that Uzbekistan needs to improve to attract foreign investment, including low economic diversification, underdeveloped banking services, and state interventionism.

23.2.3 Relation with China

Since 1992, Uzbekistan has established diplomatic relation with China. During this period there have developed numerous bilateral agreements. Particularly, these bilateral ties are marked with high degree of economic engagement.

China is Uzbekistan's second largest trading partner and the major source of investments. The main imports of Uzbekistan from China are different types of machinery (37% of total imports from China). Apart from that, Uzbekistan also imports metals, textiles and plastics—16%, 13% and 11%, respectively. The main exports of Uzbekistan to China are Mineral Products (42%) and Textiles (28%). In 2017, total imports of Uzbekistan from China composed 2.72 billion USD, and total exports to China are 1.4 billion USD.

China is one of the main sources of investments for Uzbekistan. China has already invested about $8 billion in Uzbekistan; moreover, during the 5th meeting of the Chinese-Uzbek intergovernmental committee on cooperation, which took place in summer 2019, there have been signed agreements, memoranda, and direct contracts for a total amount of 4.3 billion USD. Uzbekistan sees Chinese investments essential for its development. On the other hand, China considers Uzbekistan a key partner in development of the Belt and Road; due to this reason, China is investing heavily in Uzbekistan's infrastructure, transport and communication.

23.2.4 Dos and Don'ts

There are several general habits in Uzbekistan:

- Greetings—shaking hands (several questions regarding one's family, marriage, children and health);
- Stand nearer than an arm's length during conversations—more space is allocated between men and women;
- Regular eye contact;
- Well-groomed and wearing neatly pressed clothing.

There are no strict rules which need to be followed when doing business with Uzbek people. However, in order to make communication more efficient several things can be considered. One of the most important components of Uzbek culture is an expression of respect. It can be noted in the way they greet each other, ask about one's health and family, serve the table when invite to their homes and etc. Another aspect to be considered when doing business in Uzbekistan is that the majority of population is Muslim. If, for example, you have business lunch with your Uzbek partners, make sure that the food is "halal" (which means "lawful" or "permitted"). And the most common of "non-halal" food is pork.

23.3 Czech

23.3.1 General Information

Czech is a Central European Country that borders to the west with Germany, to the south with Austria, to the east Slovakia and the northeast to Poland. It is a landlocked country that covers 78,866 square kilometers with oceanic and continental climate in general.

Prague is the capital city. In 2017, Prague was the fifth most visited European city after Istanbul, Rome, Paris and London.

Czech is an EU member since 2004, but it does not belong to the Eurozone. It uses its own currency Czech koruna.

23.3.2 Economic Profile

In 2018, GDP of Czech is 245.23 billion USD, and GDP per capita is 23,078 USD. Czech exported 202.5 billion USD and imported 162.9 USD in 2018. The top exports of Czech include vehicles (20.4%), machinery (19.8%), electrical machinery (18.3%). The top imports of Czech are the same as top exports, with electrical machinery (20%), machinery (17%) and vehicles (10.4%). Over 80% of Czech's trade happens within EU. Germany is its largest trading partner.

In 2018, Czech attracted 164.2 billion USD of foreign investment. Czech invest 41 billion USD abroad in this year. Inward FDI mainly flow to financial and insurance activities and manufacturing. These two industries attracted about 60% of total FDI. The FDI outflow of Czech mainly flows to the financial and insurance activities, which accounts for 71.5% in 2018. The top investors in Czech are Netherlands, Luxembourg and Germany. The key sectors that worth to invest in Czech are automotive, machinery, electronic, life sciences, airplane technique and IT.

23.3.3 Relation with China

In 2016, Czech exports to China 1.9 billion USD and China exports to Czech 17.77 billion USD. FDI flow between the two countries is minor. In 2015, China invested 1.5 billion euro in Czech, mainly in the area of real estate.

23.3.4 Dos and Don'ts

There are some general habits in Czech, including:

- Many Czechs tend to have distrust, especially towards foreigners.
- Personal space is very important in the Czech Republic.
- Czechs are more individualists than collectivists, and this applies to both personal life and work.
- Being late for official events and meetings is considered very rude.
- Entering the house, Czechs remove their street shoes immediately and put on slippers. Almost every Czech house has shoes for guests.
- Many Czechs, being at home with their families, can only be dressed in underwear—this should be borne in mind if you're planning to visit your Czech friend.
- Family plays a crucial role in the life of every Czech, often several generations live side by side. It is customary to respect all the elderly, including strangers.
- In public transport, locals give up their seats to older people and pregnant women.
- Czechs use a polite form of address to strangers and unfamiliar people, as well as elders.
- Getting acquainted with someone, Czechs shake the hands, keeping eye contact. Friends are greeted the same way.
- Most Czechs are Catholics, but there are also many atheists in the country. Here faith is considered a private matter.
- Czech mentality can be called "a small country's mentality". "A small but their own"—that's what many Czechs think, preferring to pay more attention to what is happening in their country than in the rest of the world.
- Czechs highly value education and respect educated people.

In business, there are Dos and Don'ts.

- Punctuality is important in business and meetings; plan well ahead.
- English is an accepted business language but hire an interpreter for meetings outside the major cities or for negotiations.
- Address your business partner with Pan (Mr.), Pani (Ms.), plus their surname.
- Add professional titles if possible; address your partner with Pan or Pani plus their title (Professor Pan).
- Expect decision-making to be slow due to a focus on details and hierarchy.
- Do not jump to business right away; take some time for small talk.
- Meetings take place in the office or recently also during business lunches, but these could also be offered in the company canteen.
- Czech people tend to view life and judge deals from an almost ideological perspective, freedom and equality as basic principles.

- Beer and breweries is a welcome subject in any conversation; Czechs are very proud of their beer history.
- Gifts are not necessary in business relations; if you do, gifts should be modest but good (such as quality pens, imported liquor or flowers for ladies).

23.4 Germany

23.4.1 General Information

Germany (officially: the Federal Republic of Germany; German: Bundesrepublik Deutschland) is the largest country in Central Europe, covering an area of 357,582 square kilometers. Germany is considered to be the heart of Europe as no more than nine neighboring countries surround it: Denmark in the north, Poland and the Czech Republic in the east, Switzerland and Austria in the south, France in the southwest and Belgium, Luxembourg and the Netherlands in the west.

Germany is a country rich in natural beauty. Between the peaks of the Alps in the south and the North Sea and Baltic coasts, breathtaking landscapes are there, ranging from vast expanses of river and lakeland scenery, hills uplands, and densely wooded regions to agricultural plains and industrial cities. The pride of the German mountains is the Zugspitze. The Zugspitze is the highest mountain in Germany at 2,963 meters. Competing with the beauty of the mountains is the river Rhine. The Rhine is Germany's longest river, which flows the country for a total of 865 kilometers.

Berlin, located in the north part of Germany, is the capital city and the most populous city in Germany. With an area covering 344.3 square miles, people consider Berlin to be the largest city in the country. Every year Berlin attracts millions of visitors. Having played a crucial role in both World War One and Two, the town provides its tourists with the perfect fusion between past and modern history.

Germany has the second largest population of any European country. More than 90% of the people are considered to be descendants from Germanic tribes (ethnic Germans). Beginning with the 1950s, a large number of foreign workers have come to Germany from countries like Turkey, Italy, Greece, and the former Yugoslavia. Nowadays, Germany has become a country with one of the most diverse communities in Europe, making it extremely special and unique.

The nation's official language is Standard or High German, with over 95% of the population speaking German as their first language. German is also the official language of Austria and one of the three official languages of Switzerland. Apart from that, there are also German speakers in Eastern Belgium, the French region of Alsace-Lorraine,

Lichtenstein, Luxembourg, and some regions in Northern Italy. Needless to mention the fact that German is an official language of the European Union and one of the three working languages of the European Commission. But there are also many more dialects spoken throughout the country. It is essential to mention that throughout the country, there are many other spoken dialects and minority languages. For instance, Low German is spoken along the North Sea, and 60,000 people speak Baltic Sea coasts, Sorbian, which is a Slavic language in eastern Germany, Turkish (1.8% of the population) spoken by Germany's immigrant community and Frisian spoken in Nordfriesland by around 10,000 people.

In 2002, Euro became the official currency of Germany. Euro pronounced in German like OY-row has the symbol €, and it was created by a German named Arthur Eisenmenger. Currently, there are nineteen states in EU using euro as their official currency: Austria, Belgium, Cyprus, Estonia, Finland, France, Germany, Greece, Ireland, Italy, Latvia, Lithuania, Luxembourg, Malta, the Netherlands, Portugal, Slovakia, Slovenia, and Spain. The Euro is divided into 100 cents and is issued in €2, €1, 50c, 20c, 10c, 5c, 2c, and tiny 1c denominations. Banknotes are issued in €500, €200, €100, €50, €20, €10, €5 domination. Today, the Euro is considered to be one of the strongest and most stable currencies in the world. Compared to other countries, the Germans still prefer to pay cash. Around 80% of all transactions in Germany are in cash.

23.4.2 Economic Profile

Germany's economy is not only one of the largest worldwide, but it is also the largest in Europe and prognosticated to become one of the countries with the largest GDP by the year 2030. At this moment, Germany is among the world's top 20 countries with the most extensive GDP per capita. Besides in Europe, Germany is the leading country in imports and exports, and worldwide she has been surpassed only by China and the United States. Needless to mention the fact that Germany, delineate one of the highest trade surpluses worldwide. Germany's national debt adds up to around 60% of GDP, and it is continuously diminishing. Germany boasts having the lowest unemployment rate in the European Union. Everything points out to a very bright future in Germany.

In 2018, the GDP per capita in Germany reached 47,502 USD, ranking the 13th position in the world. Beginning from 1970 until 2018, Germany's GDP per capita averaged 33,711 USD. In the first quarter of 2019, Germany's GDP grew 0.4% compared to the previous quarter. The total GDP of the first quarter of 2019 was 978,769 million USD, placing Germany in the top 3 countries with the highest registered

GDP in the world. In March 2019, its GDP deflator (implicit price deflator) increased to 2.169%. In the same month, the gross savings rate of Germany has measured 28.25%.

23.4.3 Foreign Trade

Germany is the third-largest exporter and importer in the world, and it is also responsible for more than half of the European Union's international trade. On the 1st of January 1995, Germany became a member of the World Trade Organization, taking two roles, one as an individual nation and one as part of EU. Many of Germany's exported products are related to industrial market and services, in particular, German mechanical engineering products, vehicles, and chemical products. About one euro in four is earned from exports, and every fifth job depends directly on foreign trade. The exports of goods and services had a high impact on Germany's GDP. More than 52% of Germany's GDP was the result of a high flow of exported products and services.

In 2018, Germany shipped 1.557 trillion USD of goods and services around the globe, with 66% exporting within Europe. France accounts for the largest share of German total exports, 9.5%. Asia took 18% of German products and services. Ten percent of total goods and services have been shipped to North America, and smaller percentages went to Africa (1.7%), Latin America (1.6%), Oceania, and the Caribbean (0.9%).

If we analyze the data from a macroeconomic point of view, we can notice that Germany's total exported goods represented 35.7% of its total GDP for 2018 (4.356 trillion USD). If we compare the resulted percentage of 2018 (35.7%) with the one from 2014 (41%), we can notice a decrease in the rate of German products sold on international markets. Given its population of 80.5 million people, Germany's 2018 exports (1.557 trillion USD) reflects around 19,400 USD per every resident living within Germany.

The following industries groups had the highest shipment quota during 2018: machinery including computers 271.7 billion USD (17% of total exports), vehicles 263.7 billion USD (16.9%), electrical machinery, equipment 163.8 billion USD (10.5%), pharmaceuticals 96.8 billion USD (6.2%), optical, technical, medical apparatus 80 billion USD (5.1%), plastics, plastic articles 68.1 billion USD (4.4%), aircraft, spacecraft 41.4 billion USD (2.7%), articles of iron or steel 33.6 billion USD (2.2%), mineral fuels including oil 33.4 billion USD (2.1%), iron, steel 29.2 billion USD (1.9%).

In 2018, Germany had imported 1.287 trillion USD worth of goods from all around the world. Much of Germany's total imports are imported from European countries. Most of Germany's imported goods come from the Netherlands, China, and France. In 2018, Germany's imports purchased from European countries stretched to 64.3%. Imports from Asia were accounted for 22.1% of its total imports while 7.1% worth of goods were imported from North America. Smaller quantities originated from Africa 2%, Latin America 1.4%, and 0.3% from Oceania (Australia).

The most often group products imported to Germany are as follows: machinery including computers 165.5 billion USD (12.9% of total imports), electrical machinery, equipment 159.1 billion USD (12.4%), vehicles 131.1 billion (10.2%), mineral fuels including oil 117.9 billion USD (9.2%), pharmaceuticals 57.9 billion USD (4.5%), plastics, plastics articles 49 billion USD (3.8%), organic chemicals 46.4 billion USD (3.6%), optical, technical, medical apparatus 44.2 billion USD (3.4%), iron, steel 33.3 billion USD (2.6%), articles of iron or steel 25.6 billion (2%).

When it comes to Germany's regulations and bureaucratic procedures, one can think it is challenging to overcome them. When companies plan to take place in Germany's market, they also have to keep in mind that US exporters will pay very close attention to them as well. It's not about discrimination; it's about making sure that the safety standards and all requirements are being closely followed. When it comes to a different product, a thing is sure, timeless testing and specific certifications are a must. The TARIC (Tarif Intégré de la Communauté), provides the right information and helps to determine which licenses are required for different kinds of products. The European Commission maintains an export helpdesk which is specialized in providing information about restrictions on various products. Apart from these two institutions dedicated to providing information to companies that are interested in developing on the German market, many EU member states might also provide companies with their list of goods subject to import licensing. For instance, Germany's "Import List" (Einfuhrliste) stipulates which licenses are required, their code number, any applicable restrictions, and the agency that could issue the relevant permits.

23.4.4 Foreign Direct Investment

In Europe, Germany is considered by far to be the most attractive country for foreign direct investment. However, as a result of the recent global recession and Eurozone crisis, the influx of FDI got constrained. Each year more and more companies are investing in Germany. People in business around the world are very much attracted to the German secure and rewarding business opportunities. Since 2010, Germany's FDI stock market increased by more than 20% to reach an astonishing 518 billion USD in 2015. Nowadays, more than 80,000 foreign companies are operating on the German market, employing 3.7 million people. In 2018, more than 2,000 international companies opened up business in Germany.

Despite the global recession and subsequent Eurozone crisis, which have happened in the previous years, and which have influenced the influx of Germany's FDI, Germany remains an attractive country for foreign direct investment. According to the United Nations Conference on Trade and Development (UNCTAD), in 2019, Germany became one of the world's leading countries for FDI with 812 billion USD in inward FDI stocks.

New studies point out the fact that more than half of total Germany's FDI stock is claimed by the Netherlands, Luxembourg, US, and UK. Other important investing countries are Switzerland, France, Italy, Belgium, Austria, Japan, Spain, and Denmark. In recent years Asian countries are trying to increase their FDI stocks in Germany. At this moment, Germany is the country with the world's largest recipient of Chinese FDI projects. A big part of the investments is usually orientated towards professional, scientific and technical services, finance and insurance, real estate, information and communication, manufacturing, and nonetheless trade.

23.4.5 Relation with China

In the past few years, Germany's relationship with China has evolved a lot. A strategic partnership unites both China and Germany. They enjoy a very close bilateral relation settled on a high political level. What has started as a strategic partnership in 2004, has ultimately evolved into a comprehensive strategic partnership in 2014. From a political point of view, Germany points China as a significant partner and indispensable element of their bilateral negotiation projects, including high-level coordination on policy, investment, the environment, dynamic trade relations, culture, and science. On the international stage of politics, China is an influential participant, and it's very well respected. Apart from that, China is also a gigantic economic participant.

In 2017, Germany had a trading volume of over 180 billion euros with China. This fact made Germany China's most important trading partner in Europe. German businesses are well accounted for with China's manufacturing and investment potential. Apart from these two areas, China is also very well known for its increasing prospect as a research base in a variety of domains. Needless to mention the fact, that in 2019 China's impressive market took over from Germany, as the world's leading exporter country. As also mentioned before, China is one of Germany's most essential and appreciated trading partners around the globe. According to data collected from the German Chamber of Commerce, the bilateral trade between Germany and China reached an astonishing number of 154 billion euros in 2014. The same report states the fact that German exports to China have been continuously growing, with a cumulative amount of 5,200 German companies operating in China in 2015. The data also reveals the fact that Germany's exports are mainly related to automobiles and machinery industries. These two industries account for more than 50% of Germany's total exports to China. The remaining percentage, such as industries related to electrical products, optical equipment, and airplanes, complete the total export volume. At the same time, electrical products and machinery dominate Chinese products exported to Germany.

The Federal Statistics Office of Germany stipulates as well that China is the largest trading partner for imports of Germany. Regarding exports to Germany, China is ranked fifth after the United States, France, the United Kingdom, and the Netherlands. Experts have stated that the trading relationship between China and Germany is and will continuously increase by an average of 14.2% each year, doubling every five years.

From the officially released government data, it can be noticed that FDI from Germany to China continues to be active and developing and that until nowadays, Germany remains one of China's top ten foreign investors. German companies have engaged themselves in employing over 1.1 million staff in China, providing a boost to the country's economy. When it comes to challenges, human resources are still reaming the biggest challenge for German companies to overcome by operating in China. To find qualified staff is reported to be one of the most challenging obstacles to overcome in China. 82.4% of companies have reported having difficulties in finding eligible Chinese members to fit in their job requirements. One of the most challenging parts is finding Chinese citizens speaking the German language. For German companies operating in China, this is the first significant requirement which has to be conquered, when applying for a job at their companies. This challenge is closely followed by issues related to currency risks. Other vital problems which worth to be mentioned are administrative hurdles, domestic protectionism, legal insecurity, and the protection of intellectual property.

23.4.6 Dos and Don'ts

Germans will always aim to find the best way of achieving the most excellent quality outcome. They take great care to plan very methodically and spend as well many hours in deliberating all factors of a decision. When you make a proposal or negotiation suggestion, you have to make sure that everything has been written down and has been stated enough. In business, they make sure that every path they followed is correct and transparent so that it can be analyzed and controlled at any time according to the protocol. They won't accept an offer or bend to your demands based on your friendliness. Everything will depend on your arguments and data. If there are any uncertainties, expect them to ask you for clarification.

Moreover, once a decision has been taken, Germans will show very little flexibility. Never try to push a negotiation or discussion to hurry things up, nevertheless, to insist on changing the outcome/decision. After the plan has been established, everything is expected to run smoothly and continuously.

Another vital aspect is to show up at the right time. German businessmen are emphasizing a lot the importance of being on time. Don't ever show up early or late to meetings, because it is considered very disrespectful and unprofessional. To avoid any problems, show up sooner to the meeting, but wait somewhere close for the right moment or visit some nearby shops before the meeting time, to make it look that you aren't sitting there just waiting for them.

It's essential to avoid bypassing a person to reach someone of the higher status to make sure that you will get a quicker deal. German business deals are hierarchical, so please remain patient and continue working with the designated person to work with you. Always make sure to use titles and last names when speaking to someone you don't know. Try to make sure that you will remember their names in advance so you can address them during the meeting.

Usually, when doing business with German people, you don't need to bring a gift when meeting them, but if you receive one, it's customary to open it right there. When attending a business social event, it's more common to exchange gifts. When exchanging gifts, stick with office items like high-quality pens or high-quality agendas with your company logo. Wine and liquor should work as well. Should you get the opportunity to go to a business associate's home, you can bring a gift of wine or chocolates. Flowers are acceptable, but there are not recommended because there are way too many rules regarding colors and flower counts.

German business meetings are an essential part of interacting with someone to make a deal or build an everlasting relationship. To get a better understanding and to maximize the chance of closing a contract with a German company, the following "Dos and Don'ts" should be considered:

- Do: Get right to the meeting. Avoid asking any questions related to relationships and family because they are not a part of German business.
- Do: Plan meeting away ahead of time. At least two or three weeks ahead of time.

- Do: The most senior person should enter the room first and great the top person on the other side/team.
- Don't: Meeting shouldn't be scheduled/hold on a Friday afternoon. German business people like to wrap up the week and attend different social events.
- Don't: Don't schedule any meetings during July, August, or September because these are regarded as holiday months, whereabouts many events and festivals are taking place around these periods.
- Don't: Don't sit down before you have been told to do it.

Chapter 24

Countries on the 21st Century Maritime Silk Road

24.1 Republic of Korea

24.1.1 General Information

Republic of Korea is located in East Asia, on the southern half of the Korean Peninsula jutting out from the far east of the Asian landmass. Korea covers 103,290 square kilometers. Seoul is the capital city of Korea.

Korean is the language of Korea. Its currency is Korean won (KRW).

24.1.2 Economic Profile

The GDP per capita of Korea in 2019 is 31,345 USD. Korea is the 5th largest export economy in the world and the 6th most complex economy according to the Economic Complexity Index (ECI). In 2017, Korea exported 596 billion USD and imported 471 billion USD, resulting in a positive trade balance of 124 billion USD. The top exports of Korea are Integrated Circuits, Cars, Refined Petroleum, Passenger and Cargo Ships and Vehicle Parts. Its top imports are Crude Petroleum, Integrated Circuits, Petroleum Gas, Photo Lab Equipment and Coal Briquettes.

The top export destinations of Korea are China Mainland, the United States, Vietnam, China Hong Kong, and Japan. The top import origins are China Mainland, Japan, the United States, Germany, and Other Asia.

In 2017, Korea ranks as the world 20th top host economy in terms of FDI inflows. FDI stocks increased by 22% from 2016 to 2017 reaching 230 billion USD (15.4% of GDP). The main investing countries or regions in Korea are US, Cayman Islands, China Hong Kong, China Mainland, Vietnam, Luxembourg, Ireland, UK, Singapore, and Japan. Investments have been mainly oriented towards finance and insurance, trade, manufacturing, real estate, information and communication, mining and quarrying, and transportation.

Korea's appeal in terms of foreign direct investment is the result of the country's rapid economic development and the country's specialization in new information and communication technologies. However, the lack of general transparency in regulations remains a major concern for foreign investors. The World Bank esteems that the Korea is a country with a highly developed business environment as testified by its 5th position in the Doing Business 2019 ranking.

24.1.3 Relation with China

Diplomatic relations between China and Korea were formally established on August 24, 1992. In recent years, China and Korea have endeavored to boost their strategic and cooperative partnership in numerous sectors, as well as promoting high level relationship. Trade, tourism and multiculturalism, specifically, have been the most important factors of strengthening two neighboring countries cooperative partnership.

China is the top market of Korea. China accounts for 24% of all Korean exports. Among the exports to China, 79% are intermediate goods, and 27% are semiconductors. From 2001 to 2017, the average increase of trade per year is 13.9%.Chinese companies' direct investment in Korea surged 240% in 2018, boosting foreign direct investment in Korea to a new annual high.

24.1.4 Dos and Don'ts

The general habits in Korea include:

- Koreans generally prefer to concentrate on their food while eating, and to talk after the meal finished over coffee or tea.
- Unless your hosts raise it first, avoid discussing business during a meal.
- Ensure you don't serve yourself or eat before the host initiates it.
- Never pick up any food with your fingers. Fruit is eaten in slices with forks.
- Pour and receive two hands for the drinks, and turn right or left your head when you are

drinking it.
- Never sticking up your chopstick on the rice. Never!
- Don't be late!
- Don't cross your leg during the meeting.
- Don't sneeze in public!
- Business cards—Handing out business cards takes on a great importance here. When receiving a business card take a moment to look at it and if in a meeting place it neatly in front of you or put it in a place that demonstrates you value the information being given to you. Also giving and receiving business cards should be done with both hands if at all possible.
- Older people eat first, and start the meal.
- Should not hold your bowl up! Leave on the table all the way!

24.2 Myanmar

24.2.1 General Information

Sometimes known as Burma, the Republic of the Union of Myanmar—which is often shortened to Myanmar, is a sovereign state in Southeast Asia. Myanmar is the 40th largest country by area. The area is 676,578 square kilometers. Myanmar is situated in South East Asia, and is bordered on the north and northeast by China, on the east and south by the Lao and Thailand, on the south by the Andaman Sea and Bay of Bangal and on the west by Bangladesh and India.

Currently Myanmar's capital city is Naypyitaw. The city is officially replaced Yangon also known as the economic center of the country as the administrative capital of Myanmar in 2006. Naypyitaw is notable for its unusual combination of large size and very low population density. The city hosted the 24th and 25th ASEAN Summit, the 3rd BIMSTEC Summit, the 9th East Asia Summit, and the 2013 Southeast Asian Games.

The official language of Myanmar is Burmese, with some ethnic groups using their own languages.

Myanmar cuisine is mainly an amalgam of cuisines from various regions of Myanmar. It has also been influenced by various cuisines of neighbouring countries, in particular, China, India and Thailand. And most of Myanmar enjoy their lunch and dinner with rice and curry. They like sour, spicy taste. A popular Myanmar rhyme sums up the traditional favorites: "Of all the fruit, the mango is the best; of all the meat, the pork is the best; and of all the leaves, tea leaves or lahpet is the best."

24.2.2 Economic Profile

In 2018, the GDP of Myanmar is 360 billion USD, and GDP per capita is 1571.9 USD. Myanmar does not enjoy good trade relations, especially with the western countries. US does not import anything from Myanmar. Australia and EU have also imposed sanctions on the country, restricting the import of certain products. Myanmar's main export partners are China Mainland, India, Japan, Korea, Germany, Indonesia, and China Hong Kong. Myanmar's main import partners are China Mainland, Japan, India, Indonesia, Germany, France and, China Hong Kong.

In 2016-2017, Myanmar's trade deficit stood at around 5.5 billion USD, with exports lagging behind imports at 11.6 billion USD and 17.2 billion USD. Myanmar's exports fell drastically during the global economic crisis of 2008-09. Oil and natural gas dominate Myanmar's exports. The services export was 4 billion USD, while services import was 2 billion USD. Total trade as percentage of GDP is 28%. For fiscal year 2015/16, Myanmar received a record of 9.5 billion USD FDI.

24.2.3 Relation with China

China and Myanmar have shared a geopolitically strategic 2185-kilometre border. China and Myanmar have active bilateral relations with each other. China is providing extensive aid and helping to develop industries and infrastructure in Myanmar and aims to be the chief beneficiary from cultivating Myanmar's extensive oil and natural gas reserves. For strategic relation, China is the most important supplier of military aid and maintains extensive strategic and military cooperation.

For commercial relation, bilateral trade between China and Myanmar exceeds 13.54 billion USD. China is Myanmar's largest trading partner. In 2018, one third of Myanmar's export went to China and some are from border trade. The main exports of Myanmar to China are mineral fuels, oils, distillation products, rice, sugars and sugar confectionery and so on, which totaled 5.56 billion USD. The main imports of Myanmar from China are mineral fuels, iron and steel, electrical, electronic equipment, vehicles other than railway, tramway, plastic, and so on, reaching 6.22 billion USD.

China is not only its largest trading partner, but also has made a huge investment in Myanmar. China (including Hong Kong and Macao) ranked first among sources of Myanmar's FDI as of 2018. China invested 344 projects totaling 24.85 billion USD, accounting for 40% of Myanmar's FDI.

24.2.4 Dos and Don'ts

Myanmar culture is basically Buddhist and so much of the accepted etiquette pertains to Buddhist beliefs. To pay deep respect to a monk, kneel on the ground and touch your palms and forehead to the floor three times. Women should not touch a monk or give objects directly to him (instead of place the object on a table or some other surface near the monk). On buses and trains, people customarily give their seat to monks.

Most of Myanmar are devout Buddhists, and while they will not impose their beliefs on visitors, they will expect you to pay due respect to their traditional practices. Wear appropriate clothes when visiting religious sites, and don't violate their space. Avoid touching a monk's robes, and don't disturb praying or meditating people in temples. Watch what you do with your feet, too. You shouldn't point to or touch objects with them, and you should tuck them under yourself when sitting on the ground or floor. Don't sit with your feet pointing away from your body—or worse—pointing at a person or a pagoda.

Myanmar, like their religious compatriots around Southeast Asia, has strong feelings about the head and feet. The head is considered holy, while the feet are considered impure. Keep your hands off people's heads. Touching other people's heads is considered of disrespect, something to avoid doing even to children.

Businessmen will typically greet each other with a handshake. If a businesswoman offers you her hand, it is acceptable to shake it, but you should not offer your hand to a woman—a small bow is enough. In general, male to female contact should be avoided in public. The exchanging of business cards is commonplace in Myanmar. Business in Myanmar requires patience, as well as a willingness to build friendships and foster trust. Furthermore, Myanmar has a deep culture of hospitality and openness. Use people's appropriate titles when addressing them (e.g. Mr., Mrs.) unless they are children. The popular formal greeting in Burmese is "Min-ga-la-ba".

There is a strong tradition of respect for elders, throughout society and in business. When an older person enters a room, it is normal to stand up. Perhaps more uncomfortably for some westerners, junior members of staff will enter a room and bow uncomfortably deeply as they pass you.

24.3 Ethiopia

24.3.1 General Information

Ethiopia, officially the Federal Democratic Republic of Ethiopia, is a country in the northeastern part of Africa, known as the Horn of Africa. Some of the oldest skeletal evidence for anatomically modern humans has been found in Ethiopia. It is widely considered as the region from which modern humans first set out for the Middle East and places beyond.

During the late 19th-century Scramble for Africa, Ethiopia and Liberia were two nations that preserved their sovereignty from long-term colonization by a European colonial power and many newly-independent nations on the continent subsequently adopted its flag colors.

Ethiopia is a land of natural contrasts, with its vast fertile west, its forests, and numerous rivers, and the world's hottest settlement of Dallol in its north. The Ethiopian Highlands are the largest continuous mountain ranges in Africa, and the Sof-Omar Caves contains the largest cave on the continent. Ethiopia also has the most UNESCO World Heritage Sites in Africa.

Ethiopia shares borders with Eritrea to the north, Djibouti to the northeast, the de facto state of Somaliland and Somalia to the east, Kenya to the south, South Sudan to the west and Sudan to the northwest. Ethiopia covers 1,103,600 square kilometers. Its capital and largest city is Addis Ababa.

Ethiopia is a multilingual nation with around 80 ethno-linguistic groups, the four largest of which are the Oromo, Amhara, Somali and Tigrayans. Most people in the country speak Afro-asiatic languages of the Cushitic or Semitic branches. The working language of Ethiopia is Amharic.

Ethiopia uses the ancient Ge'ez script, which is one of the oldest alphabets still in use in the world. The Ethiopian calendar, which is approximately seven years and three months behind the Gregorian calendar, co-exists alongside the Borana calendar.

24.3.2 Economic Profile

In 2018, the GDP of Ethiopia was 29.9 billion USD, and GDP per capita is 951 USD. Ethiopia exported 2.6 billion USD and imported 9.6 billion USD in 2018.

Ethiopia's export is dominated by only a few numbers of agricultural commodities such as coffee, oil seeds, pulses, live animals and lather and lather products. Nowadays, Ethiopia tries to initiate value added export. The import of Ethiopia focuses on sophisticated manufacture goods, such as airplanes, helicopters, spacecraft, gas turbines, packaged medicaments, telephones and delivery trucks.

The exports of Ethiopia mainly go to Germany, Saudi Arabia, Netherlands, US, Switzerland, China, Somalia, Italy, Sudan, and Japan. Its imports mainly come from China, Saudi Arabia, India, Italy, US, Japan, Germany, Malaysia, and Pakistan.

Ethiopia is one of the top FDI destinations in Africa. In 2018, Ethiopia attracted 3.3 billion USD of FDI, accounting for 3.9% of GDP. It accounts for 18.5 % of all

FDI jobs in the continent. Almost half of FDI flows to the East African region were absorbed by Ethiopia. The top 6 FDI origins are: China, Turkey, India, Saudi Arabia, Netherlands, and UK. China has significantly increased its investment in the country over the past decade, notably in the field of construction, textile, power generation, and telecommunications sectors. The main investment area includes petroleum refining, mineral extraction, real estate, manufacturing, and renewable energy.

To encourage private investment and promote the inflow of foreign capital and technology into Ethiopian, the following incentives are granted to both domestic and foreign investors engaged in areas eligible for investment incentives.

(1) Customs Import Duty: 100% exemption from the payment of import customs duties and other taxes levied on imports is granted to an investor to import all investment capital goods such as plant machinery and equipment, construction materials as well as spare parts worth up to 15% of the value of the imported investment of capital goods provided that goods are not produced locally in comparable quantity, Top of Form Bottom of Form quality and price. Exemptions from customs duties or other taxes levied on imports are granted for raw materials necessary for the production of export goods.

(2) Exemption from Payment of Export Customs Duties: Ethiopian products and services destined for export are exempted from the payment of any export tax and other taxes levied on exports.

(3) Income Tax Holidays: Any income derived from an approved new manufacturing and agro-industry investment or investment made in agriculture shall be exempted from the payment of income tax. For the period ranging from 2-6 years profit tax holiday is granted subject to council of ministers regulation Number 8412003 issued on the bases investment proclamation No 280/2002 moreover, the council of Ministers may also award profit tax holiday for greater than seven years. The period of exemption from profit tax begins from the date of the commencement of production or provision of services as the case may be.

(4) Loss carried forward Business enterprises that suffer losses during the tax holiday period can carry forward such losses for half of the income tax exemption period following the expiry of the exemption period.

(5) Guarantees to investors

- Repatriation of capital and profits
- Guarantee against Exportation

Ethiopian is a member of the World Bank—affiliated Multilateral Investment Guarantee Agency (MIGA) which issues guarantees against non-commercial risks to enterprises that invest in signatory courtiers. Ethiopia has also signed the World Bank treaty "the International convention on the Settlement of Investment Disputes (ICSID) between States and Nationals of Other States".

24.3.3 Relation with China

The China-Ethiopia relation was established in 1970. By 2016-2018, Chinese direct investment (FDI) in Ethiopia had reached 4 billion USD and bilateral trade had grown to 5.4 billion USD.

Chinese premier Zhou Enlai visited Ethiopia in January 1964. The Ethiopian emperor Haile Selassie visited Beijing in October 1971, where he was received by Mao Zedong. Qian Qichen, China's vice-premier and minister of foreign affairs visited Ethiopia in July 1989, January 1991 and January 1994. Chinese president Jiang Zemin visited in May 1996. In June 2001 the Ethiopian deputy foreign minister visited Beijing, where he expressed support for the "One China" principle in the dispute with China Taiwan. In December 2003, Chinese premier Wen Jiabao visited Ethiopia to attend the opening of the China-Africa Cooperation Forum. In December 2004, the heads of the Ethiopian and Chinese legislatures met in Beijing and in a joint statement said that the two counties wish to expand all aspects of cooperation. In May 2007, China's Assistant Minister of Commerce Wang Chao visited Ethiopia and signed a debt relief agreement worth 18.5 million USD. In February 2008, the Chinese minister of construction met his counterpart in Ethiopia, and reemphasized the commitment of the two governments to cooperation. The Ethiopian minister welcomed the involvement of Chinese construction companies in improving Ethiopian infrastructure. In November 2008 the chairman of the standing committee of China's National People's Congress visited Ethiopia where he met senior Ethiopian officials and political leaders including President Girma Wolde-Giorgis and discussed ways to strengthen economic cooperation.

During these visits of two countries' leaders, many agreements have been reached. Agreements between the two countries include Agreement for Economic and Technological Cooperation (1971, 1988 and 2002); Trade Agreement (1971, 1976); Trade Protocol (1984, 1986, and 1988); Agreement for Trade, Economic and Technological Cooperation (1996); and Agreement for Mutual Promotion and Protection of Investment (1988). In May 2009, the two countries signed an agreement to eliminate double taxation, expected to boost trade and investment.

About 400 Chinese investment projects worth of 4 billion USD are in full operation in Ethiopia. Of the total 400 investment projects, over 100 were established in joint venture with Ethiopian partners. These projects have created over hundred thousand job opportunities in Ethiopia.

24.3.4 Dos and Don'ts

General habits in Ethiopia include:

- Unless you're at a restaurant or cafe, it is extremely rude to eat in front of Ethiopians without inviting them to join you. Unless you plan on sharing your snack with every single person on that bus or with every person you pass on the street, it's best to hold back. "Enebela" (እንብላ) means, "Let's eat!" in Amharic and is probably the single most widely used phrase in the country.
- Outside of Addis Ababa (Ethiopia's capital), it is extremely inappropriate for women to show their knees or shoulders. So girls, pack a lot of maxi dresses and scarves!
- Ninety percent of Ethiopian food is served with Enjera, a pancake-like dough, and the other 10% is served with bread, so get used to eating without silverware! However, since everyone eats off of the same plate, it is extremely rude to lick your fingers during the meal and someone will always come around with a water bucket to help you clean up after the meal.
- If you're invited to someone's house for coffee, it is rude to leave before finishing three cups.
- If you invite someone to meet for food or drinks, you are expected to pay. If they invite you, they are expected to pay.
- When meeting someone, whether for the first time or for the hundredth time, you will be expected to: shake their hand with your right hand while holding onto your right elbow with your left hand; shake their right hand while bumping your right shoulder against their right shoulder; or, if the person is an older woman whom you know well, shake her right hand while kissing her right shoulder.
- Don't be surprised to find males of all ages holding hands, feeding each other and/or cuddling. In Ethiopia, that's just how bros act like bros.
- Do not discuss homosexuality with Ethiopians, as it is outlawed and extremely taboo. If you are a homosexual couple visiting Ethiopia, you will unfortunately have to go "back in the closet" during your stay.
- If you need a waiter's attention, it is culturally appropriate to clap your hands.
- No matter how expensive your restaurant meal is, you will not be expected to tip more than five birr. Usually, anywhere from two to five birr is an acceptable tip.
- Most Ethiopians assume that sickness is caused by cold air or "bad smells", so if you open a window during a hot, crowded bus ride, don't be surprised if several people ask you to keep it closed.
- It is best to avoid using your left hand while eating Enjera, hand shaking or shopping. Using your left hand is often considered rude.
- Ethiopians are generally extremely welcoming, accommodating people who are excited

to see foreigners visiting their country. So if you have a cultural "do or don't" question during your trip, don't be afraid to ask the locals.

Dos:

- Make sure you spend some time getting to know an Ethiopian before talking about a serious matter or business.
- Be aware that tasks can take a long time to complete in Ethiopia and the pace of life is generally slower. For example, it takes hours to make brew coffee in the traditional Ethiopian way. Plan to allow more time for engagements and be patient if things last longer than expected.
- Try to refer to the Ethiopian nation, nationality or culture specifically when possible, rather than "African". It is appreciated when foreigners recognize that Ethiopia is culturally distinct from the rest of Africa.
- Show interest in the well-being of an Ethiopian's family whenever you see them (e.g. "How are your children?"). However, it is best not to enquire about a person's private life (e.g. relationships, parenting) unless they open up to you first.
- Show greater respect to elders in all circumstances and situations. Their age is thought to indicate wisdom, knowledge and experience.
- Remember that Ethiopians see themselves as progressive people and pride themselves on their country's legacy of independence. Avoid invoking stereotypes of Africa to form conclusions about Ethiopian culture.

Don'ts:

- Do not assume that all Ethiopian migrants have experienced conflict or lived in refugee camps. While this is the case for some, it does not apply to all people. Many Ethiopians migrate as skilled workers or on family visas.
- Do not criticize Ethiopia's developmental challenges. While certain things may not be as convenient to access in Ethiopia, it does not mean the culture or people are less sophisticated.
- Avoid asking questions that assume Ethiopians are uneducated, uncivilized or impoverished. Most Ethiopian migrants living in English-speaking countries are skilled, educated, urbanized and familiar with the technologies of the developed world.
- Do not assume that Ethiopians suffer from food shortages or famine. The country has not experienced famine since the 1980s and stereotypes of the people as "starving Africans" can be offensive.
- Avoid offering your opinion on local politics, ethnic tensions or Ethiopia's relationship with Eritrea. There are a lot of political overtones in Ethiopia. If the topic is raised, it is best to simply listen.

- Do not disrespect religion, be it Orthodox Christianity, Protestantism or Islam.
- Avoid directly asking someone what ethnicity they belong to. This can come across as an insensitive or divisive question. In Ethiopia, people generally ask one another what region they are from or language they speak, and make an informed guess about the person's tribe or ethnicity from there.
- Avoid complaining, raising your voice or showing public anger/frustration about petty or minor inconveniences. Ethiopians are generally tolerant and stoic people, and are very unlikely to make a scene if something aggravates them.

24.4 Djibouti

24.4.1 General Information

Djibouti is a country located in Eastern Africa that borders the Red Sea and the Gulf of Aden, with the area of 23,200 square kilometers. Neighboring countries include Ethiopia, Eritrea, and Somalia. Djibouti has a strategic location near the world's busiest shipping lanes and close to Arabian oilfields. The government system is a republic, and the chief of state is the president, and the head of government is the prime minister. Djibouti has a mixed economic system which includes a variety of private freedom, combined with centralized economic planning and government regulation. Djibouti is a member of the League of Arab States (Arab League) and the Common Market for Eastern and Southern Africa.

The capital city is Djibouti. There are several languages in Djibouti, including French (Official), Arabic (Official), Somali and Afar. The currency of Djibouti is Djiboutian franc.

24.4.2 Economic Profile

The GDP in Djibouti was worth 1.97 billion USD in 2018. The GDP of Djibouti represents less than 0.01% of the world economy. The economy of Djibouti is derived in large part from its strategic location on the Red Sea and the Gulf of Aden. As such, Djibouti's economy is commanded by the services sector, providing services as both a transit port for the region and as an international transshipment and refueling center. Djibouti is located in one of the busiest maritime trade routes and has the status of free trade zone. As a result, Djibouti is highly dependent on tax revenues from in-transit trade flow. Also, since Djibouti has very few natural resources and virtually no industry, it depends on foreign assistance.

The FDI inflow to Djibouti peaked at 286 million USD in 2013. FDI flows amounted to 165 million USD in 2017 and 265 million USD in 2018. In terms of stock, FDI represents 101.5% of the country's GDP, or almost USD 2.2 billion in 2018. The service sector receives the most FDI. The main investors are the Gulf countries, Ethiopia, Yemen, China, the U.S., France, Brazil, India and Turkey. As a member of COMESA willing to attract more FDI, Djibouti aims specifically at building closer ties with the Gulf Cooperation Council and India. Large inward FDI are expected in 2019, which will play a part in transforming the country into a regional logistics center.

In terms of business climate, Djibouti has made a remarkable jump in the 2019 Doing Business report of the World Bank. After gaining 17 positions in 2018, the country further won 55 positions in 2019, ranking 99th out of 190 economies (compared to 154th in 2018).

The reforms undertaken include creating a one-stop shop for business start-up, making property transfer easier and more transparent, strengthening access to credit, strengthening minority investor protections, making enforcing contracts easier by establishing a dedicated division within the court of first instance to resolve commercial cases and by adopting a new Code of Civil Procedure, and making resolving insolvency easier. The country's main attractive feature for investment is its strategic geographical location, situated at the maritime crossroads between the Far East, the Persian Gulf, Africa and Europe, which makes its deep-water port facilities and railway key assets. Moreover, Djibouti has a stable currency, which is freely convertible and pegged to USD. Furthermore, the government, which is implementing an ambitious infrastructure programme, offers significant tax reductions to foreign investors.

24.4.3 Relation with China

China and Djibouti established relations on January 8, 1979. China has financed a number of public projects in Djibouti. Since the First Forum on China-Africa Cooperation in 2000, Beijing has delivered 16.6 million USD in development finance to Djibouti. Chinese aid projects in Djibouti include:

- 8.2 million USD to fund the construction of a hospital in Arta.
- 2.41 million USD grant for construction of a new headquarters for the Djiboutian Foreign Minister.
- 1.75 million USD in food aid during a drought in Djibouti in 2005.

In 2016, construction began on a Chinese naval outpost in Djibouti. The site was slated to become China's first overseas military installation, with an estimated cost of

600 million USD. In 2017, China announced the launch of a cross-border potable water project between Ethiopia and Djibouti. The project will include the installation of a 102 kilometer long pipeline to draw groundwater from the Ethiopian town of Hadagalla to be provided to the towns of Ali-Sabieh, Dikhil, Arta and Djibouti city.

24.5 Kenya

24.5.1 General Information

Kenya, officially the Republic of Kenya, is a country in Africa with 47 semiautonomous counties governed by elected governors. Kenya covers 582,646 square kilometres. Kenya sits on the equator where it is bordered by South Sudan to the North West, Ethiopia to the North, Somalia to the East, Uganda to the West, Tanzania to the South and the Indian Ocean to the South-East. Kenya is one of the most varied lands on the planet. It encompasses savannah, lakelands, the dramatic Great Rift Valley and mountain highlands. It's also home to wildlife like lions, elephants and rhinos.

The capital and largest city in Kenya is Nairobi, which is famous for having the world's only game reserve in a large city. It is situated in the south-central part of the country, in the highlands at an elevation of about 5,500 feet (1,680 metres). The city lies 300 miles (480 km) northwest of Mombasa, Kenya's major port on the Indian Ocean. Nairobi is the second-largest city in the African Great Lakes area. With the suburbs included, Nairobi is Africa's 14th largest city. Other major cities include Mombasa, Kisumu, and Nakuru.

Kenya is a multilingual country. Although the official languages are Swahili and English, there are actually a total of 62 languages spoken in the country. These mainly consist of tribal African languages as well as a minority of Middle-Eastern and Asian languages spoken by descendants of foreign settlers (i.e. Arabic, Hindi, etc.).

The Kenyan Shilling (KES) is the currency of Kenya.

24.5.2 Economic Profile

Kenya has a market-based economy with a liberalized external trade system and a few state enterprises. In 2018, GDP per capita for Kenya was 1,839 USD. In 2017, Kenya exported 6.17 billion USD and imported 17.1 billion USD, resulting in a trade deficit of 11 billion USD. Kenya's chief exports are horticultural products and tea, while it mainly imports oil and mineral fuels, machinery, motor vehicles, cereals, iron and steel, and plastics. The exports of Kenya mainly go to Pakistan, Uganda, US, Netherlands, and UK. Its imports are mainly from China, India, United Arab Emirates, Saudi Arabia, Japan, and South Africa.

In 2018, FDI inflows to Kenya were 1,626 million USD. The ICT sector has attracted the most FDI. Other sectors targeted by FDI are banking, tourism, infrastructure and extractive industries. United Kingdom, Netherlands, Belgium, China, and South Africa, are the main investors in Kenya.

The Kenyan government has been actively taking measures and implementing reforms to attract FDI. As a result, the country made remarkable progress in the Doing Business ranking published by the World Bank. After it gained 16 places in the 2017 report, and 12 places in the 2018 report, it gained further 19 places in the 2019 report, reaching the rank 61st out of 190 countries. Kenya simplified procedures for business creation, and shortened the term of processing, and simplified the process to register property, and strengthened access to credit and minority investor protections and made paying taxes and resolving insolvency easier. The development of public-private partnerships as part of the "Vision 2030" strategy should also have a positive influence on FDI inflows. Kenya plays a pivotal role in the East African Community, acting as a regional economic hub.

24.5.3 Relation with China

These bilateral relations between Kenya and China started from 14 December 1963, two days after the formal establishment of Kenyan independence, when China became the fourth country to open an embassy in Nairobi. Military exchange between the two countries has been increasing in the past decade. In April 2007, the Jinchuan Group, a state-owned metal manufacturing group, became the first Chinese company to enter Kenya's mining sector, purchasing a 20% stake in Tiomin Kenya. Early in 2006 Chinese President Hu Jintao signed an oil exploration contract with Kenya. The deal allowed for China's state-controlled offshore oil and gas company, CNOOC Ltd., to prospect for oil in Kenya.

Kenyan president Mwai Kibaki visited Beijing in August 2005. In 2013, President Uhuru Kenyatta visited China. He held talks with his Chinese counterpart, Xi Jingping. Kenya and China ended up signing deals worth 5 billion USD. The Premier of China, Li Keqiang visited Nairobi on his 2014 Africa tour. He and President Kenyatta witnessed the signing of 17 multi-billion deals to fund multiple infrastructural projects and various agreements. This included the establishment of a China-Africa Development Bank.

In bilateral trade between Kenya and China, Kenya exports hides, skins, coffee, tea, titanium ores and plastics, and imports leather, rubber, machinery and transport equipment and chemicals. China is Kenya's largest trading partner. In 2017, Kenya exported to China was valued at 96.88 million USD, while it imported 3.79 billion USD in goods from China. China is also Kenya's biggest FDI source.

24.5.4 Dos and Don'ts

There are some general habits in Kenya:

- Never refuse hospitality.
- Do not buy items derived from endangered species.
- Do not ask people's tribe.
- Do not take people's picture without their consent.
- Watch what you wear.
- Never refuse a security check.

In business, there are somethings need to be aware of.

1. Greetings

A handshake is an appropriate greeting—start with the most senior person in the group and be sure to shake hands with each person present.

2. Communication style in Kenya

Blunt statements are best avoided as they may appear rude. This can make it hard to decipher people's true meaning or intentions as outright refusal is rare. Instead, evasive or subtle remarks may need to be interpreted. It's also important that expats control their emotions and avoid displaying anger or using profanities, especially in public settings.

3. Concept of time in Kenya

Meetings should begin on time, although there's little chance of an end time being adhered to. Spending time on small talk is important—rushing this aspect of a meeting will make a bad impression. The Kenyan concept of time is traditionally fluid, and expat businesspeople that value punctuality are likely to be frustrated.

24.6 Uganda

24.6.1 General Information

The Republic of Uganda, with the area of 241,550 square kilometers, is located in the heart of East Africa, with direct access to a regional market of 150 million potential customers, abundant natural resources, and a young English-speaking population. Uganda is commonly referred to as the "pearl of Africa" because of its natural beauty, good weather, and other natural resource endowments. Its capital city is Kampala. Ugandans speak English and Swahili. Uganda Shillings (UGX) is its currency.

24.6.2 Economic Profile

The GDP per capita of Uganda is 769 USD in 2018. Uganda's GDP growth rate averaged 5% over the past decade, driven in part by publicly financed infrastructure development as well as private investments in construction and telecommunications. With an estimated 1.4 billion barrels of recoverable oil, the World Bank described Uganda as the hottest inland exploration frontier in the world in 2017, attracting investments worth 8 billion USD from US, France, Britain, and China.

Agriculture plays a dominant role in Uganda's economy, employing nearly 4/5 Ugandans and contributing over 1/5 of GDP. Uganda is Africa's top coffee exporter, and the 8th largest coffee producer in the world. Other significant agricultural exports include fish, flowers, and horticultural produce.

In 2017, Uganda exported 2.79 billion USD and imported 5.84 billion USD, resulting in a trade deficit of 3.05 billion USD. The top exports of Uganda include coffee, tea, spices, gems, precious metals, cereals, fish, mineral fuels, and vegetables. Its top imports are refined petroleum, palm oil, packaged medicaments, broadcasting equipment, and cars. The top export destinations of Uganda are the United Arab Emirates, Kenya, South Sudan, the Democratic Republic of the Congo, and Rwanda. The top import origins are China, India, the United Arab Emirates, Kenya, and Japan.

Uganda is one of the countries that attract the most FDI in East Africa. FDI flows to Uganda accounted for 1.3 billion USD in 2018, an increase from 803 million USD in 2017. FDI stock also grew to 13.333 billion USD in 2018 (estimated at 47.4% of the GDP). The major recipient sectors of foreign direct investment are mining and quarrying, accounting for 49% of the total FDI. This was followed by information and communication technology (18.1%), finance and insurance (16.7%), and manufacturing (7.6%). Due to the discovery of oil reserves, new investors might be interested in the country in the future.

Also, according to UNCTAD report, some progress has been made in regulatory development in financial services (especially in insurance and capital market) and in privatization in banking for attracting FDI. On the other hand, Uganda is rich in natural resources.

24.6.3 Relation with China

China is one of the first countries to sign a joint communiqué to set up a diplomatic mission in Uganda. Since then, both countries have been maintaining cordial political relations despite the changes of internal and external situations. The exchanges of visits at the highest level have been maintained. And the mutual visits at the cabinet and other levels are very frequent. These visits have further enhanced the mutual understanding and friendly cooperation between the two countries.

For decades, the Chinese Government has continued to provide project aid to Uganda in forms of interest-free loans and grants to construct some of those projects which are at the best need of Uganda. Some of the notable Chinese projects include the Wakawaka Fish landing site, Kibimba (now Tilda) and Doho rice schemes, government buildings such as the Ministry of Foreign Affairs, the President's Office, Naguru Hospital, and the Mandela National Stadium at Nambole.

The Government of Uganda has in return, reciprocated by offering China projects such as the construction of the 600MW Karuma Hydropower Dam and the 51.4 km Kampala-Entebbe express high way.

China continues to be one of Uganda's leading trading partners. In 2012, the trade volume between the two countries came to 575.5 million USD, of which China's exports were 546.01 million USD, and imports 29.49 million USD. This indicated that Uganda exports 5% worth of what it imports from China. China imports leather, coffee, fish, and food products from Uganda and exports light industry products, farm tools, textiles, pharmaceutical products, garments, ceramics to Uganda. China has made this possible by employing a strategy that emphasizes a zero-tariff treatment to 95 percent of the products from the least developed African countries having diplomatic relations with China.

China is the largest source of foreign direct investment and the biggest infrastructure partner for Ugandan. The Chinese government has made significant investments in Uganda mainly in the areas of infrastructural development such as road construction, hospitals, railway, electrical power, and communications development.

In 2017, China invested 219 million USD in Uganda, creating 18,000 jobs. Uganda is among the top 4 investment destinations for China in Sub-Saharan Africa. There are 22 Chinese companies licensed in mining.

24.6.4 Dos and Don'ts

There are some general habits in Uganda. In Uganda, it is always best to shake hands while meeting even strangers will do you. Both men and women shake hands.

Children may kneel down upon your arrival in the home and so will women in the central part of the region. This is a cultural sign of respect.

Ugandans like to dress smart, but conservative. Ugandans find it insulting if you wearing clothes that are not neatly pressed, cleaned and in need of mending. Women should avoid wearing short shorts and mini-skirts. Modesty in dress code applies both to women and men.

Ugandans normally do not show affection in public. Kissing in public is not acceptable culturally. There is however a slow change, middle class Ugandan women will give a hug to another woman she knows well. Even the president has stated in an interview that he never kissed his wife in public.

Time in Uganda is based on the African concept of time which is based on relationships, at least most of the time.

Ugandans show respect for elders (Mzee). They are deeply respected, sought out for advice and counsel. The elderly in Uganda especially the grandmothers in villages are the backbone of Uganda.

In business, there are Dos and Don'ts in Uganda.

- Do respect the fact that people might not be used to seeing people with white skin, especially in the more rural areas. You will be called "Muzungu" which means "white". Some people might be afraid to touch you or get close because they think your skin is sensitive.
- Do make an attempt to learn some Uganda words or phrases before you come to Uganda. Being able to use a few phrases shows respect and will endear you to most Ugandans in Kampala and central areas.
- Do try to avoid constant eye contact when meeting with your business colleague. Some eye contact is acceptable but generally Ugandans prefer indirect eye contact.
- Don't be surprised if your Ugandan colleagues stand close to you during business conversations. Their personal space is smaller than in western countries.
- Don't use your right hand to greet your Ugandan associates. The right hand is believed to be unclean.

24.7 Cameroon

24.7.1 General Information

Cameroon officially known as the Republic of Cameroon is a nation in Central Africa, with the area of 475,442 square kilometers. It is bordered by the Central African Republic to the east, Chad to the northeast, Nigeria to the west, and the Republic of the

Congo, Gabon, and Equatorial Guinea to the south. The country's coastline lies in the Bight of Biafra, a section of the Gulf of Guinea, and the Atlantic Ocean.

Early settlers of Cameroon included the Baka hunter-gatherers in the south-eastern rainforest and the Sao civilization, found in Lake Chad. In the 15th century, Portuguese explorers arrived at the coast and named the region Rio dos Camarões which translates to River of Prawns. This later became Cameroon in English. In the 19th century, the Fulani soldiers established the Adamawa Emirate in the northern region of the country. A number of ethnic groups of northwest and west of the country also created powerful chiefdoms. This was in 1884 when Cameroon became a German colony referred to as Kamerun.

Cameroon has several important cities. Yaoundé is the capital city (political capital) as well as the second largest city of the country. Douala is the economic (commercial) capital of Cameroon and houses the Douala international airport and the largest port of the country. Another important city of Cameroon is Bafoussam, which is the trade center of the country. It is also the capital of the country's west region. Situated near the Benue River, Garoua is one of the most important cities of Cameroon. The city is the trading hub of the northern region of the country. It also houses Benue National Park and Waza National Park, the two important touristic attractions of Cameroon. Apart from these, other cities include: Loum, Mouloudou, Ngaoundere, Nkongsamba, Obala, Sa'a, Sangmelima, Tiko, Mamfe, Maroua, Mbandjock, Mbouda, Meiganga, Mokolo, and Mora, just to name a few.

Cameroon is often known as "Africa in miniature" due to the incredible cultural and geological diversity of the country. The country is home to over 1,738 different linguistic groups. French and English are the official languages of Cameroon. Eight out of the ten regions of the nation, housing 83% of the population of Cameroon, are Francophones. The remaining two regions, representing 17% of Cameroon's population are mainly Anglophones. However, the proportion of Anglophones in the country is gradually decreasing.

The official currency of Cameroon is the Central African CFA franc which is also used in Central African Republic, Chad, Republic of Congo, Equatorial Guinea, and Gabon. The Bank of Central African States which is responsible for the currency is based in Yaoundé, Cameroon. It is pegged to the Euro at a standard rate of 1 Euro = CFA 655.957. The franc has an equal value to the West African Franc but cannot be used in West Africa. The CFA Franc was introduced in 1945 by France to its colonies in Equatorial Africa to replace the French Equatorial African Franc. After independence, the colonies continued the use of the franc. The franc is offered in both notes and coins and is divided into centimes.

24.7.2 Economic Profile

Cameroon is a lower-middle income country in Central Africa. It is rich in natural resources such as gas, oil, timber, and minerals. The GDP for the Cameroon is 38.50 billion USD (2018) and the GDP per capita is about 1,497.80.

Cameroon is a country that is richly endowed with natural resources but whose industrial sector is still lagging. For this reason, it exports more of its raw materials in order to import more sophisticated manufactured goods that it is not yet technologically capable of producing. In 2017, Cameroon exported 4.27 billion USD and imported 5.88 billion USD, resulting in a negative trade balance of 1.61 billion USD.

The top exports of Cameroon are Crude Petroleum, Sawn Wood, Cocoa Beans, Bananas and Rough Wood. In 2016, Cameroon ranked fourth among tropical timber exporters worldwide by volume (and third by value), exporting more than any other African nation. Its top imports are Refined Petroleum, Special Purpose Ships, Rice, Crude Petroleum and Packaged Medicaments. The exports of Cameroon mainly go to China, France, Italy, Netherlands, and Spain. The imports of Cameroon are mainly from China, France, Nigeria, Thailand, and Togo.

FDI inflows to Cameroon, traditionally low compared to the potential of its economy, reached 702 million USD in 2018, decreasing significantly compared to 814 million USD registered in 2017. FDI stocks are estimated to represent 7.2 billion USD in 2018 (18.8% of GDP). Most of FDI come from European Union, particularly France and Germany and target the mining industry, including oil extraction. However, China has become a major investor in the country, carrying on large infrastructure projects.

Cameroon's economy has the potential to become one of the most prosperous and best placed to receive foreign direct investment in Africa. However, it only ranks 166th out of 190 economies in the 2019 Doing Business ranking of the World Bank (down three positions compared to the previous edition). While the country has many natural resources (oil, forestry, fisheries), as well as fertile land on which to build, it needs to improve and simplify its administration in order to boost entrepreneurship and fight against corruption. Poor infrastructure, weak rule of law and continuing inefficiencies of a large parastatal system in key sectors impede FDI growth.

Cameroon needs to attract foreign investors in order to finance its future projects of developing infrastructure and notably, the exploitation of gas. Large French companies are well-placed in these developing sectors. As part of its growing interest in Africa, China has been investing steadily in Cameroon (with total Chinese direct and indirect investments amounting to 2.43 billion USD in 2016 according to Cameroonian Ministry of Economy), allowing the construction of Kribi Port and Industrial Complex,

Memve'Ele hydroelectric dam and new football stadiums in light of the 2021 Africa Cup of Nations that is meant to be hosted by the country.

24.7.3 Relation with China

China and Cameroon established formal diplomatic relations in 1971. Since then, Chinese state-backed aid projects in Cameroon have included constructing the Cameroon parliament building, a conference center and sports stadium in Yaoundé and a women and children's hospital. A feature of the early 1980s was the Lagdo hydroelectric dam near Garoua, as well as assistance in building public hospitals, mainly in Mbalmayo and Yagoua.

The Cameroon government estimated that there was 2.86 billion USD of new investment from China in 2015, and another 2.43 USD billion in 2016. China Eximbank is the public financial institution currently financing most of the major infrastructure projects underway in Cameroon, the Memve'Ele hydroelectric dam, the deep-water port at Kribi, the Yaoundé-Douala motorway, the deployment of fiber optics by the country's telecoms operator, Cameroon Telecommunications, the "e-post" project to connect all the country's post offices, and projects to supply drinking water in four major cities. China Eximbank is also expected to help finance the construction of further sports facilities in Cameroon.

China is the second largest destination of all exports from Cameroon and the first destination in terms of wood exportation. Almost 20% of Cameroon's imports come from China, placing China at the top of the list of Cameroon's main import partners. Chinese investment in Cameroon is worth twice as much as all of Cameroon's other investment sources combined; that is, 67% of Cameroon's 5 billion USD in foreign direct investment in recent years, according to the United Nations Conference on Trade and Development. Eighty percent of Chinese investment is in infrastructure—roads, water, electricity, ports—with some in agribusiness and forestry. 12,000 jobs have been created by Chinese investments, with more than half in forest areas. China's Belt and Road Initiative has provided a new driving force for investment from China in Cameroon. This initiative is based on the theory that initial focus on infrastructure projects may pave the way for a future increase in resource extraction investments.

24.7.4 Dos and Don'ts

There are some general habits in Cameroon. Cameroonians are very welcoming people with open minds. Show respect for elders. Family is very important to

Cameroonians, even the extended family.

In business, there are some Dos and Don'ts.

- For official business meetings, business partners should always be very neatly dressed and endeavor to be on time.
- Do not underestimate female entrepreneurs. Sub-Saharan Africa has the highest rate of female entrepreneurship across the globe, with more women starting businesses in Africa than anywhere else in the world.
- In formal settings, personalities greet each other with a very warm handshake. Among close relations, it is common to see men hug each other or give pecks to the ladies on both jaws. Ladies equally do same.
- Foreign business partners should demonstrate interest in discovering Cameroon. During talks, mentioning touristic sights that they have heard of in Cameroon is definitely a plus.
- Business decisions are not necessarily based on past experiences or relations. New business partners are very welcome.

Chapter 25

Other Countries in America

25.1 Mexico

25.1.1 General Information

Mexico or the United Mexican States as its constitution dictates, besides being internationally applauded for its cuisine, pre-Hispanic culture and beautiful beaches, has come a long way from its independence in 1810, and now plays a major role in the international arena. This is mainly because it has developed numerous trade areas based on its diversity, which is why it is extremely important for you or anyone to conduct business with Mexico.

Mexico is located in North America, bordering in the north to the United States and in the south to Belize and Guatemala. Its territory extends to 1.96 million square kilometers making it the 5th largest country in the Americas and the 14th largest country in the world.

Its capital city is Mexico City, which is close to the center of the country. Mexico recognizes 68 indigenous languages and Spanish. At the present time, there are 364 indigenous linguistic variations. Almost 7 million Mexicans talk a variation of an indigenous language, and 860,000 of them speak Mayan and most of them are located in the south of the country. The currency of Mexico is Peso.

25.1.2 Economic Profile

As of 2019, the Mexican economy is the 2nd largest in Latin America and the 15th worldwide, and has grown steadily as a consequence of the application of long-term economic policies. In 2018, GDP per capita of Mexico was 9,806.821 USD.

Mexico has a free trade agreement (NAFTA) with US and Canada, which endows Mexico a preferential access position to the markets of US and Canada. Not only its own firms export to the two partners' markets, but also foreign firms that choose Mexico as an export platform.

In 2018, Mexico's total imports were 464,302.3 million USD and its exports were 450,684.5 million USD. As far as specific product goes, Mexico imports a major amount of vehicle parts, refined oil and integrated circuits. In the other side, Mexico exports flat screen TVs, fruits such as avocado and papaya and minerals like silver and gold. The main export destinations of Mexico are USA, Canada, Korea, China Mainland, Germany, Brazil, Spain, Japan, Colombia and United Kingdom. The main origins of imports are USA, China Mainland, Korea, Japan, Germany, Malaysia, Canada, China Taiwan, Brazil, and Vietnam.

Mexico is one of the most open emerging countries for foreign direct investment. In 2018, FDI inflows edged down to 33.5 billion USD, while the outflow marked 6,858 million USD. The FDI mainly come from US, Spain, Canada, Germany, and Japan. The main invested sectors include manufacturing industry, electricity, water and gas supply, retail and wholesale trade, financial services, and mining.

25.1.3 Relation with China

Mexico was one of the first Latin American countries to extend diplomatic recognition of People's Republic of China. That relationship dates back to February 14th, 1972. Formally and diplomatically, China-Mexico relationship has grown and matured substantially in the last decades. Through more than four decades of diplomatic relations, Mexico and China have established the basis of a relationship of friendship, dialogue and cooperation that has allowed them to advance in the deepening of a diverse and inclusive agenda.

In recent years, the bilateral economic relationship between Mexico and China has experienced a very particular dynamism that shows the priority that the two governments give to strengthening it. With an increasing complementarity that helps Mexico to be more competitive in the international market, China is today our second commercial partner, with exchanges close 80 billion dollars; the second source of Mexico's imports; and the third destination of Mexico's exports. In 2019, Mexico imports from China are quickly hitting the 100 billion USD mark, while the exports to China are slowly getting to 10 billion USD. This dynamism has led an increasing number of companies from both countries to explore trade and investment opportunities in Mexico's respective markets with great success.

In 2019, the investment from China to Mexico was of 1.2 billion USD, representing less than 5% of Mexican total inflows. Around 1,000 Chinese companies have discovered Mexico's potential as a platform for its internationalization. Lenovo, ZTE and Huawei (telecommunications), Hisense, Hier and Sanhua (manufacturing industry); BAIC, Minth, Minhua and JAC Motors (automotive), Sinohydro (infrastructure); Envison Energy and Jinko Solar (renewable energy); and CNOOC (hydrocarbons) represent just a few examples of successful cases that seek to be replicated by new companies and financial institutions interested in entering the Mexican market, such as ICBC, the first Chinese bank to open a subsidiary in Mexico in mid-2016. China's FDI in Mexico has concentrated in manufacturing and services related to Mexico's domestic market.

For its part, China has become an important market for some of the best and largest Mexican companies. Bimbo (bakery), Maseca (manufacture of corn and wheat products), Nemak (auto parts), Softtek (TIC), Grupo Kuo (chemical sector) and ICC, a joint venture formed by Interceramic, are some of the Mexican companies that have explored successfully the Chinese market.

Furthermore, Chinese tourists have begun to discover that Mexico is an attractive and versatile destination that can offer a wide range of experiences. Mexico is already the main destination in Latin America for Chinese visitors, whose flows have increased to double digits in recent years, making China the second source of visitors for Mexico within the Asia region. These positive results respond not only to the promotional activities that are carried out, but also to the visa facilitation measures for foreigners that have been implemented and to an increasing air connectivity between both countries that has been possible thanks to Aeroméxico, which operates a direct flight between Mexico City and Shanghai with five weekly frequencies, and China Southern, which became the first Chinese airline to operate a flight between Guangzhou and Mexico City, via Vancouver.

25.1.4 Dos and Don'ts

Just like Mexico's neighbors, the general idea of doing business with Mexicans is quite similar to doing business with anyone from the western world, you show up on time in your business suit and move to the formal, "American way" of doing business.

Mexicans greatly appreciate that their international counterparts are tolerant, friendly, accessible, comprehensive and educated. That is, they like to be treated well, their way of being is respected and they want to establish friendly relations with them. Mexicans also have low acceptance of the inexpressive attitudes of their peers. It is very likely that this is because the Mexican negotiating culture is extremely expressive.

The business hierarchy still has a great weight, so it is necessary to establish a relationship with the person of power in the company. Professional titles are also very important, so it is wise to say the professional degree of the person followed by the person's first name and first last name, if the title is unknown a common Mr. or Mrs. would be enough. Despite this, when you are introducing yourself you should not say your own professional title, as it is arrogant.

Time is required to establish a relationship with a Mexican, as they tend to be distrustful of strangers. To gain confidence, you must maintain constant communication and be courteous. To establish a good relationship, you have to make two or three visits a year. In general, the first contact is made via email.

As in almost all countries of Latin America, Mexicans always use the formal version of "You"—"Usted" (better explained in Chinese: 您) as a default treatment for other people. Of course, if negotiations are done in English, "You" would be the only option available.

The way to address a Mexican counterpart through some written via is characterized by being highly cordial and formal. That is why, when writing an email, make sure you are as pleasant as possible. State your honor and pleasure in contacting your counterpart, using expressions such as "we are honored by your trust" or, "we are at your distinguished orders".

Business appointments must be scheduled at least one week in advance. It is always convenient to confirm a meeting a few days before the scheduled meeting.

It is important that you arrive on time for meetings, although your business partners in Mexico may be up to 15 minutes late. Do not show irritation if this occurs as meetings usually get delayed a few minutes without notice.

Business cards should be exchanged at the beginning of the initial meeting. It is advisable that they contain your professional and educational qualifications. The presentation of the same, archives, reports, promotional publications, or any other type of document that is presented in the negotiations, is considered very important. Throwing documents on the table during a business meeting, or anywhere and anything for that matter, is considered a highly offensive gesture.

In a meeting and before starting the negotiation, there is usually a brief conversation between the participants in which they talk about family, country of origin, hobbies and trivial topics. Therefore, the theme of the meeting itself is as important as being personally known. However, be careful when talking about private life, because a Mexican may feel offended when someone inquires a lot about it, this includes not talking about salaries, prices of houses, cars or expensive possessions.

It is extremely important not to talk about religion or politics, if the conversation gets to that topic, politely change the subject.

The greeting with men is done with a handshake, and if it is already known, it is accompanied by a hug. With women, a formal handshake and sometimes a kiss on the cheek.

As for nonverbal language, security and confidence should be shown when speaking. Physical contact is usual.

The usual clothing in the Mexican business environment is formal, suit and tie. However, there are sectors in which clothing is not of such importance, as for example in engineering. The female costume is usually elegant and conservative.

Once the relationship is established, it is customary to conclude meetings with a lunch or dinner. Here it is important to set aside business and take advantage to gain the confidence necessary to close a deal. The business conversation can be something informal, it is not subject to protocol rules. It is important to remember that it is not only a negotiation with the company but also with a person, so the more trust is achieved, the more benefits can be generated to the company.

It is very easy for a Mexican after doing business to open his house to his counterpart. In other countries, that is unthinkable. If you receive an invitation to have lunch or dinner in a Mexican house, it is advisable to bring a present such as flowers or sweets. The packaging does not have any particular protocol, although it would be good if it contains colors with light tones and a card. Again, expensive gifts are not welcome as they create awkward situations. Do not give red flowers either, because it could lead to misunderstandings. White flowers could be a good gift and are perceived with appreciation by Mexicans. If you receive a gift, open it and react with enthusiasm and then thank with utmost courtesy.

It should be noted that Mexicans are reluctant to outright denial. Despite having no interest in a project or negotiation, they will say that they are thinking about it or that they have to check with their colleagues or superiors, because saying a definite "no" is considered impolite.

In the same topic, and given that punctuality is not a priority, there is no excess of control and appointments are usually delayed. Expressions such as "tomorrow" or "right now" are used that do not necessarily mean "tomorrow" or "now" literally. Sometimes, the postponement in time is a synonym for "no".

Having these details in mind will determine the willingness of the Mexican company to close the deal and the establishment of a business relationship over time.

Finally, to be successful in a negotiation with a Mexican, the same thing that they expect must be demonstrated by the counterpart: cordiality, openness, closeness and trust.

25.2 Ecuador

25.2.1 General Information

Ecuador is a Latin American country, located in the west coast of South America, with the area of 256,370 square kilometers. It borders Colombia, Peru and the Pacific Ocean. Ecuador is one of the most environmentally diverse countries in the world, and it has contributed notably to the environmental sciences. The first scientific expedition to measure the circumference of the Earth, led by Charles-Marie de La Condamine of France, was based in Ecuador. Research in Ecuador by the renowned naturalists Alexander von Humboldt of Prussia and Charles Darwin of England helped establish basic theories of modern geography, ecology, and evolutionary biology. Ecuador has a rich cultural heritage. Much of what is now Ecuador came to be included in the Inca Empire, the largest political unit of Pre-Columbian America.

People speak Spanish, Kichwa, Shuar and others used by indigenous people. Its capital city is Quito. Ecuador use USD as currency.

25.2.2 Economic Profile

GDP per capital of Ecuador is 5,185 USD in 2018. Trade is a very important component within Ecuador's economy. In 2018, Ecuador exported 21.6 million USD and imported 23.19 million USD, resulting in a negative trade balance of 1.587 million USD. The top exports of Ecuador are crude oil, fish and crustaceans, bananas, preparations of meat, live trees and other plants, cocoa. Ecuador's top 10 exports account for 90% of the overall value of its global shipments. Its top imports are refined oil; machinery, mechanical appliances, nuclear reactors, boilers; vehicles other than railway or tramway rolling stock; electrical machinery and equipment, sound recorders and reproducers; plastics and pharmaceutical products. The top export destinations of Ecuador are United States, Peru, China, Chile and Panama. The top import origins are United States, China, Colombia, Panama and Brazil. Considering a continental perspective, 39% of Ecuadorian exports by value are delivered to North America, 24% of them are sold to Europe, 20% is sent to Asia and 16% is going to South America. A tiny percentage (0.39%) arrives in Africa and the same percent for

Oceania.

Since 2000, the annual inflow of FDI to Ecuador is 637.9 million USD and 89.7% of the total foreign capital that entered Ecuador went to five sectors: mining and quarrying exploitation, manufacture, commerce, commercial services and farming.

25.2.3 Relation with China

The relation between Ecuador and China started in 1970 with the nations placing an office of commerce in each other's country. However, due to internal distress in Ecuador and military destabilization, the process slowed until 1980 when relations were established once more. By 1994 Cooperation Agreements began. Interesting to notice, though several head of state visited China for years, the first head of state to visit Ecuador was President Xi Jinping in 2016.

While Cooperation Agreements were signed in 2000 in 2002, strong political and economic ties between both countries escalated from 2006 during the government of Rafael Correa. Correa's administration issued the "Good Living National Plan" (GLNP), a governmental plan with several objectives. This reform related to China's position and objectives. As a result, in 2007 bilateral agreements were signed by Ecuador and China. By 2015, in a meeting with the Community of Latin American and Caribbean states (CELAC), President Xi Jinping announced an annual bilateral trade for the next 10 years with Chinese investment of over 250 billion US Dollars as well as a trade rise of up to 500 billion USD. In such meeting, Ecuador agreed for a 5.3 billion USD credit line with China Eximbank and other 2.2 billion USD in additional funding.

From 2007 until 2015, Ecuador and China signed 21 Bilateral Agreements. Most of them were directed towards mining, energy projects (from both renewable as non-renewable energy sources) and infrastructure investment projects. Ecuador and China also signed commercial agreements like the 2012 Commercial Agreement to promote trade of shrimps, bananas, cacao, lemon, pineapple and mango and the "Mutual Visa Agreement" (to abolish/diminish visa requirements for Chinese and Ecuadorians when entering the respective countries).

China has been on the top countries Ecuador exports to. With an export value of almost 800 million USD in 2017 and 1.4 billion USD in 2018, China was around 4% and 6.92% of the country's total exports those years. The main export products from Ecuador to China are crude petroleum, accounting for around 77% of the total exports in 2010 and 44% in 2017. The rest of the export matrix from Ecuador to China (as of 2017) was crustaceans (14%), bananas and animal meal (17%), precious metals (Ore) (9.2%) among other products.

China as well is one of the most significant import countries for the Ecuadorian economy, with 18.91% of imports coming from Chinese market and a net value of 4.3 billion USD by 2018. Generally, the country imports machinery products, ranging typically between broadcasting equipment (usually between 5%-6% average over 2016, 2017 and 2018), computers (constant high import with the topmost in 2014 with 8.9% of total imports), telephones and electric motors, and vehicles and cars (with a combine 4.8% in 2017).

China is one of the top investors of Ecuador. Until 2006 Chinese FDI was not so remarkable, with for example 11.6 million USD investment that year and a minus 19.6 million USD in 2005. As a result of the 2007 boost of China-Ecuador relations, FDI escalated that very same year to 84.8 million USD. Investments during the following 8 years (from 2007 to 2014) were mainly focus on infrastructure projects and mining and quarrying (more than 95% of FDI). After new commercial agreement was signed in 2015, Chinese FDI to Ecuador increased by 43% from 79.6 million USD in 2014 to 113.9 million USD in 2015. In 2017 and 2018 investments diversified more not only on mining and quarrying 51% and 78% respectively, but also services provided to companies (23.7% in 2017 and 9.19% in 2018) and construction (17.6% and 4.98% respectively).

At the early stages of Correa's government, because of the Ecuadorian financial crisis and lack of good credit markets perception together with the Chinese need to cover its tremendously increasing demand for oil, in 2009, a lending of 1 billion USD was completed by PetroChina. Later on in 2013, a 2 billion USD financing was completed to PetroEcuador. The following loans continued in 2010 by China Export-Import Bank with a loan of 1.7 billion USD and 570 million USD for several energy projects, by Chinese Development Bank with 2 billion USD loan to the Ecuadorian government and several other loans of between 1 billion and 2 billion USD respectively. At the end of 2013, the Chinese funds covered around 6.2 million USD of the Ecuadorian financing need, claiming up to 90% of the Ecuadorian oil shipments for upcoming years.

25.2.4 Dos and Don'ts

Dos:

- Bureaucratic system is a little bit slow and complex, therefore it is possible to encounter some difficulties with the customs of goods or with the obtention of certificates in the Health Registration. As a consequence, it is recommended that having a local contact that could speed up the processes with the administration.
- In most of the places in Ecuador, it is necessary to have key contacts in order to do

business. It is advised to count with a local company. If not, then a big help could be contacting with an agency of import-export or lawyers office.
- It is recommended that business meetings should be schedule with two weeks ahead of anticipation. In addition to that, it is necessary to confirm it again two or three days before.
- There is a group of businessmen who value personal and trust relationships more through of the word. In any case, it is always advisable to be protected by contracts, rules and laws.
- In general, the businessman from the coast makes the decisions faster than those from the highlands. In that sense, it is advised not to invade with national policy issues, recommendations of how to do business and/or pressure for the completion of the negotiation process.
- The language in the negotiation must be formal, direct and precise, without missing respect and cordiality.
- Before entering the subject of business, you should give time to informal conversation (travel, culture, current affairs, etc.). It is common for comments, anecdotes or personal experiences to be given during negotiations that are not directly related to what is being discussed.
- Conversations are conducted in a friendly tone. It is recommended to avoid any type of comments that could be misinterpreted, in addition to maintaining a soft tone of voice, so as not to give an impression of aggressiveness.
- In the presentations it is recommended to show specific data and figures, the profitability of the proposed businesses will be reviewed before making any decision.
- When a gift is offered, the other party should open it immediately and demonstrate an effusive reaction.
- It is recommended that when visiting the cities in the highlands, such as Quito for example, to take the necessary precautions since it is located about 2,760 meters above sea level. The altitude can cause tiredness, headaches or sleep, it is not recommended to do physical activity, or eat or drink excessively.

Don'ts:

- Ecuadorians consider that agreements are made more with people than with the companies they represent, therefore changes in the negotiating teams are not recommended, since it could cause a delay or a stoppage in the agreement.
- It is not recommended to talk about the following topics: relations with neighboring countries such as Colombia and Peru, and the indigenous population.
- To avoid misinterpretations, head movements to deny or affirm should be avoided, since not all Ecuadorians welcome these gestures. It is preferable to do it verbally.

Other facts:

- There are some regional differences. People from the capital, Quito, which is the administrative capital and basis of public institutions, tend to be more conservative, formal and reserved in business and relations with others while people from Guayaquil tend to be of a more entrepreneurial spirit, open to new business, more flexible and relaxed in the commercial relations.
- Employers usually wear formal attire (suits) for interviews or business meetings. This will also depend on the region of the country and the productive sector where it is carried out the contacts; on the coast clothing is more informal (for example, not wearing a tie is more common).
- Chamber of Commerce has a quite important representation in Ecuador and could be a good connection and introduction to the country.
- It is not customary to close deals on the first date. It is common to resort to an analysis with your team of advisers, investors or shareholders and then make a decision.
- Of course, an advantage to advance business and commercial relationships with Ecuadorian entrepreneurs is the image and experience that the company has in the field of their activities, whether regional or international.
- It is common that when an entrepreneur is interested in establishing businesses, goes from a formal interview relationship to a purely informal one, moving on to a more social one. This is a way of knowing the personal and trustworthy side that you can establish with its counterpart.
- In Ecuador, decisions are usually made based on past experiences, over the application of general rules or logical principles, and Ecuadorian negotiators do not easily change their minds.
- Negotiations are usually carried out at a slow pace. Decisions will be made at a senior executive level. It is likely that there will be several delays until the closing agreement is reached.
- It is customary for men to greet each other with a handshake, both at the presentation and at the farewell. The women greet each other verbally, and generally give a kiss on the cheek when they already know each other.
- In general, punctuality in meetings is not customary. In this sense, it is common delays of more than 15 to 20 minutes. Although at a managerial level this culture is changing and is taken into account when doing business.
- In legal documentation it is customary to use both surnames (father and mother). For presentation purposes only the paternal surname is used.
- It is customary to organize lunches to discuss business, which is given around 1:00 p.m. If the negotiations are more important or if the foreign visitor requires special attention, it

is customary to invite them to dinner.
- As for meals, the portions are usually abundant. In the highlands, it is common to offer a variety of dishes, not necessarily from the locality, such as the "fritada" (fried pork with mote, potatoes and toasted corn). On the coast, typical dishes are made with seafood or fish.
- It is common for meals to be accompanied by wine and alcohol, in the mountains, having a cold climate is more common. More beer is usually drunk on the coast.
- Depending on the geographical area of the country—interior or coast—there is a different way of dressing. In the mountains the businessperson is expected to wear a dark colored suit and tie, even on very hot days. On the coast, people are more informal, the use of the "guayabera" is common.
- Holidays are taken in different months depending on the geographical area. In the Sierra (Quito) vacations are taken during the month of August, while on the coast (Guayaquil) in January and February.
- It is mistakenly perceived that the entire country has a warm climate. In Quito it varies from temperate to cold.
- For business meetings it is customary to address the Ecuadorian businessman stating his profession. The business environment is formal, but at the same time personal.
- In recent years, the exchange of business cards is very common in the formalization of the interview.

Reading Material

The Belt and Road Initiative

Reference Answers

请扫码阅读
参 考 答 案

Bibliography

［1］孙莹. 国际商务英语［M］. 北京：经济管理出版社，2017.
［2］郭建梅. 外贸英文函电［M］. 北京：对外经济贸易大学出版社，2010.
［3］余晓泓. 外贸英文函电［M］. 北京：清华大学出版社，2017.
［4］刘卓林，孙芳，温珺. 外经贸英语函电［M］. 2版. 北京：科学出版社，2011.
［5］陈文汉. 外贸英语函电［M］. 北京：中国人民大学出版社，2013.
［6］王兴孙. 新编进出口英语函电［M］. 3版. 北京：外语教学与研究出版社，2012.
［7］赵劼. 国际商务单证实务［M］. 北京：清华大学出版社，2013.
［8］赵劼. 国际贸易实务［M］. 北京：清华大学出版社，2013.
［9］浩瀚. 商务英语外贸高频话题［M］. 北京：中国水利水电出版社，2010.
［10］查尔斯·希尔，托马斯·霍特. 国际商务（英文版·第11版）［M］. 北京：中国人民大学出版社，2018.
［11］刘白玉. 国际贸易实务［M］. 北京：清华大学出版社，2019.
［12］檀文茹. 国际贸易专业英语［M］. 3版. 北京：对外经济贸易大学出版社，2015.
［13］周燕，廖瑛. 英语商务合同长句的语用分析及其翻译［J］. 中国科技翻译，2004，11(4)，Vol.17：29-32.
［14］郑敏. 商务英语函电与合同［M］. 北京：清华大学出版社，北京交通大学出版社，2005.
［15］滕美荣，许楠. 外贸英语函电［M］. 北京：首都经济贸易大学出版社，2005.
［16］陈详国. 国际商务函电［M］. 北京：对外经济贸易大学出版社，2005.
［17］邹海峰，赵耀，Manvel Lunes. International Business Correspondence & Form Handbook［M］. 北京：对外经济贸易大学出版社，2004.
［18］诸葛霖，王燕希. 外贸英文书信［M］. 北京：对外经济贸易大学出版社，2007.
［19］张翠萍. 商贸英语口语大全［M］. 北京：对外经济贸易大学出版社，2006.
［20］耿延宏，等. 商务贸易英语口语［M］. 大连：大连理工大学出版社，2002.
［21］张立玉，何康民. 国际贸易进出口实务［M］. 武汉：武汉大学出版社，2005.
［22］仲鑫. 外贸函电［M］. 北京：机械工业出版社，2006.
［23］戚云方. 新编外经贸英语函电与谈判［M］. 杭州：浙江大学出版社，2007.

[24] 顾乾毅. 国际商贸英语 [M]. 广州：华南理工大学出版社，2005.
[25] 张军，等. 国际贸易英语政策、组织与实务 [M]. 北京：中国水利水电出版社，2006.
[26] 潘丽. 国际贸易专业英语 [M]. 哈尔滨：哈尔滨工业大学出版社，2005.
[27] 刘志伟. 国际商务函电与沟通 [M]. 北京：对外经济贸易大学出版社，2005.
[28] 陈倩. 商贸英语对话 [M]. 北京：对外经济贸易大学出版社，2005.
[29] 谢毅斌. 商务英语 [M]. 北京：对外经济贸易大学出版社，2005.
[30] 陈宁，池玫. 21世纪实用国际商务英语口语 [M]. 北京：北京大学出版社，2007.
[31] 何福胜，王玉雯. 经贸英语精选 [M]. 北京：清华大学出版社，2003.
[32] 浩瀚. 商务英语即用即查 [M]. 北京：中国水利水电出版社，2007.
[33] 谢丹焰，印丕杰. 商务英语综合教程 [M]. 北京：清华大学出版社，2004.
[34] 杨祖宪，龚晓斌. 最新商务英语读本 [M]. 苏州：苏州大学出版，2007.
[35] 凌华倍，朱佩芬. 外经贸英语函电与谈判 [M]. 北京：对外经济贸易大学出版社，2002.
[36] 滕美荣. 电子商务英语 [M]. 北京：首都经济贸易大学出版社，2002.
[37] 滕美荣，许楠. 市场营销英语 [M]. 北京：首都经济贸易大学出版社，2003.
[38] 杜凤秋. 商务英语综合教程 [M]. 北京：首都经济贸易大学出版社，2007.
[39] Nick Brieger, Jeremy Comfort. 商务英语 [M]. 刘平梅，译. 北京：清华大学出版社，1998.

请扫码阅读
更多参考资料